LEADERSHIP
Excellence

ENDORSEMENTS

Leadership is not a static concept, especially in a disruptive and connected world. It is complex and multi-dimensional. It needs to be understood and applied at contextual, operational and micro levels. Certainly it is much more than a set of competencies.

More has probably been written about and spoken about leadership than almost any other topic throughout history. However, to understand leadership is to understand the concept from multiple perspectives. That is what this very comprehensive book provides. There is no single approach to leadership and the variety of perspectives provided in this book will further enhance our understanding and practice of leadership.

An important book with highly qualified and insightful contributors which will add to the conversations about leadership for a long time to come. An essential read for leaders and those responsible for leadership in their organisations now and in the future.

Terry Meyer, Strategy & Leadership Consultant, Leadership SA

Truly a standout book that packs a real punch in the sea of books on leadership. This extraordinary book has to be the most updated, and most comprehensive and definitive compendium on leaders and leadership, written by an impressive array of prominent and respected experts in the field.

Understanding the "what" and "how" of leadership is something that most organisations continue to grapple with in these volatile, complex, uncertain and ambiguous times. This book offers advice on the toughest challenges leaders are facing in business today.

This is compulsory reading for anyone seeking to understand and distil powerful perspectives on leadership and how to become a better leader

The book provides robust perspectives on leadership fundamentals ranging from leadership theory, models and frameworks on leadership, leadership principles and philosophy, and, in addition, offers authentic, actionable examples. It is bursting with great tips and advice that are immediately applicable and anchored in research.

An indispensable and essential resource for leaders and aspiring leaders at all levels.

Shirley Zinn, Professor Shirley Zinn, Group HR Director, Woolworths

This book is rooted in the challenges facing leaders today, and offers current and future leaders a perspective to help them lead in a VUCA world. The authors take a unique view of leadership from a "value chain" perspective. They provide executives and those in the leadership development business a framework and insight into both being and building better leaders for tomorrow. I believe this book – a product of frontline leaders, will prove to be a great handbook for those who regard leadership as both an interest and a passion.

Paul Norman, MTN Group: Group Human Resources and Corporate Affairs Officer

I have read dozens of books on leadership but none of them has tackled this complex topic in the way that *Leadership Excellence* has done. This book tackles the real issues of leadership from understanding the foundations of leadership; to examining leadership within its unfolding context; to leadership identification, growth and development; to issues of leadership transitions and leadership wellbeing. The insights and models are based on research and on real experiences and I particularly enjoyed the section on leadership articles and stories – real-life leadership experiences as told by the leaders themselves.

This book is that rare mix of a treasure house of up-to-date knowledge about every aspect of leadership and at the same time full of insights and suggestions for practical implementation. It is both thought-provoking and enlightening, and a must-read for anyone trying to understand the complex issues surrounding leadership. This is one of the best books on the topic of leadership I have been privileged to read.

> *Italia Boninelli, HR Strategist, Executive Coach and Author, (recent past Executive Vice-president: People and Organizational Development, AngloGold Ashanti)*

The seminal guide to the kind of transformational leadership required in the 21st century and beyond.

> *S'ne Mkhize, Senior Vice President, Human Resources – Sasol*

What a phenomenal work!

This is the most comprehensive, insightful and well-grounded work on leadership ever published in South Africa.

It unpacks leadership in its many facets and perspectives – from individual to organisational and global leadership.

The authors are thought leaders, scientists and subject-matter experts; they ask the difficult questions and reveal the essence of leadership as an art and science.

This book is a must for everybody in leadership positions – be it the business sector, public sector, religious organisations, education, or community organisations.

An ideal reference work for the consultant or business science practitioner.

> *Dr Johan de Beer, Human Capital Executive, Africa Division, Imperial Logistics*

Leadership Excellence is a feast for scholars, students and practitioners alike who will find a comprehensive reference book on leadership theories, a diversity of the schools of thought that have influenced and continue to shape the evolution of the leadership as a fully fledged discipline that is applied to complex and changing contexts. As someone trying to master the leadership discipline and as an aspirant leadership expert myself, I was pleasantly surprised at how much there is still to know and learn about this enthralling subject called leadership.

> *Dudu Msomi, Chief Executive Officer, Busara Leadership Partners*

Given the plethora of books on Leadership, one is tempted to think, "What else can be written about leadership?"

This masterful creation crushes that thought. It is a call to choose to be a different and better leader, to stand up and … lead.

I recommend that current and future leaders, young and old, study this gem and weave the learnings into their approach to leading our most precious asset, people.

> *Leon Steyn, Group Human Resources Executive, Bidvest*

Copyright © KR Publishing, Andrew J Johnson and Theo H Veldsman

All reasonable steps have been taken to ensure that the contents of this book do not, directly or indirectly, infringe any existing copyright of any third person and, further, that all quotations or extracts taken from any other publication or work have been appropriately acknowledged and referenced. The publisher, editors and printers take no responsibility for any copyright infringement committed by an author of this work.

Copyright subsists in this work. No part of this work may be reproduced in any form or by any means without the written consent of the publisher or the author.

While the publisher, editors and printers have taken all reasonable steps to ensure the accuracy of the contents of this work, they take no responsibility for any loss or damage suffered by any person as a result of that person relying on the information contained in this work.

All cases are for illustrative purposes only and the intent is not to evaluate the performance of an organisation.

First published in 2017

ISBN: 978-1-86922-690-9 (Printed)
ISBN: 978-1-86922-691-6 (ePDF)

Published by KR Publishing
P O Box 3954
Randburg
2125
Republic of South Africa

Tel: (011) 706-6009
Fax: (011) 706-1127
E-mail: orders@knowres.co.za
Website: www.kr.co.za

Printed and bound: HartWood Digital Printing, 243 Alexandra Avenue, Halfway House, Midrand
Typesetting, layout and design: Cia Joubert, cia@knowres.co.za
Cover design: Marlene de'Lorme, marlene@knowres.co.za and Cia Joubert, cia@knowres.co.za
Editing: Adrienne Pretorius, pretorii@mweb.co.za
Proofreading: Valda Strauss: valda@global.co.za
Project management: Cia Joubert, cia@knowres.co.za

LEADERSHIP
Excellence

Edited by
Andrew J Johnson and Theo H Veldsman

2017

ACKNOWLEDGEMENTS

What a pleasure to work with authors who see the unquestionable criticality of leadership, and are passionate about the difference leadership must make in assuring a desirable, sustainable future for all. It was wonderful to have worked with each and every one of our 69 authors over such an extended period of time. Your wisdom, expertise, suggestions and time willingly shared in crafting your invaluable contribution in making *Leadership Excellence* the outstanding and trend-setting Thought Leadership Book it has turned out to be is gratefully acknowledged.

Warm word of thanks is due to:

- All of our Peer Reviewers for your valuable input and time.
- To all our Endorsees for your time given, to offer our book the cachet it deserves.
- Wilhelm Crous, Managing Director of KR, for your constant stretch and guidance; constructive criticism; ongoing encouragement; infectious enthusiasm; and advice and help in working around and through barriers, that made it such a pleasure to work on our book.
- Joann Hill for organising the peer reviews and endorsements.
- Cia Joubert, for your excellent project management of our book that was mission critical in ensuring that the right things happened at the right time and in the right way so that our book became a reality.
- Adrienne Pretorius, our technical editor, for ensuring the technical quality excellence of our book.
- Valda Strauss, for the excellent proofreading of our book after layout.

Last but not least, a warm, appreciative "Thank you" to our families for their understanding, support and sacrifices throughout the painful birth process of the book which took two years from initiation, through conceptualisation and production, to final delivery.

TABLE OF CONTENTS

FOREWORD BY *EDWARD KIESWETTER*	ii
ABOUT THE EDITORS	v
ABOUT THE CONTRIBUTORS	vi

SECTION 1: SETTING THE SCENE — 1
1. Leadership as strategic organisational capability and intervention by *Theo H Veldsman and Andrew J Johnson* — 2

SECTION 2: LEADERSHIP EXCELLENCE AND BRANDING — 11
2. Leadership excellence dimensions by *Anton Verwey, Ronel Minnaar and Paul Mooney* — 12
3. Leadership excellence across cultural settings by *Lize Booysen* — 31
4. Leadership brand modelling by *Anton Verwey* and *Sonja Verwey* — 53

SECTION 3: LEADERSHIP ATTRIBUTES — 59
5. Authentic Leadership by *Tineke Wulffers* — 60
6. Mindful leadership by *Errol Nembhard* — 73
7. Virtuous leadership by *Marius Ungerer* — 83
8. Wise leadership by *Lisa Ashton* — 99
9. Spiritual leadership by *Penny Law* — 111
10. Ethical leadership by *Leon van Vuuren* — 125

SECTION 4: LEADERSHIP TYPES — 145
11. African leadership by *Vusi Vilakati* — 146
12. Women in leadership by *Mmasekgoa Masire-Mwamba* — 177
13. Multi-generational leadership by *Graeme Codrington* and *Raymond de Villiers* — 191
14. Diversity Leadership by *Nene Molefi* — 205
15. Change leadership by *Sesh Paruk* — 217

SECTION 5: LEADERSHIP SETTINGS — 229
16. Team leadership by *Drikus Kriek* — 230
17. Entrepreneurial leadership by *Boris Urban* — 243
18. Board leadership by *Carmen Le Grange* — 249

SECTION 6: LEADERSHIP OUTCOMES AND IMPACT — 265
19. Leadership excellence measurement by *Anton Verwey, Steven Teasdale, Marzanne de Klerk* and *Francois du Plessis* — 266

SECTION 7: LEADERSHIP STORIES — 285
20. *Thuli Modonsela*: Leadership as the giant leap necessary for an inclusive, prosperous and peaceful future — 288
Shameel Joosub: Creating movement as a leader in a constantly evolving and changing environment by *Adriaan Groenewald* — 291
Mohammad Karaan: Intuition, silence, giants and the cattle herder from *Sakebeeld* — 293
Dave Macready: Leadership built on vision, belief and passion from *Sakebeeld* — 295
Hendrik du Toit: Good leaders stand or fall by their principles from *Sakebeeld* — 297
Ian Donald: Being an authentic and confident leader by *Adriaan Groenewald* — 299

SECTION 8: LOOKING AHEAD — 301
21. The future of leadership by *Andrew J Johnson and Theo H Veldsman* — 302

Index — 313

FOREWORD BY EDWARD KIESWETTER

WE TEND TO SET THE BAR FOR LEADERSHIP TOO LOW

For a role so profound in its impact, the bar sadly, is set very low for anyone who wishes to assume a leadership position, formally or otherwise. Anyone can be a leader, whether elected, elected or self-ordained to the position. In most spheres of society quite simply anyone can assume a leadership position. Modern democracies set neither formal competence nor attributes for those who get to hold powerful offices that can potentially shape our destiny. Anyone can start a church, a community organization, or a trade union, or political party. The only criteria being that they can muster a following, with no regard for the broader skills a leader may require to lead.

One would not consider going to a physician who is not professionally qualified and declared competent according to agreed standards. No significant bridge or building will be designed and built unless a professionally qualified and registered team of engineers, as well as a team of professional building and construction professionals are engaged. An accountant has to serve a period as an article clerk and demonstrate sufficient competence, and thereafter pass a board examination before being allowed to perform the work of a chartered accountant and be a competent authority to approve a set of financial statements. The same applies to lawyers, auditors, actuaries, and other professions. But there is no equivalent requirement for leadership. This is especially true for those running for political office.

I'm not necessarily simply referring to a university degree. There is no other formal qualification or professional bodies that oversee a clear set of universal standards for leadership. Even though an MBA provides a broad general exposure to business administration, it does not necessarily cover business leadership as a professional discipline in its own right. Recently regulators have insisted on fit and proper declarations for directors and for certain roles especially in the financial services sector. No registration is required, however, to be a leader. Also just the fact that one may be a world-class technical expert, does not imply that one is capable of providing leadership in that or any other discipline. The opposite is often more evident when a great technical expert goes on to become a poor leader. Across the various spheres where leadership is required, we have seen massive failures that without exception can be traced back to a leadership failure. Thankfully most organisational and institutional successes can also be linked to leadership excellence. The question is whether there is a higher level of predictability, on the basis of a set of required competencies and attributes, of leadership

This book attempts to respond explore this question, and in a way raise the bar for what is considered Leadership Excellence.

WHAT IS CONSIDERED LEADERSHIP EXCELLENCE DEPENDS ON WHO YOU ASK

What is considered as Leadership Excellence depends on what is being sought!

The conversation about Leadership Excellence, as dealt with by this book, given the many blatant leadership failures we experience, is a necessary and important one. This book quite correctly states that the question of Leadership Excellence has to be considered in relation to context.

Leadership Excellence as covered in this book is an enduring theme. It is particularly topical in the current global context of populist leaders, who have been elected without any prior experience to leadership roles of great power, and who seem to exercise that power rather carelessly. I wonder how many readers of this book would be able to name even one current leader who is truly inspirational. Apart from the current Pope Francis, I personally don't find any example of a leader that truly inspires me. Your experience may well be different. If you were indeed fortunate to identify a leader that inspires you, I would ask what were the the defining attributes of such a leader?

The state of global politics raises endless questions about the quality and integrity of political leadership. Of course the justification for the likes of Donald Trump, Rodrigo Duterte, Recep Erdogan, Vladimir Putin as well as South Africa's Jacob Zuma, could well be that each has a passionate following and support that would indicate that they resonate strongly with an issue of the day or with a segment of the population that does not find the same connection to more conventional politicians. There appears to be a proliferation of political leaders increasingly following a "strong-man" approach. Such leadership appears to be fueled more by ego-centricity that is quite at odds with the notion of public service, but who have come to power due to the perception that there is some constituency whose interest they serve.

But what yardstick should be used to rate these individuals as excellent leaders? A popular leader is not necessarily always an excellent leader but why, one could ask, does the same leader illicit extreme disgust from some, and unquestioning reverence from others? It is, as this book explains, about context.

I would suggest, in particular, that how you might define your personal interests has a strong bearing on how you would rate these leaders. It's all about where one stands. If any of these leaders happen to serve or advance your own particular interests, your assessment could very well be that the leader is excelling, regardless of the experience of others.

Politicians are not alone. Business leaders are no different. Many Chief Executives serve at the altar of short-term profits, seduced by a system of incentives and rewards that incentivises them to see the long term merely as a series of short terms.. To shareholders and analysts who focus narrowly on quarterly returns, a short-term profit driven CEO is an excellent business leader, whilst workers who feel exploited are quite likely to have a different view. Environmentalists, for example, might conclude that the same business has a negative impact on the environment. Each stakeholder would regard the same CEO in a different light, depending on their own particular set of often fairly narrow interests.

We see a similar phenomenon in other civic organisations. Religious leaders, labour leaders, and leaders of various community organizations may profess to serve a common good, but might in actuality have become drunk with a sense of self- righteousness and self-importance that has little bearing on their impact on the common good. That said, there always seems to be a group or a cause whose interest they serve, and by whom they are regarded as excellent.

This phenomena, encompassing political, business and civic leadership is not confined to present times. Human history is littered with examples of many leaders who were celebrated by a particular interest group, and accorded the status of excellence purely because they served the narrow interests of that group.

So it is not obvious that there is any universal agreement as to what is meant by leadership excellence. That notwithstanding , it would still not be possible to assess Leadership Excellence without understanding first what the leadership role seeks to achieve; what methods or tactics it may use; whether the true cost of the achievement is fully accounted for; and whether or not the unintended consequences justify the achievement in the immediate, medium or long term.

WHY DOES LEADERSHIP EXCELLENCE MATTER

No matter how noble or pure the intent of ones behavior, in the end, it's only the impact that really matters. We often justify our behavior by its stated intent, but it may pale into insignificance when what is actually achieved has severe negative consequences.

Leadership Excellence goes well beyond the work that the leader does. It is about the impact the leader has. Leaders by virtue of their role have impact. Leaders must be mindful of, and consider whether or not their impact is positive or detrimental. Leadership excellence is about consciously choosing to ensure a positive impact to a greater good. Whilst the impact of leadership action or inaction may or may not be intended, the issue of impact is real and felt by all stakeholders, directly or indirectly, immediately, or over the longer term.

In my own work on Steward Leadership, I argue that Leadership is characterised by intent, impact, insight, inspire, influence and interdependence, which I believe are implicit in *Leadership Excellence*:

Serving a higher purpose that results in positive impact for all stakeholders is the ultimate mark of Leadership Excellence.

The authors' intention with, and aspiration for, Leadership Excellence is for this book to be a "thought leadership book on understanding leadership excellence from multiple angles: leadership excellence itself; leadership brand and profile; and leadership outcomes and impact" They seek to do this by providing "cutting edge, present-into-the-future, and future-into-the-present, thinking with respect to leadership excellence, leveraged from the best currently available insights and informed views, and secondly, by providing actionable knowledge and theory-informed practice."

The editors, through their work experience and professional approach, are eminently qualified to lead a conversation on Leadership. My sense is that this book adequately delivers on this aspiration and intent. I have confidence that the reader will find *Leadership Excellence* a valuable read and will experience the impact of this book positively.

Edward Christian Kieswetter, President: Da Vinci Institute, and ex Group Chief Executive of Alexander Forbes Limited

ABOUT THE EDITORS

Dr Andrew J Johnson

Andrew is the Chief Learning Officer at Eskom's Academy of Learning. An Industrial Psychologist by profession, he holds an MSc in Occupational Psychology (Nottingham) and a PhD in Industrial Psychology from the University of Johannesburg (UJ). He has also completed formal philosophical, theological and exegetical studies at Sts. Peter & John Vianney Seminaries and St Joseph's Scholasticate.

A seasoned HR executive, his special interests are HR strategy consulting, leadership development, talent and succession management, organisational transformation, and change management. His career in Organisational Effectiveness in the private sector has seen him working for Edcon, MTN, Avmin, JSE and Liberty in senior positions, and he has consulted to other state-owned entities, private companies, and African and BRICS (Brazil, Russia, India, China and South Africa) utilities.

He held non-executive roles in FASSET, the NEF, the COJ Property Company, Transparency SA, NSFAS, & King II; currently he serves on the Advisory Committee of the Industrial Psychology Department of UJ (where he is an occasional lecturer), and the HR (Staffing) Committee of the University of KwaZulu-Natal (UKZN). Andrew is involved in the Society for Industrial & Organisational Psychology of South Africa (SIOPSA) (president in 2011/12), and the Global Forum on Executive Development and Business Driven Action Learning. He is the winner of the prestigious IPM HR Director of the Year (2014), and the recipient of the SABPP Lifetime Achievement Award (2014) and of SIOPSA's Honorary Life Membership (2012).

He is in high demand as a speaker, coach and mentor. At his core he is a deeply passionate student of human behaviour in the context of work, and how this can create a better self, team, organisation and society.

Prof Theo H Veldsman

Theo, who is regarded as a thought leader in South Africa with respect to people management and the psychology of work, has demonstrated his ability to proactively identify emerging people and leadership needs and arrive at fit-for-purpose, innovative solutions that are theoretically and practically sound.

Theo holds a PhD in Industrial Psychology and is a registered Industrial Psychologist and Research Psychologist and accredited HRM Practitioner. He prefers to call himself a Work Psychologist. He has extensive research and development, as well as consulting experience gained over the past 35 years in strategy formulation and implementation; strategic organisational change; organisational (re)design; team building; leadership/management and strategic people/talent management. He consults with many leading South African companies as well as organisations overseas, in the roles of advisor, expert and coach/mentor.

In addition to being the author of nearly 200 technical/consulting reports/articles, he has done numerous management and professional presentations and attended seminars at a national and international level. He is the author of two books, and has contributed nine book chapters.

Up to the end of 2016, when he retired, he was Professor and Head of the Department of Industrial Psychology and People Management, Faculty of Management, University of Johannesburg. Since the beginning of 2017 he is a Visiting Professor at the sam eDepartment. He has led the profession of Psychology and Industrial Psychology nationally as president on several occasions. He has been awarded fellowship status by the Society of Industrial and Organisational Psychology of South Africa (SIOPSA), and is the 2012 recipient of a Life-Long Achievement Award from the South African Board for People Practices (SABPP).

ABOUT THE CONTRIBUTORS

Lisa Ashton

Lisa, who holds an M.Com in Human Resources Management (Industrial Psychology), is a senior Industrial Psychologist with a wealth of consulting experience from a wide range of HR and Organisational Change projects and interventions.

She joined Third Foundation Systems (TFS) in 1996 prior to the formation of BIOSS SA. Lisa has worked with CPA and the Matrix of Working Relationships since 1993 and has been with BIOSS Southern Africa since 1996, where she now holds the position of Managing Director. She has worked extensively in Africa, South America, Eastern Europe and the USA. She has also lectured at the University of Johannesburg in Strategic Personnel Management, Organisational Behaviour and Psychometrics. Previous positions include Principal Consultant (MAC Consulting), primarily as part of large-scale organisational change projects, and corporate roles in the banking and telecommunications industries.

Her areas of specialty include executive assessment, succession planning, talent management, HR development, strategic HR planning and coaching. She has a special interest in diversity management, leadership and decision making in the face of complexity. She has learnt that leadership is about creating conditions for others to be successful. Her particular area of expertise is in the development of people strategies to deliver on the strategic intent of organisations.

Lize Booysen

Lize is an internationally recognised scholar-practitioner in the field of leadership, culture and diversity. She is Professor of Leadership and Organizational Behavior at the Graduate School of Leadership and Change at Antioch University, USA, Executive Leadership Coach at the Center for Creative Leadership (CCL), Greensboro, North Carolina, and Senior Research Fellow in the Department of Industrial Psychology and People Management at the University of Johannesburg (UJ), South Africa. She is past Chair of the Business Leadership Member Interest Group of the International Leadership Association (ILA).

Lize has been involved in the 12-nation Leadership Across Differences (LAD) research project steered by the CCL (2003-2010). She participated in the GLOBE 65-nations research project on leadership, national culture and organisational practices (1994-2003), steered by Wharton Business School at the University of Pennsylvania. Prior to joining Antioch in 2009, Lize was Professor at the Graduate School of Business Leadership (SBL), University of South Africa (Unisa) from 1992. She served on the SBL board of directors (1999-2006) and held the portfolios: Director HR Development, as well as Academic Director. She was the Research Manager at the SBL (2007-2008) and served as Editor of the South African *Journal of Labour Relations* (2006-2008).

Lize has received the GLOBE Research Award (1997), Best Academic Career Achievement (Unisa, 2004), Best Professor in Organizational Behavior (2011) and best paper awards (2011, 2013). She features as one of 50 role models for South African women and as leadership expert in *Inspirational women @ work* (Lapa Publishers, 2003).

Graeme Codrington

Futurist, board advisor, author and speaker, Graeme is also an expert on the future of work and disruptive change. His background and experience are rich and varied: from articles at

KPMG to an IT start-up, from work in the non-profit sector to professional speaking. As CEO of TomorrowToday Global, Graeme travels the world working with organisations in every industry and sector, helping them to identify disruptive change and what they can do to become future-fit. He has seen many different ways to succeed – and fail – in this changing world we live in.

In addition to practical experience, he has spent many hours in research, with five degrees and five best-selling books to show for it. He is a guest lecturer at some of the world's top business schools, including Duke, Cornell, London Business School and GIBS. E-mail: graeme@tomorrowtodayglobal.com, see also http://www.graemecodrington.com

Marzanne de Klerk

Marzanne, who holds a DCom in Industrial and Organisational (I/O) Psychology, currently works at the Eskom Leadership Institute, where she focuses on leadership strategy and measurement. She has a vast range of experience in change management, organisational and team development, psychometric assessments, organisational culture design and leadership measurement practices, amongst others. To date she has published two articles on identifying and selecting suitable individuals as change agents in large organisations. She also acts as external examiner for Master's and doctoral research projects and is external supervisor for a number of Master's students, in addition to working as a part-time lecturer. Her involvement in academia allows her to develop others and to gain insight into the latest research in the field of I/O Psychology.

Raymond de Villiers

Ray is a Generation Y/digital natives expert who connects at operational and executive levels of business, thanks to his global experience. He thrives in situations where a strategic understanding of the new world of work is required. He has been 'around the block' with leadership and management positions in a number of entrepreneurial and corporate organisations, both locally and internationally. He brings this to bear on his keynote presentations with relevant and engaging anecdotes which draw on this experience. This may be related (though not limited) to understanding generational dynamics, Generation Y/digital natives, the gamification of the workplace, leadership in a changing world, and being able to translate these diverse drivers of change into relevant and realistic strategies and tactical activities.

He makes effective use of humour, without being a comedian. While his content is well thought through and engaging, it is effectively supported by a style that is easy-going, comfortable, yet engrossing. As part of a team of professional speakers and consultants who all focus on areas that impact and form the new world of work, the collaborative partnership means that the content he delivers is always reflective of the most up-to-date research in the field.

Francois du Plessis

Francois studied and graduated in commerce (HR and Industrial Psychology) and completed his Master's in HR Management (Industrial Psychology). After 15 years of consulting across a wide variety of industries and in the broad organisation development and effectiveness arena, he entered the entrepreneurial world by co-founding the inavit iQ group of companies, of which he is currently Group CEO.

Francois has authored and co-authored various published works (both nationally and internationally), the most recent being *Reshaping leadership DNA* and the *Handbook for human resources in emerging markets*.

Francois' interests and hobbies include mountain biking, sailing, golf and cooking. He also holds a competent crew and level 1 sailing certificate. His passion is business, and in particular helping small and medium enterprises to become the best they can be.

Drikus Kriek

Drikus received an MA (Clin. Psych.) and an MBA (both cum laude) from the Rand Afrikaans University and the University of Stellenbosch respectively. He holds a PhD from the University of Pretoria and is a graduate of Yale University in the USA. At Wits Business School he is Director of the Leadership Development Centre, Associate Professor in Human Resource Management and Leadership, and Programme Director of the International Executive Development Programme and the International Executive Programme for Learning and Development.

His research, publications and teaching focus mainly on teambuilding, leadership and change management. He consults in organisation development and has been involved in team development, management education projects and leadership development programmes. Drikus was instrumental in introducing and advancing the adventure therapy industry in South Africa.

His extensive international work experience was gained in Namibia, Botswana, Australia, Ghana, the DRC and Eritrea. Most recently, he was involved in teambuilding interventions with companies from Slovenia, Russia, Serbia, Mozambique and Namibia. In 2006 he was Visiting Professor at the Integral Leadership Centre of the Graduate School of Management of the University of Western Australia in Perth.

Penny Law

Penny, who co-founded Regenesys with Dr Marko Saravanja in 1999, is the current Dean of the organisation. Prior to this, she worked at the University of the Witwatersrand (Wits) as a lecturer and programme manager, and was Residence Tutorial Scheme Coordinator at the University of Cape Town. She holds a Master's degree in the Psychology of Education (Wits) and a PhD in Spiritual Leadership from the University of the Western Cape (UWC).

As Director and major shareholder, she contributes to the overall strategic direction of Regenesys and its subsidiaries. As Dean, she provides strategic academic oversight and champions academic quality throughout the organisation. She is also responsible for business development and has also consulted for many local and international companies, with the aim of improving their individual and organisational performance.

Carmen le Grange

Carmen is a partner in PwC's Risk Assurance practice, based in Johannesburg. A qualified chartered accountant, she has 19 years' experience in auditing and consulting in the accounting profession.

As Business Resilience Leader for Africa, she is responsible for driving PwC's approach to solutions that cross the intersection of business strategy, governance, risk management, business operations, compliance, internal control and technology. With a strong background on advising clients on risks and controls, Carmen also delivers corporate governance, risk management, compliance and GRC technology services to clients across a number of industries in Africa. Her core competencies include external audit, internal audit, corporate governance, risk consulting, Sarbanes-Oxley, compliance and sustainability reporting.

As a member of PwC's Global Risk Leadership Network, Carmen also represents the Africa practice on the American Psychological Association (APA) and EMEA (Europe, the Middle East and Africa) Risk Leadership Network. She previously served two terms as a member of PwC's southern Africa Governing Board and served on the Clients and Markets Committee. She has served as the Diversity and Inclusion Leader for the southern Africa firm and spent a number of years as Human Capital Partner for the advisory line of service, comprising approximately 1 400 staff members, as well as being Functional Lead for resourcing and recruitment for PwC Africa.

Mmasekgoa Masire-Mwamba

Mmasekgoa served two terms as Deputy Secretary-General for the Commonwealth. As the most senior woman of the 53-country intergovernmental organisation, she actively promoted women as agents of change in leadership and at different levels throughout the Commonwealth. She is Executive Director of the Masire-Mwamba Office (TMMO), which provides high-impact capacity-building, advocacy and advisory services.

With a career spanning over 30 years, she has extensive experience in diplomacy, development, investment promotion, telecommunications and branding. She has also served on various boards and community service institutions in the fields of tourism, business, civil aviation and banking.

Mmasekgoa has an engineering background, having graduated from the University of London with a specialisation in Electronics and Physics. This is complemented by a law degree from the University of South Africa and an MBA from the University of Pittsburgh, in addition to having completed the Advanced Management Programme from IESE in Spain.

In 2015, she was awarded Distinguished International Alumni by the University of Pittsburgh. She was also recognised in the legal field by the Honourable Society of Middle Temple Inn awarding her Honorary Bencher status in 2009.

Nene Molefi

Nene is owner and MD of Mandate Molefi HR Consultants, a well-established company with a track record spanning over 16 years. She previously worked for the City of Cape Town as Executive Director for Transformation and for Eskom, where she was responsible for employment equity.

Nene has garnered a reputation as a thought leader in diversity and inclusion, values-driven leadership and transformation, leadership development and whole-system culture change. She has presented at numerous conferences across the world.

A respected author, she formed part of a global panel of experts who developed the Global Inclusion Benchmark Tool. She is a member of the Diversity Collegium, a think tank of globally recognised diversity experts. She has guest lectured for the Thabo Mbeki African Leadership Institute on value-based leadership, as Associate Lecturer on transformation at Stellenbosch Business School and on unconscious bias, diversity and inclusion at GIBS.

As a Lead Consultant, Nene has managed large-scale culture change projects and led dialogue sessions with executive teams of multinationals. She has worked with the judiciary across all nine High Courts and for Discovery, Sasol, Sapref, Fraser Alexander and Standard Bank.

Nene, a trained coach with the Coaches' Training Institute, also completed its leadership training in San Francisco. She is a skilled process work and deep democracy consultant focusing on social change, and has a wealth of experience as a former non-executive director of companies. She currently serves on the advisory structure of the Auditor General and is a member of the Professional Designation Committee of the Institute of People Management (IPM).

Nene is committed to social entrepreneurship and community involvement. She serves on the board of Meals on Wheels (a non-profit feeding scheme) and of the Community Aids Response (CARE), while coaching and mentoring young women in various stages of their career.

Errol Nembhard

Errol is Executive Director and shareholder of the Pacific Institute SA and Botswana, which is part of a global organisation whose processes and interventions at the leadership level have significantly contributed to transforming the agendas of many blue-chip organisations across the continent. He serves on the Global Advisory Committee for the Pacific Institute in Seattle, Washington.

Errol, who is originally from the UK, has for the last 18 years been at the forefront of the transformation challenges of organisations across the African continent, accumulating successful case studies and insights into the complexity of initiating and sustaining organisational growth and performance. He has developed sound and well-researched views that have been well documented and used by, amongst others, the Council for Scientific and Industrial Research (CSIR), Rand Merchant Bank (RMB), First National Bank (FNB) International, Eskom, Accenture SA/Nigeria, the National Bank of Tanzania, MultiChoice Africa, KPMG and the Office of the Auditor-General.

A continual learner, he is awaiting confirmation award of his MBA from Henley Business School.

Sesh Paruk

Sesh is a leader, integration and synthesis specialist whose global business and organisational experience includes 25 years at executive leadership level; strategic planning and scenario planning; strategic leadership advisory services and executive coaching; transformation and change management; culture change and organisational integration and synthesis; talent management and capacity building.

She has spent 20 working in the academic, research and health sectors, as well as the advanced integrative health and life coaching sectors. She has consulted to NGOs, the public and private sectors (including the Parliament of South Africa), the energy and science sector and several academic institutions. Sesh currently serves on the Governance Board of the National Consumer Tribunal, the Medical Board on Emergency Health Care, the Editorial Board of the Electronic Newsletter *Trailblazer* (a platform for open dialogue and innovation), and is a member of the United Nations Peace-Keeping Foundation and the Global Girl Up Campaign, which has reached more than 20 000 adolescent girls in developing countries.

Nominated by Chief Executive Office Communications as one of South Africa's most influential women and profiled by the Legacy Project as a significant female leader in Africa, she focuses on enterprise leadership, integration and synthesis, the management of complexity, leveraging potential leading to organisational and individual performance excellence, facilitating strategic collaboration and systemic synchronisation. She is trusted as an experienced leader due to her personal work ethic; strong driving of business results with energy, passion and vision; planning with meticulous attention to detail and skills that align with global best practice.

Steven Teasdale

Steven currently occupies an executive role in the Eskom Leadership Institute with a primary responsibility for the leadership strategy and executive talent management of the organisation. In the past he headed up the organisational effectiveness portfolio at Eskom. He was recruited in London by Eskom seven years ago, where he was Senior Manager for Strategy at an actuarial and investment consultancy. Prior to this he operated as a management consultant at a number of global organisations, including Deloitte, Aon and Mercer.

Steven is deeply passionate about supporting organisations to become highly effective systems and firmly believes the role of leadership is the fundamental component to executing organisational strategy. He holds an MBA (Creativity, Innovation & Change and Strategic Finance) from Open University Business School (OUBS), UK.

Marius Ungerer

Marius is Professor of Strategic Management at the University of Stellenbosch Business School (USB). He is also a visiting Professor at Nagoya University of Commerce & Business in Japan, and the University of Johannesburg in South Africa. He previously worked in financial services, manufacturing, information technology, aviation, education and training.

He completed an honours degree in Industrial Psychology at the University of Stellenbosch, an MCom and DCom at the Rand Afrikaans University, and a MBA at Potchefstroom University. He has published in journals such as *International Business Review, Southern African Business Review, African Journal of Business Management* and *South African Journal of Industrial Psychology and Sustainability*. He is the co-author of five books on strategic management and leadership.

Boris Urban

Boris, a Professor at the Graduate School of Business Administration (WBS), University of the Witwatersrand, has practised, taught and researched strategy, organisational behaviour and entrepreneurship. The first appointed Chair in Entrepreneurship (Lamberti) at Wits, he is a rated researcher.

With more than 70 publications in high-impact academic journals, his work is increasingly cited in the field. He is the editor and co-author of the prescribed book series 'Perspectives in entrepreneurship: A research companion', and co-authored *Entrepreneurship theory and practice* (3rd ed.). He has presented papers at, amongst others, the Academy of Management and the International Council of Small Business (ICSB). He serves on the editorial board of the *Journal of Social Entrepreneurship* (Oxford), the *Journal of Social Business* (UK) and local journals.

Boris holds a PhD in Entrepreneurship (University of Pretoria). He has served on the EMAA NRF Specialist Committee (2014–2018), as Acting WBS Director (2009), Research Director (2013) and on the Wits Senate (since 2010). As Programme Director at WBS, Boris introduced the Master of Management in Entrepreneurship (Ranked in Top 100 Best Masters.com). His research theme leads the Centre for Entrepreneurship (Cfe) at the WBS, serves as a platform for research fellows and provides access to international networks. He has contributed to initiatives such as the World Economic Forum (YGL), EY G20 Entrepreneurship Monitor Report, *Sunday Times* Directors' Event, and MIT Global Start-ups panels. He also sits on the Executive Board of the Africa Business and Entrepreneurship Research Society, and presented his research findings to the Office of the SA Presidency.

Through training and consulting, he has delivered interventions to clients in the private, NGO and public sectors. His primary research agenda is to integrate the personal and social foci of causation within a unified explanatory structure to understand entrepreneurial behaviour at individual, organisational and societal levels.

Leon van Vuuren

Leon is Executive Director: Professional and Business Ethics at the Ethics Institute. Prior to joining the institute in July 2014, he was Professor in Industrial Psychology in the Department of Industrial Psychology and People Management (IPPM) at the University of Johannesburg, where he taught industrial psychology and business and professional ethics for 26 years. He is professionally registered as a Psychologist (Category: Industrial) with the Health Professions Council of South Africa (HPCSA). He serves on the Professional Board for Psychology of the HPCSA where he is, amongst others, Chairperson of the Committee for Preliminary Inquiry (Ethics Committee).

Anton Verwey

Anton holds a DCom (Leadership and Change) from the Rand Afrikaans University. He takes a different perspective to the much-studied subject of leadership, focusing on leadership instead of on the individual leader. He has experience in a wide range of industries in the fields of business strategy, organisation and work architecture, leadership talent development and human capital processes and systems. For the past two decades his focus has primarily been on leadership capacity-building strategies and processes. In this context, he has worked with organisations ranging from SMEs to listed companies, as well as state-owned enterprises.

He is the co-author of two books: *Reshaping leadership DNA* (VDM Verlag, Germany) and *Reshaping leadership DNA: A field guide* (Knowledge Resources). He is also the author and co-author of a number of articles and has supervised (in a part-time capacity) more than ten Master's and doctoral studies. Anton is the Executive Chairman of inavit iQ (Pty) Ltd who oversees the Business Development and Solutions Crafting portfolios for the group. E-mail: amverwey@mweb.co.za

Sonja Verwey

Sonja is Head of the School of Communication at the University of Johannesburg. She is also the Head of the Department of Strategic Communication, one of three departments within the school. She specialises in the field of organisational communication/communication management, having obtained both her Master's and doctorate in this field. She is past and present editor of *Communicare*, the official journal for Communication Sciences in southern Africa, and has served on the editorial boards of *Communicatio*, *Communitas* and *African Communication Review*. She currently serves on the editorial boards of the *International Journal of Strategic Communication* and *Communicatio*.

Sonja was the first female president of the Southern African Communication Association and is currently a member of the board of the Council for Communication Management. She has published various academic articles and is the editor/author of several chapters/academic textbooks. She has taught across a broad range of communication disciplines at both local and overseas universities. She consults on a part-time basis in several private sector companies, mainly within the field of communication management.

Vusi Vilakati

Vusi was born and raised in Mbabane, Swaziland, and has lived and worked in South Africa as a religious minister in the Methodist Church of Southern Africa (MCSA) since 2000. He graduated from the Swaziland College of Technology with a Diploma in Construction Studies (1998). His undergraduate theological studies were at John Wesley Theological Seminary and his postgraduate honours and MA in Biblical and Religious Studies were completed at the University of Pretoria (2006). He obtained an MPhil in Human Resource Management (cum laude) in Personal and Professional Leadership (2012) and is currently pursuing a PhD in Leadership in Performance and Change from the University of Johannesburg.

Vusi's experience covers a number of leadership, pastoral and policy formulation roles within the MCSA: being the District Secretariat, Adjunct Lecturer at the Methodist Seminary, a member of the HR unit, as well as serving on the Doctrine, Ethics and Worship committee within the MCSA. His current interests and research include African consciousness in leadership coaching, the role of business in society, corporate citizenship, outcomes-based and ethical leadership, holistic leadership development, and the economic and human advancement of Africa.

Tineke Wulffers

Tineke divides her time between her practitioner and academic work. She is Director of the Moya Institute of Authentic Leadership Effectiveness. Her senior organisational leadership clients have told her the organisational world can 'squeeze the self out of the self'. In response, her passion is to facilitate the development of individual and team authentic leadership effectiveness for the greater good of themselves, their organisations and stakeholders. Her work allows leaders to enhance their leadership authenticity, inter-relational trust, and individual and team leadership effectiveness, which has a positive effect on their results.

As an academic she is affiliated with both the University of Stellenbosch Business School (USB) and the Wits Business School (WBS) where she supervises and examines the work of postgraduate students. She obtained her PhD in Personal and Professional Leadership in the Faculty of Management at the University of Johannesburg in 2014, having completed her Master's (cum laude) in Professional Coaching with Middlesex University (UK) in 2009. She regularly writes academic articles on authentic leadership development, and is the author of *Authentic Leadership Effectiveness for Individuals and Teams: A Coaching Approach*. For more information, see www.moyatf.co.za

SECTION 1
SETTING THE SCENE

Chapter 1

ORIENTATION

Theo H Veldsman and Andrew J Johnson

On many fronts, and in many ways, our insight into and the exercise of leadership is under severe scrutiny because of a radically changing and significantly different world; reinventing organisations; and working persons with significantly different, or significantly shifting, needs, expectations and aspirations. Without doubt, leadership is in the overheating crucible of a reframed/reframing world that is in the throes of fundamental and radical transformation.

The current fierce debate about leadership and leadership excellence (or lack thereof) may be one of the most important issues of our present time, alongside issues such as demographic shifts, the distribution of economic prosperity, food and water security, world peace, global warming, and sustainability. It could even be argued that these issues in and of themselves are but symptomatic of poor leadership; or, at worst, of the inability and/or a lack in the commitment to lead.

The clarion call is clear and unequivocal. At this critical juncture in our history, the search is on for better *and* different leadership. Leaders and leadership have to reinvent themselves if they wish to be successful in the unfolding world of tomorrow. Old recipes and conventional ways of leading will no longer suffice. They may even be detrimental and destructive. It can be argued that those nations, societies, communities and organisations that are able to demonstrate leadership excellence consistently will dominate and inherit the future, in particular in the case of emerging countries in Africa. Our very future is predicated on the quality of our current and future leadership who will either make us architects or victims of the future.

Without any doubt leadership is *the* critical strategic capability of nations, societies, communities and organisations, making them sustainably future-fit. The primary trigger for *Leadership Excellence* is therefore to be found in the snowballing crisis around leadership, and the consequential imperative for better and different leadership.

The Strategic Leadership Value Chain Perspective: A Meta-framework From Which to View Leadership

Leadership is a critical organisational capability and intervention. To the best of our knowledge no overall, systemic, integrated and holistic perspective is available in the literature viewing leadership from a Strategic Leadership Value Chain perspective. Such a perspective would provide a meta-framework from which to look at leadership systemically and holistically as an organisational intervention. Such a perspective would assist one not only in bringing order to the overwhelming, exploding leadership literature, but also serve as an overall, integrative map for organisations in engaging with leadership. At best numerous, piecemeal treatises are available dealing with specialised leadership intervention topics, e.g. leadership assessment, leadership development, or leadership well-being but no overarching meta-framework exits.

Figure 1.1 provides our take on the make-up of the Strategic Leadership Value Chain in terms of which leadership as a mission-critical, strategic organisational capability and intervention can be viewed.

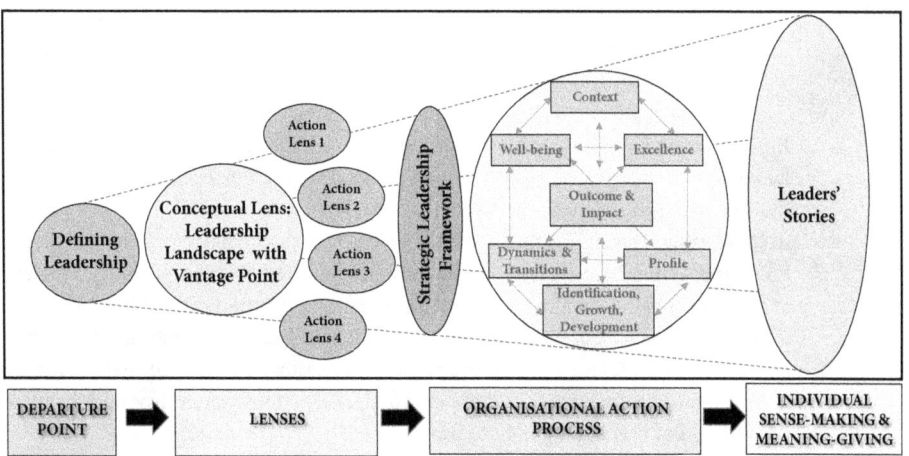

Figure 1.1 A Strategic Leadership Value Chain Perspective on leadership as an organisational capability and intervention

The make-up of the Strategic Leadership Value Chain

With reference to Figure 1.1, the Strategic Leadership Value Chain is composed of the following elements:

- *Departure point: Defining leadership*

    In crafting an organisation-specific leadership thinking framework, the organisation as a starting point must formulate explicitly and intentionally what they understand "leadership" as a phenomenon to be conceptually, in order to correctly demarcate the territory called "leadership". An incorrect definition of leadership can delineate the phenomenon either too narrowly, consequently excluding essential elements of leadership; or too broadly, resulting in the inclusion of unrelated elements ("noise") in its definition.

- *Lenses*

    Having demarcated the territory called "leadership" by defining it, the organisation must next construct and/or select the lenses it will use to map, make sense of, and give meaning to the demarcated leadership territory. The lenses represent the "toolbox" the organisation will use in engaging with the leadership territory. Three types of lenses can be discerned:

    o **Conceptual lens:** This represents the organisation's meta-view – its 'Google map' - of what building blocks (= 'towns with their suburbs') with their interdependencies (= 'roads') make up the demarcated leadership territory. We call this meta-conceptual view the 'Leadership Landscape'.

    The value of the Leadership Landscape as meta-conceptual view of the leadership territory is three-fold:
    - *to simplify*, organise and integrate at a meta-level the complexity of the field of leadership with its ever-expanding and overwhelming literature;
    - *to provide* a common meta-language for an all-inclusive, coherent leadership dialogue about leadership, for example in teaching, or in an organisation; and

- *to structure* an organisation's conversation about leadership, enabling it to arrive at a customised Strategic Leadership Framework (see below) for the organisation that will direct and guide its thinking, decisions and actions regarding leadership as a strategic organisational capability and intervention.
    o *Interpretative Lens:* A Vantage Point next must be chosen by which the Leadership Landscape with its building blocks will be interpreted. For example, Appreciative Inquiry or Critical Management Theory.
    o *Action Lenses:* Having mapped the leadership territory, and having chosen a Vantage Point, the Action Lenses serve as enabling tools selected by the organisation to deal and work with the various building blocks making up the Leadership Landscape. Action tools represent various disciplines and theoretical/ practical approaches that can be used to engage with the leadership territory in order to make sense of it. Examples of such action tools are neuroscience, action science, psychodynamics, narratives, and psychobiographical profiling.

- *Strategic leadership framework*

    In proceeding along the Strategic Leadership Value Chain (see Figure 1.1), the organisation next has to make choices regarding its specific position on each of the building blocks making up the Leadership Landscape as Conceptual Lens, based on how it strategically wants to position leadership in its organisation.

    For example with respect to some of the building blocks of the Leadership Landscape, the choices are:

    o Its chosen *Leadership Stance* regarding leadership for the organisation: Does leadership need to be task- and/ or people-centric? Must leadership be present or/ and future focused?
    o Its desired *Leadership Style(s)*: Tell, Consultative, Co-determination and/ or Self-Governance?
    o Its repertoire of expected *Leadership Roles*: Resources, Coach, Guide, Networker?
    o *Leadership Talent Management*: its make-up; strategic talent timeframe; and talent pools.

    The Strategic Leadership Framework therefore forms the reference point and basis regarding all the organisation's decisions and actions with respect to leadership. Its sits as a bridge between the organisation's Leadership Thinking Framework on the one hand, being part of the Thinking Framework itself. And, on the other hand, the Framework directs and guides how 'things' must happen in the organisation with respect to leadership.

- *Organisational action processes*

    The organisational action process refers to the frontline decisions and actions the organisation has to take on a daily basis regarding leadership. This process is made up of an integrated, reciprocally interdependent, set of organisational actions, embedded in an organisational change navigation process (represented in Figure 1.1 by the circle in which these actions are contained). The actions are as follows:

    o **Action 1:** Understanding the unfolding *Leadership Context* with its leadership challenges, demands and requirements;
    o **Action 2:** Formulating a context relevant, *Leadership Excellence* model;
    o **Action 3:** Generating a future-fit *Leadership Brand and Profile*;

- o   **Action 4:** *Identifying, Growing and Developing* the organisation's leadership talent;
- o   **Action 5:** Managing the ongoing, everyday *Leadership Dynamics and Transitions* in the organisation;
- o   **Action 6:** Ensuring and enhancing *Leadership Well-being* (and countering leadership mal-being); and
- o   **Action 7:** Monitoring and tracking *Leadership Outcomes and Impact*

- *Individual sense-making and meaning-giving: Leadership stories*

  In the final instance, leaders have to be prolific, enticing storytellers. Through the stories they construct and share, leaders make sense of and give meaning to their leadership experiences, for themselves and others. Hopefully and ideally speaking, leadership experiences are transformed into information; information into knowledge; and knowledge into wisdom. In turn, the distilled wisdom can be applied to ground, enhance and enrich in a recursive fashion the preceding Strategic Leadership Value Chain elements as elucidated above.

This book – *Leadership Excellence* – forms part of a five book series covering the respective elements of the Strategic Leadership Value Chain. The accompanying box gives a list of the books in the series, and what portion of the Strategic Value Chain they address.

Book	Portion of Strategic Leadership Value Chain Addressed (Refer back to figure 1.1)
Book 1: Understanding Leadership	Departure Point: Defining Leadership Lenses: Conceptual, Interpretive, Action Strategic Leadership Framework
Book 2: Leadership in Context	Organisational Action Process • Action 1: Understanding the unfolding Leadership Context with its leadership challenges, demands and requirements
Book 3: Leadership Excellence (This book)	Organisational Action Process • Action 2: Formulating a context relevant, Leadership Excellence Model • Action 3: Generating a future-fit, Leadership Brand and Profile • Action 7: Monitoring and tracking Leadership Outcomes and Impact
Book 4: Building Leadership Talent	Organisational Action Process • Action 4: Identifying, growing and developing the organisation's leadership talent
Book 5: Leadership Dynamics and Well Being	Organisational Action Process • Action 5: Managing the ongoing, everyday Leadership Dynamics and Transitions in the organisation • Action 6: Ensuring and enhancing leadership well-being (and countering leadership mal-being)

Book	Portion of Strategic Leadership Value Chain Addressed (Refer back to figure 1.1)
Leadership Stories	Throughout the above five books stories by prominent SA leaders are given to illustrate how they have made sense of and given meaning to leadership

Purpose and Structure of *Leadership Excellence*

The purpose of *Leadership Excellence* is to address Leadership Excellence (Section 1), Leadership Brand and Profile (Section 2) and Leadership Outcomes and Impact (Section 3) as action domains in the Organisational Action Process. The location of the Organisational Action Process within the Value Chain, and the action domains discussed in *Leadership Excellence*, are indicated by arrows in Figure 1.2. (To note: all of the actions making up the Organisational Action Process are encapsulated in an organisational change navigation process, represented in Figure 1.2 by the circle enclosing these actions).

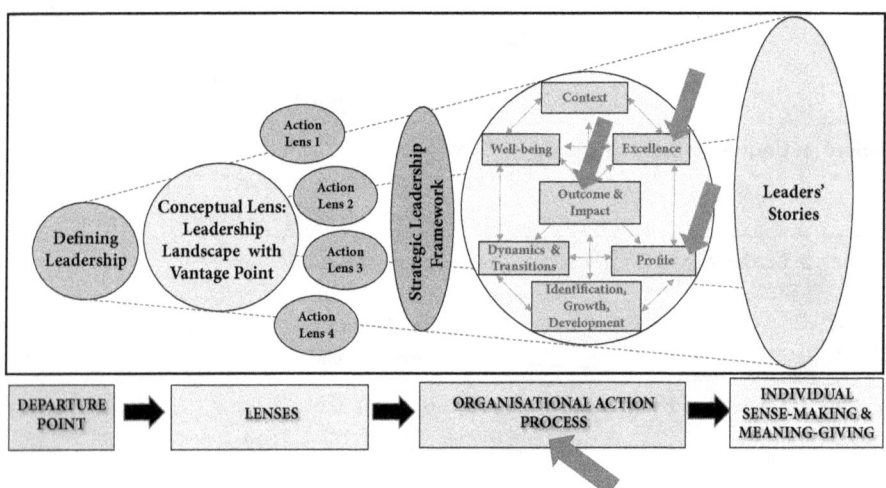

Figure 1.2 Organisational Action Process of the Strategic Leadership Value Chain: Excellence

Relative to the Context action domain of the Organisational Action Process (see Figure 2.1), the organisation needs to craft a *Leadership Excellence Model*: what will it take for leadership to be successful in the demarcated, unfolding Leadership Context, in the present and going into the future? The Excellence Model acts as reference and comparison point in the organisational dialogue about what leadership the organisation needs to be sustainably, future-fit.

Leadership Excellence is covered in *Leadership Excellence* from two angles:

- a generic *Leadership Excellence Model* using the Service Profit Chain as frame of reference from which leadership excellence dimensions are derived.
- *cross-cultural differences in and preferences for desirable leadership attributes*, and hence Leadership Excellence, given that in a global world organisations are global/ globalising with

a consequentially increasingly diverse work force. Key to global leadership excellence is cross-cultural leadership at the individual, team, organisational and societal levels.

The next action in the Organisational Action Process is to *Brand* and *Profile* tomorrow' leaders as required by the organisation relative to the unfolding Leadership Context, and its crafted Leadership Excellence Model.

Four elements are essential in considering the Branding and Profiling of tomorrow's leadership as depicted in Figure 1.3.

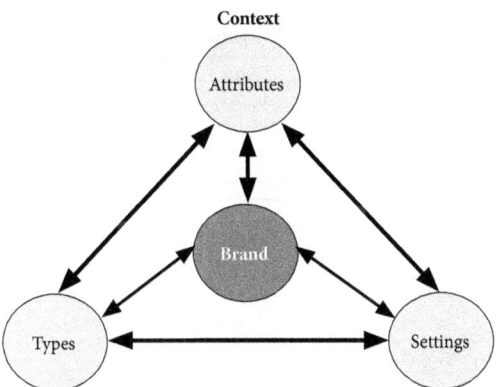

Figure 1.3 Leadership Brand, Attributes, Types and Settings to be considered with respect to tomorrow's leadership

The four elements in Figure 1.3 can be described as follows:

- Leadership Brand: The identity and reputation of leaders throughout an organization
- Leadership Attributes: The critical qualities with constituent capabilities of tomorrow's leaders
- Leadership Types: Specific categories of tomorrow's leaders
- Leadership Setting: Particular settings of tomorrow's leaders

The choice of topics for Leadership Excellence were made on the basis what was believed will be of relevance for tomorrow's leadership, now and going into the future.

In the previous action of the Organisational Action Process we have addressed Leadership Brand and Profiling. Next to consider in this process is *Leadership Outcomes and Impact*: what, how and when must leadership success be measured? This action sits at the center of the total Action Process as can be seen in Figure 1.2.

Based on the above discussion of the pertinent Action Process Steps, and Figure 1.3, the topics addressed in *Leadership Excellence* are given in the accompanying box.

SECTION	TOPICS ADDRESSED	CHAPTER
Section 2: Leadership Excellence and Branding	Leadership excellence dimensions	2
	Leadership excellence across cultural settings	3
	Leadership brand modelling	4
Section 3: Leadership Attributes	Authentic Leadership	5
	Mindful leadership	6
	Virtuous leadership	7
	Wise leadership	8
	Spiritual leadership	9
	Ethical leadership	10
Section 4: Leadership Types	African leadership	11
	Woman leadership	12
	Multi-generational leadership	13
	Diversity Leadership	14
	Change leadership	15
Section 5: Leadership Settings	Team leadership	16
	Entrepreneurial leadership	17
	Board leadership	18
Section 6: Leadership Outcomes and Impact	Leadership excellence measurement	19

Leadership Stories (Section 7: Chapter 20)

In this section prominent leaders express their personal views on leadership from the front line where it is happening for them, , illustrating may of the topics discussed in *Leadership Excellence*.

The future of leadership (Section 8: Chapter 21)

In this chapter we would like to gaze in the crystal ball by answering the question: If there is a need for better and different leadership going into the future? If yes, and what would it look like with the conditions attached to such future-fit leadership?

Our intention with and aspirations for *Leadership Excellence* – Ambitious and bold, but humble

Our intention with and aspiration for *Leadership Excellence* is for the book to be a thought leadership book on understanding leadership excellence from multiple angles: leadership excellence itself; leadership brand and profile; and leadership outcomes and impact. *Firstly*, by providing cutting edge, present-into-the-future, and future-into-the-present, thinking with respect to leadership excellence, leveraged from the best currently available insights and informed views. *Secondly*, by providing actionable knowledge and theory-informed practice about leadership excellence where it matters at the organisational front line.

Both in our intention and aspiration we realise we may be overly ambitious and bold by deciding what we believe are some of the more important Contexts in which leadership is embedded. Simultaneously, however, we are fortuitously humbled by the depth, richness and diversity of the overwhelming, exploding body of knowledge regarding different Leadership Contexts. In no way can we claim, or wish to claim, that we therefore have covered all of the possible/ potential Leadership Contexts. That would be arrogant.

The Intended Audience of *Leadership Excellence*

In the first place, *Leadership Excellence* intends to assist executives and leadership specialists within organisations, whether public or private, to direct, guide and build – confidently and with well-grounded insight – leadership as a mission critical organisational capability and intervention in their organisations, using a Strategic Leadership Value Chain perspective. In this way we hope that they will be able to ensure a future-fit organisation and leadership who are able and willing to be architects of the future they so ardently desire.

In the second place, *Leadership Excellence* aims to assist academics and their students in the teaching and studying of leadership as a critically important subject. In the third place, the topics covered in *Leadership Excellence* may also provide creative triggers to future leadership research.

The Intended Use of *Leadership Excellence*

The intended use of *Leadership Excellence* is to serve as a handy daily "desktop" reference book on leadership lenses to our intended audience:

- for ongoing referral as and when ways of understanding leadership matters arise in an organisation, and
- where input from a thought leadership source is desired and necessary on available leadership lenses.

Thus *Leadership Excellence* is not intended to "Rest in Peace" on the bookshelf but to be a "Working Manual" by being an ever-present companion for continuous, daily consulting, referral and advice. Also in a similar fashion assist as a reference for teaching on and research into leadership.

The Expected Value-add of *Leadership Excellence*

We hope *Leadership Excellence* will provide you as the reader with seven overriding insights (or Lessons-to-be-Learnt):

Leadership Excellence

- Without a well thought through, organisationally entrenched, understood and accepted *Leadership Excellence Model* to direct and guide the organisation's thinking, its decisions and actions regarding success criteria for future-fit leadership will be confused, conflicting, and at cross-purposes.
- In a global world with global/ globalizing organisations, the organisation's Leadership Excellence Model has to incorporate *cross-cultural leadership excellence* dimensions and criteria in order to take account of cross-cultural differences in and preferences for desirable leadership attributes.

Brand and Profile

- The criticality of establishing and maintaining a *clear, distinct identity of and reputation for leaders, a Brand*, throughout the organisation and beyond its boundaries.
- The required leaders tomorrow for an organization have to be profiled multi-dimensionally according to *attributes, types and settings relative to the unfolding Context* in which they have to lead.
- *Congruent, integrated leadership profiles* in terms attributes, types and settings of tomorrow's leaders have to be generated.

Leadership Outcomes and Impact

- The degree to which leadership is successful depends almost entirely on the Leadership Context within which the question is asked, of whom, and by whom. Different stakeholders have different definitions and criteria, and therefore different perspectives on *Leadership Excellence Outcomes and Impact*. This will most definitely change as we move into the future within a VUCA context. The formulation and assessment of Leadership Excellence Outcomes and Impact hence will be a moving target going into the future.
- The *Service Profit Chain Model* provides a useful perspective from which to view *Leadership Excellence*. It ties together in an integrated, systemic way: organisational capacity; external stakeholder requirements; the organisation's fit to its competitive landscape; the internal organisational brand (or culture); employee engagement; stakeholder delight (or satisfaction); business performance; and the organisation's external brand.

We wish you a stimulating, enriching and capacitating journey through *Leadership Excellence*

SECTION 2

LEADERSHIP EXCELLENCE AND BRANDING

Chapter 2

LEADERSHIP EXCELLENCE DIMENSIONS
Anton Verwey, Ronel Minnaar and Paul Mooney

The title of this chapter is meaningful as the two key words *Leadership* and *Excellence* imply *success*. Each one of these words is subject to very personal interpretation and meaning, and we will attempt to be as clear and precise as we can be about the meaning we attached to them for the purposes of this chapter and *Leadership Excellence*.

From the overall perspective of *Leadership Excellence*, this chapter begins to pull together the ideas shared in how we think about leadership and how the context within which leadership plays out raises specific challenges. When reading this chapter, the reader may want to refer also to the following chapters:

- Chapter 4: Leadership brand modelling; and
- Chapter 19: Leadership excellence measurement

The purpose of this chapter is to elucidate the dimensions of Leadership Excellence. In doing so, the chapter will cover the following topics: what is 'success'; the service – profit chain model as a logical model for organisational cause and effect; Leadership Excellence dimensions; a practical approach to developing the 'Being' of leadership; and finally the 'Doing' of leadership.

What is "Success"?

In many respects, this is a very complex question to answer, as the degree to which leadership is successful depends almost entirely on the context within which the question is asked and of whom. One may make, for example, the assumption that if shareholders are satisfied with return on investment that (i) the organisation is successful and therefore (ii) its leaders are successful. For the same company, another group of stakeholders may, however, consider the organisation and its leaders to be unsuccessful as they are causing harm to the environment.

Of course, the fact that different stakeholders have different criteria and therefore different perspectives on success should not be new to the readers of *Leadership Excellence*. What one may want to reflect on is how criteria of success of institutions and their leadership will shift as we move ahead. What we can be fairly certain of is that stakeholders will determine the definition of success in ways we have not even considered as yet, using criteria we are not aware of yet.

Success, in our view, is therefore a constantly shifting set of expectations being formulated and reformulated based on constantly changing groupings of stakeholders. To some degree at least, this means that organisations and their leadership have simultaneously to focus on what they consider to be success and to be open to the possibility that this may change. The perspectives of some leaders may be useful in exploring this thinking:

- While we tend to think of success along two metrics — money and power — we need to add a third: *"To live the lives we truly want and deserve, and not just the lives we settle for, we need a third measure of success that goes beyond the two metrics of money and power, and consists of four pillars: well-being, wisdom, wonder, and giving."* – Arianna Huffington
- *"Success in life could be defined as the continued expansion of happiness and the progressive realization of worthy goals."* – Deepak Chopra

The Service-Profit Model Chain as a Logical Model for Cause and Effect

Figure 2.1 depicts a model positioning leadership as the driver of strategy and employee engagement which clearly includes elements of both the external and internal experience of leadership (in other words, the brand).

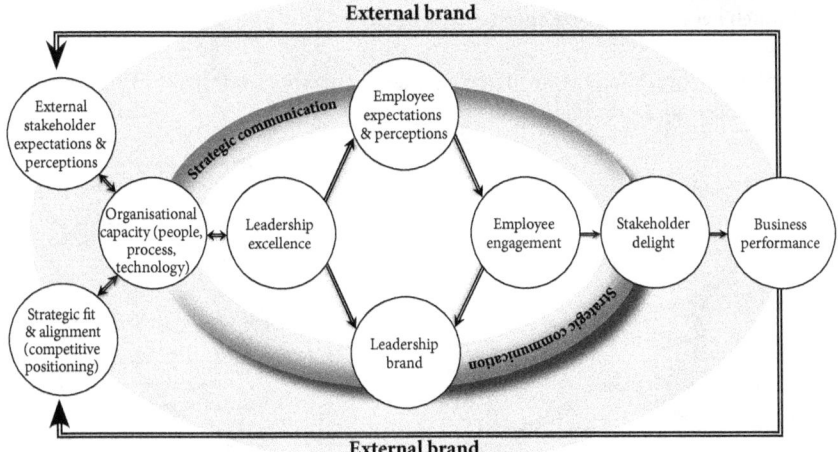

Figure 2.1: Modified service profit chain

In essence, this model suggests that:

1. **Leadership Excellence** is in the first instance about the creation of the required **organisational capacity** (people, process and technology) (i) to meet the **requirements of all external stakeholders** and (ii) to ensure **current and future fit to its competitive landscape**;
2. Leadership Excellence is then simultaneously the driver of the **internal brand** (or culture) which is determined by the degree to which (i) the leadership brand is able to meet the **expectations of employees** so that (ii) high levels of **employee engagement** (commitment) are achieved;
3. Employee engagement drives **stakeholder delight** or satisfaction; which
4. Leads to **business performance** that serves as an input to both external stakeholder perceptions and competitive positioning and in this manner creates the **external brand**.
5. It is of key importance that a deliberate process of **strategic communication** be implemented to ensure alignment between the internal leadership brand and the external organisation brand.

Leadership Excellence Dimensions

Given that leadership plays a central role in the model proposed above and therefore in the achievement of success, it may be useful to explore exactly what Leadership Excellence may look like.

The dimensions

Keeping in mind the context created by Figure 2.1, the following questions arise:

- What does leadership look like that can formulate strategy that will ensure sustainable competitive advantage?
- What does leadership look like that can create the organisational capacity to execute the strategy effectively and efficiently;
- Through people who are committed and engaged?

In our experience, organisations are increasingly asking questions that may be summarised as in Figure 2.2: *Leadership Dimensions*

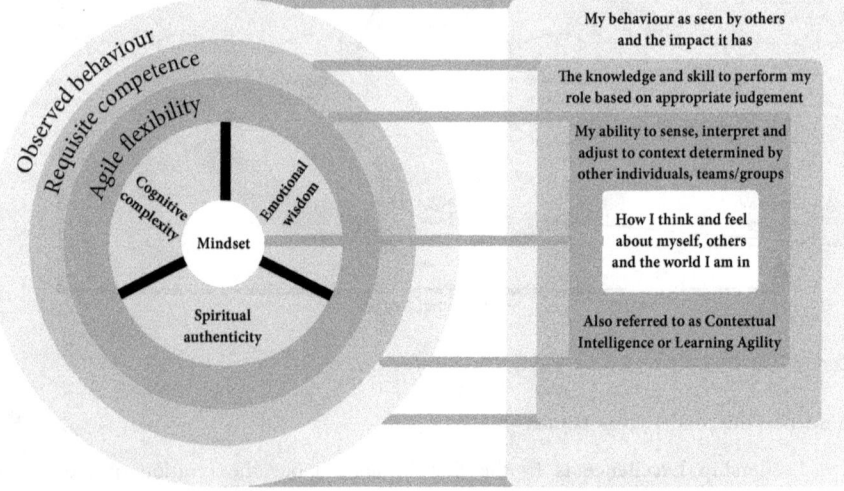

Figure 2.2: Leadership dimensions

What is suggested is that the leaders who can address the questions posed in Figure 2.2 above have mastered the following:

- They have great clarity on exactly who they are, and how they think and feel about other people, as well as the external context within which they work;
- They are able to understand the context of others, sometimes referred to as contextual intelligence (or learning agility);
- They have the knowledge and skill to exercise judgement appropriately; and
- They consistently behave in a manner that creates positive impact.

We are mindful that these simple points in fact assume a wide range of demands being placed on leadership (and the leader). In our work with clients, we have begun to use a specific language to clarify the thinking contained in these points.

The "Being" of leadership

Firstly, we use the term "leadership capability" to include four aspects, these being:

- The *mind-set* of the individual leader and/or of the leadership community, including values, beliefs, worldviews;

- The ability to generate *cognitive complexity* appropriate to their role, informed by the Levels of Work Theory;
- The *emotional wisdom* to be able to engage the hearts and minds of people – all having their own perspectives and dreams – and to realise and recognise the impact of behaviour and actions on those around us;
- The *spiritual authenticity* to remain a constant in an ever-changing world so that trust is based on predictability; and
- More recently, we have come to the conclusion that for a number of reasons, leaders and leadership need the ability to move across different contexts quite rapidly and frequently. The ability to do so is referred to as *agile flexibility*.

The balance of this chapter will explore these elements of leadership so as to lay the foundation for the next chapter that will focus specifically on competence.

Leadership mindset

"For individuals, character is destiny. For organisations, culture is destiny." We argue that the character leaders display as individuals and collectively as a leadership community, over time define the predominant culture within the organisation they lead. It is therefore critical to understand what character is and what it entails. Sweeney and Fry analysed various definitions of leader character and as a result, they suggest leader character entails the following: (1) core moral beliefs, (2) actions consistent with these moral beliefs, and (3) the psychological strengths that allow leaders to move from beliefs and intentions to moral actions. They furthermore propose that a leader's actions that are internally motivated to maintain consistency with their core moral beliefs and identities, and promote the greater good of the community, reflect their true character.

What is mindset, what does it consist of, and how does it link to character? Numerous authors have written about this subject over past decades. Literally it can be seen as a way of thinking and some refer to it as a mental inclination or a frame of mind. Mindset is a collection of our values and beliefs that shape our attitude. Attitude affects how we think and feel, and what we do. Mindset can also be seen as our worldview, the frame of mind from which we experience our reality and form perceptions of it. The cornerstones of our mindset are the fundamental assumptions we form about our reality and the core beliefs we have about ourselves, others and life in general.

According to Sweeney and Fry, leadership and psychological literature suggests that a leader's core values and belief system are the foundation of their character. Core values and beliefs are the cognitive structures that influence leaders' awareness of moral and ethical issues, judgement, intentions and moral and ethical behaviour. The degree to which leaders integrate their core values, beliefs and moral standards into their self-identities will influence the consistency of their moral and ethical behaviour.

> "You cannot not model. It's impossible. People will see your example – positive or negative – as a pattern for the way life is to be lived."
> – Stephen Covey

In a number of his publications Stephen Covey[1] refers to the fact that we cannot hide or disguise our deepest self. He argues that no matter how skilful we are in pretending and posturing, our real desires, values, beliefs and feelings come out in a thousand ways.

Leaders' own personal example – the consistency and integrity of their own life – gives credibility to everything they try to do and accomplish. As other people see in their lives the model of what they are trying to encourage in the lives of others, people will feel that they can believe in and trust their leaders because they are trustworthy.

In light of the shared perspectives in the preceding paragraphs, the realisation must be that our mindset and how it leads to the character we display, is dynamic and complex. Awareness is the critical first step, but will not lead to sustaining success unless a leader creates and owns the motivation to change and improve his/her mindset and those aspects it entails, such as worldviews, beliefs, values and attitude. Sweeney and Fry suggest that there are supporting character strengths available to a leader for facilitating integration of core values and beliefs into self-identify, enhancing judgement, and increasing consistency in behaviour. These supporting strengths are: (i) sense of agency, (ii) self-awareness, (iii) self-motivation and (iv) self-regulation.

Through a *sense of agency*, the leader assumes responsibility for his/her own mindset, believing that one has the ability to guide the development of mindset (self-efficacy) and makes a commitment to constantly strive towards improved worldviews, values, beliefs and attitudes.

Self-awareness assists leaders with gaining understanding of who they truly are and who they want to become. It develops mindfulness about one's thoughts and feelings when engaging in day-to-day activities. This mindfulness about the present is enhanced through engaging in reflection and introspection, developing self-knowledge and gaining insights regarding one's thoughts, feelings and desires and how they affect behaviour. Through self-awareness leaders also develop a sense of their readiness and openness to change.

Self-motivation highlights the importance that motivation for aligning mindset with the required behaviour a leader wants to display, has to be drawn from internal sources. Internal motivation is drawn from leaders assuming ownership and believing in their ability to influence their own development and shape their external environment.

The last strength applicable here is *self-regulation*. Self-regulation refers to the ability to understand and control one's emotions, thoughts and behaviours to achieve the desired outcomes through self-directed influence.

During engagements with leaders in our client systems, a view often uttered is that it is seen as hard and difficult work to be busy with ourselves and the thoughts, beliefs and attitudes we entertain. For some leaders, it requires hard work and practice just to establish a habit of reflection and introspection that will lead to developing self-awareness. Leaders often battle with translating this self-awareness they have developed into actions that will affect their worldviews, beliefs, values and attitudes in such a way that the desired behaviour change is seen and sustained. We have also worked with leaders who just cannot adjust their mindsets and as a result sustained change in leadership behaviour is just not possible.

Leaders who have great clarity on who they are, and who have developed an understanding of how they think and feel about other people and the external context within which they work, display the leadership capability to adjust quite rapidly to different contexts.

Cognitive complexity

In 1967, Schroeder et al[2] defined cognitive complexity as the degree to which an individual can differentiate and integrate information. In 1972, Janis[3] shared his view that cognitive complexity must be recognised as a construct having significant impact on managerial decision-making and action.

Various authors since the early 1960s have written about the characteristics of individuals who have the ability to generate higher levels of cognitive complexity. According to Harvey et al,[4] an individual who is able to generate higher levels of cognitive complexity is more comfortable with ambiguity and tends to seek and process higher amounts of information. In 1986, Streufert and Swazey[5] reported that higher cognitive complexity may lead to an increased ability to reconceptualise problems, enabling an individual to be better at planning and strategic thinking. According to Schwenk,[6] an individual with higher cognitive ability is able to integrate acquired information in the decision-making process with increased effectiveness. It is therefore expected that leaders with the ability to generate higher levels of cognitive complexity will use more information and operate with less rigid mental models, allowing them to adapt more easily and think strategically.

According to Larson and Rowland,[7] individuals with the ability to generate higher cognitive complexity, perceive more differences in their context and are better positioned to assimilate and deal with contradictions. On the other hand, individuals with the ability to generate lower levels of cognitive complexity perceive and evaluate their environment more simplistically. They apply a few and fairly rigid rules of integration and may not be able to see and understand how many diverse elements fit together in order to produce a meaningful whole.

According to Jacques,[8] complexity is determined by the number of factors, the rate of change of those factors, and the ease of identification of the factors in a situation. According to him, there are two constructs of importance when considering complexity in the context of work:

- The complexity of the information which has to be handled in carrying out a task by means of a particular method; and
- The complexity of the processes which an individual can apply in handling the complexity of a task.

Through a study Jacques and Kathryn Cason performed in 1994,[9] the major conclusion was that "[t]he existence of the managerial hierarchy is a reflection in organisational life of discontinuous steps in the nature of human capability". According to him, this conclusion and the work that followed can be seen as providing a solid foundation for achieving a method of making an accurate match between individual capability and role complexity in filling positions and therefore also laying the basis for effective managerial leadership.

Gillian Stamp[10] at BIOSS International has for more than 25 years spent time listening to people from different age groups, backgrounds and levels of responsibility in a vast range of industries, talking about their working lives. As result of this work, a process for creating an understanding of two constructs, complexity and capability, emerged. This process of appreciation is known as Career Path Appreciation.[11] Through the work of BIOSS International, the construct **complexity** must be understood as follows:

- "Work is the application of knowledge and the exercise of discretion within prescribed limits in order to achieve a goal within a stated completion time. Complexity is introduced when new and uncertain conditions have as a result that an individual needs rely more on judgement, as his/her knowledge and experience may not be relevant to the new challenge presented."

- In the work environment, an increase in complexity becomes a function of (i) increased levels of uncertainty, diversity of stakeholders and the time span of consequences; (ii) an environment that is more abstract and the variables to juggle become more diverse; and (iii) the use of judgement and insight becomes more predominant than known data, detailed knowledge, skill, experience, and prescription.

In order to understand the level of complexity that an individual is comfortable dealing with, the second construct, **capability**, needs to be understood:

> "Capability is the decision-making process in the face of uncertainty. Capability exhibits the property of individuals' perspectives about a situation and how they scan and read a setting or context; how they exercise judgement in a particular way; and how their capability tends to grow and unfold over time." – Gillian Stamp[12]

When engaging with leaders in our client systems, increasingly, the importance of making the right decision regarding the selection and placement of leaders with the ability to generate cognitive complexity appropriate to their role is realised. Our thinking and work is informed by the application of Requisite Organisation principles and the Levels of Work Theory as a methodology to define the required cognitive complexity within the organisational operating model and structure.

Once role complexity has been defined, a critical success factor is the selection of capable individuals to perform these roles. Career Path Appreciation as a methodology to guide leaders within the organisation with this very important task enables a formalised review and monitoring of employees' decision-making capability as well as ensuring that complexities associated with a particular level in the organisation are dealt with by individuals with the appropriate level of cognitive capability.

Emotional wisdom

Florence[13] describes emotional wisdom as being, among others:

- The creative outcome of knowledge and experience that have become integrated and joined together,
- Dependent upon our capacity to listen to and understand our emotional experience,
- An internal journey dependent upon our ability to trust our own inner experience and our own inner voice and to be responsive to this,
- Dependent upon our capacity for reflective thought,
- Resulting from a healthy relationship between our emotions and our mind, and for this relationship to flourish we will need to learn a fluent emotional language and a good emotional vocabulary, and
- A state of well-being which is not static; it is a continual process of evolution, a natural process of continual growth and integration.[14]

Daniel Goleman is known for his work in the field of emotional intelligence. In 2002 he and two other authors, Boyatzis & McKee, published an article, entitled "Primal Leadership: The Hidden Driver of Great Performance" in the *Harvard Business Review*, presenting a deeper analysis of their earlier assertion that a leader's emotional intelligence creates a certain culture or work environment. *Harvard Business Review* again published this particular article as one of the ten must-reads on emotional intelligence. They report that a leader's mood and accompanying behaviours are potent drivers of business success. Therefore a leader's principal task is emotional leadership.

Goleman et al report in this particular article that high levels of emotional intelligence create climates in which information-sharing, trust, healthy risk-taking, and learning flourish. Low levels of emotional intelligence create climates rife with fear and anxiety. Because tense and terrified employees can be very productive in the short term, their organisation may post good results, but these never last.[15]

For most people, it is their most difficult challenge and, together with that, gauging how their emotions affect others. Goleman et al[16] argue that the implication of primal leadership requires executives to determine through reflective analysis how their emotional leadership drives the moods and actions of the organisation and then, with equal discipline, to adjust their behaviour accordingly.

Emotionally intelligent leaders:

- Monitor their moods through self-awareness;
- Change them for the better through self-management;
- Understand their impact through empathy; and
- Act in ways that boost others' moods through relationship management.

Ovans, in a summary of research on publications on emotional intelligence, makes the clear point that although research indicates the importance of emotional intelligence for leadership, it certainly is not the only way to be successful in leadership roles.[17] Goleman et al agree with Ovans when pointing out that, although it is said that managing your mood and the moods of followers is the task of primal leadership, it is not meant to suggest that mood is all that matters. Actions are critical, and mood and action together must resonate with the organisation and with reality.

Table 2.1 gives the five components of emotional intelligence at work.[18]

Table 2.1: The components of emotional intelligence

Component	Definition	Hallmarks
Self-awareness	The ability to recognise and understand your moods, emotions and drives, as well as their effect on others	Self-confidence Realistic self-assessment Self-deprecating sense of humour
Self-regulation	Ability to control or direct disruptive impulses and moods Propensity to suspend judgement – to think before acting	Trustworthiness and integrity Comfort with ambiguity Openness to change
Motivation	A passion to work for reasons that go beyond money or status A propensity to pursue goals with energy and persistence	Strong drive to achieve Optimism, even in the face of failure Organisational commitment
Empathy	The ability to understand the emotional make-up of other people Skill in treating people according to their emotional reactions	Expertise in building and retaining talent Cross-cultural sensitivity Service to clients and customers
Social skill	Proficiency in managing relationships and building networks An ability to find common ground and build rapport	Effectiveness in leading change Persuasiveness Expertise in building and leading teams

> "The skills required to conquer adversity and emerge stronger and more committed than ever before, are the same ones that make for extraordinary leaders."
> – Bennis & Thomas

Bennis and Thomas believe that what makes a great leader has something to do with the way people handle adversity.[19] They have found that one of the most reliable indicators and predictors of true leadership is an individual's ability to find meaning in negative events and to learn from even the most trying circumstances.

Resilience is the virtue that enables people to move through hardship and become better. No one escapes pain, fear and suffering. Yet from pain can come wisdom, from fear can come courage, from suffering can come strength – if you have the virtue of resilience.[20]

Bennis and Thomas[21] interviewed more than 40 leaders in business and the public sector and discovered that all of them had endured intense, often traumatic, experiences that transformed them and became the source of their distinctive leadership abilities:

- The ability to engage others in shared meaning;
- A distinctive and compelling voice;
- A sense of integrity (including a strong set of values); and
- Adaptive capacity – the ability to transcend adversity, with all its attendant stresses, and to emerge stronger than before. This critical skill comprises two qualities: (i) the ability to grasp context; and (ii) hardiness – the perseverance and toughness that enable an individual to emerge from devastating circumstances without losing hope.

Engaging with leaders in our client systems reveals, more than ever before, that the expectation that leaders will have the ability to deal with adversity is of increasing importance. Developing personal resilience within individual leaders assists them with the capacity: (i) to accept and look hard at reality; (ii) to find meaning in some aspects of life; (ii) to re-establish their values; and (iv) to improvise and find solutions.

Spiritual authenticity

Burckhardt[22] defines spirituality as that which gives meaning to one's life and draws one to transcend oneself.[23] Spirituality is a broader concept than religion, although that is one expression of spirituality. Vaughan suggests that spiritual intelligence is one of several types of intelligence and that it can be developed relatively independently.[24] Spiritual intelligence calls for multiple ways of knowing and for the integration of the inner life of mind and spirit with the outer life of work in the world.

Authenticity is a term used to describe the degree to which one is true to one's own personality, spirit, or character, despite external pressures. The conscious self is seen as coming to terms with being in a material world and with encountering external forces, pressures and influences that are very different from, and other than, itself. An interesting perspective on authenticity is shown in Figure 2.3.[25]

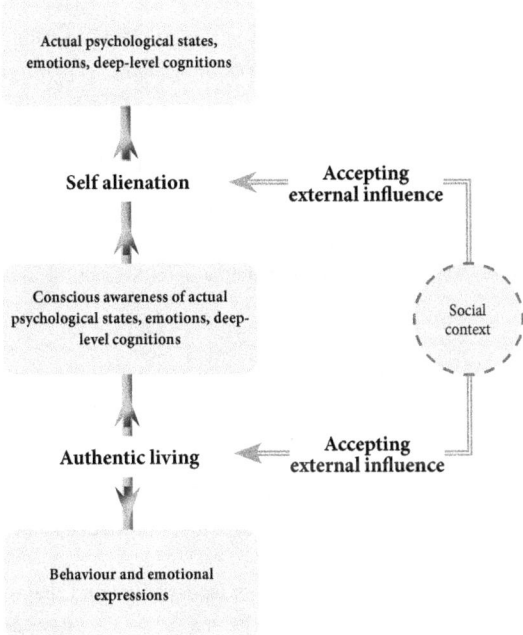

Figure 2.3: Authenticity

Bringing together the ideas about spirituality and authenticity, Greenberg makes the following points about "authentic spirituality":

- It involves an *emotional response*, which can include feelings of significance, unity, awe, joy, acceptance, and consolation.
- The spiritual response helps meet our affective needs for both celebration and reconciliation.
- It often involves a *cognitive context*, a set of beliefs about oneself and the world which can both inspire the spiritual response and provide an interpretation of it.
- By contemplating such beliefs we are temporarily drawn out of the mundane into the realisation of life's deeper significance, and this realisation generates emotional effects.
- But equally, the spiritual response generated is itself interpreted in the light of our basic beliefs; namely, it is taken to reflect the ultimate truth of our situation as we conceive it.
- The cognitive context of spirituality and the spiritual response are therefore linked tightly in reciprocal evocation and validation.[26]

However, we are not suggesting that spirituality, and specifically authentic spirituality, is primarily or only a cognitive process. We are of the view that it is the result of being deliberately and mindfully **conscious** of yourself and the context within which you find yourself.

Fundamentally, spiritual authenticity will lead to a perception of consistency (and therefore predictability). In our view, it is this perceived and experienced consistency that leads to the building of trust in leaders and leadership.

Agile flexibility

The concept of agile flexibility is based on conversations with and observations of dynamics in a number of client systems, locally and abroad. The shift at play seems to be that, in contrast to organisational life up to the 1990s (where "leaders" had specific roles and accountabilities), it is becoming increasingly important for leaders and leadership to:

- Work across different levels of complexity;
- Engage people with differing levels of emotional maturity and wisdom;
- Who have very different perspectives on spirituality; and
- Have very divergent worldviews.

Good & Yeganeh describe cognitive agility as being composed of three core elements, these being:

- *Focused attention* as the capacity to oppose incoming distraction;
- *Openness* to noticing and searching for new information in the context; and
- *Cognitive flexibility* as the capacity to switch mental activity in favour of what is more appropriate.[27]

From the perspectives of spiritual authenticity and emotional wisdom, we have similarly concluded that these are expressed through wisdom and compassionate action in the world. Both emotional and spiritual "intelligence" are necessary for discernment in making judgements that contribute to organisational health. To some degree at least, these two "intelligences" seem to be related to the construct called "Contextual Intelligence" which can be described as the ability to understand the limits of our knowledge and to adapt that knowledge to a context different from the one in which it was developed.[28]

On any single day, a leader or community of leaders may find themselves in very diverse contexts within which they rapidly have to shift behaviour so as to have deliberate (purposeful and mindful) impact. It is within this highly dynamic context that the exercise of appropriate judgment becomes so challenging – there is simply not that much time to adjust. A practical example – given in Table 2.2 – illustrates what we mean.

Table 2.2: Examples of agile flexibility

Situation	Adjustments to be made

From 08h00 to 10h00 you attend a Board Meeting to finalise the decision to close a plant as it does not meet strategic intent any longer and is not generating the cash flow anticipated	- **Cognitive Complexity**
	  ○ Work at the level of strategic intent
	- **Emotional Wisdom**
	  ○ Take yourself out of the situation
	- **Spiritual Authenticity**
	  ○ Consider whether the way things are done aligns to personal and organisational values

From 10h00 to 11h00 you meet with your own team to give feedback on the Board Meeting	- **Cognitive Complexity**
	  ○ Work at the level of complexity with which your team is comfortable
	- **Emotional Wisdom**
	  ○ Be aware that some people may feel threatened
	  ○ Question yourself as to how you should adjust your words to connect at an intellectual and emotional level
	- **Spiritual Authenticity**
	  ○ Consider what you can and cannot share with your team and still retain integrity

Situation	Adjustments to be made

From 11h00 to 13h00 you meet with a number of providers who are dependent on the plant to be closed. They have asked to meet with you because processing of their payment is slow and payment is now overdue	- **Cognitive Complexity**
	  o Work at the level of complexity with which they are comfortable
	- **Emotional Wisdom**
	  o Be aware that some people may feel angry
	  o Be aware of your obligation not only to these people but also to other providers, and the external perceptions of your company
	  o Question yourself as to how you should adjust your words to connect at an intellectual and emotional level
	- **Spiritual Authenticity**
	  o Consider what you can and cannot share with these individuals and still retain integrity
	  o Question yourself as to how you can also be respectful of their agendas

From 13h00 to 13h30 you have time to reflect on the fact that your job is on the line as the plant to be closed is your accountability	- **Cognitive Complexity**
	  o Question yourself as to how you should think about your work, and what you should be accountable for
	- **Emotional Wisdom**
	  o Question yourself as to how you should deal with your own anxiety at the workplace, at home, and with friends
	- **Spiritual Authenticity**
	  o Ask yourself what your reflection tells you about yourself
	  o Ask yourself what your self-talk is about, and what it is like

How do you retain your own well-being while, during a span of less than six hours, working across different levels of complexity, each requiring different emotional maturity and an acknowledgement of different spiritual demands? At a simplistic level, you may want to consider resilience as a personal attribute. Our own sense is that the inherent capability to work across these different contexts is equally as, if not more, important. People who do not have this capability find it almost impossible to be resilient, and the behaviour patterns that become evident are:

- Avoidance or withdrawal;
- Defensiveness; or
- Anger and destructive behaviours.

At the level of the leadership community, these patterns often form the basis for so-called "toxic leadership".

Ironically, our advice to leaders and leadership is to *slow down*. Do not schedule back-to-back meetings, but provide time and space to plan each engagement in a mindful manner. If you have a personal assistant, let him/her help you with this (they will also be grateful to be under less pressure!).

Section summary

In this section on the "being" of leadership, we have outlined some perspectives on the core dimensions of leadership capability, these being the ability:

- To generate appropriate complexity;
- To develop emotional wisdom;
- To be spiritually authentic; and
- To demonstrate agile flexibility.

The key issue at play is, of course, that without these capabilities, leaders and leadership will simply not be able to build the competence required to exercise good judgment.

A Practical Approach to Developing the 'Being' of Leadership

A key aspect to consider is the meaning of the word "leadership". Much of the content of this chapter can easily be read from the perspective of an individual leader. In our view, this perspective, while valid, may also be limiting, and you may also want to take a perspective on Leadership Excellence being an organisation-wide attribute. This relates to the concepts of leadership community and leadership brand that are simultaneously: (i) an aggregate of the capability and competence of individual leaders, and (ii) a contextual variable in the creation of internal and external brand.

From a practical perspective, the question then clearly becomes one of: "How do we build leadership community and brand based on a clear sense of the 'being' of leadership?" An approach to this question, developed using the principles of cohesion, is described in this section of this chapter.

In 1965, Bruce Tuckman[29] described a collective dynamics theory that showed how leaders could relate to groups in that they (i) Form, (ii) Storm, (iii) Norm, and (iv) Perform. Following development work from Professor Michael Marquardt of George Washington University in the field of Action Learning,[30] this paradigm has been upgraded to show that groups can (i) Form, (ii) Norm, (iii) Storm, and (iv) Perform. The theory behind the shift is that the standard is raised before the chaos of brainstorming begins.

Underpinning the group dynamic theory is that action is formed from energy. The energy of the people in the room, their cognitive constructs, their emotional charges, their memories, their spiritual intelligence, and their combined psychological states all go towards manifesting possibility from potential. This leads to the notion of Dialogue[31] as a method to uncover all of these energies.

If this theory is assumed to be correct, then what are the systems and processes that can record Energy Utility within a group and within an organisation? Can this system relate the Energy Utility to the more traditional measuring of Economic Utility only? One such system suggests that Energy Utility and Economic Utility in a system can be worked with together, raised, and then measured. This system is named Cohesion,[32] and it has four stages.

Stage 1: Individual leader maturity

The first stage is to work with the leader one-on-one in a process called Leader Maturity. This process takes place over a two- to three-month period and brings the leader into a twenty-hour individual process, led by a trained guide. The guide works with the leader in a private capacity to help them move from their current state of ego maturity into the next stage of their ego maturity. The phases of ego maturity are based on the work of Rooke and Torbert,[33] and the scale and assessment instrument used was developed by Dr Susan Cooke-Greuter.[34] By helping the individual leader understand their own action logic, they can begin the journey of developing their own and the organisational capacity to lead.

Stage 2: Executive resilience

The second stage is to work with up to eight executives who report to the leader in a 2,5-day process called Executive Resilience. The leader is, of course, included in this process. During this breakaway, the group work together through a process called a 'container' that brings them on a journey through the MetaResilience maximisers of Personal Persistence, Personal Efficiency, Experience of Adversity, and Openness to Change; as well as the MetaResilience Minimisers of Obstacles to Adaptation, Instability of Environment, Personal Vulnerability, and Low Self Esteem. During these 2,5 days, the group learns Dialogue techniques that will contain and challenge the executive group and which can be used with other members of the cluster, after the workshop is completed.

Stage 3: Learning the R.E.A.L. Dialogue method

The third stage is to bring every member of the cluster into a one-day Dialogue method where each person learns a sixty-minute dialogue process called R.E.A.L. Dialogue (Relationships, Engagement, Action, Learning).

- Following the one-day immersion, several members of the cluster are trained to be R.E.A.L. Dialogue guides. They continue the process for a period of one to two months within the system under supervision.
- The R.E.A.L. Dialogue method works at the level of: (i) Leadership Intention, (ii) System Themes, (iii) Member Perspectives, (iv) Problem Presenter Actions, (v) Leadership Intention Feedback, (vi) Learning, (vii) Application of Learning, and (viii) Group Reflection. A Dialogue Scribe gathers the data in real time into an application that then tags the data in real time at an enterprise level. This dashboard is available for all in the system to review and analyse.
- Additionally, each member of the Dialogue Circle is invited to download and run an Application called Action Learning Coach (ALC), which records each item of their learning, and helps them to convert that learning into action. Each action is stored on the enterprise database. In this way, members of the system can see how learning is converted into action in real time, and across all the dialogue circles.

Stage 4: Energy2Economics

Once the R.E.A.L. Dialogues have become a systemised way of doing business, Stage 4 is the implementation of a continuous listener process called E2E (Energy2Economics). This online and smart-device data-gathering system continually tracks 85 given and 15 customised items in the cluster. The items are coded for either (i) Energy, or (ii) Economics. They are secondarily coded for (iii) Service, (iv) Revenue, (v) Margin, (vi) Efficiency, (vii) Productivity, and (viii) Resilience. They are thirdly coded for (ix) Leader, and (x) and (xi) Organisation.

The data is stored on a relational database which is presented in real time on a monitor that gives all members of the system a click-through view of the data that are continually entered by them.

Such a practical approach to the use of a Cohesion process allows the individual and the leadership community, individually and collectively, to build the "being" of leadership in a manner that directly and visibly also links the leadership community to the "doing" of leadership.

The 'Doing' of Leadership

Assuming that leaders and leadership have the 'Being' in place (or have at least made progress on the journey of getting there), there is also a requirement to take ownership of action. In Figure 2.2, this is referenced by the two outer circles, namely requisite competence and observed behaviour.

Chapter 4 (Leadership brand model) will specifically focus on defining requisite leadership competencies for the future, and will therefore not be explored in any detail here.

Suffice it to say that:

- The notion of competence is an ever-shifting one, simply because we live in a world of increasingly rapid change; with
- An openness and interdependence that destroys fixed ideas about boundaries and control; so that
- Leadership Excellence is increasingly about the ability to influence.

None of this would be possible at the individual or collective leadership level without the constant awareness and development of the "being" side of leadership.

Conclusion

In this chapter, we specifically explored the idea of Leadership Excellence within the context of success. We have illustrated that the idea of success is probably better understood within the broader context of an expanded service-profit chain (see also the Business Value Model© in Chapter 19) that provides the following specific thinking parameters:

- Business success is better understood when a perspective of broad business benefits realisation is adopted; and
- Leadership Excellence does not have a direct linear relationship to business benefits realisation, but is mediated by the ability of the leadership to:
    o   Build the organisation capacity to execute strategy:
        - People;
        - Process;
        - Structure;
        - Technology; and
        - Culture; so as to gain:
    o   Employee engagement and commitment;
    o   That will enable stakeholder delight;
    o   To ensure sustainable business benefits realisation.

We have also shown that Leadership Excellence is a combination of the "being" of leadership and the "doing" of leadership, as is shown in Figure 2.4.

Chapter 2: Leadership excellence dimensions

Figure 2.4: Chapter Summary

From the perspective of the individual leader, Rosen makes a very similar point when referring, among others, to emotional health, intellectual health, spiritual health, social health, and vocational health.[35]

The reader is also reminded that this chapter forms the basis for Chapter 4: Leadership brand modelling. Together with Chapter 19: Leadership Excellence measurement, these chapters create the context for the chapter on *Leadership Excellence*'

Endnotes

1. Covey, 1989, 2004.
2. Schroeder, Driver & Streufert, 1967.
3. Janis, 1972.
4. Harvey, Hunt & Schroeder, 1961.
5. Streufert & Swazey, 1986.
6. Schwenk, 1988.
7. Larson & Rowland, 2001.
8. Jacques, 1998.
9. Cason & Cason, 1994
10. Stamp, 2004.
11. Stamp, 2009.
12. Gillian, 2009.
13. Florence, 2014.
14. Florence, 2014.
15. Goleman, Boyatzis & McKee, 2015.
16. Goleman, Boyatzis & McKee, 2015.
17. Ovans, 2015.
18. Goleman, 2015.
19. Bennis & Thomas, 2002.
20. Greitens, 2015.
21. Bennis & Thomas, 2002.
22. Burkhardt, 1989.
23. Burkhardt, 1989.
24. Vaughan, 2002.
25. Wood, Linley, Maltby, Baliousis & Joseph, 2008.
26. Greenberg, N. 2014.
27. Good & Yeganeh, 2012.
28. Khanna, 2014.
29. Tuckman, 1965.
30. Marquardt, 2011.
31. Bohm, 2004.
32. Mooney, 2015.
33. Rooke & Torbert, 2005. Torbert & Rooke, 2004.
34. Torbert, 2004.
35. Rosen, 2014.

References

Bennis, WG & Thomas, RJ. 2002. 'Crucibles of leadership'. *Harvard Business Review*. September.

Bohm, D. 2004. *On dialogue*. New York, NY: Routledge Classics.

Burkhardt, M. 1989. 'Spirituality: An analysis of the concept'. *Holistic Nursing Practice*, 3(3):69-77, May.

Cason, JE & Cason, K. 1994. Human capability: A study of individual potential & its application. Virginia: Cason Hall & Co.

Chopra, D. 1994. *The Seven Spiritual Laws of Success: A Practical Guide to the Fulfillment of Your Dreams*. San Rafael, CA: New World Library/Amber-Allen Publishing.

Covey, SR. 1989, 2004. *The 7 Habits of Highly Effective People: Powerful Lessons in Personal Change*. New York, NY: Simon & Schuster.

Florence, J. 2014. *Emotional Health, The Voice of Our Soul* (audio recordings). A-Z of Emotional Health Ltd. [Online]. Available: http://www.a-z-of-emotionalhealth.com/index.html. [Accessed 1 July 2016].

Goleman, D. 2015. 'What makes a leader?' In D Goleman, R Boyatzis & A McKee (eds). A *HBR's 10 must reads on emotional intelligence*. Boston, MA: Harvard Business School Publishing Corporation.

Goleman, D, Boyatzis, R & McKee, A. 2015. 'Primal leadership: The hidden driver of great performance'. In D Goleman, R Boyatzis & A McKee (eds). *HBR's 10 must reads on emotional intelligence*. Boston, MA: Harvard Business School Publishing Corporation.

Good, D. & Yeganeh, B. 2012. 'Cognitive agility: Adapting to real-time decision making at work'. *OD Practitioner*, 44(2):13-17.

Greenberg, N. 2014. *Can spirituality be defined?* University studies interdisciplinary colloquy on spirituality and critical inquiry. Knoxville, TN: University of Tennessee.

Greitens, E. 2015. *Resilience: Hard-won wisdom for living a better life*. New York, NY: Houghton Mifflin Harcourt.

Harvey OJ, Hunt DE & Schroeder, HM. 1961. *Conceptual systems and personality organization*. New York, NY: Wiley.

Hsieh, T. 2010. *Delivering happiness: A Path to profits, passion, and purpose*. New York, NY: Grand Central Publishing.

Huffington, A. 2014. *Thrive: The third metric to redefining success and creating a life of well-being, wisdom, and wonder*. New York, NY: Harmony Books.

Jacques, E. 1998. *Requisite organization: A total system for effective managerial organisation and managerial leadership for the 21st century*. Arlington, VA: Cason Hall & Co.

Janis, IL. 1972. *Victims of groupthink*. Boston, MA: Houghton-Mifflin.

Khanna, T. 2014. 'Contextual intelligence'. *Harvard Business Review*. September.

Larson, LL & Rowland, KM. 2001. 'Leadership style and cognitive complexity'. *Academy of Management Journal*, 17(1): 37-45.

Marquardt, MJ. 2011. *Optimizing the power of action learning: Real-time strategies for developing leaders, building teams and transforming.* Boston, MA: Nicholas Brealey Publishing.

Mooney, P. 2015. 'Meta-resilience: The alchemy of burnout'. Unpublished Doctoral thesis. London, UK: Middlesex University.

Ovans, A. 2015. 'How emotional intelligence became a key leadership skill'. *Harvard Business Review*, April.

Rooke, D & Torbert, WR. 2005. 'Seven transformations of leadership'. *Harvard Business Review*, April.

Rosen, B. 2014. *Grounded. How leaders stay rooted in an uncertain world.* San Francisco, CA: Jossey-Bass.

Schroeder, HM, Driver MJ & Streufert S. 1967. *Human information processing: Individuals and groups functioning in complex social situations.* New York, NY: Holt Rinehart & Winston.

Schwenk, CR. 1988. 'The cognitive perspective on strategic decision-making'. *Journal of Management Studies*, 25: 41–55.

Stamp, G. 2004. 'The individual, the organisation and the path to mutual appreciation'. First published in *Personnel Management*; amended BIOSS.

Stamp, Gillian. 2009. CPA manual version 2009. BIOSS International Southern Africa. Bedfordview, Johannesburg.

Streufert, S & Swazey, RW. 1986. *Complexity, managers and organisations.* Cambridge, MA: New York Academic Press.

Sweeney, PJ & Fry, LW. 2012. 'Character development through spiritual leadership'. *Consulting Psychology Journal: Practice and Research*, 64(2):89–107.

Torbert, WR. 2004. *Action inquiry: The secret of timely and transforming leadership.* San Francisco, CA: Berrett-Koehler.

Tuckman, B. 1965. 'Developmental sequence in small groups'. *Psychological Bulletin.* 63(6):384–399.

Vaughan, F. 2002. 'What is Spiritual Intelligence?' *Journal of Humanistic Psychology*, 42(2):16-33, Spring.

Wood, AM, Linley, PA, Maltby, J, Baliousis, M & Joseph, S. 2008. 'The authentic personality: A theoretical and empirical conceptualization and the development of the authenticity scale'. *Journal of Counseling Psychology*, 55(3):385-399.

Chapter 3

LEADERSHIP EXCELLENCE ACROSS CULTURAL SETTINGS

Lize Booysen

In the world of increasing globalisation, hyper-diversity and the multicultural workforce in which leaders have to operate, a specific focus on global mindsets has become imperative. I believe global leaders and organisations do not need to be conversant in cross-cultural research and theory in order to lead effectively. They do, however, need to understand how culture influences leadership; to know how to leverage cultural differences; to bridge cultural boundaries; and to avoid cultural misunderstanding.

Cross-cultural leadership is a process that takes place on a systemic level within a micro, meso and macro level context and is key to global leadership excellence. It is not simply a matter of national cultural influences on leaders' and followers' expectations – it has to do with the relationship between:

- Leaders and followers as individuals (micro level);
- Within specific social groups and in specific organisational settings (meso level);
- Embedded within particular societal and national cultural contexts and historical, socio-political and legal landscapes (macro level).

In this chapter I will show how culture in its broadest sense *influences leadership and follower expectations*. I will explain *Culturally Endorsed Implicit Leadership Theory (CLT)*, and discuss *universal and cultural-specific leadership based on the GLOBE research*, with specific reference to *South Africa*. I will then discuss *the landscape and scope of global leadership,* dimensions of a *global mindset,* and *the multiple intelligences needed for global leadership excellence.* I will conclude by speculating about *an ethic of responsible global leadership* as the way forward for leadership excellence globally.

As a compass to guide the reader through my chapter, the main arguments offered overall in the chapter are illustrated graphically in Figure 3.1. The figure depicts in an integrated fashion the landscape, scope and context of global leadership excellence to be discussed in this chapter.

According to Figure 3.1:

- **Block I** shows that cultural influences permeate all levels of leadership from leading the self and others to leading globally, as explained by the Levels of Cultural Influences on Leaders and Followers, and the Implicit Leadership Theory (CLT) (see also Figures 25.2 and 25.3, and Tables 25.1 and 25.2).
- The **inverted pyramid** and **Levels of Leading** indicate that leading globally includes the whole scope of leading individuals, groups or units, whole, multiple, merged, multinational and global organisations and contexts.
- **Block II** indicates that high levels of the six intelligences, Cognitive, Emotional, Social, Spiritual, Culture and Contextual, are needed in order to be a successful global leader (as summarised in Table 3.4 and linked with the level of work in organisations in Figure 3.4).
- The broad scope of global leadership leads to **Extreme Contexts** of **increased levels** of competing commitments, paradox, polarities, culture and contextual influences, diversity, interdependencies, complexity, multiplicity, uncertainty, ambiguity, and responsibility. It also leads to **decreased levels** of knowing, power, control, predictability, and certainty.

- The **Competencies** needed for leadership excellence across cultural settings are a Global Mindset, Cultural Agility, Strategic Agility, Relational Agility, Contextual Agility, Global Knowledge, Boundary Spanning and Organisational Agility (summarised in Table 3.3).

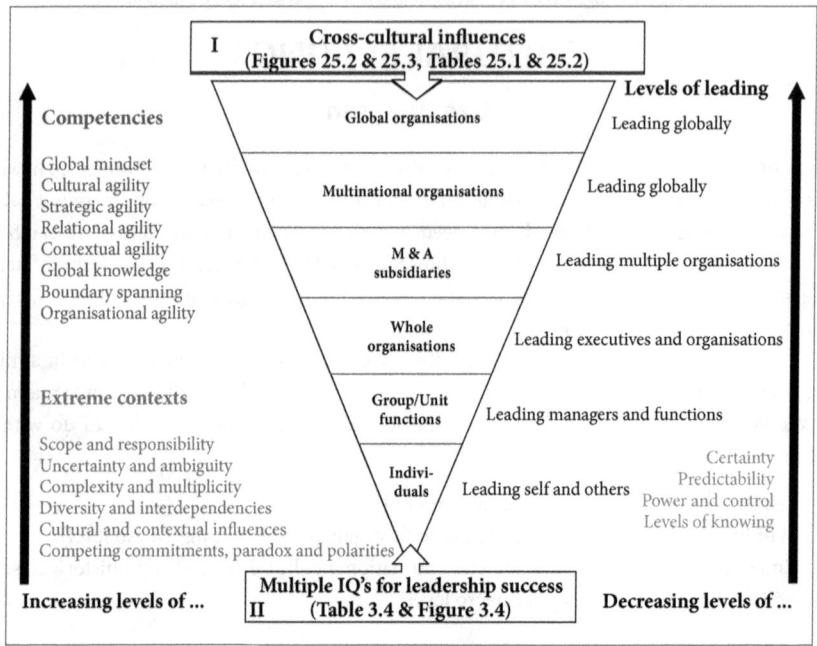

Figure 3.1: *The landscape, scope and context of global leadership excellence*

Cultural Influences on Leadership Processes and Follower Expectations

Culture is generally used to refer to a shared set of ways of thinking and being of groups that differentiate them from other groups in meaningful ways and that culminate in behavioural patterns of doing.[1] Research has shown that leadership is a universal phenomenon found in all societies, and that cultural forces influence many aspects of leadership. The basic question under study in cross-cultural leadership is: *To what extent is leadership influenced by culture?*[2] Let us first unpack the different aspects of culture.

National Culture, Sub-Cultures and Social Identities

The *Global Leadership and Organisational Behavior Effectiveness* study (or Project-GLOBE[i]) defined culture as "*shared motives, values, beliefs, identities, and interpretations or meanings of significant events that resulted from common experiences of members of collectives and are transmitted across age generations.*"[3] This is what we know about culture:

---

i GLOBE is based on the assumption that leader effectiveness is contextual and that it is embedded in the societal and organisational norms, values, and beliefs of the people being led. Their key research question was: What is the relationship between culture and leadership attributes? GLOBE phases 1 and 2 investigated 62 national cultures and examined both practice (as is) and values (should be). GLOBE included 170 international country co-investigators, and sampled 17 300 middle managers. GLOBE used a mixed-method research design including media analyses of unobtrusive leadership measures, in-depth individual interviews, focus groups, and survey research using a questionnaire that measured nine universal cultural dimensions and 112 leadership attributes in each country.

- Culture is learned through socialisation processes, and not inherited;
- It is a socially constructed shared system of meaning which permeates all aspects of our thinking, doing and being;
- Leadership practices, follower expectations, and organisation culture and practices are influenced by culture;
- Culture is not stable. It is evolving and constantly adapting to changing contexts; and
- Culture is not absolute. It is relative, each culture is relative to other cultures' way of perceiving the world and doing things.

Most cross-cultural leadership studies focus on the influence of national culture on leadership, or cross-national differences, like Hofstede's, and the GLOBE study. Yet national *culture is multi-dimensional* and contains different *sub-cultures and social categories* such as age, gender, race, ethnicity, generational differences, language, religion, and sexual orientation.

There is also consensus among cross-cultural leadership scholars that cultural measures can predict behaviours of a specific group, but not necessarily the behaviour of separate individuals in that specific group.[4] Personality can predict individual behaviour much more accurately than culture. In other words, while culture might be an important force shaping leadership and follower expectations, it is an unpredictable and unreliable factor in determining any particular individual's values or behaviour. This means:

- Culture is about groups;
- It is a collective phenomenon, and not about individual behaviour;
- There are wide variations in individual values and behaviour within each culture; and
- There are also numerous shared similarities among cultures.

This is important to understand, because when leaders work across cultures, they interact with individuals across national cultures and social categories, each with a unique individual personality.[5]

Social Identity: The Bridge Between Personal Identity, Sub-groups and National Culture

A relatively new concept in cross-cultural research that can help us understand the interface between national culture, social category and individual personality is Social Identity.[ii] It explains how individual identity, group-level identity and national culture identity integrate. It views social identity as part of a person's cultural constellation.[6] Social identity is an individual's sense of who he/she is, based on his/her group membership(s). It is concerned with both the psychological and sociological aspects of group behaviour.

Social identity explains the psychological basis of:

- Group behaviour and group association;
- Intergroup discrimination;
- In-group favouritism and out-group derogation;
- Stereotyping; and
- Social identity conflict.

---

ii Some of the most prominent intergroup theories explaining group identity effects on human behaviour have been self-categorisation (Turner, 1987), Social Identity Theory (Tajfel, 1974), and the extension on Social Identity Theory by Tajfel & Turner in 1979, Ellemers & Haslam, 2012, and Turner & Reynolds, 2012. See Booysen, 2015.

Individuals within specific national cultures belong to different categories and sub-cultures and have *unique individual and collective social identities* that influence their behaviour. Moreover, social identity is characteristic of both the individual and the cultural identity group of members sharing the same social identities.

Based on the above discussion I want to extend Hofstede's well-known three levels of mental programming[7] – human nature, culture, and individual personality – to five levels, by expanding the cultural dimension into three separate levels of influence: (i) national culture, (ii) sub-culture/social category, and (iii) social identity level, and link it to levels of influence, as depicted in Figure 3.2.

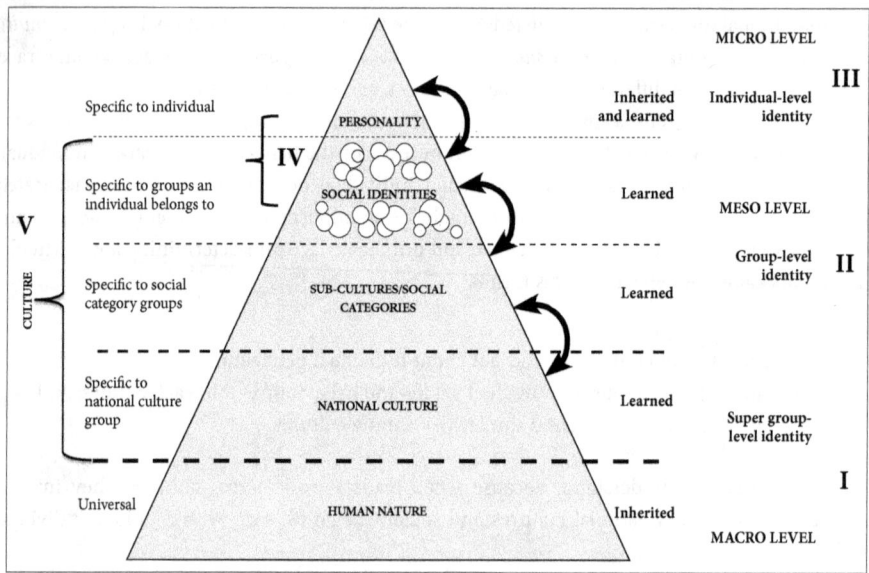

Figure 3.2: Levels of cultural influences on leaders and followers[8]

From Figure 3.2 we can see that:

- The pyramid indicates five levels of cultural influences on leaders and followers:
  o Human nature;
  o National culture;
  o Sub-cultures/social categories
  o Social identities; and
  o Personality.
- *Level I: Macro:* **Human nature** and **national culture** inform an individual's super group-identity on a macro level. Human nature is universal and inherited. National culture is specific to a national culture group and learned.
- *Level II: Meso:* **Sub-cultures/social categories and social identities** inform group level identity on a meso level. Sub-cultures/social categories and social identities are specific to a social category or group an individual belongs to and learned, and
- *Level III: Micro:* **Personality** is specific to an individual, learned and inherited, and informs individual level identity on a micro level.
- *Level IV: Social Identity:* **Social identity** is the bridge between individual and group identity, and the circles indicate the simultaneous nature, cross-cutting and differing prominence and power differences of social identities.

Chapter 3: Leadership excellence across cultural settings

- *Level V: Culture:* **Culture** refers to the national culture, sub-culture/social category and social identity levels.

It is also clear that the boundaries between the levels of identities are not solid but permeable, especially the boundary between **Social Identity** and **Personality**. The arrows show the reciprocal nature of how each level of culture informs each other, and how social identity informs personality and *vice versa*.

So it is clear that *cross-cultural leadership in its broadest sense*, speaks not only to the *super group level diversity* or difference, (e.g. national cultures, multi-national organisations, geographical difference) but also to *sub-cultural difference* (e.g. race, gender, ethnicity, religion, sexual orientation), and *social-identity difference* (specific group identification of individuals in the organisation), as well as *individual personality differences.*

Cultural Influences on Leadership: Insights from Research

Now that we have discussed all the different levels of cultural influences, let us return to the question being studied in cross-cultural leadership: *To what extent is leadership influenced by culture?*

In this section I will focus on the GLOBE study that shows how culture impacts leadership. I will discuss the universal cultural dimensions, country clusters and leadership attributes found by the GLOBE study. I will look at leadership attributes that are seen as desirable and undesirable across cultures, and highlight the South African GLOBE findings and some subsequent South African leadership research. I will then focus on executive leadership effectiveness across cultures, and the role of organisational and societal contingency factors. This section will conclude with specific societal contingency factors that influence South African leadership practices.

The impact of cultural values on leadership

Hofstede's research on the consequences of culture on organisations demonstrated the significance and influence of cultural values on leadership and organisational behaviour. The GLOBE study extended Hofstede's work. Despite critique of the GLOBE project,[9] it is still seen as the most comprehensive empirical cross-cultural leadership study to date.

The GLOBE Project distilled the following nine bipolar *universal cultural dimensions*, described in Table 3.1.

Table 3.1: The GLOBE universal culture dimensions[10]

Performance Orientation:	the degree to which a society encourages high standards of performance and rewards innovation and improvement
Assertiveness:	the degree to which individuals are assertive, tough, dominant and aggressive in social relationships
Future Orientation:	the extent to which members of a society or an organisation believe that their actions will influence their own future
Humane Orientation:	the degree to which a collective encourages and rewards individuals for being fair, altruistic, generous, kind and caring to others

35

Institutional Collectivism:	the extent to which a society's organisational and institutional norms and practices encourage and reward collective action and collective distribution of resources
In-group Collectivism:	the degree to which individuals express pride, loyalty or cohesiveness in their organisations and families
Gender Egalitarianism:	the degree to which the collective minimises gender inequality
Power Distance:	the extent to which a society accepts and endorses authority, power differences and status privileges
Uncertainty Avoidance:	the extent to which a society, organisation or group relies on social norms, rules, and procedures to alleviate the unpredictability of future events

While the dimensions in Table 3.1 are discussed in isolation, in reality they are *inter-related and have reciprocal effects* on one another.

These different "**cultural patterns**" mediate the way in which dimensions show up in leadership. For example, it is expected that group work in a collectivist culture should involve active interaction and discussion of issues, because everyone should work towards shared outcomes. However, in a collectivist culture such as sub-Saharan Africa, with high humane orientation and average power distance, collective work shows up rather differently. The group is more likely to proceed with respectful interaction and a concern for expressed harmony, based on the high humane orientation level. The average power distance will influence the group process to search for public consensus aligned with the apparent wishes of authority figure(s).

GLOBE also developed and tested the Culturally Endorsed Implicit Leadership Theory,[11] (CLT). In short, the CLT theory proposes:

1. That culture influences organisational practices and leader attributes and behaviours that are most frequently enacted, accepted, expected and effective in that culture.
2. Organisational contingencies also affect organisational culture and practices, as well as leader behaviours, acceptance and effectiveness, and *vice versa*.

The most important findings of the GLOBE project are briefly summarised in Table 3.2.

Table 3.2: GLOBE Phases 1 and 2: Findings in a nutshell[12]

Leadership Characteristics and Attributes
Ten Country Clusters: Leadership Characteristics
Anglo: Competitive and results-orientated *(South African white sample)*   **Confucian Asia**: Result-driven, encourage group working together over individual goals   **Eastern Europe**: Forceful, supportive of co-workers, treat women with equality   **Germanic Europe**: Value competition and aggressiveness and are more result-oriented   **Latin America**: Loyal and devoted to their families and similar groups   **Latin Europe**: Value individual autonomy   **Middle East**: Devoted and loyal to their own people, women afforded less status   **Nordic Europe**: High priority on long-term success, women treated with greater equality   **Southern Asia**: Strong family and deep concern for their communities   **Sub-Saharan Africa**: Concerned and sensitive to others, demonstrate strong family loyalty *(South African black sample)*

Six Universal Leadership Clusters
Charismatic/value-based leadership: Reflects the ability to inspire, to motivate, and to expect high performance from others based on strongly held core values. **Team-orientated leadership:** Emphasises team building, collaboration and common purpose among team members. **Humane-orientated leadership:** Emphasises being supportive, considerate, compassionate, and generous. **Participative leadership:** Reflects the degree to which leaders involve others in making and implementing decisions. **Autonomous leadership:** Refers to independent and individualistic leadership, which includes being autonomous and unique. **Self-protective leadership:** Reflects behaviours that ensure the safety and security of the leader and the group.
Twenty-two Universally Endorsed Leadership Attributes
Trustworthy, having foresight, positive, confidence builder, intelligent, win–win problem solver, administratively skilled, excellence-orientated, just, plans ahead, dynamic, motivational, decisive, communicates, co-ordinates, honest, encouraging, motive arouser, dependable, effective bargainer, informed, team builder **Conclusion:** A leader with high levels of integrity, who is value-based and charismatic, and has good interpersonal skills will in all probability be universally accepted and seen as effective.
Eight Universally Undesirable Leadership Attributes
Loner, irritable, ruthless, asocial, non-explicit, dictatorial, non-cooperative, egocentric **Conclusion:** A leader who is asocial, malevolent, and self-focused will in all probability be universally perceived as ineffective. The way in which these universally endorsed and undesirable leadership attributes manifest behaviourally is culture contingent, and they look different in different cultures!

Table 3.2 shows that GLOBE found that the **62 nations** could be categorised into **10 unique regional country clusters**. GLOBE distilled **six universal leadership dimensions** that linked with the country clusters' cultural values and practices. Lastly, GLOBE isolated **22 universally endorsed** and **eight universally undesirable leadership attributes.**

One of the most intriguing findings from the GLOBE study is that certain aspects of universal leadership (leadership that is common across cultures), such as humane and/or participative leadership (see Table 3.2) **are culture-specific and not shared by other cultures**. In other words, what humane or participative leadership looks like in practice will vary in different cultures.[13] For cross-cultural leaders, this means becoming aware of those leadership values and practices that are universally shared across cultures, and leadership styles that are unique to a specific country.

The South African GLOBE findings

The South African sample for the GLOBE study presented two sub-groups in South Africa, white males and African black males. The results of the white sub-sample aligned with the Anglo country cluster (Canada, Australia, England, Ireland, New Zealand, USA), which is competitive and results-orientated. The African black sub-sample aligned with the sub-Saharan (Zimbabwe, Namibia, Zambia, Nigeria) country cluster, which is concerned and sensitive to others and demonstrates strong family loyalty. Figure 3.3 shows how the South African sample scored on the six universal leadership dimensions.

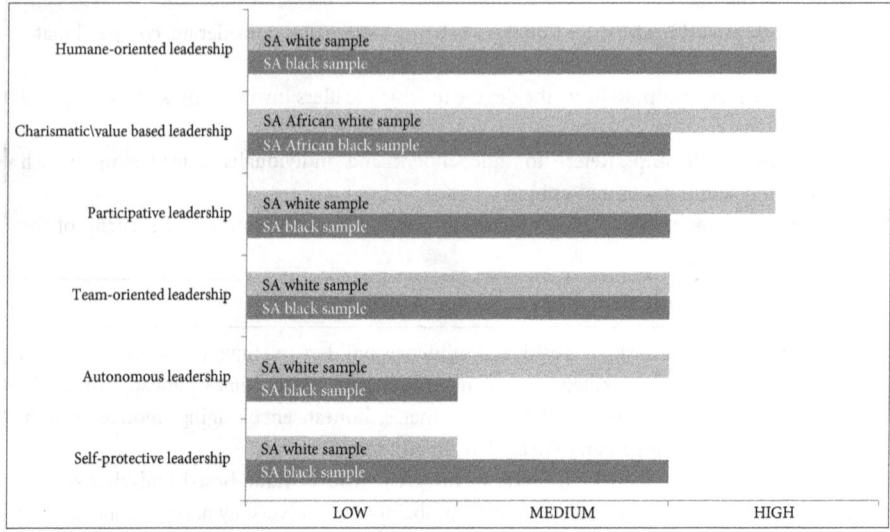

Figure 3.3: The South African scores on the GLOBE universal leadership dimensions[14]

Figure 3.3 shows that the GLOBE study found that:

- In general, South African leaders seem to be supportive, considerate, compassionate, and generous (high levels of **Humane Leadership Orientation**).
- The ability to inspire, to motivate, and to expect high performance from others based on strongly held core values (**Charismatic/Value-based leadership**) are also valued. The white sub-sample shows high levels of Charismatic/Value-based leadership orientation (the highest of all the country clusters). Black counterparts showed medium levels of Charismatic/Value-based leadership orientation.
- **Participative leadership** – the degree to which leaders involve others in making and implementing decisions – is highly valued by white South African leaders and moderately valued by Black South African leaders.
- South African leaders in general showed medium levels of **Team Orientation Leadership**. They invested in team building, collaboration and creating common purpose among team members.
- Black South African leaders seem to be less autonomous (low level) than white South African leaders, who showed medium levels of **Autonomous leadership**, which reflects their more individualistic nature.
- Black South African leaders showed medium levels of self-protective leadership, compared to low levels of white South African leaders. **Self-protective leadership** reflects behaviours that ensure the safety and security of the leader and the group.

Subsequent GLOBE-related research done in the late 1990s[iii] found an Afrocentric and Eurocentric duality between white and African black South African leaders. South African black leaders were found to be more humane-orientated and participative than South African white leaders, which is aligned with the higher levels of collectivism found in South African blacks. Also, different from the GLOBE results, recent research[15] done in 2011 showed that both black and white managers in South Africa value charismatic/value-based leadership equally highly.

The above shows that there are some conflicting results on desirable and undesirable leadership attributes for South African black and white leaders. More research in this regard is needed. It is important to note that the GLOBE data was collected in 1994-1995, coinciding with the advent of democracy and huge changes in the fabric of the South African society. Therefore subsequent research may reflect more accurate findings of the current state of South African leadership.

In conclusion, based on the above, South African leaders tend to emphasise:

- High levels of Humane Leadership Orientation and Charismatic/Value-based leadership
- Medium-high levels of Participative leadership
- Medium levels of Team Orientation, and
- Medium-low levels of Autonomous and Self-Protective leadership.

Executive leadership effectiveness

Phase 3 of the GLOBE study[iv] focused on Executive Leadership Effectiveness. It found that **Charismatic/Value-based leadership**, which includes vision, inspiration, performance orientation, decisiveness and high integrity, is the global leadership behaviour which has the most impact. This behaviour is universally desirable across all the countries in their study. **Team-Orientated Leadership** is the **next most important global leadership behaviour**, being especially administratively competent, a team integrator, diplomatic, and collaborative. This makes intuitive sense because even in individualistic cultures, team performance is crucial to organisational effectiveness. Team-orientated leadership is most sensitive to societal expectations, and how it will be enacted in cultures depends on the culture's CLT. **Humane Orientation** – being supportive, considerate, compassionate, and generous – **is the third most important global leadership behaviour.** It is also sensitive to societal expectations.

This means that, to be effective, CEOs need to behave in particular ways and at the same time, need to act according to the leadership expectations of their societies, and/or the society in which they work. Interestingly, it seems that there is a large amount of overlap between effective CEO leadership expectations and preferred leadership emphasised by South African leaders. In both cases, **charismatic leadership, team-orientated leadership** and **humane orientation** are valued.

---

iii Booysen (1999, 2001, in Booysen & van Wyk, 2007) did an in-country study in South Africa using the GLOBE questionnaire and found the white management group profile congruent with western or Eurocentric management, which tends to emphasise competition and performance orientation, free enterprise, liberal democracy, individual self-sufficiency, self-fulfilment and development, exclusivity, planning, methodology and structure. The black South African management group reflected an Afrocentric management, which emphasises collective solidarity, inclusivity, collaboration, consensus and group significance, concern for people as well as working for the common good, structure through rituals and ceremonies, patriarchy, respect, and dignity.

iv Phase 3 of the GLOBE study (2014) included 24 countries, 1 015 domestic organisations and Chief Executive Officers (CEOs), and more than 6 000 managers in the top management teams.

The role of organisational contingency factors in cross-cultural leadership

Now, I want to circle back to the second part of the GLOBE's CLT theory focusing on organisational contingency factors. This theory shows that apart from cultural forces, other forces such as political, economic, social, technological, legal and environmental (setting) stability and uncertainty (PESTLE forces), and organisational task and mission, are also major influences on organisational practices and leadership behaviour. So, in addition to culture, societal and organisational contextual forces are important aspects in cross-cultural leadership.

The Center for Creative Leadership's (CCL) Leading Across Differences (LAD[16]) framework extends the CLT theory and illustrates how these myriad contextual forces influence leadership practices. As with CLT, it takes the **individual, organisational and societal levels of reciprocal influences** into account.

Of particular interest in this framework is the focus on how different groups and sub-groupings on all three levels can cause **"geological fault-lines"**[17] that create friction when the boundaries rub against each other, which has repercussions throughout the whole system. These fault-lines can pull groups apart, grind and collide, and create conflict.

This LAD framework suggests that:

1. *Fault-lines* (sub-groupings such as national culture, race, gender, language, and religion) function on the *societal level* and spill over into the *organisational context*.
2. The *societal landscape* (which includes the demographical, historical, and PESTLE contexts) influences leaders' and followers' *individual level identity development and awareness.*
3. *Individuals* (followers and leaders) carry these *fault-lines* into their **organisational context** and specifically **leadership practices and expectations**. For instance, identity group history, and intergroup anxiety and conflict all spill over into the organisational context.
4. The *organisational context* includes yet another level of *cultural influences, organisational culture; shared values*, both espoused and enacted; the *organisational climate* and *practices; human* and *other resources;* and the *organisation's vision, mission, strategy, strategic intent,* and *practices.*
5. Over and above *societal-level fault-lines,* organisations also create their own *organisational fault-lines* **(or "Us" and "Them" groups),** for instance, interdependent divisions and departments, functional silos, competitive teams, competing organisational cultures, and employee hierarchies (tops, middles, and bottoms).
6. Lastly, another important factor we need to consider is that there are *perceived power differences* **between** *fault-lines groups,* where some groups are seen as **in-groups**, dominant and the norm, and others are viewed as subordinate or marginalised.

Leaders need to understand how their own cultural and social identity dynamics impact on their roles as leaders, and engage in practices to off-set being caught up in these dynamics. The CCL identified the following role demands for leaders.[18] Leaders are:

- ***Often pulled in many directions*** between conflicting intergroup values, viewpoints, and beliefs. Leaders need to be unbiased and need to be respectful of everyone's needs and viewpoints.
- ***Commonly pushed to one side***. Any specific leader is a member of only particular groups, which will influence others' perceptions of them. Therefore leaders should focus on fairness and equity to show that they are not partial to their own group(s).

- *All too frequently caught out of the loop.* This is due to the leader's lack of critical awareness concerning fault-lines and social identity dynamics, as well as information filtering. Leaders need first to be accessible in order to be in the loop, and they need to be sensitive to group dynamics, to create a setting of trust and safety.

While both black and white South African managers value the **"credibility triad"** of **competence, honesty** and **inspiration** (charismatic or value-based leadership), key differences along organisational and contextual fault-lines exist between managers and employees and sub-groups, such as age, education and level of management.[19]

South African societal fault-lines

The following societal fault-lines influence South African workplaces, leadership practices and follower expectations:[20]

- The *ineffectiveness of affirmative action and employment equity* in South Africa, arising from tokenism, reverse discrimination, negative stereotyping of black affirmative appointees, a backlash against affirmative action appointees, and appointment of foreign nationals in order to make equity targets.
- *Racial polarities obscure gender parity.* Women, and black women specifically, are still not represented proportionally in leadership positions.
- *Class inequality* is especially evident in the wealth of a few and the devastating poverty of the majority. Uneven development along race lines can be seen in terms of the lack of material security, which is more uneven now than it was during the apartheid era. The number of *young unemployed,* specifically black South Africans, in turn gives rise to poverty.
- The unprecedented *high levels of violent crime,* the *HIV/Aids epidemic* and a low life expectancy are added factors which affect the country's economy and stability.
- The *skills gap, brain drain* and *skills wastage* all result in a crucial *skills shortage* in the country.
- *Generational differences* between South Africans are vast:
  - *The Apartheid Generation* (born 1938-1960) grew up knowing a system that favoured whites.
  - *The Struggle Generation* (1961-1980) took part in the fight against the apartheid regime.
  - *The Transition Generation* (1981-1993) grew up in apartheid South Africa, socialised with older friends and family who were part of the struggle era, and now are caught in an economy with few job opportunities.
  - *The Free Generation* (born 1994-2014) was never subject to the apartheid regime; their only lived experience has been that of a democratic and more globally and socially integrated South Africa.
- Minorities such as *foreign nationals* from neighbouring countries and South African whites *are not being fully integrated* and experience discriminatory practices which fuel hostility between ethnic groups.
- Despite South Africa's progressive constitution, *rising homophobic sentiments* and occurrences of "corrective rape" are rife. This can possibly be ascribed to key players in the ANC, pressure groups such as CONTRALESA, and evangelicals, as well as various other African nations' criminalisation of homosexuality.
- *As a result of the radical power shifts* since 1994, primary identities and perceptions of

inclusivity are shifting in society and workplaces. ***New social identities are developing*** coupled to profession, education, workplace, and identities other than race.

Summary: Cross-cultural Influences on Leadership

To conclude the section on cross-cultural influences on leadership, I want to highlight again that national culture's influence on leadership is only one of several other cultural influences, as can be seen in Figure 3.2. The GLOBE study is useful for national country comparisons and speaks to **group level behaviour** and ***not* individual behaviour**. The understanding of cross-cutting intra-national diversity, sub-cultural, social categories and social identities, and individual differences, can be even more challenging for leaders. The LAD framework is useful because it shows how **societal and organisational contextual factors and fault-lines intersect in organisations** and influence leadership expectations and leadership role demands. Lastly, I highlighted some of the important **fault-lines impacting South African workplaces**.

How Can We Lead Effectively in Multicultural Organisations?

Let me offer some practical guidelines that follow from the research discussed.

- *Understand how culture impacts leadership*

    Leaders need to understand how culture impacts their roles as leaders, their own leadership practices, and follower expectations. Leaders need to take care not to get caught up in cultural fault-line dynamics, so that they are not experienced as being biased and engaging in self-protective leadership.

- *Knowledge of most effective and least effective leadership attributes across cultures*

    Leaders that will be seen as effective in most cultures: have high levels of integrity, are value-based and fair, competent, excellence-orientated, charismatic, team-orientated, humane-orientated, and have good interpersonal skills.

Leaders who are perceived as **ineffective in most cultures**: are **asocial, malevolent, egocentric, in-group focused,** and **non-co-operative**.

- *Cultivating a Global Mindset in order to understand better across differences*

    Leaders also need to know that that the ways in which the desired and undesirable leadership attributes manifest are not necessarily the same across cultures, and may look different in different cultures. Cultivating a global mindset will help leaders to leverage these cultural differences, bridge cultural boundaries, and avoid cultural misunderstanding. (This will be the focus of the next section.)

- *Focus on mission-driven leadership*

    Leadership is a process that directs and aligns employees towards commitment to the mission of the organisation. This becomes more difficult if we work in multicultural organisations where follower expectations vary across cultures. Yet the shared mission of the organisation still acts as the common denominator for all employees, despite their cultural differences. Therefore, when leading across cultural differences, strong mission-driven leadership is imperative. In this way, the focus is on the shared outcome and not on the perceived differences. Outcomes and expectations must be explored together and spelled out clearly. Assumptions must be tested continuously, and effective communication is key.

- *Create inclusive organisational cultures*

    Organisational culture (the underlying shared assumptions, values and beliefs that affect the way in which work is done and people behave) is a powerful force in accomplishing commitment, and acts as the glue that keeps the organisation together. Organisational culture is also a holding space in which leadership takes place. Inclusive organisational cultures are more conducive to leveraging difference. When leaders create inclusive organisational cultures and workplaces where all people from diverse cultural backgrounds feel safe, valued, respected, recognised and treated fairly, higher levels of commitment will be achieved.

The Scope and Context of Global Leadership

Global leadership can be defined as the process of directing the thinking, attitudes, and behaviours of global communities in order to work together synergistically toward a shared vision and common goals in a committed way.[21] In order to do this, global leaders need to consider the national macro contexts and societal fault-lines carefully, and pay attention to managing cultural differences, in addition to the several other boundary-spanning practices in which they need to engage. In fact, cross-cultural leadership is a subset of global leadership.[22]

The term "global" actually reflects the context in which leadership operates. Global leadership needs to be defined in terms of the manifestation of the levels of complexity and boundary spanning, since it functions in an extreme context of complexity. It involves the creation and navigation of linkages across a myriad boundaries.[23]

The CCL identified five common levels of boundaries global leaders have to negotiate:

1. *Vertical* – across levels and authority;
2. *Horizontal* – across functions and expertise;
3. *Stakeholder* – across external groups and interests;
4. *Demographic* – across diverse groups and differences; and
5. *Geographic* – across markets and distance.

These boundaries function on a cultural, sub-cultural and divisional level, and add to the complexity of the global leaders' work landscape exponentially, depending on how many different boundaries are crossed per level.[24]

Complexity also involves the interplay of:

- **Continuous multiplicity**, for instance more and different PESTLE influences, stakeholders, cultures added for each country/geographical area;
- **Interdependence, mutual interplay and connectedness** of, for example, different organisations, departments, customers;
- **Ambiguity** (convergence of multiplicity and interdependence); and
- **Flux** – constant motion, white water of change, just-in-time actions.

Boundary spanning in a global context also includes:

- **Flow** which refers to relational aspects using human networks and social capital to run smooth operations; and
- **Presence** which refers to the degree to which managers must actually "geographically co-locate" (physically or virtually) in order to perform effectively in their roles.

Individuals with a global mindset have the ability to deal with the complexity, ambiguity, and polarities of cultures and sub-cultures without being paralysed, intimidated or frustrated by the differences. They do not presume to have the answers, but remain curious, open minded, and humble in their mindful inquiry about others.

Dimensions of a Global Mindset

A global mindset rests upon open-mindedness and a deep awareness of diversity across cultures and contexts, and on the capability to integrate and synthesise the polarities and cognitive complexities of these diverse viewpoints and contexts.

Researchers from Thunderbird Business School[25] interviewed over 200 global executives and surveyed over 6 000 managers. They identified a set of individual qualities that are critical for the leaders of tomorrow, which they called a Global Mindset:

- Leaders with a global mindset are **knowledgeable about cultures and doing business in the global arena**.
- They understand **PESTLE systems in the countries** in which they operate, and understand how the global industry works.
- They are passionate about **leveraging cultural difference** and are willing to step out of their own comfort zones and stretch themselves.
- They are comfortable with **being uncomfortable in uncomfortable settings** – they are able to withstand the tensions of polarities.

Research[26] has indicated that having a global mindset requires the competencies listed in Table 3.3.

Table 3.3 Global mindset competencies

Competency	Description
Global intellectual capital	A manager's knowledge base and how he/she leverage it. Global business savvy and competence, cognitive complexity, and cosmopolitan outlook
Global psychological capital	A manager's willingness to engage in a global setting. A passion for diversity, adaptability, optimism, quest for adventure, inquisitiveness, resilience, self-assurance, and confidence
Global social capital	The ability to show intercultural empathy, cultural sensitivity, interpersonal impact, diplomacy. The ability to create consensus among divergent views, and multicultural teams
Global ethical relational practice	Being relationally skilled, practising mindful inquiry and curiosity. The ability to build trusting relationships despite difference, by showing integrity, fairness, dignity, respect, empathy, and humility
Global systems competencies	The ability to lead change, foster innovation, make complex ethical decisions, influence stakeholders and build community and social capital

Global leadership development is hard work. At its core, global leadership development is an individual affair. It needs to fit the specific gap of the manager's unique existing competency configuration and the positional (contextual) demands for competency deployment in a current or future job.[27] This brings us to what is needed for global leadership excellence.

Multiple Intelligences for Global Leadership Excellence

It is well established that basic intelligence (IQ) is important to deal with cognitive complexity in the workplace. It is moderately related to attaining a leadership position and only slightly related to being successful as a leader.[28] Other forms of intelligences are also needed for leadership success.

Two multiple intelligence theories that gained popularity in management studies in the 1980s and 1990s are Gardner's Theory of Multiple Intelligences (1983)[v][29] and Sternberg's (1997)[30] Triarchic Theory of Intelligence.[vi] Goleman and others' work[31] on the importance of Emotional intelligence (EQ) in leadership success paved the way for leadership studies to explore other forms of relational intelligences related to leadership success on a local and global level.

Table 3.4 summarises the six intelligences, when used in combination, that in my opinion, hold the most promise for global leadership excellence.

Table 3.4: Six intelligences for global leadership excellence

Type of IQ	Definition	Components
Cognitive Intelligence (IQ)	Ability to apply and understand abstraction, to do complex problem solving both fluid and concrete, to see causalities and to master new learning material	Verbal competency Non-verbal competency (2D and 3D) Analytical and abstract thinking Job knowledge and competencies
Emotional Intelligence (EI)	Ability to accurately perceive, understand and regulate emotions, and to effectively apply emotions as a source of energy, information, connection and influence	Self-awareness and self-management Motivation and empathy Relational management Emotional expressiveness, sensitivity and control
Social Intelligence (SQ1)	Ability to perceive and accurately interpret the intricacies of social situations and to select appropriate behavioural responses	Social expressiveness, sensitivity and control Adaptability and flexibility Collaboration and co-operation Influencing and leading others Effective listening

---

v Gardner (1983) maintained human beings exhibit multiple intelligences that work in combination and not in isolation in a particular context or cultural setting. He identified seven distinct modalities of intelligences: linguistic, logical-mathematical, spatial, musical, bodily kinaesthetic, interpersonal, and intrapersonal, and added two more modalities, existential and moral intelligence as non-cognitive abilities. Gardner argued that leaders exhibit high levels of linguistic intelligence, interpersonal intelligence, and intrapersonal intelligence.

vi Sternberg's (1997) Triarchic Theory of Intelligence for Leadership Success is based on (i) analytical intelligence which equates to basic cognitive intelligence, (ii) practical or contextual intelligence, and (iii) creative intelligence, which is the ability to produce novel and useful ideas, solutions and behaviour.

Table 3.4: Six intelligences for global leadership excellence (continued)

Type of IQ	Definition	Components
Spiritual Intelligence (SQ2)	Ability to maintain inner and outer peace, be mindful, see meaning, and act with wisdom and compassion, regardless of the circumstances	Sense-making and sense of belonging Spiritual presence Transcendental awareness Critical self-reflection and reflexive thinking Existential wisdom
Cultural Intelligence (CQ1)	Ability to function effectively in a diverse context where assumptions, values and traditions of one's upbringing are not uniformly shared with those with whom one needs to work	Motivational CQ – interest, drive, and energy to adapt cross-culturally: *Drive* Cognitive CQ – level of cultural knowledge: *Understanding* Metacognitive CQ – making sense of culturally diverse experiences: *Strategy* Behavioural CQ – ability to act appropriately in cross-cultural situations: *Action*
Contextual Intelligence (CQ2)	The ability to understand the limits of our knowledge and to adapt that knowledge to a setting different from the one in which it developed	Acute awareness of internal and external contextual variables Awareness of relevant past events Intuitive grasp of preferred future A global perspective in the midst of local circumstances

Based on the information in Table 3.4, the respective intelligences must be understood in the following way:

- *Cognitive Intelligence (IQ)* is the first type of intelligence needed to be effective as a global leader. It aids leaders to learn and acquire work knowledge and competencies, and to deal with cognitive complexity, analytical thinking, problem solving, and decision-making. It is also safe to say that higher levels of cognitive job complexity would probably require higher levels of IQ. Yet, *cognitive agility* alone is not enough. Multiple forms of intelligences are needed to deal with all the contextual factors and complexities encountered in global leadership.
- *Emotional Intelligence (EI or EQ)* can be seen as the second basic building block for effective global leadership. High levels of EQ lead to intra- and interpersonal awareness and understanding. It is the ability to use emotions, your own and others', as a driving force to direct and align behaviour and keep people motivated and committed – in short, *emotional agility*.
- *Social Intelligence (SQ1)* can be referred to as everyday intelligence or *social agility*. It is the ability to understand social situations, formal and informal social norms, rules and roles, and to act appropriately in social situations.[32] In a global setting, it is particularly important for leaders to be able to be adaptable and flexible, in order to focus on relational practice and to manage multiple social realities.

- **Spiritual Intelligence (SQ2)** or **spiritual agility** is "... *the intelligence with which we address and solve problems of meaning and value, the intelligence with which we can place our actions and our lives in a wider, richer, meaning-giving context, the intelligence with which we can assess that one course of action or one life-path is more meaningful than another*".[33] The transformational power of SQ2 distinguishes it from IQ, EQ and SQ1. It is the human capability ultimately to ask questions about the meaning of life and to experience simultaneously seamless connection between each of us and the world in which we live.
- **High levels** of EQ or **emotional agility**, SQ1 or **social agility** and SQ2 or **spiritual agility** in combination leads to higher levels of relational agility. *Relational agility* is the intentional practice of utilising emotional energy and social contexts in a mindful way in order to build meaningful and positive relationships.
- **Cultural intelligence (CQ1)** or **cultural agility** is the ability to leave behind intelligent behaviours learned in one cultural context when what is intelligent in another cultural context differs.[34] *CQ1* is a relatively new development in leadership studies and builds on and extends EQ, SQ1 and SQ2. CQ1 is based on:
    o *Self-awareness* – understanding the impact of one's own culture and background in terms of the values and biases one brings to the workplace.
    o *Social awareness* – understanding others and their comparable values, biases and expectations, and managing multiple cultural realities.
    o *Behavioural adaptability* – being able to display appropriate, adaptable and flexible behaviours and expectations in cross-cultural situations.
    o *Curiosity and confident action* – showing interest in, enjoying cultural encounters, and confidently practising new behaviours.
    o *Respectful inquiry* – showing respect for other cultures and being humble about one's own culture.

CQ1 can be developed through multicultural experience and cultural exposure. Rather than expecting individuals to master all the norms, values, and practices of the various cultures encountered, CQ1 helps leaders to develop an overall perspective and repertoire that helps them deal with cultural complexity and ambiguity.

- **Contextual intelligence (CQ2)** is also a relatively new development in leadership studies, and leads to *contextual agility*. The contextually intelligent practitioner has the ability to recognise and diagnose quickly and intuitively the dynamic contextual variables. He/she is knowledgeable about how to do something (in other words, he/she has technical knowledge from formal education and observation). More importantly, this leader is wise enough, based on intuition and experience, to know what to do, to adapt if needed, and do whatever it is differently in another context.[35] Global leaders must translate and transfer knowledge and practices from one setting to another on a constant basis.

Figure 3.4 shows on which level of work each of the six IQs is most applicable.

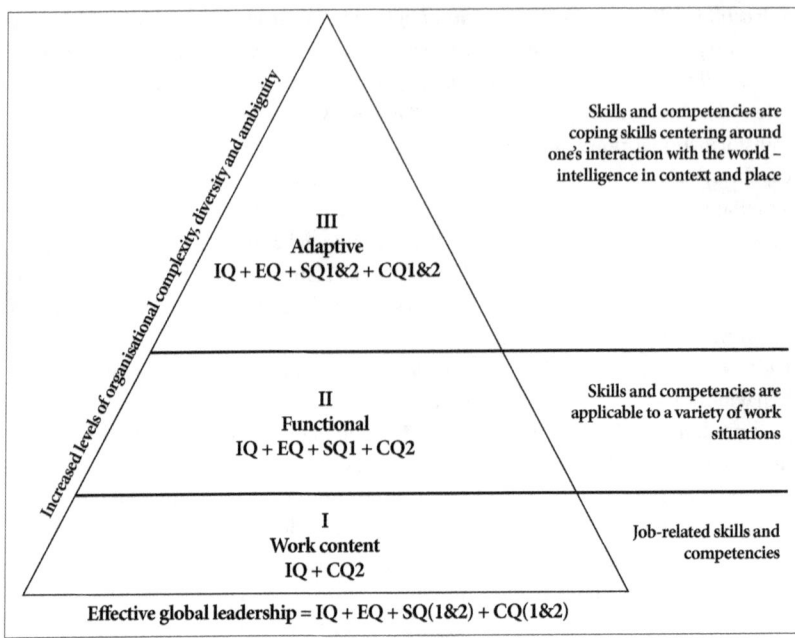

Figure 3.4: Multiple intelligences linked with level of work in organisations

Figure 3.4 shows that:

- IQ and CQ2 are most important on a work content level.
- IQ, EQ, SQ1 and CQ2 are most important on a functional level.
- All six intelligences are needed on an adaptive level of work in organisations.
- Adaptive level competencies are at the apex of global leadership and comprise the largest part of global leadership effectiveness.

Figure 3.4 also shows that an increase in organisational complexity, diversity and ambiguity needs increased adaptive functioning. Lastly, the combination of Cognitive Agility (IQ), Emotional Agility (EQ), Social Agility (SQ1), Spiritual Agility (SQ2), Cultural Agility (CQ1), and Contextual Agility (CQ2) equals effective global leadership.

The Way Forward: An Ethic of Responsible Global Leadership

"Be ashamed to die until you have won some victories for humanity."
– Horace Mann[36]

What is local has an impact on what is global, and what is global needs responsible leaders to be stewards of our world and our future. Global leaders and global corporations have the widest reach and footprint and are in the best position to influence and effect positive social change, and to model responsible global leadership. It is also no longer enough just to act locally and think globally. In the extreme contexts of complexity, diversity, ambiguity and flux in which leaders operate, we must think and act globally, while *living and acting* locally.[37]

Recent leadership research in South Africa[38] showed that there is a quest for a new type of leadership that speaks to sustainability, ethical practice, social justice, fairness, and preservation of resources with a large stakeholder base – **responsible leadership**. Responsible leadership focuses on both social responsibility, which includes corporate social responsibility, and leadership on local and global levels.

Responsible global leaders need to engage in dialogue courageously about how to have a positive impact with regard to the moral dilemmas we are facing today, such as:

- How do organisations maximise profits and at the same time maximise their contributions to addressing societal problems?
- Can inclusive, equitable workplaces and societies be created within a capitalist economic system?
- How do we view our fellow (local) and global citizens and peacefully integrate opposing beliefs and value systems?
- How do we ensure that people are treated as humanely as possible, with inalienable rights, rather than as instruments towards profit?
- What kind of world do we want both to live in and leave for the better?

Responsible global leaders are ethical leaders committed to making a difference in the world, who are agents of positive social change for the common good of all. Responsible Global leaders need to ask the crucial questions – leadership for what…? What kind of leader do I want to be …?

Endnotes

1. Hofstede, 1980, 1991; Hofstede, Hofstede & Minkov, 2010; House et al., 2004; House et al., 2014.
2. House et al., 2004, 2014, p. 11.
3. House et al., 2004, 2014.
4. Hofstede et al., 2010; House et al., 2004, 2014.
5. Hannum, McFeeters & Booysen, 2010.
6. Tajfel & Turner, 1979; Ellemers & Haslam, 2012; Booysen, 2015.
7. Hofstede, 1991.
8. Synthesised from Hofstede, 1980, 1991, 2010; Booysen, 2015; Tjafel and Turner (1979).
9. Hofstede, 2006, 2010; Minkov & Hofstede, 2011; and others.
10. Booysen, (2007), based on an original discussion from Dorfman, (1996); Hofstede, (1980, 1991, 1996); House et al., (2004), cited in Booysen, 2015.
11. Lord & Maher (1991), Hofstede (1991, 1996), McClelland (1985) and Donaldson (1993), in House, 2004.
12. Booysen, 2015.
13. Javidan, House, Dorfman, Hanges & de Luque, 2006.
14. Compiled from Booysen & van Wyk, 2007, and House et al., 2004.
15. Lee, 2011.
16. Ruderman, et al., 2010, in Hannum et al., 2010.
17. Lau and Murnigham (1998, 2005) brought the fault-line analogy into leadership studies and explained it as hypothetical dividing lines that can split organisations (and societies) into "us" and "them" groups. See Hannum et al., 2010.
18. Ruderman et al., 2010, in Hannum et al., 2010; Booysen, 2015.
19. Lee, 2011.
20. Booysen & Nkomo, 2014; Lee, 2011.
21. Mendenhall & Bird, 2013; Javidan & Walker, 2013; Booysen, 2015.
22. House, et al., 2004, 2014.
23. Mendenhall & Bird, 2013.
24. Ernst & Yip, 2009.
25. Javidan, Teagarden & Bowen, 2010.
26. Javidan et al., 2010; Bird et al., 2010; Mendenhall & Bird, 2013; Javidan & Walker, 2013.
27. Mendenhall & Bird, 2013.
28. Riggio, Murphy & Pirozzolo, 2002.
29. Gardner, 1983.
30. Sternberg, 1997.
31. Goleman, McKee & Boyatzis, 2002.
32. Riggio et al., 2002.
33. Zohar & Marshall, 2000.
34. Van Dyne, Ang & Livermore, in Hannum et al., 2010; Offerman & Phan, 2002; Riggio et al., 2002.
35. Kutz & Bamford-Wade, 2013; Khanna, 2014.
36. Horace Mann
37. Howard, 2010.
38. Gleason, Nkomo & De Jongh, 2011.

References

Bird, A, Mendenhall, M, Stevens, MJ & Oddou, G. 2010. 'Defining the content domain of intercultural competence for global leaders'. *Journal of Managerial Psychology*, 25(8):810–828.

Booysen, LAE. 2015. 'Cross-Cultural Coaching'. In D Riddle, E Hoole & E Gullette (eds). *The center for creative leadership handbook of coaching in organizations*. San Francisco, CA: John Wiley & Sons/Jossey-Bass. 241–288.

Booysen, LAE & Nkomo, SM. 2014. 'New developments in employment equity and diversity management in South Africa'. In A Klarsfeld et al. (eds). *International handbook on diversity management at work: Country perspectives on diversity and equal treatment (Vol. 2)*. 2nd ed. Cheltenham, UK: Edward Elgar Publishing. 241–265.

Booysen, LAE & van Wyk, MW. 2007. 'Culture and leadership in South Africa'. In JS Chhokar, FC Brodbeck & RJ House (eds). *Culture and leadership across the world: The GLOBE book of in-depth studies of 25 societies*. New York, NY: Taylor & Francis. 433–473.

Dorfman, PW. 1996. International and cross-cultural leadership research. In B.J. Punnett, & O. Shenkar (Eds.) Handbook for international management research, pp. 267-349. Oxford UK: Blackwell.

Ellemers, N & Haslam, A. 2012. 'Social identity theory'. In PAM van Lange, AW Kruglanski & ET Higgins (eds). *Handbook of theories of social psychologies (Vol. 2, Part Five)*. Thousand Oaks, CA: Sage Publications, Inc. 379–398.

Ernst, C & Yip, J. 2009. 'Boundary spanning leadership: Tactics to bridge social identity groups in organizations'. In TL Pittinsky (ed). *Crossing the divide: Intergroup leadership in a world of difference*. Boston, MA: Harvard Business School Press. 87–99.

Gardner, H. 1983. *Frames of Mind: The theory of multiple intelligences*, New York: Basic Books. The second edition was published in Britain by Fontana Press. 466 + xxix pages.

Gleason, D, Nkomo, SM & De Jongh, D. 2011. *Courageous conversations: A collection of interviews and reflections on responsible leadership by South African captains of industry*. Pretoria: Van Schaik Publishers.

Goleman, D, McKee, A & Boyatzis, R. 2002. *Primal leadership: Realizing the power of emotional intelligence*. Boston, MA: Harvard Business School Publishing.

Hannum, K, McFeeters, BB & Booysen, LAE. 2010. *Leading across differences: Cases and perspectives*. San Francisco, CA: Pfeiffer.

Hofstede, G. 1980. *Culture's consequences: International Differences in Work Related Values*, Newbury Park, CA: Sage.

Hofstede, G. 1991. *Cultures and Organizations: Software of the Mind*. New York, NY: McGraw-Hill.

Hofstede, G. 2006. What did GLOBE really measure? Researchers' minds versus respondents' minds. *Journal of International Business Studies*, 37, 882-96.

Hofstede, G, Hofstede, GJ & Minkov, M. 2010. *Cultures and organizations: Software of the mind*. 3rd ed. New York, NY: McGraw-Hill International.

Horace Mann. (n.d.). BrainyQuote.com. Retrieved July 21, 2016, from BrainyQuote.com.[Online] Available: http://www.brainyquote.com/quotes/quotes/h/horacemann133541.html [Accessed 16 July 2016]

House, RJ, Hanges, PJ, Javidan, M, Dorfman, PW & Gupta, V. 2004. *Culture, leadership, and organizations: The GLOBE study of 62 societies*. Thousand Oaks, CA: Sage Publications, Inc.

House, RJ, Dorfman, PW, Javidan, M, Hanges, PJ & Sully de Luque, MF. 2014. *Strategic leadership across cultures: The GLOBE study of CEO leadership behavior and effectiveness in 24 countries*. Los Angeles, CA: Sage Publications, Inc.

Howard, A. 2010. 'A new global ethic'. *Journal of Management Development*, 29(5):506–517.

Javidan, M., House R.J., Dorfman P., P. Hanges P., & Sully deLuque M. 2006. Conceptualizing and measuring cultures and their consequences: A comparative review of GLOBE's and Hofstede's approaches. *Journal of International Business Studies*.

Javidan, M, Teagarden, MB & Bowen, DE. 2010. 'Managing yourself: Making it overseas'. *Harvard Business Review*, 109–113, April.

Javidan, M & Walker, J. 2013. *Developing your global mindset: The handbook for successful global leaders*. Edina, MN: Beaver's Pond Press, Inc.

Khanna, T. 2014. 'Contextual intelligence'. *Harvard Business Review*, 92(9):58–68.

Kutz, MR & Bamford-Wade, A. 2013. 'Understanding contextual intelligence: A critical competency for today's leaders'. *Emergence: Complexity & Organization*, 15(3):55–80.

Lee, GJ. 2011. 'Mirror, mirror: Preferred leadership characteristics of South African managers'. *International Journal of Manpower*, 32(2):211–232.

Mendenhall, ME & Bird, A. 2013. 'In search of global leadership'. *Organizational Dynamics*, 42(3):167–174.

Minkov, M & Hofstede, G. 2011. "The evolution of Hofstede's doctrine". *Cross Cultural Management: An International Journal*, Vol. 18 no. 1, 10-20.

Offermann, LR. & Phan, LU. 2002. Culturally intelligent leadership for a diverse world. In R. E. Riggio, S. E. Murphy, & F. J. Pirozzolo (Eds.), Multiple intelligences and leadership (pp. 187-214). Mahwah, NJ: Erlbaum.

Riggio, RE, Murphy, SE & Pirozzolo, FJ. 2002. *Multiple intelligences and leadership*. London, UK: Lawrence Erlbaum Associates.

Sternberg, RJ. 1997. *Successful intelligence*. New York, USA: Plume.

Tajfel, H. 1974. Social identity and intergroup behavior. *Social Science Information*, 13 (2), 65-93.

Tajfel, H & Turner, JC. 1979. 'An integrative theory of intergroup conflict'. In WG Austin & S Worchel (eds). *The social psychology of intergroup relations*. Monterey, CA: Brooks & Cole. 33–47.

Turner, JC, Hogg, MA, Oakes, PJ, Reicher, SD. & Wetherell, MS. 1987. *Rediscovering the social group: A self-categorization theory*. Oxford and New York: Basil Blackwell.

Turner, JC, & Reynolds, K. 2012. Self-categorization theory. In P.A.M. van Lange, A. W. Kruglanski & E. T. Higgings (Eds) *Handbook of theories of social psychology* (Vol. 2. pp. 399-418). London: Sage.

Zohar, D & Marshall, I. 2000. *Spiritual intelligence: The ultimate intelligence*. London, UK: Bloomsbury Publishing Plc.

Chapter 4

LEADERSHIP BRAND MODELLING

Anton Verwey and Sonja Verwey

Traditionally, the term 'brand' referred to aspects such as corporate identity and marketing campaigns. More recently, the research and literature on leadership includes the notion of 'leadership brand', which may be defined as "the identity and reputation of leaders throughout an organisation".[1]

The purpose of this chapter is to discuss and propose a leadership brand model. To this end, the following topics are discussed: the concept 'brand'; brand promise; brand promise and leadership; leadership brand; and the right leadership brand.

The Concept 'Brand'

Historically, the use of the term 'brand' can be traced back to the Old Norse word '*brandr*', meaning 'to burn', which bore reference to the 'branding' of livestock as a means of identification.[2,3] Further historical evidence of branding includes the unique symbols used by brick makers in ancient Egypt to differentiate their work, and the use of heraldic symbols in Scotland and England.[4,5,6] While branding in the form of the use of a mark or symbol may have been prevalent throughout history, generations past only glimpsed the power of brands and branding exercised and experienced today.

Notions of what constitutes a brand have undergone significant reconceptualisation away from seeing brands only as tangible trademarks or logos serving to identify products and services, to a concept enabling differentiation and distinction between products and services. Such differentiation is based not only on tangible aspects, but also on the intangible psychosocial associations which add value to the tangible attributes by imbuing them with emotional, social, and even spiritual resonance.

A brand can therefore be regarded as comprised of both emotional and rational elements. The *emotional elements* stem from how the brand expresses itself, and what it shows, tells, or promises. These elements set the brand's tone, character, mode, style, and mood of execution, and are less visible and, in turn, more difficult to express directly and to measure.[7] The *rational elements* stem from what the brand is telling, doing, and showing. These rational elements embody the content and theme of the brand's communication, promise, and proposition. They are the most visible part of the brand, and therefore the easiest part to articulate and measure.[8]

The Brand Promise

Brand success and value thus resides in the promise on which the product or service will deliver. Branding adds a spirit and a soul to what would otherwise be "a robotic, automated, generic price-value proposition".[9] This value-add involves "delivering a consistent set of customer experiences through the product or service, the advertising and communication, and the human representatives of the brand".[10] Experiences and interactions create a perception of the brand by all stakeholders involved, and collectively this ultimately results in the brand image. Along with the perception of the brand comes an expectation of what the brand promises to deliver, which is based on an individual's assessment of and association with the visual, auditory and kinaesthetic sensory drivers. Brand delivery may be in the form of what the individual feels or experiences after an interaction with a brand, especially if the experience doesn't live up to the expectation.

A brand is therefore nothing more than a promise that is made and kept or not kept, and which expresses an organisation's commitment to its stakeholders. The extent to which that promise is perceived to be kept is dependent upon the quality of the experience with the brand. This experience is largely reliant on employee behaviour, and the extent to which the expectations of customers are met during these critical interactions. The way in which employees behave has a direct influence on the reputation of a brand, and ultimately influences the overall success of the organisation.

From a management point of view, brand-consistent behaviour becomes an important success factor, because individual employees form the link between the organisation and its customers and stakeholders. The onus is on the leadership of the organisation to define its brand values clearly, and to encourage individual employees to act in accordance with them. Corporate branding is an important concept that "embodies the organisation values and a promise of value to be delivered. It may be used to differentiate the organisation from its competitors based on its strengths, its corporate culture, corporate 'style' and future direction".[11] Although employees experience the corporate brand on a daily basis, internal branding assists in establishing the connection between individual employees' contributions and the organisation's external reputation.

Internal branding is an organisational alignment effort designed to make sure an organisation can, and will, effectively deliver on its brand promise to customers. Internal branding ensures that the entire organisation understands and actively pursues the delivery of the brand promise.[12] As such, internal branding translates the corporate brand into internal behaviour and systems that support the individual employee in turning the brand promise into the reality of customer experience.

The Brand Promise and Leadership

In essence, this shift in perspective is an acknowledgement that leadership effectiveness is a function of the degree to which both external and internal stakeholders perceive leadership behaviours that are consistent with, and aligned to the strategy of the organisation. Colville and Murphy observe that "it is clear that the driving force connecting strategy and organisation can only be leadership: and leadership at multiple levels".[13] Another relevant shift is a move away from the focus on the individual leader towards leadership as an enterprise-wide capacity. In this context, leadership brand is the capability of leaders at every level to connect customer expectations to employee and organisational behaviour.[14] Vallaster and de Chernatony also make this link, highlighting the importance of the role leaders play in shaping internal organisational culture: "Based on our research, we postulate that leaders play an active role during the brand building process when it comes to 'translating' the brand's promise into action".[15]

Branding efforts within organisations enable organisations to build co-operation, collaboration and alignment with their internal and external customers on the policies, products and performance of the organisation. In brand-led companies, structures, processes, and incentives are required to enable and encourage brand-orientated employee behaviour. A successful leadership brand will connect employee actions with customer needs by developing the right collective leadership behaviours to drive and support the brand. By connecting the collective leadership behaviour inside the organisation to customer expectations outside the organisation, leadership branding is not concerned only with the collective role of leaders inside the organisation, but also with their impact on the customer.

Leadership Brand

Figure 4.1 depicts the portfolio of Leadership Brand Behaviours.

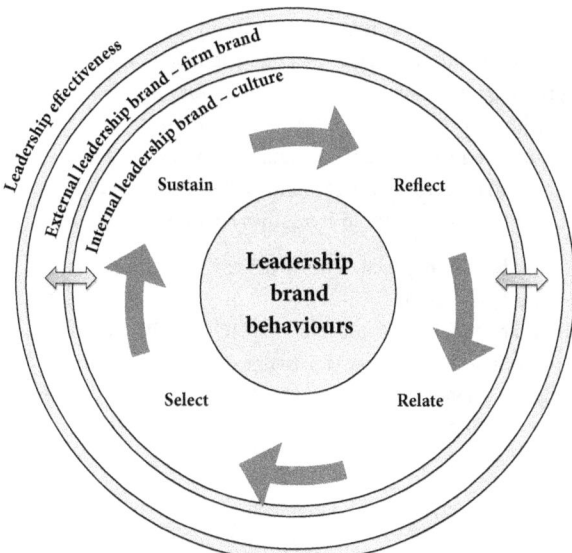

Figure 4.1: Leadership Brand Behaviours

As shown in Figure 4.1, shifts in perspectives on branding lead to questions such as:

- How do we define our unique leadership brand behaviours so that they reflect our unique market positioning?
- How do we establish these leadership brand behaviours in individual leaders?
- How do we extend and entrench these behaviours so that they create an enduring culture?
- How do we make our leadership behaviours part of our strategic intent and unique competitive advantage?
- How do we make these behaviours visible to external stakeholders so that they become an identifiable part of our firm brand?
- How do we ensure alignment (authenticity) between internal and external perceptions of our leadership brand?

A key aspect to keep in mind is that there are multiple stakeholders which influence and are influenced by one's leadership brand. One is usually quite comfortable thinking about leadership behaviours that drive profitability, customer delight, quality, and so forth. These are easy to justify to investors, shareholders and customers.

However, once we also consider stakeholder interests at the level of purpose beyond profit (such as people and planet), we are in the challenging domain of conflicting expectations (emphasising short-term profits works for investors, but not for sustainability activists). Formulating a leadership brand that can consistently and authentically talk to both internal and diverse groups of external stakeholders is therefore a challenging task, requiring deep, meaningful reflection by the executive leadership of the organisation.

The point was made earlier that the process of defining the leadership brand behaviours of the organisation is in reality the first phase in creating a unique leadership brand perspective for any organisation. In the recent past, organisations have typically worked from lists of leadership "competencies", or have developed their own particular leadership "competence framework", which is essentially based on an approach that assumes that there is specific knowledge and skills sets that leaders should have and master. While these kinds of approaches are certainly not without merit, the experience with client systems to date is that the transition from individual leader ability to broader leadership brand is not easily accomplished. Having said this, the question can still be posed as to what such a set of leadership brand behaviours might look like.

Figure 4.2 provides an example of Leadership Brand Behaviours which is based on research conducted, both locally and overseas, by Van der Merwe[16] and Von Eck,[17] among others. In addition, work done by Engage Leadership (Pty) Ltd and its associates in a number of organisations in South Africa across a range of industries seems to confirm that leadership brand behaviours may cluster broadly into three areas, these being:

- Leadership brand behaviours related to PURPOSE (where increasingly the conversation is about purpose beyond profit);
- Leadership brand behaviours related to RELATIONSHIPS (where increasingly the issue is how to position yourself in a dynamic network of networks); and
- Leadership brand behaviours related to IMPLEMENTATION (where the conversation is still about value × velocity).

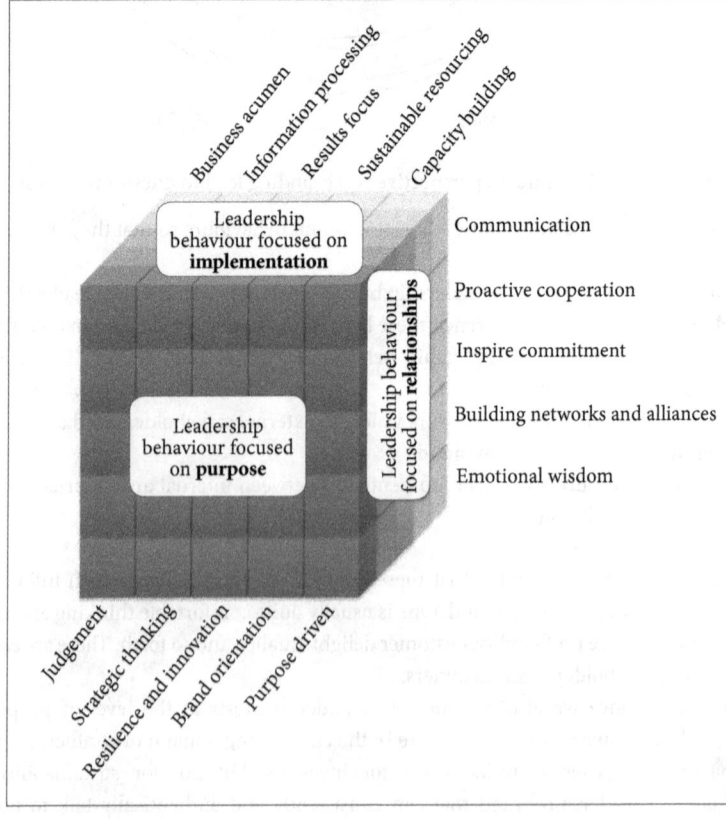

Figure 4.2: Example of leadership brand behaviours

The Right Leadership Brand

In the final instance, organisations may have to articulate their leadership brand with much greater clarity so that it becomes part of the identifiable firm brand, and enhances the unique value proposition of the business. "Once you have consensus that the organisation wants to have a leadership brand, deciding on the right brand is the critical first step. Learning leaders should bring leaders from across the organisation together to answer the question, 'what do we want to be known for?' "[18]

McLaughlin & Mott also note the importance of the authenticity of leadership culture in attaining a competitive position: "The final principle is that your leadership brand needs to be part of the leadership fabric across the organisation before it has the power to be a competitive external driver of equity".[19] These perspectives on leadership brand clearly have a significant impact on how organisations should think about their own approach to leadership and the identification or assessment of leadership, as well as how leadership is developed and entrenched.

Conclusion

The way that organisations and their leadership think about leadership brand, and act on it as a deliberate component of competitive strategy and means of differentiation, must be viewed in relation to the perspective that is adopted on what constitutes effective leadership and how the impact (= brand value) of such leadership may be measured. This chapter should therefore also be read in conjunction with chapter 3 "Leadership Excellence Dimensions" and chapter 19 "Leadership excellence measurement."

Endnotes

1. Rao, 2010.
2. Keller, 1998.
3. Cheverton, 2002.
4. Yan, 2005.
5. Batey, 2008.
6. Balmer & Gray, 2003.
7. de Chernatony, 2001.
8. Grimaldi, 2003.
9. Blumenthal, 2001.
10. Stanier, 2001.
11. Conference Board, 2002.
12. Tosti & Stotz, 2002.
13. Colville & Murphy, 2006.
14. Ulrich & Smallwood, 2008.
15. Vallaster & de Chernatony, 2006.
16. Van der Merwe, 2006.
17. Von Eck, 2007.
18. Cohen & Sinha, 2008.
19. McLaughlin & Mott, 2009.

References

Balmer, JMT. & Gray, ER. 2003. 'Corporate brands: What are they? What of them?' *European Journal of Marketing*, 37(7/8):972–997.

Batey, M. 2008. *Brand meaning*. New York, NY: Routledge.

Blumenthal, D. 2001. *Internal branding: Does It improve employees' quality of life?* [Online]. Available: http:www.institueforbrandleadership.org. [Accessed 1 July 2016]. http://museum.brandhome.com/docs/P0087_Internal%20Branding.pdf]

Cheverton, P. 2002. *Strategies, tools and techniques for marketing success*. London, UK: Kogan Page.

Cohen, E & Sinha, A. 2008. 'Develop a winning leadership brand'. *Chief Learning Officer*, 7(9):66.

Colville, ID & Murphy, AJ. 2006. 'Leadership as the enabler of strategizing and organizing'. *Long Range Planning*, 39(6):663–677.

Conference Board. 2002. *Engaging Employees Through Your Brand*. [Online]. Available: https://www.conference-board.org/topics/publicationdetail.cfm?publicationid=461 [Accessed 1 July 2016].

de Chernatony, L. 2001. 'A model for strategically building brands'. *Brand Management*, 9(1):32–44.

Grimaldi, V. 2003. *The fundamentals of branding*. [Online]. Available: http:www.interbrand.com/features_effect.asppf_id=183. Cited in C. le Roux & C. du Plessis. 2014. *An exploratory Q study of corporate brand identity elements governing corporate brand image formation*. [Online] Available: http://www.unisa.ac.za/contents/faculties/service_dept/docs/Sabview_18_3_Chap%206.pdf [Accessed 21 July 2016].

Keller, KL. 1998. 'Branding perspectives on social marketing'. In JW Alba & JW Hutchinson (eds). *Advances in consumer research (Vol 25)*. Provo, UT: Association for Consumer Research.

McLaughlin, V & Mott, C. 2009. 'Building leadership brand equity'. *Chief Learning Officer*, 8(8):46–48.

Rao, MS. 2010. *How do you build your leadership brand?* [Online]. Available: http://profmsr.blogspot.com/2010/07/how-do-you-build-your-leadership-brand.html.

Stanier, MB. 2009. Living the brand at Airtours Holidays: Making the connection between brand, culture and employee satisfaction. *Corporate brand and corporate reputation*.

Tosti, DT & Stotz, RD. 2001, 'Brand: building your brand from the inside out', *Marketing Management*, Vol. 10, No. 2, pp. 28-33.

Ulrich, D & Smallwood, N. 2008. 'Aligning firm, leadership, and personal brand'. *Leader to Leader*, 47:24–32.

Vallaster, C & de Chernatony, L. 2006. 'Internal brand building and structuration: The role of leadership'. *European Journal of Marketing*, 40(7/8):761–784.

Van der Merwe, L. 2006. *Leadership meta-competencies for the future world of work: An explorative study in the retail industry*. PhD thesis. Johannesburg, ZA: University of Johannesburg, Faculty of Economic and Management Sciences.

Von Eck, C. 2007. *Change dynamics and related leadership competencies: Leading people through change and uncertainty*. PhD thesis. Johannesburg, ZA: University of Johannesburg, Faculty of Management Sciences.

Yan, J. 2005. *Beyond branding*. London, UK: Kogan Page.

SECTION 3
LEADERSHIP ATTRIBUTES

Chapter 5

AUTHENTIC LEADERSHIP
Tineke Wulffers

The current state of leadership points to a crisis in leadership, caused by a lack of positive gravitas and ethical behaviour in leadership behaviour. This has resulted in a lack of trust in leadership, both in the global corporate and political contexts. In response, in the last decade there has been a call for a better quality of positive leadership that can reinstate the stakeholder trust that has been lost. It is actually possible to be both an ethically positive and an effective leader. I believe that such leadership is found in authentic leadership, which can be regarded as the root of positive forms of leadership.

In this chapter I briefly discuss the current state of leadership, the need for better leadership, followed by what Authentic Leadership (AL) is and the impact such quality leadership can have. I offer important criteria for consideration when wishing to develop this type of leadership in organisations, followed by an outline of an AL programme that has been scientifically tested in a doctoral study, for both its appropriateness and effectiveness. Two well-known leaders, namely Archbishop Desmond Tutu and former President Nelson Mandela, are viewed through the lens of AL, in order to give more meaning to this notion.

The Current State of Leadership

In recent years, as problems have continually surfaced in various well-known international organisations, the extent of the leadership crisis has become apparent, creating a widespread erosion of trust in business leaders. We are continually reminded of the immensely negative impact of unethical leadership. For instance, a few years ago, international news headlines highlighted that there had been an extreme lack of integrity in the executive leadership of the global parent company of one of South Africa's top five financial institutions. This resulted in the immediate resignation of Bob Diamond, the CEO of Barclays Bank, and even when having to report to the British parliament, he was accused of prevaricating while responding to the questions in parliament. The impact of such lack of integrity affected not only the parent company, but also the local financial institution and its employees.[1] More recently, reputable international organisations such as Volkswagen, who have admitted to cheating in emissions tests in their diesel cars in the USA,[2] and again Barclays in the Libor rigging scandal,[3] received considerable press exposure due to their extremely unethical behaviour.

However, these examples are not limited only to profit-seeking organisations. They extend to politics as well. In South Africa, the unethical behaviour of political leadership continually makes the headlines of newspapers. For some time now, the president of South Africa has been under the spotlight,[4] over his excessive use of public funds for private gain, in the form of expenditure on his private residence for himself, his five wives, and his approximately 20 children. Even so, he has consistently refused to accept accountability for these and other continual wrongdoings, resulting in an investigation by the South African Public Protector and a damning judgment from the South African Constitutional Court in 2016, finding him guilty of violating the Constitution in his use of excessive State funds for the upgrade of his private home. Despite consistent national calls for his impeachment, he has refused to do the honourable thing and step down, and his refusal has been made possible only as a result of the support that he still receives from his political allies, who have placed their own political party interests above the interests of the people of South Africa, whom they have committed themselves under oath to serve.[5] Unfortunately, this type of behaviour trickles down to those who regard him as a role model, leading to unethical behaviour permeating South African society.

The Need for Better Leadership

Not all leadership positions are filled by leaders, and by the same token, one does not have to fill a leadership position in order to be experienced as a leader. This means that there is not a one-on-one relationship between leadership positions and leaders. "True" leadership has always been more difficult to maintain in challenging times, but the unique stressors facing organisations throughout the world today call for a renewed attention to what constitutes true and moral leadership. These challenges have resulted in renewed focus on how our leaders can restore confidence, hope, and optimism. Leaders, whether in corporate or political organisations, need to be resilient and be able to respond appropriately to catastrophic and extraordinary events. At the same time, they also need to help those important to them in their search for meaning and connection by fostering new self-awareness, and by genuinely relating to all stakeholders, whether these are employees, customers, suppliers, and even communities.[6]

There is a need for leaders who lead with purpose, values, and integrity; who build enduring organisations; who motivate their staff to provide superior customer service; and who create long-term value for stakeholders.[7] What the world is searching for now is a way of leading that is based on character and substance rather than style of leadership, on integrity and presence rather than merely position. These qualities equip leaders to rebuild trust within themselves and others, a prerequisite to creating well-functioning and effective organisations.

I facilitate the development of authentic leadership effectiveness in various private and public organisations, mainly in South Africa, and have experienced a strong desire among my clients to work in a values-based leadership culture. Numerous leadership clients wish to develop moral courage, an aspect of AL, in order to allow them to respond to unethical challenges in an ethical manner. This requires a strong sense of self, a strong commitment to self, and a strong moral compass. It furthermore requires 360° leadership, meaning that they sometimes need to lead upwards as well, especially in state- and municipal-owned enterprises, which are continually exposed to unethical, politically-connected requests for favours.

The need for strong and positive leadership is not only in response to organisational scandals attributed to poor and unethical leadership. The more they are in senior leadership positions in organisations, the more leaders need to deliver through others. This means that they need to be able to inspire, influence, and empower others to deliver to the best of their ability. Because of the continual pressure often experienced at senior levels in organisations, many skilled and accomplished executives often feel that they are not good enough, which can have an adverse effect on their self-esteem at the expense of their careers and organisations.

While there are enormous responsibilities placed on senior leaders to deliver and meet business targets through others, they are often not appropriately equipped to do so. What I have often noticed is that leaders are promoted to more senior leadership positions as a result of their previous successes, which is often due to their business or technical acumen rather than leadership skills. While they might have studied for years to equip themselves for those previous successes, they are expected to develop leadership skills almost by osmosis, which is an unrealistic expectation. They then feel frustrated and disempowered with themselves as leaders, and they start becoming autocratic and bullying leaders in order to force others to deliver. This can lead to what is called role compression in those who are on the receiving end, as they go below the radar to avoid the wrath of the leader. This then further impacts adversely on performance, resulting in the opposite of what the leaders hope to achieve. Those below them may then be sent for further development or coaching, while the leaders themselves, very sadly, are often unavailable for such programmes. I call this inappropriate invulnerability.

However, all is not lost! While it is ideal to start at the top with the development of improved leadership, my experience has shown that it is prudent to be pragmatic, and to start with where leader development readiness is in place. Often, as those leaders become more effective, they impact positively upwards as well on relational leadership dynamics.

While I have thus far referred mostly to individual leaders, it is also important to consider leadership teams. Patrick Lencioni, founder and president of The Table Group, who focus on team development and organisational health, takes this further, stating that "it is not finance, not strategy, not technology, but teamwork that remains the *ultimate* competitive advantage, both because it is so powerful and so rare."[8] Such teamwork can be developed only with a true leader at the helm, who can both be a role model and facilitate the process of developing authentically effective teams.

While "good leaders navigate through all weather; profound leadership occurs during a storm"[9]. True leadership is tested when a profound crisis occurs within organisations or societies. I believe that it is this type of leadership that is required in times of uncertainty in South Africa and internationally, and it is important to understand how this type of leadership can be developed. Authentic leadership has been defined not only as the root construct of positive forms of leadership;[10] it also meets the requirements for the highest level of effective leadership, as defined by Eigel and Kuhnert,[11] and as the following will illustrate.

Root of Positive Leadership: Authentic Leadership Defined

In my experience, authentic leaders are leaders who not only know themselves, but are also true to themselves. Furthermore, they are true to their leadership positions, with a strong moral underpinning (and a good dose of moral courage), for the greater good of all. More specifically, Avolio et al.[12] define authentic leaders as leaders who know who they are and what they believe in; who display transparency and consistency between their values, ethical reasoning and actions; who focus on developing positive emotional states such as confidence, optimism, hope, and resilience within themselves; and who are widely known and respected for their integrity.

This requires authentic leaders to understand who they are before they can self-regulate to ensure that they display transparency and consistency with regard to their values, ethical reasoning and actions. In particular, authentic leaders need to understand the internal identity, leadership purpose, and vision that drive them. Furthermore, they need to understand their values, their beliefs about self and others, and their internal thoughts and psychological states that drive their behaviours.[13] These combined elements make up what can be called the self-schema of the "current self", which initially may not always be sufficiently aligned to create a congruent expression of the self that others can trust and wish to follow.

This is where the second step of self-regulation becomes important. In order to align these elements and to ensure that limiting aspects are transformed into empowering ones towards increased leadership authenticity, self-regulation, reflected in behaviour, needs to take place. These elements and processes allow any authentic leader to grow an internal moral compass that focuses them on staying true to the self and the leadership position, for the greater good of all.

Avolio and Gardner[14] performed a study in which they compared the components of AL development theory also present in theories underpinning other positive forms of leadership such as transformational, charismatic, servant, and spiritual leadership. These AL components pertained to positive moral perspectives, leader self-awareness, self-regulation processes, and behaviours. This was further extended to include follower (those with whom the leader interacts) self-awareness and development, and organisational performance. The study confirmed that the development of AL formed a strong foundation for positive forms of effective leadership.

Impact of Authentic Leadership

The underpinning rationale that AL builds intrapersonal and inter-relational trust, and that the development of inter-relational trust and trustworthiness builds and strengthens individual and team leadership effectiveness,[15] is discussed as follows.

On inter-relational trust

One of my epiphanies as an AL practitioner was that everything starts with self, including the development of trust. It is near impossible to trust unknown entities, and as one of my clients had shared with me, "Often, the most unknown entity is the self." Therefore, before we can trust others, or be worthy of trust by others, we need to trust ourselves. An antecedent to being able to trust oneself is the presence of self-awareness and self-knowledge of one's 'internal AL Compass, which happens through the dynamic process of continuous introspection and reflection, and further allows regulation of one's thoughts, feelings, and behaviours.

This then leads to the question of how this trust extends to followers. Inter-relational trust between leader and follower is developed when a leader is willing to be appropriately vulnerable.[16] This means that the leader is comfortable enough within to reveal self-referential information that might be helpful to others, and such vulnerability could therefore be referred to as strength-based vulnerability. Leaders who are willing to reflect relational transparency develop relationships of trust and mutual respect with their followers. Followers are then prepared to display vulnerability to that leader, knowing that the leader leads with integrity, in alignment with organisational values and vision, for the greater good of the organisation.

Individual leadership effectiveness

While AL is posited as the root construct of positive leadership, it also equates to the highest level of leadership development levels (LDL), reflected in the most effective forms of leadership. Eigel and Kuhnert,[17] having done research on the link between authentic development, LDL, and executive leadership effectiveness, found a direct link between AL and leadership effectiveness. For instance, AL is related to characteristics such as self-awareness, self-esteem, trustworthiness, integrity, respect for others, and high emotional intelligence, which are the characteristics that one expects to find in highly effective leaders.

Followers are able to recognise the difference between veritable and false authenticity in a leader. Veritably authentic leaders are confident, optimistic leaders of high moral character who are aware of their own thoughts and feelings, abilities, values, and behaviours, and who are also attentive to these in others and the situational context in which they operate. These aspects allow them to be effective at commanding follower loyalty, trust, and respect, and as a result, these leaders are able to assert a powerful influence in extraordinary times, such as when there is uncertainty regarding the organisation's survival.[18]

Furthermore, in business, leadership is often approached as a skill with which to increase the effectiveness of the organisation and increase the bottom line. Such an approach is inherently transactional, because the primary motivation is known to be profit-based. People in extreme circumstances move beyond transactional concerns; coercive leaders are eventually ignored, and bonuses or promises or other tangible rewards become less relevant when they have to place their future in the hands of the leader. Business leaders who find it difficult to make the transition from transactional to a more authentic and perhaps transformational leadership may gain both understanding and inspiration from authentic leader role models.

Team leadership effectiveness

Leadership, both individually (formal leader) and collectively, is central to team effectiveness,[19] as team effectiveness depends not only on the task skills that members contribute, but also on high levels of cohesion and associated positive states, such as inter-relational trust, which are required to sustain productivity. The foundation of any effective leadership team is that each member is worthy of trust. Based on Lencioni's[20] observation of ineffective teams, insufficient attention to results is often due to an absence of trust, which leads to a fear of conflict and therefore a lack of commitment, which in turn results in avoidance of accountability, as reflected in Figure 5.1.

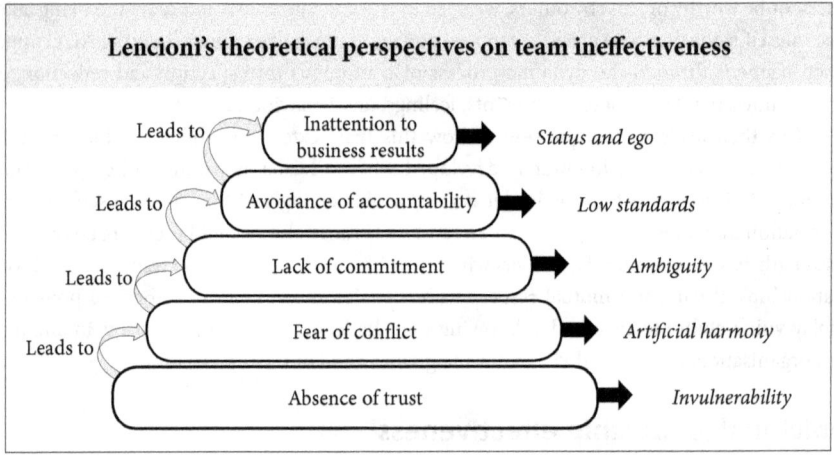

Figure 5.1: Team ineffectiveness

It therefore follows that the pyramid of strength in any effective leadership team is based on a solid foundation of trust at the bottom of the pyramid. This leads to the freedom to have healthy disagreements, a commitment to a course of action, and a willingness to be accountable, which leads to achieving and often exceeding expected results,[21] as illustrated in Figure 5.2.

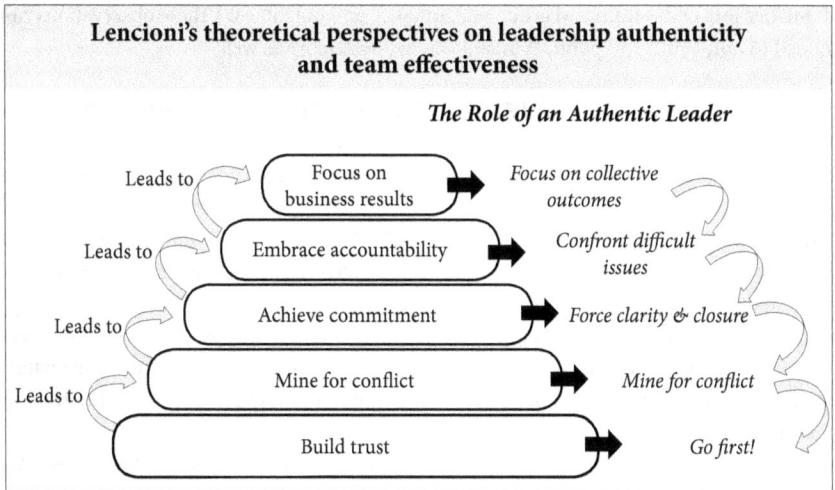

Figure 5.2: Team effectiveness

In authentic team leadership, there is a shared leadership approach, where all team members, including the leader, share responsibility, and there is a strong reliance on shared mental models, knowledge, and cognition within the team.[22] Leadership roles and responsibilities are shared and distributed throughout the team, depending on contextual requirements at any time, fostering faster agreements on problem definitions and strategic decisions, resulting in enhanced team effectiveness and efficiency.

This becomes possible when team members develop a collective belief structure and a value system that are shared and adhered to by all team members. By further promoting relational transparency and balanced processing of information among team members, a rapid and more accurate transfer of information occurs among them, resulting in the development of trusting relationships, which then have a further positive impact on individual and team performance. Therefore, AL is an antecedent to team authenticity and effectiveness.[23]

Organisational outcomes

Walumba et al.[24] point out that there is a strong link between leadership authenticity, individual positive psychological capital, collective or follower positive psychological capital, inter-relational trust, and individual and group citizen behaviour and performance. Individuals in groups that have more trusting relationships, are willing to be more transparent, exchange information and knowledge, are willing to learn from one another's expertise, and are motivated to work hard to maintain their relative standing in the group, as well as improve their performance. Authentic leaders therefore seem to have a positive influence on group performance, as they use their values, beliefs, and behaviours to become role models to others in making the best choices.

Leadership teams do not work in isolation, and any expected results are typically delivered through individuals outside the immediate leadership team, usually by those who report to the team leaders. The trust that needs to be in place needs to be both horizontal and vertical, meaning that there first needs to be peer-to-peer inter-relational trust within the leadership team, but also between each leader within the team and his or her reporting followers, individually and collectively, and others within the organisation. Trust has the ability to impact positively on interpersonal communication, follower attitudes and behaviours, and employee engagement,[25] with further impact on team and group performance and outcomes.[26] These observations can be extended to non-profit and political organisational leadership as well.

Criteria for Developing Authentic Leadership

Chan, Hannah and Gardner,[27] pointing out that the level of authenticity within any leader varies along a continuum, from complete inauthenticity to full authenticity, divided their research on AL development and the emergence of AL behaviour into (1) the intrapersonal processes, followed by (2) the effect of that on self, others, and outcomes. They illustrated a process model of the emergence of authentic behaviour, starting with self, and then continued by pointing out that every leader forms part of a bigger system, and that they interact, influence, and receive feedback from other members in their system. Although they did not elaborate on the nature of the required leadership programme, they did indicate that the process starts with a leadership programme.

AL development needs to start with self. As every leader interacts with others, those others, also called *followers*, will observe the leader's behaviour, and try to make sense of the authenticity of that behaviour; the degree of perceived authenticity then has an impact on the quality of the leader–follower relationships, with underpinnings such as trust, transparency, predictability, and integrity. This, in turn, results in veritable effects on the followers, with the leader receiving diagnostic feedback through the follower feedback loop and various forms of performance and feedback. This process helps leaders to self-verify authenticity and impact, and, finally, aids the formation and reinforcement of an authentic organisational culture.

There is no silver bullet for the development of such leadership. The metric of time for development of AL is typically very long, as it usually takes time for all the AL characteristics to emerge.[28] Also, perceptions of authenticity that occur may be instantaneous (self-awareness), while the development and execution of actual AL behaviours may take longer (self-regulation). Conventional leadership interventions, often of short duration and training-based, would therefore be insufficient for the transformative nature of developing AL. A study by Reichard and Avolio[29] was not able to include any research on leadership authenticity programmes, and they encouraged researchers to bridge the practitioner–researcher divide by conducting a greater number of high-quality field programme studies. In response to their call, one such study was completed in 2014, and is discussed as follows.

Example of a Programme Journey towards Authentic Leadership Effectiveness

The following example of an AL programme was scientifically evaluated during a doctoral study with an executive leadership team who participated in the programme. It was found to be effective in the development of AL, inter-relational trust, individual and team AL effectiveness.[30] As illustrated in the pyramid of positive leadership in Figure 5.3, the actualisation of AL in organisations requires the underpinnings of interpersonal and, more importantly, personal leadership. The underpinning rationale is that the achievement of positive leadership needs to start with mastering personal leadership, before focusing on being able to lead others and, ultimately, an organisation or society, as the complexity in leading increases at each level. It is not possible to lead others successfully, for instance, if self- or personal leadership has not yet been mastered.[31]

Chapter 5: Authentic Leadership

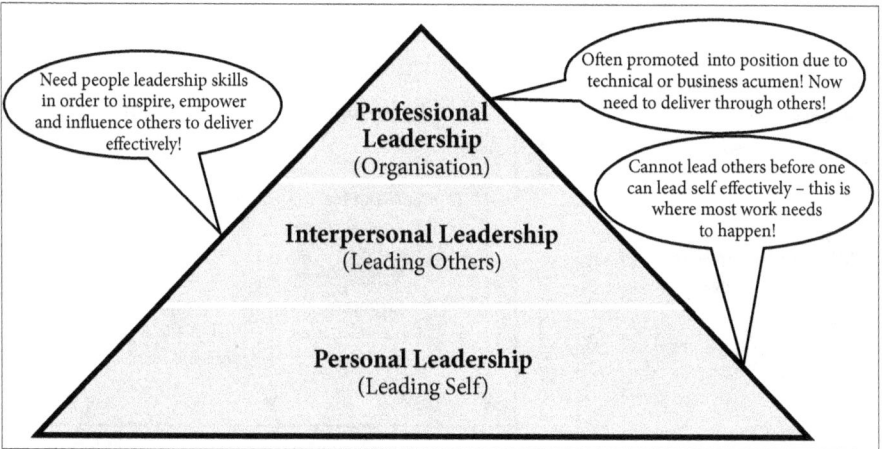

Figure 5.3: The pyramid of positive leadership

As each leader is unique, a coaching style of facilitation is particularly fitting in such a programme as it allows participants to develop a deeper understanding of what AL entails for them in particular. It allows participants to develop a deeper self-awareness of their current internal compasses comprising their internal identity, purpose, vision, legacy, values, beliefs about self and others, and their psychological states, and how these have an impact on their behaviour. It also allows them to commit to further development on all of these aspects in order to create a more congruent internal compasses towards their next level of their possible self, which they need to endeavour at all times to reflect in their behaviour. Coaching holds the philosophy that individuals are talented and competent, which aligns with a positive psychology and strengths approach to developing leadership authenticity.

This overall AL programme starts with six individual leader development sessions, approximately two weeks apart, which focus specifically on the development of personal AL, followed by three team sessions one month apart, to enhance inter-relational trust, and individual and team leadership effectiveness. Figure 5.4 illustrates the horizontal and vertical AL dimensions that underpin the individual sessions. Once leaders have identified the leadership outcomes they wish to achieve, the programme helps them to create awareness and knowledge of themselves along a continuous horizontal time-line, from their past-, through their current-, to their future selves. At the same time, they explore along a vertical line aspects below the soil-line, such as their values, and beliefs of self and others, that inform their past and current behaviour, and how those would need to align and inform their future behaviour and performance. This work also helps them to understand their internal leader identity, their leadership purpose, vision and legacy that they wish to stay true to, and the psychological states that they would need to step into towards authentically becoming who they can be.

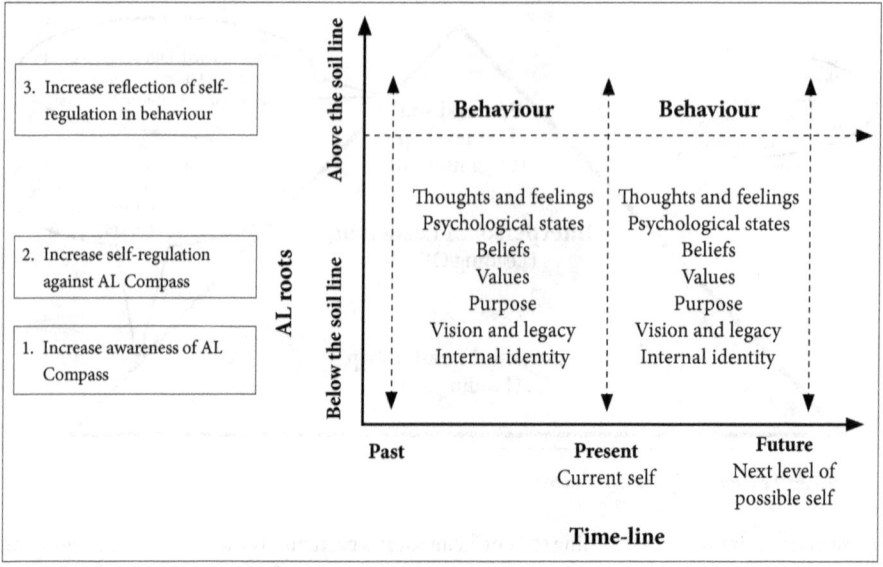

Figure 5.4. Vertical and horizontal aspects of authentic leadership development journey

Once that awareness and self-knowledge has been created, self-regulation can be implemented, leading to a more congruent desired self, which can then be reflected in behavioural outcomes, in line with Chan et al's[32] model of AL emergence. This forms the crux of the development work that allows leaders to develop the below-the-soil-line AL roots and the "true-north" inner compass that will further ground them as positive and effective leaders, especially in times of stormy weather.

Once the development of personal authentic leadership is in place, the team sessions allow for the development of interpersonal and organisational authentic leadership. The first of the three team sessions usually takes place towards the end of the individual sessions, once self-leadership has been developed. The rationale for this is that by this time, each participant should be well on their way towards developing leadership authenticity. Any fear and trepidation in anticipation of such a team session, combined with inappropriate invulnerability that often accompanies any team with challenging team dynamics, would by this time have been replaced with cautious optimism, and balanced vulnerability.

During the team sessions the focus is on building inter-relational trust, followed by introducing the skills appropriate to conducting crucial conversations in order to allow teams to embrace healthy conflict. The programme then continues from interpersonal leadership skills towards enhancing their professional leadership, leading the team members towards a whole that is bigger than the sum of its parts. It does so by assisting teams to commit to action, and by enhancing individual and mutual accountability through the development of a team authentic leadership effectiveness charter. It focuses on achieving team and organisational results while adhering to this charter. Leaders, individually and collectively, then have an AL toolkit in place to support them in sustaining individual and team authentic leadership effectiveness.

Well-known Examples of Authentic Leaders

While a leadership programme can fast-track the development of AL considerably, this type of leadership can be developed by means of introspection during a life-time of experiences and leadership episodes. Two of the best-known examples of influential and effective South African leaders are Archbishop Desmond Tutu and former President Nelson Mandela. The following considers their leadership effectiveness through the lens of AL.

Archbishop Desmond Tutu

Archbishop Desmond Tutu is a retired South African Anglican cleric who is well known for his role in the opposition to apartheid in South Africa. He received the Nobel Peace Prize in 1984 as the head of the South African Council of Churches "not only as a gesture of support to him and to the South African Council of Churches of which he is leader, but also to all individuals and groups in South Africa who, with their concern for human dignity, fraternity and democracy, incite the admiration of the world."[33] Tutu's efforts contributed considerably to South African apartheid coming to an end in 1994, when Nelson Mandela was elected as the first black president of democratic South Africa. President Mandela appointed Tutu to head a Truth and Reconciliation Commission tasked with investigating and reporting on the atrocities committed by both sides in the struggle against apartheid.

Viewing Tutu through the lens of AL, he understood his leadership purpose as a clergyman and global leader, as he spoke out very publicly against the pain and suffering that the less powerful suffered at the hands of the more powerful minority. He consistently had the moral courage and determination to tell the truth as he saw it, even if in the years of apartheid it also made him public enemy number one to some whites, and at times the subject of death threats. However, he did not restrict his critical stance only towards the apartheid "enemies", as whites were seen to be at the time. He became as watchful a critic of his erstwhile allies in the struggle against apartheid, as corruption started setting in once they came into power.[34]

Former President Nelson Mandela

Much has been written about the leadership of former President Nelson Mandela, affectionately known by all of us as Tata Madiba. For me, Madiba is not only the best-known but also one of best examples of an authentic leader. He was a leader beyond position, and I always think of the three 'pr's that defined his leadership. Whether he was a 'pr'esident or 'pr'isoner, was irrelevant, as it was his 'pr'esence that resulted in everyone, friend and foe, regarding him as a leader. His was a leadership beyond position, defined by the essence of his authentic presence, which was informed by his internal leadership identity, his purpose and vision, his values, and his empowering belief system.

It is important, as we view Mandela through the lens of AL, to understand that authentic leaders are not perfect human beings. By his own admission, Mandela, in response to being described as a saint, said that he should not be regarded as a saint, unless a saint was a sinner who never stopped trying to grow into a better person.[35] It is this quality that is usually present in AL, the quality of introspection, appropriate vulnerability, with a willingness to grow.

Inspiration differs from motivation. Inspiration by nature is intrinsic, whereas motivation is extrinsic. Motivation is about motivating others to do what I want them to do, whereas others will decide whether they feel inspired by me. In the case of Madiba, it was his authentic leadership behaviour that caused many people across the world to be inspired by him. He truly displayed the behaviour that he wished to see in others in the world. He had a strong purpose and vision for a South Africa wherein no one race or group dominated another. For that purpose and vision, he was prepared to leave his family, whom he loved so much, to go to and remain in prison for 27 years. Although he was offered numerous opportunities to leave prison earlier, he did not accept any of these offers until he was able to manifest what he stood for and went to prison for. He lived and hoped to see his vision come true, knowing that for this, he was prepared to die, if that was what was required. His espoused values were his enacted values, and his purpose was his highest value.

Conclusion

The world that our children are inheriting is in crisis in many respects! I believe that the wellness of any system, be it a country, a political, corporate, academic or even a religious institution, is dependent on the quality of its leadership. Poor and unethical leadership has an impact on the very fibre of society, as I have been witnessing in my own country, where headlines are currently dominated by reports of individual and collective unethical political leadership, combined with an outcry for more ethical and positive leadership, as we experienced in Nelson Mandela.

However, it is not only unethical official leadership that has an impact on the fibre and wellness of any society. Each one of us is a leader in our own right, and as such we continually need to endeavour to grow towards our highest potential self, and replacing limiting with empowering belief systems, among others, plays a critical part in progress towards this goal. Ferial Haffajee, the current editor-in-chief of *City Press*, a leading South African newspaper, argues that twenty years into the democracy of South Africa where everyone is equal in the eyes of the law, black South Africans who in 2014 comprised 80.2% of the nation, at times still see themselves as inferior to white South Africans, who at that time comprised 8.4%.[36] Continuing to adhere to such a limiting belief system in a country that is ruled and run by a black government has an adverse impact on moving forward, both individually and collectively.

Mandela and Tutu would never have been as influential and effective as leaders had they bought into such self-limiting belief systems. Both Tutu and Mandela have always endeavoured to be true to themselves, and true to their leadership positions, with strong moral underpinnings, for the greater good of all. For this, they both needed empowering belief systems, considerable moral courage, and strong moral compasses. They were not perfect; no one is; but they were always prepared to be introspective, and realign to their "true north" where and when necessary. These are the qualities, also found in authentic leadership, that have inspired so many others globally to follow their examples and keep their legacies alive. The sense that leadership authenticity, the root construct of positive self- and people leadership, could be the answer to the crises in South Africa and internationally, is becoming more and more evident.

Endnotes

1	SAPA, Reuters & Business Day, 2012.	19	Hannah, Walumbwa & Fry, 2011.
2	Hotten, 2015.	20	Lencioni, 2002.
3	Stapleton, 2015.	21	Ibid.
4	De Vos, 2014.	22	Yammarino et al., 2008.
5	Grootes, 2016.	23	Hannah et al., 2011.
6	Avolio & Gardner, 2005.	24	Walumbwa et al., 2011.
7	George, 2003.	25	Hannah, Avolio & Walumbwa, 2011.
8	Lencioni, 2002, p. vii.	26	Walumbwa et al., 2011.
9	Meyer, 2007.	27	Chan et al., 2005.
10	Avolio & Gardner, 2005.	28	Chan, 2005.
11	Eigel and Kuhnert, 2005.	29	Reichard & Avolio, 2005.
12	Avolio, Gardner & Walumbwa, 2005.	30	Wulffers, 2014.
13	Wulffers, 2014.	31	Barrett, 2010.
14	Avolio & Gardner, 2005.	32	Chan et al., 2005.
15	Wulffers, 2014.	33	Biography.com, 2015.
16	Chan et al., 2005.	34	Tutu, 2011.
17	Eigel and Kuhnert, 2005.	35	Mandela, 2010.
18	Kolditz & Brazil, 2005.	36	Haffajee, 2015.

References

Avolio, BJ & Gardner, WL. 2005. 'Authentic leadership development: Getting to the root of positive forms of leadership'. *The Leadership Quarterly*, 16(3):315–338.

Avolio, BJ, Gardner, WL & Walumbwa, FO. 2005. Preface. In WL Gardner, BJ Avolio & FO Walumbwa (eds). *Monographs in leadership and management, Vol 3: Authentic leadership theory and practice: Origins, effects and development*. Amsterdam, NL: Elsevier. xxi–xxvii.

Barrett, R. 2010. *The new leadership paradigm*. Summerseat, UK: Barrett Values Centre.

Biography.com. 2015. *Desmond Tutu*. [Online]. Available: http://www.biography.com/people/desmond-tutu-9512516. [Accessed 23 July 2015].

Chan, A. 2005. 'Authentic leadership measurement and development: Challenges and suggestions'. In WL Gardner, BJ Avolio & FO Walumbwa (eds). *Monographs in leadership and management, Vol 3: Authentic leadership theory and practice: Origins, effects and development*. Amsterdam, NL: Elsevier. 227–252.

Chan, A, Hannah, ST & Gardner, WL. 2005. 'Veritable authentic leadership: Emergence, functioning and impacts'. In WL Gardner, BJ Avolio & FO Walumbwa (eds). *Monographs in leadership and management, Vol 3: Authentic leadership theory and practice: Origins, effects and development*. Amsterdam, NL: Elsevier. 3–42.

De Vos, P. 2014. 'Nkandla report exposes president Zuma's personal involvement in the project'. *Constitutionally Speaking*, 20 March.

Eigel, KM & Kuhnert, KW. 2005. 'Authentic development: Leadership development level and executive effectiveness'. In WL Gardner, BJ Avolio & FO Walumbwa (eds). *Monographs in leadership and management, Vol 3: Authentic leadership theory and practice: Origins, effects and development*. Amsterdam, NL: Elsevier. 357–386.

George, B. 2003. *Authentic leadership: Rediscover the secrets to creating lasting value*. San Francisco, CA: Jossey-Bass.

Grootes, S. 2016. 'ANC's top six have yet to meet after "damning" Nkandla judgment'. *EWN Eyewitness News*, 1 April. [Online]. Available: http://ewn.co.za/2016/04/01/ANC-confirms-no-meeting-yet-after-Nkandla-ruling. [Accessed 23 July 2015].

Haffajee, F. 2015. *What if there were no whites in South Africa?* Johannesburg, ZA: Picador Africa.

Hannah, ST, Avolio, BJ & Walumbwa, FO. 2011. 'Relationships between authentic leadership, moral courage, and ethical and pro-social behaviors'. *Business Ethics Quarterly*, 21(4):555–578.

Hannah, ST, Walumbwa, FO & Fry, LW. 2011. 'Leadership in action teams: Team leader and members' authenticity, authenticity strength, and team outcomes'. *Personnel Psychology*, 64(3):771–802.

Hotten, R. 2015. 'Volkswagen: The scandal explained'. *BBC News*, 10 December. [Online]. Available: http://www.bbc.com/news/business-34324772 [Accessed 12 November 2015].

Kolditz, TA & Brazil, DM. 2005. 'Authentic leadership in *in extremis* settings: A concept for extraordinary leaders in exceptional situations'. In WL Gardner, BJ Avolio & FO Walumbwa (eds). *Monographs in leadership and management, Vol 3: Authentic leadership theory and practice: Origins, effects and development*. Amsterdam, NL: Elsevier. 345–356.

Lencioni, P. 2002. *The five dysfunctions of a team: A leadership fable*. San Francisco, CA: Jossey-Bass.

Mandela, N. 2010. *Conversations with myself*. London, UK: MacMillan.

Meyer, T. 2007. 'The nature of leadership: Perspectives'. In T Meyer & I Boninelli (eds). *Conversations in leadership: South African perspectives*. Johannesburg: Knowledge Resources.

Reichard, RJ & Avolio, BJ. 2005. 'Where are we? The status of leadership intervention research: A meta-analytic summary'. In WL Gardner, BJ Avolio & FO Walumbwa (eds). *Monographs in leadership and management, Vol 3: Authentic leadership theory and practice: Origins, effects and development*. Amsterdam, NL: Elsevier. 203–226.

SAPA, Reuters and Business Day. 2012. 'Absa feels Barclays' pain'. Fin24, 3 July.

Stapleton, J. 2015. 'What is the Barclays Libor rigging scandal'. *LBC*. [Online]. Available: http://www.lbc.co.uk/the-barclays-libor-rigging-scandal-explained-56812. [Accessed 12 November 2015].

Tutu, D. 2011. *God is Not a Christian*. London, UK: Random House.

Walumbwa, FO, Luthans, F, Avey, JB & Oke, A. 2011. [Retracted article]. 'Authentically leading groups: The mediating role of collective psychological capital and trust'. *Journal of Organizational Behaviour*, 32(1):4–24.

Wulffers, MCC. 2014. *Evaluating a leadership authenticity programme*. PhD thesis. Johannesburg, ZA: University of Johannesburg, Faculty of Management.

Yammarino, FJ, Dionne, SD, Schriesheim, CA & Dansereau, F. 2008. 'Authentic leadership and positive organizational behavior: A meso, multi-level perspective'. *The Leadership Quarterly*, 19(6):693–707.

Chapter 6

MINDFUL LEADERSHIP
Errol Nembhard

Why the need for Mindful Leadership? Would it not be great if everyone were continually alert and paid attention to even to the smallest changes in the work context, and then were instantly able to act at the least sign of anything going awry? Think how safety, productivity and quality would improve!

This is the lure of mindfulness, the simple act of noticing or "seeing" new things, which has lately captured many leaders' attention and hopes – even *Time Magazine* caught on to the idea of The Mindful Revolution.[1] Globalization 3.0 has meant the emergence of more complex, varied, and unpredictable organisational contexts, and greatly expanded ecosystems of internal and external stakeholders, characterised by a myriad localised opportunities and threats. To be clear, "Globalization 1.0" occurred from 1492 until about 1800. In this era, globalisation was centred on countries. It was about how much horsepower, wind power, and steam power a country had, and how creatively they were deployed. The world shrank from size "large" to size "medium".[2]

"Globalization 2.0" occurred from about 1800 until 2000, interrupted only by the two World Wars. In this era, the dynamic force driving change was multinational companies. The world shrank from size "medium" to size "small". "Globalization 3.0" is our current era, beginning in the year 2000. The convergence of the personal computer, fibre-optic Internet connections, and software has created a "flat-world platform" that allows small groups and even individuals to go global. The world has shrunk from size "small" to size "tiny." What is the impact of Globalization 3.0? Here is a trendy managerial acronym: VUCA, derived from the initial letters of *volatility, uncertainty, complexity,* and *ambiguity,* sums up the uncharted territory facing many organisational leaders, and it will raise the intellectual challenge for organisational leaders to grow in new ways.

The call for mindfulness has become especially popular in organisations that have established safety basics and are looking to move toward the highest levels of performance and culture. This is particularly true where competition is fierce or organisations have seemingly tried everything to rocket above the gravitational pull of ingrained human habitual ways of thinking, thinking that continues to see the world within familiar categories that are comfortable.

There are equally those organisations whose change initiatives end up going nowhere. Such initiatives do not fail because they lack grand visions and noble intentions. They fail because leaders are unable to "see" the threats they face and the imperative to change. The signals of threat are always abundant and recognised by many, yet somehow they fail to penetrate the corporate immune system response to reject the unfamiliar.

Heifetz[3] distinguishes two classes of challenge that leaders are likely to face: *technical problems* and *adaptive challenges*. The distinctions between these two types can help to identify potential tools for facing them. *Technical problems* may be complex and difficult, but they can be addressed with existing ways of perceiving and understanding. They are known problems with known solutions based on past experience.

Adaptive challenges, on the other hand, differ from technical ones because both the problem and the solution may not be recognised and understood within current schemas. Adaptive challenges call upon leaders to grow towards more sophisticated ways of *seeing* and *thinking, acting* and *relating*.

Such deep and intricate transformational change will be both deeply personal and inherently systemic. Mindful leadership represents a largely unexplored territory in current management research into acquiring new ways of seeing and thinking. Leaders will need to be the agents of this change; in fact, the ultimate mission of leadership is change. They will need to do this in a way that engages employees, helping people to improve how they work, both individually and together. In this way, they will operate with greater mindfulness towards safety, quality, creativity, efficiency and morale without the organisation losing sight of intended results.

Given the emergence of increasing complexity, how can leaders reach this next frontier of upgrading their and their workers' personal abilities and efficiencies in order to perform with greater awareness, decision-making, cohesiveness, and consistency?

On another level, assuming that leadership can be enhanced through mindfulness, this would significantly potentiate communications in the form of the powerful but intangible quality of presence – being able to listen fully, make seamless contact, and generate the best influence on others. This would be an incredibly potent, personal, and leadership attribute. One may argue that in an increasingly complex world where work cuts across all types of institutional boundaries, the leader's only task may be to promote and harness "distributed" mindfulness.[4]

Is this more than wishful thinking? Not if you bear in mind that *practical mindfulness* is more than an airy concept of "unplugging" or being "blissed out", which would have limited application. In fact, the right mental state is critical to all high-level performance, whether that is presenting, negotiating, delivering evaluations, or deciphering financial statements. Team-based sports players must be able to sense and vary appropriately the power and angle of their shots in order to accommodate their changing distance from the goal while simultaneously evading opponents' flexing defence. Drivers must assess and then modify how much space they have to avoid being clipped by a swerving car.

The basis of this chapter, "*Mindful Leadership*", is contextual to my 17-year journey across countries, organisations and leaders, along with experiences at the front line, where there are those leaders who seem to have such attributes, tending towards mindfulness, with outstanding cognitive and decision-making skills. Yet more often than not there are those leaders who demonstrate that along with increasing organisational complexity comes increasing mindlessness, resulting in poor decisions and potentially drastic mistakes.

While other developing countries and regions have grown over the past 50 years, Africa has become adept at externalising blame and holding others responsible for its failings. Yet leadership, not a lack of capital, access to world markets, or technical expertise, is wholly to blame for the continent's under-development. What is the determinant that makes the difference?

Firstly, opening our awareness to some of the barriers that lower the shift towards "seeing" will be the initial focus, followed by examining the profile, competency thinking and practices of those who are increasingly moving towards becoming more mindful leaders fitted to meet the future challenges of increasingly complex contexts.

Barriers to "Seeing"

Awareness is the ability to know and perceive directly, to feel, or to be conscious of events, objects, thoughts, emotions, or sensory patterns. It is on this basis that I will be discussing the following elements that block us from seeing reality: power distance; minding the gap; thinking, fast and slow; and the unseen world of biases.

Power distance and leadership impact

Power distance is the extent of a society's tolerance for hierarchy and power structures. Hofstede[5] defines a high-power distance culture to mean that inequalities of power and wealth have been allowed to grow. Members of this type of culture depend on their superiors or leaders. Leaders of high-power distance cultures therefore prefer to adopt an authoritarian management style. The leadership style of low-power distance cultures is decentralised, and rewards and remuneration are based on performance.

What becomes important is the extent to which high-power distance cultures increase levels of ambiguity with regard to communication. This is commonly known as "mitigated speech", which is a linguistic term describing deferential or indirect speech inherent in communication between individuals of perceived high-power distance.

Gladwell[6] refines the definition of mitigating speech further as "any attempt to downplay or sugar-coat the meaning of what is being said", especially when there are perceived or real negative consequences for giving critical feedback in a high-power distance organisational culture. Gladwell brings the concept to life in the context of how crews related to each other in the cockpit of a commercial airliner, graphically illustrating the degree to which mitigated speech can be detrimental in high-risk situations that require clear communication. This relates to Korean Air and their disastrous record held for airline crashes between the period 1988–1998. Statistically, the airline loss rate was 4.79 per million departures, which was seventeen times higher in the same period than American carrier United Airlines, which has 0.27 per million departures.

In investigating the causes behind the failure rates, Gladwell references the research of Fischer and Orasanu,[7] where they describe five degrees of mitigation with which crew members make suggestions to authority when faced with circumstances that could lead to adverse effects in safety. He found overwhelmingly that most took the most mitigated alternative. They hinted:

1. *Crew Obligation Statement:* "*I think we need to deviate right about now.*" Notice the use of the "we" and the fact that the request is not specific.
2. *Crew Suggestion:* "*Let's go around the weather.*" Implicit in that statement is: "*We're in this together.*"
3. *Query:* "*In which direction would you like to deviate?*" That's even softer than a crew suggestion, because the speaker is conceding that he's not in charge.
4. *Preference:* "*I think it would be wise to turn left or right.*"
5. *Hint:* "*That return at twenty-five kilometres looks mean.*" That's the most mitigated speech of all. [8]

The Pacific Institute runs workshops which focus on leadership development. The concept of mitigated speech has been introduced into the questions:

- How easy is it to give clear, honest, goal-corrective feedback between yourselves and leadership? Answer: Not easy.
- What do you do when you believe it is difficult to give clear, honest feedback? Answer: Sugar-coat, or simply not give at all.
- Why would you mitigate? Answer: Self-preservation is more important than giving feedback.
- What are the implications of failing to give or, equally, receiving negative feedback? Answer: We cannot set course correctly towards any goal, which inevitably leads to multiple situations of a project "crash", or "near miss" as a result of a lack of critical information.

The implications and insights derived over the years have been significant in demonstrating the effects of high-power distance cultures and the role mitigation plays on organisational performance. Organisations that display high degrees of mitigated speech generally have high levels of self-preservation, leading to low levels of employee engagement and subsequent inertia.

In *"Changing the Mind of the Corporation"*, Roger Martin[9] speaks of four discernible stages to a company's demise: the final two are "the deterioration of necessary feedback" and the "proliferation of leadership and organisational defensiveness". This diminishes "seeing" the truth as it really is, demonstrating that leadership and organisational defensiveness are simply the corporate immune systems' re-enacted habits of pre-established mental models primed to reject the unfamiliar, and thereby remaining secure in the cocoon of their own worldview.

Many leaders interviewed knew that the problem of mitigation existed but were not mindful of the full effects of how the leadership culture and practice contributed towards accelerating levels of mitigation and how this fuelled the probability of poor decisions. Many easily identifiable and even catastrophic outcomes were observed in frank retrospective reflections, ranging from the underperformance of many State-owned entities that have had an impact on the economic outlook, to private corporations experiencing significant challenges to competition.

What was of greater concern to many leaders was that, if mitigation was so invisible and pervasive within the organisational culture, then what "crashes" were emerging that were not presently noticeable? How could they begin to see what they were failing to see?

Mind the gap

Psychologists have long striven to pick apart the moments when we make decisions, and much of the focus has been on our rational mind and our capacity for logic. A great deal of leadership research and training tacitly carries the assumption that leaders are knowingly conscious, clearly perceiving, and rationally acting.[10]

Daniel Khaneman and the late Amos Tversky[11] saw the decision process differently. They saw a much more powerful role for the other side of our minds, and at the heart of their research was the conflict between logic and intuition that leads to mistakes. This kicked off a flurry of experimentation and observation in an effort to understand the meaning of these mistakes. A coherent body of work and evidence has continued to emerge, demonstrating that intuition departs from the realm of logic, and that some of the best clues come not when we get things right, but when we get things wrong.

Emerging out of their work among others was the notion of in-attentional blindness – the failure to see visible and otherwise salient events when one is paying attention to something else – has been proposed as an explanation for various real world events. As an example, while watching team sports such as soccer, one often cannot help wondering why the player with the ball did not pass to a much better positioned teammate, even though this player seemed to be right in his/her field of vision. When the coach or a teammate asks the player after the game why he/she did not pass the ball to the free player, the player typically responds that he/she had not seen the other player.

A well-known experiment was done where observers in these experiments were faced with the task of counting the number of passes made among three basketball players. What was impressive about this experiment was that some did not even notice that a gorilla or a woman with an umbrella was moving through the group as the game was played. These studies enabled the researchers to show that many observers did not perceive an unexpected object in a dynamic setting, even though the unexpected object was right in front of them. So one primary hallmark of in-attentional blindness is that increasing the effort required by a primary task decreases the capacity to notice unexpected events.[12]

This being the case, how do we manage to navigate our way through the complexities of daily life if we are failing to "see" visible and otherwise salient events?

Thinking, fast and slow

The publication of psychologist Daniel Kahneman's book[13] *Thinking, Fast and Slow* was considered to be a major intellectual event. The broad theme of this research is that human beings are intuitive thinkers and that human intuition is imperfect, with the result that judgements and choices often deviate substantially from the predictions of normative statistical and economic models.

Kahneman's book is organised around two ways of thinking, based on the metaphor of System 1 and System 2:
- *System 1* is powerful, effortless, intuitive, automatic, unconscious, and answers questions quickly through associations and resemblances. It is non-statistical, gullible, and heuristic – enabling a person to discover or learn something for themselves – and takes shortcuts. The world around us provides sensory stimuli, and we respond to them through System 1.
- *System 2* is everything that you are aware of in your own mind – the voice in your head – that is, conscious, slow, controlled, deliberate, effortful, statistical, suspicious, and lazy: costly to use. It provides reasons, rationalisations, which are not necessarily the true reasons for our beliefs, our emotions, our intentions and what we do. So when we have to pay attention to a tricky problem, we engage slow but logical System 2, where we have to follow rules and think sequentially. Our heart rate increases, and our pupils dilate while performing System 2 operations. As an example, try counting backwards in 7s from 100 while walking!

Having an opinion about whether you like or dislike someone is something you quite often have no control over. When later asked for reasons why this is the case, it is easy to invent reasons. A lot of what System 2 does is to provide reasons and rationalisations that are not necessarily the true reasons for our beliefs, emotions and intentions. *This suggests that when we come to make decisions, we do not evaluate the decision in itself. Instead, what we unconsciously do, is to try to look at other similar decisions we have made in the past. We consider those decisions as if they were good decisions and because we have made a decision about this issue before, there is no need to go ahead and solve this present decision. Rather, we use what was done before and repeat it with some modifications.*

We make such decisions using fast System 1 when we should be using slow System 2. This is why we make the mistakes we do. These systematic mistakes are known as cognitive biases which are tendencies to think in certain ways that can lead to systematic deviations from a "standard of rationality" or good judgement.

The Unseen World Of Biases

The human brain is capable of 1 016 processes per second – that is far more powerful than any computer currently in existence. That does not mean that our brains do not have major limitations. The lowly calculator can do maths calculations thousands of times faster and better than we can. Our memories are often less than useless. We are subject to cognitive biases, those annoying glitches in our thinking that cause us to make questionable decisions and reach erroneous conclusions.

A cognitive bias is a genuine deficiency or limitation in our thinking, a flaw in judgement that arises from errors of memory, social attribution, and miscalculations (such as statistical errors, or a false sense of probability).

Since Khaneman's research, over 150 cognitive biases have been identified. Here are some of the common biases.

Confirmation bias

We love to agree with people who agree with us. It is why we visit only websites that express our political opinions, and why we mostly hang around people who hold similar views and tastes. We tend to be put off by individuals, groups, and news sources that make us feel uncomfortable or insecure about our views. This is what the behavioural psychologist, Leon Festinger, called cognitive dissonance.[14] It's a preferential mode of behaviour that leads to confirmation bias, the often unconscious act of referencing only those perspectives that fuel our pre-existing views, while at the same time ignoring or dismissing opinions, no matter how valid, that threaten our world view. And paradoxically, the Internet has only made this tendency even worse.

Observational selection bias

This is the effect of suddenly noticing things we have not noticed that much before and wrongly assume that the frequency has increased. A perfect example is what happens after we buy a new car and we inexplicably start to see the *same car* virtually everywhere. A similar effect happens to pregnant women who suddenly notice a lot of other pregnant women around them. Or it could be a unique number, or a song.

It is not that these things are appearing more frequently, it is that we have – for whatever reason – selected the item in our mind, and in turn are noticing it more often. The trouble is that most people do not recognise this as a selection bias. They actually believe that these items or events are happening with increased frequency. That can be a very disconcerting feeling. It is also a cognitive bias that contributes to the feeling that the appearance of certain things or events could not possibly be a coincidence, even though it is.

Status quo bias

We humans tend to be apprehensive of change. This often leads us to make choices that guarantee that things remain the same, or that they change as little as possible. Needless to say, this has ramifications in everything from politics to economics. We like to stick to our routines, political parties, and our favourite meals at restaurants. Part of the perniciousness of this bias is the unwarranted assumption that another choice will be inferior or make things worse. The status quo bias can be summed up with the saying, "if it ain't broke, don't fix it", an adage that fuels our conservative tendencies.

Projection bias

As individuals trapped inside our own minds 24/7, it is often difficult for us to project outside the bounds of our own consciousness and preferences. We tend to assume that most people think just like us, although there may be no justification for it. This cognitive shortcoming often leads to a related effect known as *false consensus bias*. This bias is where we tend to believe that people not only think like us, but that they also agree with us. It is a bias where we overestimate how typical and normal we are, and assume that a consensus exists on matters when there may be none. Moreover, it can also create the effect where the members of a radical or fringe group assume that more people on the outside agree with them than is the case.

Reports and studies over the past decade indicate that biases have played a role in significant corporate failures, notably in the realm of financial crisis.[15] The gap between what we say versus what we actually think in our decision-making processes demonstrates a set of unconscious biases of optimism, overconfidence and confirmation.

Bridging the Gap

How do we bridge the gap of our unawareness of the unconscious routines of leadership defensiveness that limits our "seeing"? Here are a few guidelines to begin the journey, based on an emerging profile of competencies to be required of a mindful leader within our new, emerging context.

Accept the truth of your own limitation to "see"

There is an emerging body of evidence that demonstrates leaders who through experience and thoughtful reflection have concluded that the extent of their ability to be mindful, for example, noticing what has not been noticeable, is contingent on the extent to which they have become *mindful of their own limitations towards being fully mindful.*

This is well expressed by Goleman:[16]

> *"The range of what we think and do is limited by what we fail to notice. And because we fail to notice that we fail to notice, there is little we can do to change; until we notice how failing to notice shapes our thoughts and deeds."*

By first accepting the truth of the universal limits of our capacity to notice fully and that our biases skew our capacity to be fully aware, *we accept that what we don't know and therefore can't do far exceeds what we know and can do.* Awareness and acceptance of this truth increases the possibility of moving on from fixed schemas that have resulted in a diminished perception of possibilities and rigid responses in the face of changing circumstances.

Embrace the virtue of humility

Since what we do not know and cannot do far exceeds what we know and can do, embracing humility, then, is hardly rocket science; it is common sense.

The work of Dickinson in *"Humilitas"*[17] suggests that displaying humility does not mean being a doormat for others, having low self-esteem, or curbing your strengths and achievements. Jim Collins's work, *"Good to Great"*,[18] reminds us that it is possible to be humble, iron-willed and successful. Having strong opinions is no hindrance to humility, either. One of the failings of contemporary western culture is to confuse conviction with arrogance. So what is humility if it is not surrendering to our convictions, strengths and achievements?

Firstly, humility presupposes your dignity. Someone being humble acts from a height, so to speak. True humility assumes the dignity of the one possessing the virtue, which is why it should not be confused with having low self-esteem or being a doormat for others. In fact, I would go as far as to say that it is impossible to be humble in the real sense without a healthy sense of your own worth and abilities. At the writing of this chapter, South African Public Protector Advocate Thuli Madonsela, who received the Transparency International Integrity award in Germany in 2014, is a prime example of personal humility coupled with an iron will.

Secondly, humility is *willing*. It is a choice. Otherwise, it is humiliation. Finally, humility is *social*. It is not a private act of self-deprecation, but is about redirecting your powers. It is a willingness to hold power in the service of others.

So what does a dose of humility do to help in the development of a mindful leader? Perhaps the most obvious outcome of practising humility is that you will learn and grow and thrive, and begin to "see". The logic is again simple: *People who imagine that they know most of whatever is important to know are hermetically sealed from learning new things and receiving constructive criticism.*[19]

> "Arrogant managers," writes JP Kotter of Harvard Business School, "can overevaluate their current performance and competitive position, listen poorly, and learn slowly."[20]

Take Molefe, the newly appointed CEO of an IT firm. He had previously been a hotshot senior manager in a fast-growing telecoms company. So his move to the computer software industry seemed an easy transition to himself and others. He soon learned that a talent for seeing the big picture and a flair for motivating teams would take one only so far. Within a year he was feeling out of his depth. Telecommunications is not IT. There were industry subtleties he had overlooked and technical information he had failed to study. He realised he was guilty of competency extrapolation. This is the malady of conflating self-opinion with genuine expertise. If he were to have his time over again, he would execute the transition with more grace and a listening ear.

Often those who are boastful, protective and unwilling to listen are actually the most insecure. It is a compensation mechanism, a way to hide true feelings of inadequacy. Humbly acknowledging limitations and refusing to engage in competency extrapolation are not signs of weakness. They demonstrate realism and are therefore strengths. By contrast, the logic again is simple. In reflecting humility, it demonstrates that one has a robust view of oneself. One does not need others to affirm it, at least not as often. Humility is therefore not an ornament to be worn; it is an ideal that transforms.

Humility in the context described will allow one to invite criticism from friends and colleagues. This is not the easiest thing. I am constantly surprised at the frequency with which chief executives feel threatened by open challenges to their ideas as though the source of their authority, rather than specific ideas, were at issue. I am not advocating a horizontal approach to leadership; I firmly believe that lines of responsibility and authority should be respected in healthy organisations. I am simply pointing out that allowing constructive criticism and encouraging it at team level is one powerful way to foster a little humility.

Practice suspension

Peter Senge (2005)[21] in his book *Presence* suggests that seeing freshly starts with stopping habitual ways of thinking and perceiving. As mentioned earlier, when we come to make decisions, we do not generally evaluate the decision in itself. Instead what we unconsciously try to do is to look at other similar decisions we have made in the past. Then we take those decisions as if they were good decisions. Because we have made a decision about it before, there is no need to go ahead and solve this present decision. Rather we use what was done before and repeat it with some modifications.

According to cognitive scientist, Francisco Varela,[22] developing the capacity for this sort of stopping involves "suspension", removing oneself from the habitual stream of thought. "Suspension," he continues, "is considered the first basic gesture in enhancing awareness.

Suspending does not mean the destruction of existing mental models but rather it's the hanging of our assumptions in front ourselves and by doing so we begin to notice our thoughts and mental models. Suspension allows you to see your seeing."

A good example of bringing the concept into concrete view is by the physical practice of sitting on a chair and grabbing the sides. By holding the side of the chair tightly, notice how your body feels as you hold tightly to the chair, the tension in your arms, shoulders back, stomach and neck. Now release your hold on the chair slowly and feel all those muscles relax. The lesson demonstrates that often we hold our thoughts in in much the same way. Suspension starts when we release the hold and simply notice our current thoughts.

Until leaders can start to see their habitual ways of interpreting a situation they cannot really step into a new awareness. Practising suspension requires patience and a willingness not to impose pre-established frameworks and mental models on what we are seeing. If we simply observe without forming conclusions as to what our observations mean and allow ourselves to sit with all the seemingly unrelated bits and pieces of information we see, fresh ways to understand a situation can eventually emerge.

We may have heard the saying: "If you want to understand an organisation's culture, go to a meeting." I am often invited by teams simply to come and sit in on team discussions and observe their ways of working. It is interesting to watch who speaks and who does not; who is listened to and who is not; and which issues are ignored or addressed by innuendo. All these are powerful clues for a leader to know how an organisation actually functions. You can learn to pay attention to the "external" dynamics of the meeting as well as your own thoughts and feelings. When the meeting is over, look at the incident that engaged you emotionally. Using your imagination takes time to re-create how you felt and what you thought as the incident played out.

If you do this carefully for several incidents, you will learn a lot about yourself and your organisation. You will see where you felt safe and where you felt threatened. You'll see where you were conflicted and where you were aligned with what was happening around you. You'll see where you were distracted and where you were fully present. As you practise this with a dose of humility, you will be able to engage your imagination more actively to "see" the details of your experience.

Conclusion

This is mindfulness: the more penetrative awareness that sees beyond the surface of what is going on in your field of awareness. Mindfulness makes it possible to see connections that may have not been visible before. Seeing these connections does not happen as a result of trying; it simply comes out of stillness.

I initially began the journey of exploring mindful leadership from the perspective of being fully conscious and aware in the present moment, but I have appreciated that it is more to do with deep listening, of being open beyond one's preconceptions and historical ways of making sense.

Endnotes

1	Pickert, 2014.	12	Simons & Jensen, 2009.
2	Friedman, 2005.	13	Kahneman, 2011.
3	Heifetz, 1994.	14	Festinger, 1957.
4	Langer, 2010.	15	Shefrin, 2015.
5	Hofstede, 1980.	16	Goleman, 1985.
6	Gladwell, 2008.	17	Dickson, 2011.
7	Fischer & Orasanu, 1999.	18	Collins, 2005.
8	Ibid.	19	Senge, 1994.
9	Martin, 1998.	20	Kotter, 1996.
10	Kegan, 1994.	21	Senge et al., 2005.
11	Kahneman & Tversky, 1984.	22	Varela, Thompson & Rosch, 1991.

References

Collins, JC. 2005. *Good to great and the social sectors: Why business thinking is not the answer.* Boulder, CO: HarperCollins.

Dickson, JP. 2011. *Humilitas: A lost key to life, love, and leadership.* Grand Rapids, MI: Zondervan.

Festinger, L. 1957. *A Theory of cognitive dissonance.* Stanford, CA: Stanford University Press.

Fischer, U & Orasanu, J. 1999. *Cultural diversity and crew communication.* Paper presented at Astronautical Congress, Amsterdam; American Institute of Aeronautics and Astronautics.

Friedman, TL. 2005. *The world is flat: A brief history of the twenty-first century.* New York, NY: Farrar, Straus and Giroux.

Gladwell, M. 2008. *Outliers: The Story of Success.* 1st ed. New York, NY: Little, Brown and Company.

Goleman, D. 1985. *Vital lies, simple truths: The psychology of self-deception.* New York, NY: Simon & Schuster Paperbacks.

Heifetz, RA. 1994. *Leadership without easy answers* (Vol. 465). Cambridge, MA: Harvard University Press.

Hofstede, G. 1980. *Culture's consequences: International differences in work-related values.* Newbury Park, CA: Sage Publications.

Kahneman, D. 2011. *Thinking, fast and slow.* New York, NY: Farrar, Straus and Giroux.

Kahneman, D & Tversky, A. 1984. 'Choices, values, and frames'. *American Psychologist*, 39(4):341–350.

Kegan, R. 1994. *In over our heads: The mental demands of modern life.* Cambridge, MA: Harvard University Press.

Kotter, JP. 1996. *Leading change.* Boston, MA: Harvard Business School Press.

Langer, E. 2010. *A call for mindful leadership.* HBR Blog Network.

Martin, RL. 1998. 'Changing the mind of the corporation'. *Harvard Business Review on Change*, 117–125, Nov–Dec. Cambridge, MA: Harvard Business School Press.

Pickert, K. 2014. 'The mindful revolution'. *Time*, 23 January.

Senge, P, Scharmer, CO, Jaworski, J & Flowers, BS. 2005. *Presence: Exploring profound change in people, organizations and society.* London, UK: Nicholas Brealey Publishing.

Senge, PM. 1994. *The fifth discipline: The art and practice of the learning organization.* New York, NY: Doubleday/Currency.

Shefrin, H. 2015. *The behavioural paradigm shift.* [Online]. Available: rae.fgv.br/sites/rae.fgv.br/files/the_behavioral_paradigm_shift.pdf. [Accessed 21 July 2016].

Simons, DJ & Jensen, M. 2009. 'The effects of individual differences and task difficulty on inattentional blindness'. *Psychonomic Bulletin & Review*, 16(2):398–403.

Varela, F, Thompson, E & Rosch, E. 1991. *The embodied mind: Cognitive science and human experience.* Cambridge, MA: The MIT Press.

Chapter 7

VIRTUOUS LEADERSHIP
Marius Ungerer

Leadership is a natural and necessary task wherever social beings have to co-operate. As reflected in *Leadership Excellence*, we can think about and describe this activity in various ways. In this chapter we will explore leadership from a virtuous perspective where the compass of the leader is her or his set of core values. We use the lens of virtues to give a deeper meaning and substance to the concept of core personal values.[1]

The overriding effect of upper-level leadership as a predictor of lower-level leadership practices has been confirmed by research.[2][3] Leaders have a substantial effect on followers, both positive and negative. Our collective memory and context are filled with stories of business, political and societal leaders who conducted themselves in questionable ways through deceptive decisions and practices that raised ethical issues. The images of leaders who misuse power and who deploy corrupt practices are too often a feature of our daily news coverage. Surveys[4] have also shown that the *behaviours of superiors*, meaning C-level executives and senior management, are the most highly-rated factors connected with unethical decision-making – an example of negative outcomes associated with the practices of leaders.

Organisations are all keen to show and communicate their business values to stakeholders, but what about the internal moral and ethical compass of the leaders who are supposed to uphold the espoused organisational values? This is the space the concept of virtuous leadership wants to occupy to assist and guide leaders towards a virtuous state of being and doing. By adding virtues to the leadership equation we can address the core of the ethical leadership challenges we face in a more fundamental way.[5]

The Concepts of Virtue and Virtuous Leadership

The roots of virtuous leadership are based in both Confucian and Aristotelian concepts[6] as well as Positive psychology. Confucianism is a philosophy with a strong emphasis on ethics and is not value-neutral. Confucians state that a leader should be not only knowledgeable, but also virtuous.[7] The key questions Aristotle wanted to answer in his writings were: *How can I make my life a success?* and *What makes life worth living?*[8] Positive psychology focuses on the study of the circumstances and processes required for optimal functioning of people, teams and organisations. Positive psychology thinking was born from the realisation that traditional psychology was not producing enough *knowledge of what makes life worth living.*[9]

The term "virtue" is thought to have originated from the Greek word *arete*, which in its most basic sense means "excellence".[10][11] A virtue is defined as *moral excellence and righteousness; goodness;* and *a particular efficacious, good or beneficial quality; advantage.*[12] Virtue is seen as a trait of character or intellect that is morally laudable and presents an ideal to which all good living aspires.[13] Virtues (as there are many) represent principles of moral character that motivate and guide behaviour[14] towards positive ethical outcomes. Virtues are accepted as dispositions that are part of (or not) an individual that could be measured and cultivated. Virtues assist us to achieve our full potential by being ethical[15] and represent the best human beings can be.[16]

The general scheme we use to classify and identify virtues relies on six overarching universal virtues that are endorsed by almost every culture across the world.[17] The six broad universal virtues[18] are: Wisdom and knowledge; Humanity; Justice; Courage; Temperance; and Transcendence (see also Table 7.1).

There is currently no general agreement in scholarly literature regarding the definition and attributes associated with the concept of virtuousness.[19] Virtuousness is related to constructs such as values, virtues, morality and ethics.[20] In this chapter, the views associated with positive psychology and virtue ethics are presented. "*Virtuousness possesses an affirmative bias and focuses on elevating, flourishing, and enriching outcomes.*"[21] One of the interesting attributes associated with the construct of virtuousness is that it cannot be exceeded,[22] which means it always represents a future aspiration to live up to – there is no end-line, just many new beginnings in order to live a more virtuous life. Virtues are practised at all times,[23] which means that it is a way of living. Virtuousness also represents a stable and universal standard of good[24] for us.

Two types of virtuousness can occur. Where organisational features exist that facilitate virtuousness, it occurs by organisations; and where individual members demonstrate virtuous behaviours, it happens in organisations.[25] Virtuous organisations are institutions that enable and support virtuous activities such as good habits and desires of its members.[26] These organisations promote virtuous relationships between their members and focus on being good and doing good in strategic choices; for example, downsizing as a last option is done with the utmost care and compassion.

The constructs of virtuous leadership are linked in the literature to related concepts such as moral, ethical, servant, spiritual, inclusive, authentic, transformative, transformational, and responsible leadership.[27] Virtuous leadership is described as a focus "*on the highest potentiality of human systems that is oriented toward being and doing good*".[28] A more pragmatic description states that virtuous leadership involves distinguishing right from wrong, taking steps to ensure justice and honesty, influencing and enabling the pursuit of righteous and moral goals, and connecting to a higher purpose.[29]

A description of virtuous leadership that emphasises both the ethics component and the behaviour aspects of virtue is as follows: Virtuous leadership represents a *leader–follower relationship wherein a leader's situational appropriate expression of virtues triggers follower perceptions of leader virtuousness, worthy of emulation*.[30] This description of virtuous leadership also emphasises the content, context and process elements of leadership. The virtues that virtuous leaders exemplify have the following common content characteristics: they have a disposition for "good" character traits; they are cross-culturally sensitive and reflect both Aristotelian (Western) and Confucian (Eastern) traditions; they are interrelated and manifest simultaneously where required; and they are seen as contributors to both ethical and effective leadership.

The context of dependency in which virtuous leadership is embedded relates to the argument that holding and claiming a virtue consists of showing and expressing it across a broad spectrum of situations.[31] The key processes through which virtuous leadership influences followers are perceptually-driven attribution and modelling. Attribution theory[32] states that people make judgements about the cause of a person's behaviour based on perceived behaviour consistency over time. This suggests that a leader with virtuous characteristics and competencies is expected to demonstrate virtue consistently, although followers have only restricted observation opportunities. The result is that some leaders might be perceived by followers as being less or more virtuous than others based on the array of virtues which the leader exemplifies.[33] By behaving in a virtuous manner, leaders are viewed by their subordinates as role models with a positive influence.[34] Followers observe and imitate virtuous behaviour of leaders and practise these behaviours until they become habitual.

Compared to the vast array of virtue possibilities, the focus of virtuous leadership is on a smaller set of behaviour-based virtues that are specifically relevant to leadership[35] (see the discussion on measurement).

Key Departure Points

In this part, the arena of virtuous leaders is further explored by looking at some critical departure points and assumptions associated with it.

The loss of confidence and trust in key actors (for example, business leaders, political leaders, union leaders, sports administrators) and institutions (for example, banks and related financial institutions, government institutions, sports bodies) in society and the subsequent investigations into unethical and fraudulent actions of the involved parties have created a renewed interest in business ethics, personal morality, and private ethics.[36] The practices associated with virtuous leadership allow leaders to set themselves new, ambitious goals and, in achieving these, to create normative examples of leadership actions and behaviour that serve the interests of many in a beneficial and positive way.

A virtuous leadership perspective is therefore a vision for leadership in practice,[37] where the moral and ethical base is restored as a key ingredient of positive leadership influence and results. It is not about Utopia or a new theory of perfection, but about creating a positive expectation around the leadership impacts and effects for current and future generations of business leaders as eminent, powerful societal actors; politicians as public representatives; union leaders as responsible co-value creators; and public officials as servants of communities. Are leaders busy creating value for all, or are they destroying value by pursuing short-sighted, narrow self-interests? This re-awakening and rekindling of the aspiration for enduring excellence, good and goodness is central to virtuous leadership practices.

Three important assumptions are associated with the concept of virtuousness:[38]

- An inclination exists in all humans to lean towards moral goodness. This tendency has been confirmed by various scholars.[39] [40] [41] Human beings naturally strive to do good;
- The impact of virtuousness extends beyond mere self-interest as virtuous leadership is not a means to achieve another end, but is an end in itself; and
- Virtuousness creates and fosters sustainable positive energy.

The positive reinforcing effect of virtuous leadership is created in the following way. The virtuousness of a leader manifests and is lived through values. Values such as justice, courage, temperance, and prudence create a moral 'skeleton'[i] for the individual. The values of a leader resonate within him/her, and the leader's behaviour sets up a virtuous reinforcing loop between leader and followers. Virtuous leadership influences the wellbeing of followers, and this positive experience of followers affects the wellbeing of leaders.[42] Virtuous leaders create positive conditions for followers to be virtuous. Virtuous leaders also establish the conditions of trust and openness that are essential for the creation and transformation of knowledge within organisations.[43]

Living a life based on virtues is much easier than we think. Many of us have been indoctrinated since a young age to believe that a virtuous life is difficult, reserved only for a few 'moral geniuses', something that happens after a lifetime of striving, and essentially impossible for 'normal' human beings who are worried about the next down-payment and the kids' braces.[44] This (non-virtuous) view has been given the lie by recent insights into our mammalian heritage.[45] Mark Solms argues that virtuous behaviour is the most basic instinct we all possess. He says that we are compelled to act in ways that make us feel good, so much so that it is an ancient part of

---

i An 'inner structure' that allows the rest of the personality structure to 'hang together'. The philosopher-psychologist Karl Jaspers called this Existenz – the inner structure of existence, but also the force which allows one to escape the boundaries of 'mere existence'. It is a shell that creates a refuge and comfort against the traumas of life, but one that can be transcended – 'traded in' for another, 'higher' existence. See, *inter alia*, Jaspers, 1971; Koestenbaum, 2006; Salamun, 2006; Peach, 2008; Miron, 2012.

the structure of the brain – the so-called PAG structure,[46] which developed in vertebrates before mammals split off. When Peterson and Seligman did their research they stumbled upon these same feel-good factors (see the next part, dealing with an integrated framework).

The practice of virtuous leadership is not at odds with the traditional business focus of profits and efficiency. *Rather, there is reason to expect that virtuous leadership will facilitate the economic livelihood and longer term sustainability of the organization. Accordingly, by exemplifying virtues, leaders are "doing well by doing good".*[47]

The following statement by KPMG CEO Stephen Butler in 1997 supports this mutually beneficial interaction between virtue ethics and business profits:

> "I want to stress at the outset that the strongest argument for raising the ethics bar boils down to self-interest. I believe that good business ethics is good for the bottom line and good for shareholder value … if we don't behave well, we can be regulated, we can be sued, all sorts of bad things can happen to us. … Today companies cannot afford negative publicity. Loss of confidence in an organization is the single greatest cost of unethical behaviour. Once the media gets hold of the story your customers will avoid you like the plague." [48]

It is expected that the appropriate application of virtue practices in the business would positively contribute to enhanced company profits and the wellbeing of employees.[49] This coalescence of virtue and profits is, however, possible only when we have daring, creative and insightful business leadership who accept business to be in service of society as a whole.

Virtuous behaviour becomes habitual through learning and continuous practice. Habits, however, can be lost because of a lack of practice. This implies that once a leader has mastered a virtue practice, it can be sustained only through repetitive practice.[50]

By focusing on virtues as the key content for leadership behaviour, the emphasis is on the best human beings can be – where virtue is the source of goodness and happiness in a person's life.[51]

Virtuous organisations engage in virtuous practices in the service of a higher value – a socially conscious focus of doing well while doing good.[52] The continuous contribution towards the creation of a sustainable society and environment is an integral part of the core strategic choices a virtuous organisation (and leader) makes.

An Integrated Framework for Virtue Themes and Competencies

Peterson and Seligman[53] developed a classification framework in which they classified 24 individual strengths linked to the six broad universal virtues described below. These virtues transcend national and cultural boundaries. Although they do not claim universality with this framework, they represent a claim of ubiquity – the identified virtues and associated individual strengths are commonly present in all people in the world. While not everyone will be aware of theses virtues or will call them by different names, they are present (for example, *ubuntu* consists of competencies such as empathy, social awareness, recognition of the wisdom of elders, and valuing personal relationships).[54]

The six broad universal virtues consist of the following virtue strengths and competency areas:

- **Wisdom and knowledge,** which include the cognitive competencies of creativity, curiosity, open-mindedness, love of learning and perspective.
- **Humanity**, which includes the social competencies of kindness, love and social intelligence.

- **Justice**, with the associated social competencies of fairness, leadership and teamwork.
- **Courage**, which includes the personal and emotional competencies of authenticity, bravery, persistence and zest.
- **Temperance**, with personal competencies of forgiveness, modesty, prudence and self-regulation.
- **Transcendence**, which is the sixth and final broad universal virtue, and includes the personal competencies of appreciation of beauty, gratitude, hope, humour, and religiousness.

According to De Vries, the concept of competency is used in the following way: *"As character traits are expressed in certain behavioural patterns, they can also be called competencies."*[55]

The six broad universal virtues with their associated 24 virtue strengths and competency areas are reflected in Table 7.1.

Table 7.1: Virtue strengths and competency areas

Universal virtue theme	Virtue strengths and competency areas	Short description	Reflective prompts[56]
Wisdom and knowledge	1. Creativity	Thinking of novel and productive ways to do things	Thinking of new ways to do things is a crucial part of who you are. You are never content with doing something the conventional way if a better way is possible.
	2. Curiosity	Taking an interest in all ongoing experiences	You are curious about everything. You are always asking questions, and you find all subjects and topics fascinating. You like exploration and discovery.
	3. Open-mindedness	Thinking things through and examining them from all sides	Thinking things through and examining them from all sides are important aspects of who you are. You do not jump to conclusions, and you rely only on solid evidence to make your decisions. You are able to change your mind.
	4. Love of learning	Mastering new skills, topics, and bodies of knowledge	You love learning new things, whether in a class or on your own. You have always loved school, reading, and museums – anywhere and everywhere, there is an opportunity to learn.
	5. Perspective	Being able to provide wise counsel to others	Although you may not think of yourself as wise, your friends hold this view of you. They value your perspective on matters and turn to you for advice. You have a way of looking at the world that makes sense to others and to yourself.

Universal virtue theme	Virtue strengths and competency areas	Short description	Reflective prompts[56]
Humanity	6. Kindness	Doing favours and good deeds for others	You are kind and generous to others, and you are never too busy to do a favour. You enjoy doing good deeds for others, even if you do not know them well.
	7. Love	Valuing close relations with others	You value close relations with others, in particular those in which sharing and caring are reciprocated. The people to whom you feel most close are the same people who feel most close to you.
	8. Social intelligence	Being aware of the motives and feelings of self and others	You are aware of the motives and feelings of other people. You know what to do to fit into different social situations, and you know what to do to put others at ease.
Justice	9. Fairness	Treating all people the same according to notions of fairness and justice	Treating all people fairly is one of your abiding principles. You do not let your personal feelings bias your decisions about other people. You give everyone a chance.
	10. Leadership	Organising group activities and seeing that they happen	You excel at the tasks of leadership: encouraging a group to get things done and preserving harmony within the group by making everyone feel included. You do a good job organising activities and seeing that they happen.
	11. Teamwork	Working well as member of a group or team	You excel as a member of a group. You are a loyal and dedicated teammate; you always do your share.
Courage	12. Authenticity	Speaking the truth and presenting oneself in a genuine way	You are an honest person, not only by speaking the truth but by living your life in a genuine and authentic way. You are down to earth and without pretence; you are a "real" person.
	13. Bravery	Not shrinking from threat, challenge, difficulty, or pain	You are a courageous person who does not shrink from threat, challenge, difficulty or pain. You speak up for what is right even if there is opposition. You act on your convictions.

Universal virtue theme	Virtue strengths and competency areas	Short description	Reflective prompts[56]
Courage	14. Perseverance	Finishing what one starts	You work hard to finish what you start. No matter the project, you "get it out through the door" in timely fashion. You do not get distracted when you work, and you take satisfaction in completing tasks.
	15. Zest	Approaching life with excitement and energy	Regardless of what you do, you approach it with excitement and energy. You never do anything halfway or half-heartedly. For you, life is an adventure.
Temperance	16. Forgiveness	Forgiving those who have done wrong	You forgive those who have done you wrong. You always give people a second chance. Your guiding principle is mercy, not revenge.
	17. Modesty	Letting one's accomplishments speak for themselves	You do not seek the spotlight, preferring to let your accomplishments speak for themselves. You do not regard yourself as special, and others recognise and value your modesty.
	18. Prudence	Being careful about one's choices; not saying or doing things that may later be regretted	You are a careful person, and your choices are consistently prudent ones. You do not say or do things that you might later regret.
	19. Self-regulation	Regulating what one feels and does	You self-consciously regulate what you feel and what you do. You are a disciplined person. You are in control of your appetites and your emotions, not *vice versa*.
Transcendence	20. Appreciation of beauty	Noticing and appreciating beauty, excellence, and/or skilled performance in all domains of life	You notice and appreciate beauty, excellence, and/or skilled performance in all domains of life, from nature to art, to mathematics, to science, to everyday experience.

Universal virtue theme	Virtue strengths and competency areas	Short description	Reflective prompts[56]
	21. Gratitude	Being aware of and thankful for the good things	You are aware of the good things that happen to you, and you never take them for granted. Your friends and family members know that you are a grateful person because you always take the time to express your thanks.
	22. Hope	Expecting the best and working to achieve it	You expect the best in the future, and you work to achieve it. You believe that the future is something that you can control.
	23. Humour	Liking to laugh and tease; bringing smiles to other people	You like to laugh and tease. Bringing smiles to other people is important to you. You try to see the light side of all situations.
	24. Spirituality	Having coherent beliefs about the higher purpose and meaning of life	You have strong and coherent beliefs about the higher purpose and meaning of the universe. You know where you fit in in the larger scheme. Your beliefs shape your actions and are a source of comfort to you.

If one looks at the description of the different strength and competency areas of virtue, it is clear that they represent universal and transcendent qualities that would assist leaders in their quest for a positive impact and influence. These competency areas span and infuse all other leadership competencies (such as the competency to read a balance sheet, or run a meeting). These competency areas also represent the "best" virtues that mankind can strive for. If we could develop a cadre and generations of leaders with these qualities, organisations, societies, and the world would be a better place.[57]

Measuring Individual Virtue Competencies

Next we explore the aspect of measuring virtues to create a baseline perspective for a leader. An individual may possess a variety of virtues, and this could be reflected in his/her leadership approach, impact and influence in a context. How can we identify virtue strengths and development areas in order to assist leaders to become more virtuous?

An overt intent to measure and develop virtuous leadership qualities is a clear signal to organisation members as to what is valued and also as to what to contribute in order to reinforce those values.[58] The measurement of virtuous leadership competencies should be a part of the leadership selection and development processes in an organisation. In this part, the direct measurement of virtuous leadership capabilities is described.

The measurement instrument described in this chapter represents an extension of previous work done in this area.[59] The majority of the universal virtues as described above (Table 7.1) were used as a set of virtues to develop and validate an 18-factor behaviour-based Virtuous Leadership Questionnaire (VLQ).[60] The VLQ enables us to develop a view on the virtuous leadership state of a leader based on multidimensional measures of leader virtues. Followers use the 18-item VLQ to evaluate their leader on each virtue category and item. An overall score is derived by totalling the scores of each of the five virtues. The main virtue categories that are measured are: Humanity, Justice, Courage, Temperance, and Prudence.

The overall reliability (Cronbach's alpha) of the VLQ is 0.96. The VLQ results show a lack of association with age, gender and education, which contributes to validity. The VLQ also shows positive associations with follower and leader ethical behaviour, life happiness and satisfaction, as well as workplace effectiveness. The VLQ also accounts for 60% of the variance in ethical behaviour among leaders. The 18 question items for the five virtue categories of the VLQ are shown in Table 7.2.

Table 7.2: Virtuous Leadership Questionnaire items

Leadership virtue category	Definition	Question items
Likert-type response format (1=Never; 5=Always)		
Humanity	A character trait underlying leaders' love, care, and respect of others	17. My supervisor shows concerns for subordinates' needs 7. My supervisor shows concern and care for peers 2. My supervisor expresses concern for the misfortunes of others
Justice	A character trait motivating respectful recognition and protection of rights of others to be treated fairly, in accordance with uniform and objective standards	9. My supervisor allocates valued resources in a fair manner 1. My supervisor respects individual interests and rights when allocating responsibilities 12. My supervisor resolves conflicts in a fair and objective fashion
Courage	A character trait enabling leaders to do without fear what they believe is "right"	3. My supervisor acts with sustained initiative, even in the face of incurring personal risk 4. My supervisor speaks up on matters of injustice and personal conviction, despite risking "backlash" 13. My supervisor initiates a long-term and worthwhile project despite risking personal reputation 16. My supervisor leads fundamental change though it may entail personal sacrifice and personal risk
Temperance	A character trait helping leaders control their emotional reactions and desires for self-gratification	15. My supervisor avoids indulging his/her desires at the expense of others 6. My supervisor behaves unselfishly even when there are opportunities to maximise self-gain 18. My supervisor prioritises organisational interests over self-interests 5. My supervisor downplays personal successes to avoid discomforting less successful others

Leadership virtue category	Definition	Question items
Prudence	A character trait enabling leaders to make "right" judgements and choose the "right" means to achieve the "right" goals	10. My supervisor exercises sound reasoning in deciding on the optimal courses of action 14. My supervisor efficiently and effectively assesses requirements demanded by any given situation 11. My supervisor grasps the complexity of most situations when making judgements 8. My supervisor uses only the resources necessary in responding to the demands of any given situation

Apart from getting information from subordinates about a leader, the collection of data via the VLQ can also include peers, suppliers and key customers to expand the scope of data sources. This expands the perspectives used to create a view on the virtuousness of a leader through the eyes and experiences of others. The questions in Table 7.2 can also be adjusted from "my supervisor" to "I" to allow for a leader to do a self-evaluation of his/her virtuous leadership practices. Comparing these results with those of others is also a source of enquiry and potential development.

The inherent limitation associated with leadership measurements is acknowledged – we must rely on the ratings of others to determine a particular leader's virtues. What is really measured are perceptions of these constructs, as opposed to the actual possession of the virtues.[61] Nonetheless, creating a measurement baseline on the virtuous practices of a leader based on the perceptions of followers and partners assists leaders in developing and reinforcing strengths and in being aware and sensitive to weaker virtue areas.

Developing Individual Virtue Competencies

The practical aspects of creating an awareness of virtue strengths and development areas through direct measurement interventions have been described above. We now turn to the need for the development of virtues.

Being aware of one's personal, deeply held beliefs, preferences, emotions, wants, and needs are all part of living with a higher sense of consciousness.[62] This heightened awareness assists us as people and leaders to present ourselves in a more genuine way. An awareness of my capacity to embrace virtue-based thinking and actions is a starting point for developing virtue character competencies. This development process is about leaders leading themselves to their own authentic virtuous core.[63] The following warning in this regards makes the necessity of this learning journey more relevant: "*Until an authentic virtuous core is discovered by individual leaders, no matter how rationally they are constrained by legal limits, structures, and punishments, they will forever be vulnerable to the slings and arrows of corruption that have toppled many of our most prominent executives.*"[64]

Developing virtues of character is the same as learning a skill. Virtues are developed through practice and habituation.[65] It is only through practising the virtues that one becomes virtuous. But how can we develop this capacity in individuals? We start by recognising that developing virtuous leadership is *less* about a means to just another material or financial end and *more* about creating an ultimate good.[66] This distinction is important to prevent using virtuousness only to achieve only economic and market-desirable outcomes, but to rather focus the whole leadership effort on producing substantially better results with goodness and sustainability as key features. At the very least, it demonstrates the insight that profit is a result and not a cause. Another important leverage point is self-empowerment through reflective learning.

Developing knowledge is not only a theoretical activity. Knowledge is also socially constructed – we ourselves have made the world of our knowledges, beliefs and convictions and can therefore – thankfully – remake them. In a sentence, the roots of reflective learning are expressed in this statement by Professor Donald Schön: *"I have come to feel that [the] only learning which significantly influences behaviour is self-discovered, self-appropriated learning."*[67] We learn best by reflecting on our experience, on our own practice. We learn better through an internal process of self-discovery than through externally induced processes such as expert teaching.

The benefits of reflective learning[68] as a development practice are multiple. These include:

- Understanding your own strengths and weaknesses better;
- Identifying and examining your underlying values and beliefs;
- Acknowledging and challenging possible assumptions that cause many of your ideas, feelings and actions;
- Recognising areas of potential bias or discrimination;
- Acknowledging your fears; and
- Identifying possible inadequacies or areas for improvement.

The results from the VLQ are a strong stimulus to set in motion the practice of reflective learning. Based on their VLQ results, leaders can write down their reaction to the following questions in order to create a basis for reflection over time (see Table 7.3). They should use these first reaction responses and reflect regularly on them to develop new insights and principles for them to apply in their personal, unique leadership practice.

Table 7.3: Virtuous Leadership reflective practice

Reflections on VLQ results	
Question	**Responses**
What are your overall impressions of the results?	
What virtue character strengths do you have, and how can you further enhance them?	
What areas stand-out as development areas which you should be sensitive to? How can you minimise the effects of these non-strengths?	
How can you improve the positive effects of each of the following virtue and competency areas: • **Humanity** • **Justice** • **Courage** • **Temperance** • **Prudence**?	
What can you do less of in order to be a more virtuous leader?	

Below is another example of a reflective exercise that can assist you to develop your own reflective abilities. Use the framework at <http://www.thehappinessinstitute.com/freeproducts/docs/The%20VIA%20Classification%20of%20Character%20Strengths.pdf> to reflect on your current strengths.

You will get a list of the six universal virtues with their associated strengths descriptions and you are asked to identify your personal strengths. Also use Table 7.1 to guide your reflection on each universal virtue theme. What patterns are emerging from your evaluations of yourself? Write down your insights and reflect on these over time to deepen your understanding about your virtue strengths and development areas. How can you use these insights to be a more virtuous leader in your context? Virtuous practices are formed by repetitive practices. What new leadership practices should you engage with to build your virtuous leadership capacity?

We can listen to and hear ourselves only when we are still. By reflecting on our virtuous leadership practices and results, we speak to ourselves through the "voice in our head". This is artful leisure by engaging our consciousness. Reflective learning allows us to learn in a socially interactive way with ourselves. The opportunity is always there.[69]

The practice of reflection based on silence, self-generated insights and physical inactivity is a far cry from the current business and societal focus on action, constant movement, productivity, and profits. Busyness has become the norm in an always connected world. Deliberate slowing down to make time for reflective learning practices is a big challenge. Allocating time for personal learning and reflection in our diaries is a pragmatic way of dealing with this opportunity.

Benefits and Outcomes Associated with Virtuous Leadership

We live in a world of constant change and turbulence. For us to manage change successfully, we paradoxically need two conditions – change and stability. Virtuous leadership is a stable reference point[70] to orientate towards in an uncertain, volatile and ambiguous world. Ethical standards often change and evolve over time and with circumstances. Virtuous leadership creates the stability to guide us through challenging times because virtuousness represents the best humans can be, and these unchanging universal aspirations assist us to make decisions and to manage changes.

There are limits to rule-based controls and in high-velocity environments – the rules need to be reinvented as new situations emerge. There is a difference between avoiding the bad and pursuing the good.[71] Virtuous leadership sets up a stable expectation of ethical and moral behaviour standards that far exceed the best codes, standards and rules of governance to prevent harm and wrongdoing.

Research indicates that virtuous behaviour is associated with desirable outcomes. In this regard, "*honesty, transcendence, meaning, caring and giving behaviour, gratitude, hope, empathy, love and forgiveness, among other virtues, have been found to predict desired outcomes, such as individuals' commitment, satisfaction, motivation, positive emotions, effort, physical health, and psychological health*".[72] Another study indicates that the composite of the virtues hope, resilience, optimism, and efficacy was significantly related to work performance and satisfaction.[73]

Studies showed that organisations with higher leadership virtuousness scores significantly outperform lower virtuousness organisations on aspects such as profitability, productivity, quality, customer retention, and employee retention.[74] Virtuous leadership also predicts a higher organisational commitment[75] – a crucial lead indicator of future organisational performance potential. Another study[76] concludes that the virtue of leader humanity predicted employees' psychological wellbeing, organisational citizenship behaviours, and affective trust. It is clear that encouraging evidence is mounting and the potential positive impacts caused by virtuous leadership cannot be ignored any longer.

Practical wisdom is seen as a key ingredient in decision-making processes, and leaders should therefore embrace this capability. Leadership based on virtues, as described above, culminates in practical wisdom as a core part of leading successfully in a complex world.

Conclusion

The message associated with virtuous leadership is a message of hope – the focus is on fostering an environment which emphasises the application of best practices in order to assist businesses to be great, without making moral compromises.[77] The results and impact of leaders who practise a virtuous leadership approach strike out against all injustice. The ideal of a wholly just worldwide community based on virtuous leadership practices is now a real possibility.

Leaders who role-model virtuous behaviour contribute to improving the general ethical climate in their work environments and at the same time add to the wellbeing of employees. This goes much further than promoting ethical behaviour only through ethical codes.[78]

Endnotes

1. Manz et al., 2008.
2. Bass, et al., 1987.
3. Pearce & Sims, 2002.
4. Brenner & Molander, 1977.
5. Manz et al., 2008.
6. Wang & Hackett, 2015.
7. Li, 2009.
8. Flynn, 2008.
9. Seligman & Csikszentmihalyi, 2000.
10. Wang & Hackett, 2015.
11. Cameron, 2011.
12. Stanford Encyclopedia of Philosophy, 2014.
13. Flynn, 2008.
14. De Araújoa & Lopes, 2014.
15. Flynn, 2008.
16. Cameron, 2011.
17. Dahlsgaard, Peterson & Seligman, 2005.
18. Peterson & Seligman, 2004.
19. Cameron & Winn, 2012.
20. Thun & Kelloway, 2011.
21. Cameron, 2011.
22. Ibid.
23. Riggio et al., 2010.
24. Cameron, 2011.
25. Thun & Kelloway, 2011.
26. Cameron, Bright & Caza, 2004.
27. Wang & Hackett, 2015.
28. Cameron, 2011.
29. Pearce, Waldman & Csikszentmihaly, 2006.
30. Hackett & Wang, 2012.
31. Wang & Hackett, 2015.
32. Kelley, 1972.
33. Wang & Hackett, 2015.
34. Ibid.
35. Ibid.
36. Flynn, 2008.
37. Ibid.
38. Cameron, 2011.
39. Dutton & Sonenshein, 2007.
40. Tangney, Stuewig & Mashek, 2007.
41. Krebs, 1987.
42. Ungerer, Herholdt & Le Roux, 2013.
43. Pearce et al., 2006.
44. Ungerer et al., 2013.
45. Solms, 2011.
46. Ibid, p. 44.
47. Wang & Hackett, 2015.
48. Butler, 1997.
49. Flynn, 2008.
50. Wang & Hackett, 2015.
51. Flynn, 2008.
52. Manz et al., 2011.
53. Peterson & Seligman, 2004.
54. Ungerer et al., 2013.
55. De Vries, 2001.
56. VIA Institute on Character, n.d.
57. Ungerer et al., 2013.
58. Pearce et al., 2006.
59. Riggio et al., 2010.
60. Wang & Hackett, 2015.
61. Riggio et al., 2010.
62. See footnote i on p. 415.
63. Manz et al., 2008.
64. Ibid.
65. Flynn, 2008.
66. Cameron, 2011.
67. Schön, 1987.
68. Monash University, 2015.

69	For a more detailed description on reflective learning and virtue practices, see Ungerer et al., 2013.	73	Luthans et al., 2007.
		74	Cameron, 2011.
70	Cameron, 2011.	75	De Araújoa & Lopes, 2014.
		76	Thun & Kelloway, 2011.
71	Ibid.	77	Flynn, 2008.
72	Ibid.	78	Wang & Hackett, 2015.

References

Bass, BM, Waldman, DA, Avolio, BJ & Bebb, M. 1987. 'Transformational leadership and the falling dominoes effect'. *Group & Organization Management*, 12(1):73–87.

Brenner, SN & Molander, EA. 1977. 'Is the ethics of business executives changing?' *Harvard Business Review*, 55(1):57–71.

Butler, S. 1997. *Business ethics and corporate responsibility: Good for the bottom line*. Speech delivered at an awards luncheon to recognize 100 Florida companies, Orlando, Florida, 28 February.

Cameron, K. 2011. 'Responsible leadership as virtuous leadership'. *Journal of Business Ethics*, 98(1):25–35.

Cameron, K, Bright, D & Caza, A. 2004. 'Exploring the relationships between organizational virtuousness and performance'. *American Behavioral Scientist*, 47(6):1–24.

Cameron, KS & Winn, B. 2012. 'Virtuousness in organizations'. In KS Cameron & GM Spreitzer (eds). *Oxford handbook of positive organizational scholarship*. New York, NY: Oxford University Press. 231–243.

Dahlsgaard, K, Peterson, C & Seligman, MEP. 2005. 'Shared virtue: The convergence of valued human strengths across culture and history'. *Review of General Psychology*, 9(3):203–213.

De Araújoa, MSG & Lopes, PMPR. 2014. 'Virtuous leadership, organizational commitment and individual performance'. *TÉKHNE – Review of Applied Management Studies*, 12(1):3–10.

De Vries, MK. 2001. *The leadership mystique: A user's manual for the human enterprise*. London, UK: Prentice-Hall.

Dutton, JE & Sonenshein, S. 2007. 'Positive organizational scholarship'. In S Lopez & A Beauchamps (eds). *The encyclopedia of positive psychology*. Malden, MA: Blackwell Publishing. 737.

Flynn, G. 2008. 'The virtuous manager: A vision for leadership in business'. *Journal of Business Ethics*, 78(3):359–372.

Hackett, RD & Wang, Q. 2012. 'Virtues and leadership: An integrating conceptual framework founded in Aristotelian and Confucian perspectives on virtues'. *Management Decision*, 50(5):868–899.

Jaspers, K. 1971. *Philosophy of existence*. Philadelphia, PA: University of Pennsylvania Press.

Kelley, HH. 1972. 'Attribution in social interaction'. In EE Jones et al. (eds). *Attribution: Perceiving the causes of behavior*. Morristown, NJ: General Learning Press.

Koestenbaum, P. 2006. 'Karl Jaspers'. *The encyclopedia of philosophy (Vol 4)*. (2nd ed.) (Editor-in-chief D Borchert.) Farmington Hills, MI: Thompson Gale.

Krebs, D. 1987. 'The challenge of altruism in biology and psychology'. In C Crawford, M Smith & D Krebs (eds). *Sociobiology and psychology: Ideas, Issues, and applications*. Hillsdale, NJ: Lawrence Erlbaum. 81–118.

Li, C. 2009. 'Where does Confucian virtuous leadership stand?' *Philosophy East & West*, 59(4):531–536.

Luthans, F, Avolio, B, Avey, J & Norman, S. 2007. 'Positive psychological capital: Measurement and relationship with performance and satisfaction'. *Personnel Psychology*, 60(3):541–572.

Manz, CC, Anand, V, Joshi, M & Manz, KP. 2008. 'Emerging paradoxes in executive leadership: A Theoretical interpretation of the tensions between corruption and virtuous values'. *The Leadership Quarterly*, 19(3):385–392.

Manz, CC, Manz, KP, Adams, SB & Shipper, F. 2011. 'Sustainable performance with values-based shared leadership: A case study of a virtuous organization'. *Canadian Journal of Administrative Sciences*, 28(3):284–296.

Miron, R. 2012. *Karl Jaspers, from selfhood to being*. New York, NY: Amsterdam Press.

Monash University. 2015. *The reflective learning process – Language and learning online*. [Online]. Available: http://www.monash.edu.au/lls/llonline/writing/medicine/reflective/3.xml. [Accessed 1 July 2016].

Peach, F. 2008. *Death, 'deathlessness' and Existenz in Karl Jasper's philosophy*. Edinburgh: Edinburgh University Press.

Pearce, CL & Sims, HP, Jr. 2002. 'Vertical versus shared leadership as predictors of the effectiveness of change management teams: An examination of aversive, directive, transactional, transformational, and empowering leader behaviors'. *Group Dynamics: Theory, Research, and Practice*, 6(2):172–197.

Pearce, GL, Waldman, DA & Csikszentmihaly, M. 2006. 'Virtuous Leadership: A Theoretical Model and Research Agenda'. *Journal of Management, Spirituality & Religion* 3(1–2):60–77.

Peterson, C & Seligman, M. 2004. *Character Strengths and Virtues: A Handbook and Classification*. New York, NY: Oxford University Press.

Riggio, RE., Zhu, W, Reina, C & Maroosis, JA. 2010. 'Virtue-based Measurement of Ethical Leadership: The Leadership Virtues Questionnaire'. *Consulting Psychology Journal: Practice and Research* 62(4):235–250.

Salamun, K. 2006. 'Karl Jaspers' conception of the meaning of life'. *International Journal in Philosophy, Religion, Politics and Arts*, 1(1/2), 1–8.

Schön, D. 1987. *Educating the Reflective Practitioner*. San Francisco, CA: Jossey-Bass.

Seligman, M & Csikszentmihalyi, M. 2000. 'Positive psychology: An introduction'. *American Psychologist*, 55(1):5–14.

Solms, M. 2011. 'Neurobiological foundations'. In JW De Gruchy (ed.). *The humanist imperative in South Africa*. Stellenbosch, ZA: Sun Press, Stellenbosch University. 41–55.

Stanford encyclopedia of philosophy. 2014. *Virtue Ethics*. [Online]. Available: http://plato.stanford.edu/entries/ethics-virtue/. [Accessed 1 July 2016].

Tangney, JP, Stuewig, J & Mashek, DJ. 2007. 'Moral emotions and moral behavior'. *Annual Review of Psychology*, 58(1):345–372.

Thun, B & Kelloway, EK. 2011. 'Virtuous leaders: Assessing Character strengths in the workplace'. *Canadian Journal of Administrative Sciences*, 28(3):270–283.

Ungerer, M, Herholdt, J & Le Roux, J. 2013. *Leadership for all: Virtue practices to flourish*. Randburg, ZA: Knowres Publishing.

VIA Institute on Character. n.d. *VIA classification of character strengths*. [Online]. Available: http://www.viacharacter.org/www/Character-Strengths/VIA-Classification. [Accessed 5 July 2015].

Wang, D & Hackett, RD. 2015. 'Conceptualization and measurement of virtuous leadership: Doing well by doing good'. *Journal of Business Ethics*, 8 February, doi 10.1007/s10551-015-2560-1.

Chapter 8

WISE LEADERSHIP
Lisa Ashton

> "... if there is anything the world needs, it is wisdom ... without it, I exaggerate not at all in saying, that very soon, there may be no world ..." – Robert J Sternberg

The realities of the world of work have become dynamic, complex, exposed, uncertain, and unpredictable. In fact, Former US Secretary of State Madeleine Albright said: *"There are an awful lot of things going on that need understanding and explanation. To put it mildly: The world is a mess."*

As the geopolitical situation the world over spins out of control, investors, governments and leaders at all levels are questioning how best to position their governments, organisations and institutions in order to survive the growing global turmoil. In these volatile times, we have witnessed depressed oil prices, a slowdown in key economies, conflict in Syria, the violent rise of extremist groups, and an ever-growing list of fears, which are creating a climate of global insecurity. Add to this a technological background that continuously develops, changes and innovates, and potentially paints a risky backdrop for the rest of our concerns. We are dealing with crises such as global warming and a deadly Ebola outbreak in Africa that threatened to spread worldwide. There is a real scarcity of resources, in a world where consumerism and capitalism are peaking – the most worrying deficit is the scarcity of water. And let us not forget that the recovery of the global market from the financial crisis of eight to nine years (2008) ago has not been nearly as strong as originally anticipated. The world is indeed a mess!

As the world melts into chaos and threats to the sustainability of humankind on our planet increase, serious questions need to be asked about the common sense, judgement and leadership of those in power. Leaders seem to be making decisions that are self-serving. Politicians seem more interested in being re-elected for their next term instead of making decisions that will serve the common good of the people and that are focused on the longer term.

Robert J. Sternberg, President of the American Psychological Association and one of the major researchers on wisdom, writes *"the need for wisdom is greater today than ever"*, and goes on to say, *"If there is anything the world needs, it is wisdom. Without it, I exaggerate not at all in saying that very soon, there may be no world…"*. The human community has no choice but to take responsibility for the fate of the Earth, as it is humans who have the power to save or destroy our planet. Humans have become so powerful that in one lifetime we have seen how we can change the Earth on a vast scale: we alter climate and genetic structures; we harbour weapons that can annihilate the planet. Human power has grown so great that if we do nothing, the effect on our future will be as drastic as it will be unplanned, and often determined by leaders who display narrow, short-term interests. Our leaders and indeed the world have become more occupied with the direction of the NASDAQ and the JSE, and in corporations, long-term thinking has declined.

As organisations become more complex and the world faces "wicked" problems that threaten our sustainability as a planet, the demand for wise leadership intensifies. Great leadership is not necessarily about intelligence, expertise or popularity. Rather, it is about wisdom, sound judgement and collaboration. So how do leaders make decisions, use their judgement, and discern what to do under such complex and uncertain conditions? What do they do when there is no precedent, when knowledge and experience do not suffice? How can they tell when their judgements are accurate? And what is meant by wisdom?

Wisdom Defined

Defining the construct of wisdom remains a major challenge as researchers continue to find it difficult to discover approaches to wisdom that embrace its complexity. Wisdom has a long and lingering history, and references to and papers on this topic go back to the ancient philosophers such as Aristotle and Plato, religious scriptures, the writings of psychologists old and new, and many views out of the western world, the East, and Africa.

In *"The Nicomachean Ethics"*, Aristotle described three kinds of knowledge, the first being *Phronesis*, which he emphasised was essential for human affairs. Phronesis is the practical wisdom we use in a particular situation when we do not and cannot *know* what to do. When analysis is not sufficient, and there is no technique that we know will work, we must draw on inner resources to make a judgement. Stamp contends that in order to make a judgement, it is necessary to detach – to stand back and above – and not be constrained by others telling you what to think. When we judge in uncertain and ambiguous contexts, we are not sure that our decision will bring about the right outcome. In the words of Jaques (1998): "We judge that it will, but we are not sure. Only time will tell." This, Aristotle claimed, was wisdom.

Traditionally, the Western concept of wisdom was heavily weighted toward cognitive abilities, placing emphasis on knowledge, experience, intelligence, judgement and reasoning abilities. The eastern conceptualisations of wisdom emphasise spiritual introspection, enlightenment, and social behaviour, including benevolence and compassion. We have, however, learnt over time that wisdom is a complex, multi-faceted construct, balancing intra-, inter- and extrapersonal interests, as well as a desire to attain a common good.

Paul Baltes, for example, writes that wisdom is "easily recognised when manifest", and he describes the key properties of wisdom as follows:

- Wisdom addresses important and difficult questions and strategies about the conduct and *meaning of life*.
- It embodies a truly superior level of *judgement and knowledge* – knowledge with scope, depth and balance. It also includes knowledge about the limits of knowledge.
- Wise individuals have achieved a synergy of mind and *character*, particularly caring, benevolence and compassion.

Csikszentmihalyi and Rathunde write that the term has three different dimensions of meaning: a cognitive process; a virtue (a social value); and a good condition (personal value). Ardelt defines wisdom as a personality characteristic, "an integration of cognitive, reflective and affective dimensions".

All evidence seems to suggest that wisdom is holistic and may share many characteristics with other psychological constructs. It also suggests that it draws on many cognitive, reflective, affective and social abilities.

I may summarise that there are many different components to the construct of wisdom, and sources of wisdom (western, African, eastern, Biblical writings) associate the construct with so much more than cognitive skills, knowledge and experience. Research has indicated that the following characteristics are all associated with wisdom. These are by no means exhaustive, but they provide good insight into the traits commonly associated with wisdom:

- **Competencies and knowledge** – such as: a passion for truth and knowledge; clarity of thought; well-developed mental abilities; good judgement; breadth and depth of knowledge and experience; critical thinking; intelligence; intuition.

- **Comfort with ambiguity and uncertainty** – the ability to deal with complex problems and little information.
- **Benevolence and compassion** – it is good-hearted; brings about joy and harmony; empathy; virtuous character.
- **The desire to attain the greater good for all** – creating win–win situations; benevolent capitalism; respect for all life; non-exploitative.
- **Social skills** – self-control; autonomy; humour; collaborative; emotionally intelligent.
- **Openness and reflectiveness** – enjoys life fully, with a sense of contentment; able to think about all aspects of things; self-knowledge, knowledge of limits; serenity.
- **Modesty and unobtrusiveness** – not showy, conceited, or arrogant; humility.

It is interesting that almost all theorists agree that wise leaders do things that are good for all. The common goal of wisdom is therefore to attain the common good. Yang, for example, emphasised that a wise person is able to bring harmony to home and society, and Levitt, in her study of Tibetan Buddhist monks, found that wisdom is associated with altruism and compassion, distinguishing good from evil, self-examination and monitoring of behaviour; and with personal characteristics such as honesty, humility, and respect for all creatures. To gain direct personal benefits of wisdom seems self-contradictory for these practitioners, as "by definition, the wise person acts to meet the needs of others".

So, if this is wisdom, what does a wise leader look like?

McKenna and, Rooney have set out five characteristics of wise leaders:

1. Wise leaders must have *cognitive complexity*, a capacity to deal with complex and ambiguous phenomena in complex environments.
2. Wise leaders must be *rational and deep thinkers*, having the capacity to seek out the "facts" of a situation and to deal with them rationally. However, they also need to understand and question their assumptions and where the facts originated from.
3. Wise leaders display *creativity*, and draw on the non-rational judiciously as appropriate; they also have the capacity to acknowledge the potential worth of one's own instincts in making judgements.
4. Wise leaders display *long-term vision and virtue*, having a proved commitment to the long-term welfare of not just immediate stakeholders, but of humanity in general. To care for humanity, one must be committed to virtue, to that which is intrinsically decent.
5. Finally, a wise leader is *articulate*, having a proved capacity to reach people through word, affect and action.

They also argue that wise leadership is domain-specific, or *contextualised*. That is, people may be wise when dealing with certain issues but less wise, even foolish, when dealing with other issues. This is evident in the common phrases about people being "wise in the ways of the world" or "wise in matters of the heart".

Drawing on the discussion above, Figure 8.1 depicts the characteristics of a Wise Leader.

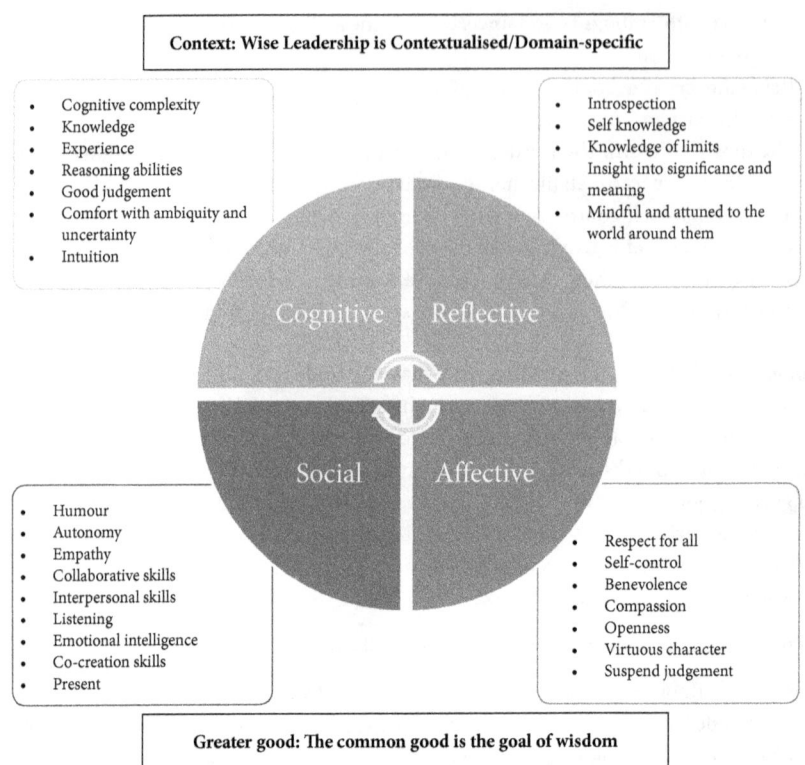

Figure 8.1: The wise leader

Wise Leaders and the Management of Social Institutions

The literature describes different kinds of wisdom, or to put it another way, different functions of wisdom. Deidre Kramer[1] distinguishes five functions: Solutions of problems confronting self, Advising others, Management of social institutions, Life review, and Spiritual introspection.

This section will focus on the role of the wise leader in social institutions.

Shaping strategic intent

One of the key deliverables that leaders are accountable for is longer-term planning, anticipating tomorrow in order to put plans in place proactively in order to ensure the long-term sustainability of their organisations. This is not a new phenomenon. From their very beginnings, human beings tried to anticipate tomorrow. They noted the cycles of the seasons and fertility; they noted the phases of the moon, the changing of the tides. They consulted seers and witch-doctors, looked for omens, and strove to find their fate in the stars.

I have already discussed the volatile and chaotic world in which we find ourselves today, as well as the power that humans have to change the earth on a vast scale. Technological progress has also resulted in change accelerating to a point where its effects have become visible in a single lifetime.

Following from the above, is it then still possible to predict the future? Do we have the ability to do so in this incredibly fast, ever-changing and turbulent world in which we live? In the past, many great futurists came surprisingly close to the mark with their predictions. They foresaw things such as: *"each well-to-do man will have a telephone in his residence"*; *"we will navigate the air"*; and *"the entire world will be open to trade"*. But then, things changed. Major events such as the world financial crisis and many technological and political events took us by surprise. Executives argue that the rate of change is too rapid, that the world has become too complex and that predicting the future is no longer possible.

Complexity theorists (diverse top-level people from many fields and disciplines) at the Santa Fe Institute developed tools and theories to understand the concept of complexity. Their shared focus was to understand the common underlying structural and behavioural features of complex systems, which display properties such as self-organisation. They tried to understand how patterns emerge out of total randomness, and they drew on lessons from diverse phenomena such as ant colonies, Internet traffic and consumer patterns.

This work on complexity has not solved the intrinsic difficulties in looking ahead, but has brought something important to the effort: a sense of humility and awe before the difficulty of the task, and a better understanding of the limits of human cognition. It has revealed that trend extrapolation, and mechanistic models and views of the world, are ineffective. It highlights the need to capture and understand the inherent uncertainties of open non-linear systems with complex feedback loops, in which small perturbations can sometimes cause large and unpredictable effects.

With this understanding, wise leaders have realised that we will never again be able to predict the future with a high degree of accuracy. They have come to realise that there are better approaches to dealing with surprise, disruption and uncertainty. They understand that they must prepare for the unexpected. To do this, they have learnt that they must constantly revise their awareness of the present, while simultaneously working towards creating the kinds of long-term outcomes they want by crafting well-considered images of the future. Yes, they craft or **shape the future**.

So how do Wise Leaders do this?

Wise leaders are truly present. They are attuned to the world around them, and they listen with interest to both the spoken and unspoken words of people at all levels, from all walks of life. This is one of the best insurance policies against a surprise-filled future. How do these wise men and women excel at "managing the unexpected"? They ensure that they distribute decision-making throughout their organisations. They make sure that the experts are heard and not just those people at the top of the food chain. They excel at listening and are able to suspend judgement. They co-operate and co-create. They communicate. These wise leaders are "mindful" and better able to detect surprises when these are new, small and insignificant.

Through quality dialogue and widely shared co-created images of what they want the future to look like for the organisation, a shared picture of the future is created. Through this envisioning process, new realms of behavioural possibilities are opened up and chain reactions of self-organising change are created. The economist Kenneth Boulding summarised this view effectively:

> *"The human condition can almost be summed up in the observation that, whereas all experiences are of the past, all decisions are about the future. The image of the future, therefore, is the key to all choice-orientated behaviour. The character and quality of the images of the future which prevail in a society are therefore the most important clue to its overall dynamics."*[2]

Another important lesson for thinking about the future was summed up by Alan Kay, who created the computer interface that became the model for the first Apple Macintosh and then the basis for Windows: "*The best way to predict the future,*" Kay said, "*is to create it.*"[3]

Collaboration

Nancy Roberts[4] wrote about the rise of what she called *wicked problems*, and that leaders are encountering a class of problems that defy solution, despite the use of the most sophisticated analytical tools. She maintains these problems are "wicked" because they have the following characteristics:

1. There is broad disagreement on what "the problem" is. Consider crime in South Africa. Is it unemployment, education, the economy? The truth is we cannot agree on the true problem.
2. Without a definitive statement of the problem, the search for solutions is open ended. Stakeholders – those who have a stake in the problem and its solution – champion alternative solutions and compete with one another to frame "the problem" in a way that directly connects with their preferred solution and their preferred problem definition.
3. The problem-solving process is complex because constraints, such as resources and political ramifications, are constantly changing.
4. Constraints also change because they are generated by numerous interested parties who "come and go, change their minds, fail to communicate, or otherwise change the rules by which the problem must be solved".[5]

The problem-solving process when dealing with wicked problems is experienced as ambiguous, fluid, complex, political, and extremely frustrating.

Roberts postulates that the only way to cope with wicked problems is to employ collaborative strategies.

So what do wise leaders do? They *collaborate*.

Wise leaders know that they can solve complex or "wicked" problems only through collaboration. How do you solve "crime in South Africa" or "world hunger" or "global skills shortages" if not through collaboration? We need to work together, involving numerous and diverse stakeholders. We need to collaborate across industries, across countries, and even across religions if we are serious about finding sustainable solutions.

Ultimately, wise leaders have learned that to lead, facilitate and participate in such collective undertakings requires an act of faith. It begins with the hope that there is a better way of doing things, a recognition that failure is possible, and a willingness to "trust the process" without guarantees of a particular outcome. It is sustained by personal reserves that enable people to remain calm and centred in the face of the unknown and the unknowable. These are important lessons for all of us to learn.

The greater good

Of late, the term "benevolent capitalism" has been used more and more frequently. It has been associated with terms such as fair play, doing no harm, and creating a positive impact beyond financial return. Wise leaders have learnt that money alone does not optimise how the world works. Modern society functions because capitalism exists, and capitalism is starting to get its act together when it comes to addressing the world's wicked problems. Individual contributions from people like Bill Gates and Warren Buffett are well recognised.

According to Gitsham and Wackrill,[6] a generation ago, the prevailing attitude was that it was the role of political leaders, not business leaders, to address the big societal issues of the day. Some business leaders engaged in philanthropic activities, either as individuals or through company contributions, but most would have argued that such concerns would only be a distraction from their core role and a source of unnecessary cost.

Wise leaders have a very different attitude. They believe that it is essential for senior executives to have a nuanced understanding of the major societal forces shaping our world, and to know where and how to respond to these through the way they go about their core business, in a way that benefits both their business and wider society. A sizeable cohort of business leaders now evidently believe that playing a leadership role in understanding and addressing the major forces shaping society – far from being a source of cost – is now central to how they create value.

Wise leaders share the following vital characteristics: They:

- Have the ability to see the connections between external trends and the implications for core business,
- Create the conditions to enable leadership to emerge throughout the business,
- Encourage innovation and frame challenges that inspire it,
- Use language and symbols effectively,
- Influence mindsets and culture,
- Recognise and reward positive new behaviours and outcomes, and
- Have the courage to raise difficult issues in the face of vested interests, and make sure that they have support in the places where they need it.

Wise leaders lead beyond the traditional boundaries of their organisation, proactively leading change in consumer and supplier behaviour, industry norms and government policy, for the mutual benefit of their organisations and wider society. Some are leading collaboratively with industry competitors, NGOs and government, where challenges need to be tackled and only collective, systemic solutions will do.

Treating people as human beings

There is an emerging call to restore humanity in the workplace, and this appeal is not only coming from the Generation Y and Millennium kids. "Old school" management practices which make employees feel bored, powerless, disempowered, infantilised and "not important" are increasingly perceived as being tools of the incompetent "leader". Wise leaders are those who make employees feel respected, trusted, worthy and honoured. They are the leaders who encourage and inspire others to become a better version of themselves. It will be these wise leaders who will lead in the future.

This view is shared by Umair Hague,[7] who says: "*Leaders lead us not to a place, but to a different kind of destination: to our better, truer selves.*" He goes on to say that "*Leaders – true leaders, those worthy of the word – do the very opposite: they lead us to truth, worth, nobility, wonder, imagination, joy, heartbreak, challenge, rebellion, and meaning. Through love, they lead us to lives that matter.*"

Hague also has the opinion that leaders inspire us because they bring out the best in us. For him, they evoke in us our fuller, better, truer, nobler selves. This is the reason that we love our leaders – not merely because they paint portraits of better lives, but because they impel us to be the creators of our own.

Developing Wise Leaders

Is it possible to develop wisdom?

Any attempt to tackle the construct in its aggregate form may seem like a daunting, if not impossible task. However, if we address each of those components that collectively make up wisdom – components such as collaboration, listening skills, social skills and mindfulness, then we may just get there. It is not that easy to develop these skills but it is my firm belief that they can be developed – albeit with effort. I believe that we need to start young, at school level, and slowly build a generation of wise leaders.

Collaboration, for example, is not a default instinct in us. Competition is a far more powerful one, and people love to judge what is "best". Consider the medals awarded at competitions, how we vote on who is best and who is worst on TV shows, how massive the business of professional sport has become. We revere the rich and the famous and often try to emulate them.

So what does it take to rise above the instinct for competition and to collaborate as a first instinct? Perhaps you remember your coach saying that there is no "I" in the word "team"? And of course it is true that a winning team is usually the one where the players co-operate the best. We have watched the business sector evolve into larger and larger entities where people have to cooperate to make them work. Maybe it is awareness of the bigger picture and of the inter-relatedness of things that leads us to be able to achieve so much more when we work together instead of against one another. Being co-operative is actually not easy. We like having our own way; we don't like to compromise with others. Everyone says they are in favour of open innovation and co-creation, we have all heard about the wisdom of crowds, bringing the outside in, and we have bought the t-shirt which states that "none of us is as smart as all of us".

It's easy for the C-suite to sign up to collaboration and co-creation. But it often goes against the grain of how they built their careers initially, and it usually does not come naturally. So where to start? Collaboration is a skill and one that can be taught, but first its value needs to be understood. Perhaps by rewarding team effort and success, and placing a greater emphasis on collaborative work, rather than self-actualisation and self-improvement, we will begin to instil the mind-set that collaboration is a vital and imperative pursuit and not something that can be overlooked, when one is pursuing individualistic goals and growth. By increasing the value placed on co-operation and joint pursuits, it is not far-fetched to assume (even if simplistic) that general trends will begin to skew in favour of collaborative environments and efforts.

Listening is another component that should be developed in leaders at all levels. Effective listening is a skill that underpins all positive human relationships and perhaps the building blocks of success. Good listening skills can lead to better customer satisfaction; greater productivity with fewer mistakes; increased sharing of information and collaboration that in turn can lead to more creative and innovative work. Many great disasters could have been prevented if leaders had "just listened". It is my firm belief that the Marikana events in the platinum industry of South Africa in 2014 could have been prevented if leaders had listened.

Many successful leaders and entrepreneurs credit their success to effective listening skills. Richard Branson, for example, frequently quotes "listening" as one of the main factors underpinning the success of Virgin. Rachel Naomi Remen summarises this well, by saying: *"The most basic and powerful way to connect to another person is to listen. Just listen. Perhaps the most important thing we ever give each other is our attention."*[8] Listening is another skill that can be taught.

Mindfulness is another skill that more and more leaders all over the world are interested in learning. Mindfulness is the skill of being able to be completely present with your actions, your environment or your companions and it makes other skills such as listening and collaboration so much easier.

Sciandra[9] said the following: *"If you are depressed you are living in the past. If you are anxious, you are living in the future. If you are content, you are living in the present"*.

According to Sciandra, these are some of the things that can happen when you are living in the present:

- Anger has little energy.
- Carrying a grudge is difficult.
- Worrying is not possible.
- Time slows down.
- The creative mind is set free.
- Physical pain diminishes and sometimes disappears.
- Every day becomes richer and more enjoyable.
- Slipping into the present moment is a gift you give to yourself.

Perception is often said to be reality, so a key step towards changing behaviour is to change the perception of what is imperative, worth pursuing, or of vital importance and value. Cultivating a shared perception of the urgency of developing such skills as discussed (collaboration, listening and mindfulness) may be the first step in creating and developing wise leaders.

In summary, in this new world we live in, leaders are required to develop skills in areas that historically have not been a conventional part of the business leader's repertoire. Examples of these are: contributing to public debate with an informed point of view; proactively leading change in consumer and supplier behaviour, industry norms and government policy; relating well to multiple constituencies; engaging in dialogue in order to understand and empathise with groups and communities with perspectives contrary to one's own; and engaging in multi-stakeholder collaboration with unconventional partners. Developing collaboration, listening, mindfulness and social skills will go a long way towards creating a new generation of wise leaders.

Conclusion

A new generation of leader is emerging: the wise leader.

The time for a new generation of leader has already come. From the discussion above, it is clear that the wise leader understands that he/she does not have all the answers; that they cannot sustain the organisation on their own; and that they understand the limits of human cognition. They are prepared for the unexpected, they hold the torch of hope high when things are uncertain, and they build resilience in their people.

Wise leaders are attuned to the world around them and they ensure this by listening with interest to both the spoken and unspoken words of people with whom, the customers they serve, and the communities in which they exist. They distribute decision-making down and around. They make sure that the experts are heard, not just the boss. They listen, they suspend judgement, they co-operate and co-create, and they communicate. Successful leaders are "mindful" and better able to detect surprises when they are new, small and insignificant.

The wise leader works towards creating long-term outcomes by crafting well-considered and co-created images of the future. They do this through dialogue and quality conversations and understand that it is these co-created images of the future that guide choices and goal-directed behaviour.

They make people feel respected, trusted, worthy and honoured – and most of all, they encourage and inspire others to become a better version of themselves.

Wise leaders understand their work within the context of the planet, the world, the communities they operate in, and the people they serve. They are aware that their work and businesses impact people, societies and the environment, and they strive towards "doing no harm", being fair, ethical and responsible. They lead people towards a more co-operative, humane and positive future!

Endnotes

1   Kramer, 1990.
2   Boulding, 1981, p. 44.
3   Kay, 1971.
4   Roberts & Bradley, 2005.
5   Roberts, 2014.
6   Gitsham & Wackrill, 2012.
7   Hague, 2013.
8   Remen, 1997.
9   Sciandra, 2015.

References

Ardelt, M. 2003. 'Empirical assessment of a three-dimensional wisdom cale'. *Research on Aging*, 25(3):275–324.

Baltes, PB & Kunzmann, U. 2004. 'The two faces of wisdom: Wisdom as a general theory of knowledge and judgment about excellence in mind and virtue vs. wisdom as everyday realization in people and products'. *Human Development*, 47(5):290–299.

Boulding, K. 1981. 'Basic evolutionary model'. In K Boulding (ed.). *Evolutionary economics*. Beverly Hills, CA: Sage. 23–47.

Csikszentmihalyi, M & Rathunde, K. 1990. 'The psychology of wisdom: An evolutionary interpretation'. In RJ Sternberg (ed.). *Wisdom: Its nature, origins, and development*. Cambridge, MA: Cambridge University Press. 25–51.

Gitsham, M & Wackrill, J. 2012. *Leadership in a rapidly changing world: How business leaders are reframing success*. Berkhamstead, UK: Ashridge.

Hague, U. 2013. 'How and why to be a leader (not a wannabe)'. *Harvard Business Review*, 8 July. [Online]. Available: https://hbr.org/2013/07/how-and-why-to-be-a-leader-not. [Accessed 6 April 2016].

Jacques, E. 1998. *Requisite organization: A total system for effective managerial organization and managerial leadership for the 21st century*. Gloucester, MA: Cason Hall.

Kay, A. 1971 [Speech at a 1971 meeting of PARC] . [Online]. Available: https://en.wikiquote.org/wiki/Alan_Kay . [Accessed 6 April 2016].

Kramer, DA. 1990. 'Conceptualizing wisdom: The primacy of affect-cognition relations'. In R Sternberg (ed.). *Wisdom: Its nature, origins and development*. Cambridge, MA: Cambridge University Press. 279–309.

Levitt, HM. 1999. 'The Development of wisdom: An analysis of Tibetan Buddhist experience'. *Journal of Humanistic Psychology*, 39(2):86–105.

McKenna, B & Rooney, D. 2005. *Wisdom management: Tensions between theory and practice in practice*. Paper presented at the Knowledge Management Conference in the Asia Pacific [KMAP], November. Wellington, NZ.

Remen, RN. 1997. *Kitchen table wisdom: Stories that heal*. New York, NY: Riverhead Books.

Roberts, N. 2014. 'Wicked problems and network approaches to resolution'. *International Public Management Review*, 1(1):1–19.

Roberts, NC & Bradley, RT. 2005. 'Organizing for peace operations'. *Public Management Review*, 7(1):111–133.

Sciandra, K. 2015. *The mindfulness habit: Six weeks to creating the habit of being present*. Woodbury, MN: Llewellyn Publications.

Stamp, G. 2005. *The day of judgement*. Bioss. [Online]. Available: http://bioss.com/gillian-stamp/the-day-of-judgement-or-in-praise-of-leprechauns/. [Accessed 24 July 2016].

Sternberg, RJ. 1998. 'A balance theory of wisdom'. *Review of General Psychology*, 2(4):347–365.
Sternberg, RJ. 2003. *Wisdom, intelligence and creativity synthesized*. Cambridge, UK: Cambridge University Press.
Yang, S-Y. 2001. 'Conceptions of wisdom among Taiwanese Chinese'. *Journal of Cross-cultural Psychology*, 32(6): 662–680.

Chapter 9

SPIRITUAL LEADERSHIP
Penny Law

Ethical scandals, globalisation, technological advances and the environmental crisis are creating unprecedented challenges for 21st century organisations. The economic context is characterised by volatility, uncertainty, complexity and ambiguity, forcing organisations to transform radically the way they do business and manage people if they want to become or remain globally competitive.

Despite global companies' legal and ethical obligation to follow good corporate practice, corruption remains a grave challenge.[1] According to the World Bank, the cost of corruption is estimated around $1-trillion annually. Transparency International says bribes of up to $40-billion are paid to corrupt officials in developing countries each year.[2] A Global Economic Crime Survey conducted by PWC in 2016 revealed that 69% of South African companies experienced some form of economic crime as opposed to the global average of 36%.[3] These alarming statistics, alongside a rising tide of Fortune 500 scandals, signify the extent to which our moral fibre has decayed, and also cast doubt on the efficacy of current leadership models to resolve ethical challenges.

Attempts to remain globally competitive have contributed to additional stressors that hamper organisational performance. Unacceptable levels of staff attrition, absenteeism, poor work morale and increasing incidents of stress-related diseases such as hypertension, depression, insomnia, obesity, diabetes, cardiac arrest, cancer and burnout[4] cost the South African economy billions of Rands. It is estimated that absenteeism alone costs R12- to R16-billion a year in South Africa.[5]

The degenerating health of individuals, and seemingly ubiquitous unethical behaviour, is not just knocking organisational performance. It is triggering a crisis of meaning. Employees, who generally spend more time in the workplace than at home, are questioning their purpose in life. They want to experience meaning in the workplace, where they can at least feel fulfilled and inspired by their work, and at best feel that they are making a difference in society.

Most contemporary leaders have failed to address organisational ailments and existential concerns because they are still operating in a mechanistic paradigm. A new type of leader is required, one who can traverse a more complex organisational terrain where the focus has shifted from only generating profit to being concerned about the triple bottom line: people, planet and profit. Employees are becoming increasingly discerning and want to work in organisations that promote employee wellness, encourage work-home balance, drive social responsibility initiatives, and actively contribute to genuinely caring for the environment.[6]

Because of this, spiritual leadership is proposed as the type of leadership required for 21st century organisations. This chapter discusses the relevance of spiritual leadership in the modern world of work; juxtaposes spiritual leadership with emerging leadership theories; and introduces an integrated spiritual leadership model from which critical leadership competences will be extrapolated, necessary to create a thriving organisational environment.

Relevance of Spiritual Leadership

Before examining spiritual leadership in more depth, the distinction between spirituality and religion must be established. Some authors construe these notions synonymously, while others regard them as distinct but related notions.

Spirituality and religion

Spirituality may be construed as a process where individuals search for a universal truth, find meaning in and purpose to life, experience a connectedness to a greater purpose related to a higher power, and strive to reach their highest potential.[7] Religion, on the other hand, concerns being a member of a specific religious community that follows rules, rituals, and belief systems.[8]

Even though there is a conceptual difference between religion and spirituality, they are interrelated. One does not have to be religious to be spiritual, as an individual could experience spirituality within or outside a religious context.[9] Fry[10] notes that "spirituality is necessary for religion but religion is not necessary for spirituality". Altruistic love serves as a bridge between religion and spirituality. In this regard, religion may be perceived as comprising institutionalised faith, while spirituality is closely associated with the living-out of positive values.

Need for spiritual leadership

Traditional leadership theories have generally failed to address 21st century challenges because they tend to focus on transformation from the outside in as opposed to changing from the inside out.[11] Transforming from the inside out turns conventional leadership theory upside down. It posits that in order to change someone else, one needs first to change oneself. Because the change of one system has a ripple effect on other interconnected systems, a leader changing from the inside out therefore has the power to transform others. This will most likely result in changes in the organisation and its performance and, ultimately, on society.

Spiritual leadership is therefore relevant because these leaders can transform others, organisations, and society by transforming themselves first. Strong *and* spiritual leadership, directed by a clear purpose and positive values, is therefore required to uproot corrupt practices and promote good corporate governance. Ethical, socially responsible leaders who lead by example are required. Organisations such as Google, 3M, Starbucks and Procter and Gamble have developed business models that promote "ethical leadership, employee wellbeing, sustainability and social responsibility".[12] They believe that the triple bottom line can be achieved while still yielding high profit, performance and quality.

Spiritual leadership encourages the experience of meaning and purpose at a personal and professional level. Feeling fulfilled in the workplace is, for some employees, even more important than earning a higher salary. When employees feel fulfilled in the workplace by being part of a values-based organisational context and practice, their performance tends to improve, which in turn improves financial performance and profit. Studies conducted in more than a hundred organisations show that spiritual leadership increased organisational commitment and productivity in these organisations.[13] Spiritual leaders tend to establish value-based organisations that are highly successful, profitable and productive because the high level of engagement fosters greater commitment among employees.[14]

Spiritual leaders operate within an entirely new organisational paradigm that replaces mechanistic organisational practices with dynamic spiritual practices. Organisations tend to achieve long-term sustainable success when they are socially responsible and guided by spiritual principles.[15] A study conducted by Collins and Porras revealed that organisations such as 3M, Hewlett-Packard, Disney and Marriot experienced sustainable growth and outperformed the stock market over a 64-year period because they were guided by a core purpose and values.[16]

Comparison between Spiritual Leadership and Emerging Leadership Theories

An alternative to a leader who operates within a mechanistic paradigm is a leader who operates within a spiritual paradigm. There are several emerging leadership theories that can be classified within a spiritual paradigm, including servant leadership, transformational leadership, authentic leadership, ethical leadership and spiritual leadership.

A *servant leader* is a leader who is dedicated to meeting the needs of others by serving others first, instead of either being driven by power or ego or wanting to lead first.[17] However, the problem with this leadership construct is that it values the needs of the followers above the needs of the organisation.[18] While this is noble, it may prove detrimental to an organisation, especially if the needs of either the followers or the employees are based on self-centred values.

According to Burns, *transformational leaders* strive to raise the level of morality and motivation of leaders and followers[19] by empowering them instead of keeping them weak and dependent.[20] However, transformational leadership theory is criticised for not determining the leader's motives, which may be based on selfish values.[21]

Authentic leaders are leaders "who are deeply aware of how they think and behave and are perceived by others as being aware of their own and others' values/moral perspective, knowledge and strength; aware of the context in which they operate and who are confident, hopeful, optimistic, resilient and high on moral character".[22] Authentic leadership is premised on the congruence between a leader's behaviour and internal values. The conceptual flaw is that a person's internal values may not be virtuous by nature. So dictators and rogues can be classified as authentic leaders as long as there is alignment between their behaviour and value systems.

Ethical leadership refers to leaders who seek to benefit followers, organisations and society by living in accordance with a system of normative beliefs and judgments as opposed to self-interest.[23] However, despite the fact that ethical leadership promotes trust and integrity in organisations,[24] its conceptual focus is so confined to ethical issues that it fails to cater for organisational performance issues that are unrelated to ethics.

Spiritual leadership has emerged from, and to a large extent embodies, many of the principles of the leadership theories operating within a spiritual paradigm. However, it has also overcome their conceptual shortfalls. Spiritual leaders operate from a positive value system, and their motivation for developing others is based on both a higher purpose and on values that are founded on a set of universal values.[25] In addition, spiritual leaders achieve congruence between the values, thoughts and behaviours of the leaders and employees in organisations.[26] Spiritual leaders are committed to improving themselves and learning from their mistakes by changing from the inside out and by emphasising self-transcendence. Although, essentially, spiritual leaders are driven by spiritual intelligence, they also acknowledge the value of emotional, physical and mental intelligence. Spiritual intelligence enables spiritual leaders to address 21st century concerns where individuals have lost their sense of purpose and meaning because of greed, power struggles, corruption, loss of trust, stress, and demotivation in their workplaces.[27]

Spiritual leaders promote and harness workplace spirituality which, in turn, is characterised by a strong sense of purpose. This sense of purpose inspires and provides meaning for others; promotes virtuous values such as trust, honesty, ethics and respect; applies humanistic work practices; and is tolerant of employees expressing their emotions without fear of reprisal.[28]

An Integrated Spiritual Leadership Model

The proposed Integrated Spiritual Leadership (ISL) model aims to provide a framework to help leaders address organisational problems and improve productivity through spiritual leadership. It is significant because it reflects the expected inputs, processes, outputs and outcomes of spiritual leadership, and can be used as a foundation for developing a spiritual leadership training or mentoring programme.

Purpose

The ISL model is driven by two core purposes. *Firstly*, the *key purpose* of the model is to promote the internal transformation of a leader. This is achieved by establishing the higher purpose and core positive value system that guides leaders' behaviour and enables them to make decisions. *Secondly*, the application of the four personal intelligences – rational intelligence (IQ), physical intelligence (PQ), emotional intelligence (EQ), and spiritual intelligence (SQ) – ensures that the leader will approach self-transcendence in a holistic and integrated manner.

Development

The ISL model has adapted and incorporated the common attributes and unique features that emerged from evaluation of a number of spiritual leadership models listed in Table 9.1.

Table 9.1: Evaluation of spiritual leadership models

Spiritual leadership model	Description
Zohar and Marshall's[29] 12 Transformative Principles Model	Developing spiritual intelligence by following 12 transformative principles
Kevin Cashman's[30] Seven Pathways Leadership Model	Developing leadership from the inside out
Stephen Covey's[31] Whole Person Leadership Model	Holistic leadership development by harnessing the four personal intelligences
Gilbert Fairholm's[32] spiritual leadership model	Conceptualisation of moral and selfless leaders who are committed to stewardship and service
The not-for-profit health group Memorial Hermann's[33] spiritual leadership model	Focusing on values; allowing employees to explore and express their spirituality; planning for and encouraging community involvement
Ferguson and Milliman's[34] spiritual leadership approach	Framework for effective organisational values, which emphasises authenticity, service to others and an alignment between personal and organisational values
Louis Fry's[35] spiritual leadership causal model	A model of the causal relationship between hope, faith, vision and altruistic love, which may instil a sense of calling and membership in others. In turn, this may improve organisational performance

Chapter 9: Spiritual leadership

Spiritual leadership model	Description
Margaret Benefiel's[36] organisational transformation model	Spiritual transformation
Sangeeta Parameshwar's[37] spiritual leaders with ego-transcendence	How spiritual principles contribute to the process of ego-transcendence
Cindy Wigglesworth's[38] 21 skills of spiritual intelligence	How to guide a leader's journey towards higher spiritual intelligence

Explanation

The ISL model comprises three core levels: spiritual leadership, the team, and the organisation, with the intention of improving performance at all three levels. The components of the ISL model and their interrelationships are set out in Figure 9.1.

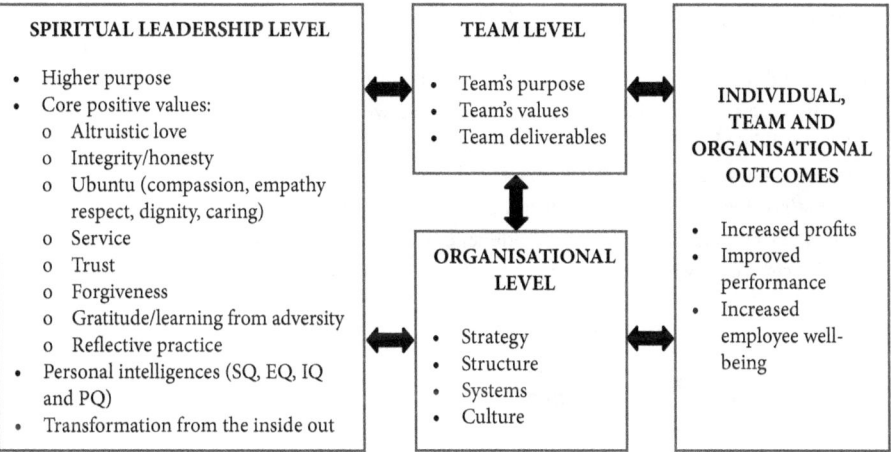

Figure 9.1: Integrated Spiritual Leadership Model

Spiritual Leadership Level

The spiritual leadership level comprises four key attributes, which form a collective whole and are necessary conditions for the successful functioning of a spiritual leader. The four key attributes of spiritual leadership are discussed in relation to the way in which they can be acquired and applied.

Higher purpose

Higher purpose refers to the way in which one expresses oneself and adds value in relation to following one's calling in life.[39] Purpose creates value as it inspires individuals to make a positive difference in the lives of others and the world. Purpose fosters authenticity by encouraging congruence between a person's purpose and actions. Purpose serves as a compass, keeping you on track with your life's course by directing one towards one's true north. Unlike a goal that is achievable, a purpose involves a life-long journey of self-discovery. Purpose should not be confused with a profession. Although it is preferable that there should be alignment between the two, a purpose extends beyond a profession in that it serves to direct all aspects of your life.

Having meaning and purpose is instrumental in transcending adversity.[40] People who have a clear purpose and meaning are able to transcend problems and are regarded by Frankl[41] as the primary motivation in life.

Asking the following questions can help one determine one's higher purpose:

- If money were of no concern in your life, how would you spend your time?
- What is your *raison d'être*, your reason for existing?
- What are your key strengths and talents, identified by you and others?
- What deeply motivates and inspires you?

Core positive values

Values refer to a set of core beliefs that define the way in which one ought to behave in a variety of situations.[42] Values are important in the context of spiritual leadership because they help spiritual leaders and their followers to live their higher purpose and find meaning at work, while offering moral guidance on their behaviour.[43] A core positive value system refers to values that are virtuous, ethically based and spiritual in nature. Positive values help the spiritual leader to transcend the ego and serve others.[44] Operating from explicit core positive values separates spiritual leadership from other leadership theories, in that the motives of a spiritual leader are founded and remain based on genuine and pure intentions.[45]

The core positive values set out in Figure 9.1 were selected on the basis that they have all been validated empirically. Many are exhibited by both spiritual and traditional leaders. However, values that are generally associated with spiritual leadership such as altruistic love, gratitude/positive use of adversity, forgiveness/acceptance and reflective practice were included to distinguish this model from other leadership models governed by values.

The eight core values for a spiritual leader as expanded are given in Table 9.2.

Table 9.2: Eight core values for a spiritual leader

Core values for a spiritual leader	Description
Altruistic love	Being selfless and giving unconditional love that is based on genuine care and wanting happiness for others[46]
Integrity/honesty	Being truthful and demonstrating complete congruence between one's values and behaviour[47]
Ubuntu	Embracing core spiritual leadership values such as compassion, respect, dignity, empathy and humility, with the intention of strengthening a community[48]
Service	Placing the interests of others before one's own interests, and giving generously of one's time, care and compassion[49]
Trust	Establishing a reciprocal relationship based on one person's confidence in another's integrity and reliability[50]
Forgiveness/ acceptance	Showing acceptance and gratitude rather than being weighed down by negative thoughts and experiences such as jealousy, gossip, failed expectations, hatred and revenge[51]

Core values for a spiritual leader	Description
Gratitude/positive use of adversity	Showing appreciation of a positive outcome, even if the positive outcome is perceived as either not earned or deserved,[52] and extracting positive lessons from a difficult experience
Reflective practice	Engaging in introspective practices such as journaling, meditation, prayer and being in nature to reframe your experience from a wider perspective[53]

Are your top five values as a reader consonant with these values? Reflecting without judgment on why there might be dissonance between the two sets of values should provide invaluable insight into the reasons for the manifestation of your current reality. Conscious and reflective application of the core positive values will alter your thoughts, behaviour and decisions, which will in turn transform your reality.

Personal intelligences

Despite the fact that spiritual intelligence may be regarded as the core intelligence, its harmonious functioning with the emotional, mental and physical dimensions of intelligence is crucial. An imbalance in one can adversely affect the effective functioning of the other dimensions.[54] The driver of the four dimensions is the spiritual dimension which serves as a compass and helps to direct attitudes and behaviours.[55]

However, each of the personal intelligences performs a critical, albeit different, role in ensuring that the spiritual leader changes from the inside out in a way that inspires others and makes a positive impact on organisations. Fostering the four intelligences contributes to the development of balanced leaders who possess the spiritual fortitude, emotional awareness, analytical abilities and physical agility required to overcome organisational problems.

A leader who applies the personal intelligences will demonstrate the following behaviours:

- Being driven by meaning, vision and values;[56] using intuition;[57] using higher purpose to overcome adversity;[58] and recognising their interconnectedness with everything in the universe;[59]
- Being aware of and able to regulate his/her own and other people's emotions;[60] and establish authentic relationships;[61]
- Applying rational, logical, analytical, metacognitive and problem-solving abilities;[62] and
- Healthy eating, exercise, and understanding the metaphysical reasons for illnesses in order to achieve balance in life.[63]

Wigglesworth[64] asserts that the four personal intelligences interrelate on several levels. The intelligences develop separately: a person who is highly developed in terms of mental intelligence may have poorly developed emotional and spiritual intelligence, and *vice versa*. However, the development of these intelligences is interdependent and interconnected. The development of one intelligence may "create a 'necessary but not sufficient condition' for growth" of another intelligence.[66] For example, some degree of cognitive development is required to attain advanced stages of spiritual development: a person with a high SQ is able to perceive issues from a multiplicity of perspectives. On the other hand, EQ development is necessary for SQ development because it is incumbent on a person with a high SQ to manage her or his own emotions effectively, as well as those of others, and to show empathy. In addition, the development of PQ is necessary for SQ development because the body serves as a barometer for spiritual, mental and emotional misalignments.

Transforming from the inside out

Transforming from the inside out refers to changing oneself first in order to effect change in others. Traditional leaders focus on changing the behaviours, attitudes and skills of others, with little or no emphasis on changing themselves. In contrast, spiritual leaders believe that in order to change others, one needs to change oneself first. An inside out approach is driven by spiritual leaders who live out their spirituality as opposed to talking or thinking about it. This in turn results in ethical wellbeing.[66]

Operating in accordance with an inside out approach implies that individuals take responsibility for their thoughts, actions and responses.[67] 'Victim' thinking is replaced by taking responsibility for one's own actions instead of blaming others, and being proactive in finding solutions.[68] In addition, according to Cooper,[69] the "inner attracts the outer" in the sense that one's internal and underlying values and thoughts attract lessons within the external context. If a situation in the external world is not desirable, one should first examine oneself, and then shift one's values, beliefs and feelings in order to alter one's reality.[70]

The inside out approach is based on a quantum reality in terms of which everything in the universe is made up of energy and is intrinsically interconnected.[71] Scientific advances in the area of brain plasticity in the fields of neurobiology and quantum physics have demonstrated that human beings are able to change the hardwiring of their brains.[72] By changing our thoughts, reframing events and experiences, we are able to rewire our brains.[73] From a quantum perspective, beliefs are vibrating energy patterns within an energy field, where a change of belief causes the quantum energy field to change.[74] Accordingly, positive thoughts, actions and feelings will create a positive reality. Negative thoughts, actions and feelings will create a negative reality.[75] Spiritual leaders operating from an inside out approach do not only accept that they have created their own reality – be it positive or negative – but also feel empowered to transform their reality and the realities of others.

Transforming one's beliefs involves two core processes: *firstly,* uncovering one's conscious and shadow beliefs, and, *secondly,* developing helpful beliefs. Conscious beliefs are beliefs one is aware of. Shadow beliefs are subconscious or hidden beliefs that are suppressed because they are too painful to face. Jung, who coined the notion of shadow beliefs, contended that they fall into two categories: *firstly*, the light shadows – hidden positive potentials such as unknown talents and gifts – and *secondly*, the dark shadows, which are problematic, destructive, and stop us from moving forward in life.[76]

Shadow beliefs often operate insidiously and sabotage conscious beliefs, plans and goals. For example, if one finds oneself never having the job or relationship that one desires, it could be because the shadow belief of "I'm not good enough" is overriding one's conscious belief. Jung argues that shedding light on shadow beliefs creates the opportunity to deal with the issue instead of permitting it to undermine your efforts continuously.

Uncovering shadow beliefs requires being conscious of how one's feelings and thoughts are projected onto others. It is common to project one's repressed thoughts onto others as a means of disassociating oneself from the negative thought. For example, if one believes that "my manager is controlling and mean", it could be an indicator of an unresolved shadow. We judge and criticise others because it is too painful to resolve the issues that we are attempting to suppress. However, when others reflect these behaviours, it brings strong emotions to the surface, and we often respond disproportionately to the situation.

If one identifies a pattern of people – former bosses, romantic partners and friends – who display this behaviour, then it is a clear indication that one has identified a shadow. One's animosity towards one's manager for being controlling and mean could, for example, have roots in one's own unresolved and subconscious beliefs about oneself as either being controlling and mean, or, on the contrary, being a pushover and unassertive, which might underpin a belief of being weak and worthless. The adage "if you spot it, you've got it" highlights that people we dislike are often our best teachers, because they provide us with invaluable opportunities to heal ourselves.[77] We inadvertently create experiences where we attract into our lives people who mirror our shadow beliefs as an attempt to heal subconscious thoughts and painful wounds.[78]

Changing beliefs is a relatively simple process but requires steadfast diligence and perseverance. Once the shadow belief has been exposed, it should be replaced by a helpful and supportive belief. The helpful belief must be developed based on the following principles:

- It should always be stated in the present tense so that you create the reality that you desire. Example, the belief "I **am** assertive" will be experienced in the current reality, as opposed to the belief "I **want to be** assertive" which would not be experienced in the present situation because it is phrased in the future state.
- It should be crafted as a positive statement. Phrasing the belief as "I am assertive" is preferable to "I am not weak", because the brain tends to focus on key words such as "weak" and tend to overlook minor words such as "not".
- It should be short and simple so that it can be repeated easily and effortlessly.

These helpful beliefs should be repeated extensively a minimum of 100 times a day. Even though there may be resistance to repeating these helpful beliefs initially, one should persevere. The subconscious mind does not know what is real and not real, even if the conscious mind can make this distinction. With constant repetition the subconscious mind establishes a vibrational pattern to create the desired thought so that the helpful belief is eventually accepted by the conscious mind as real.[79] Therefore, transforming from the inside out involves changing one's beliefs in order to change one's reality.

Team level

The team level depicted in Figure 9.1 refers to an area in which spiritual leaders are able to influence employees in the workplace. This level comprises team members and employees whose performance is guided by the team's purpose and values. The spiritual leadership level influences performance at a team level. In turn, the team level may influence both the behaviour of the spiritual leader and performance at an organisational level. Quantum physics has proven that everything is intrinsically interconnected.[80] This implies that the spiritual leader can affect the team, which in turn will affect the organisation.

The inspiration that flows from spiritual leadership should result in enhanced commitment and calling in the workplace. This in turn would lead to team members' greater sense of belonging, bolstering their work ethic and improving performance.

Organisational level

The organisational level represented in Figure 9.1 pertains to the leader's influence in the organisation both as an individual and through a team. Organisational performance refers to an organisation meeting its strategic targets and delivering services through managing the organisation's strategy, systems, structure and culture effectively. Organisational performance may be observed by an organisation meeting its targets; adhering to good corporate governance principles; improving service delivery; using funds in an efficient and effective way (getting more done with less); being environmentally friendly; and improving the lives of its employees and communities.

The organisational level comprises the organisational elements of strategy, structure, systems and culture. These elements are based on McKinsey's 7-S framework, which depicts seven key interrelated organisational elements: strategy, structure, staff, systems, skills, style and shared values.[81] These elements are categorised as hard elements (strategy, structure and systems) and soft elements (shared values, style, staff and skills).[82] The collection of soft elements is referred to as organisational culture. Organisational strategy should determine the development and operation of the organisational structure, systems and culture, while the organisational elements are influenced by the actions of the spiritual leadership and the teams. Likewise, the organisational elements may influence the functioning of the spiritual leader and the teams.

The spiritual leadership, team and organisational levels are therefore interconnected in a dynamic and synergistic manner. While the spiritual leader should influence the direction of the teams and the organisation, the team and the organisational levels also influence each other as well as the spiritual leader. The role of the spiritual leader is to ensure that leadership, teams and organisation are aligned in terms of purpose and values, and to involve relevant stakeholders at multiple levels to promote buy-in to the ISL model.

Individual, team and organisational outcomes

In Figure 9.1 the application of the four attributes of a spiritual leader – higher purpose, core positive values, transformation from the inside out, and personal intelligences – all promote individual, team and organisational outcomes. This extends beyond financial bottom-line indicators to fostering self-transcendence; increased employee satisfaction; and establishing ethical businesses that operate on environmentally sustainable principles. The spiritual leader's influence on the team contributes to increasing feelings of calling and membership as employees feel that they are making a difference to the workplace and to communities, which in turn has a positive impact on the organisation as a whole.

Conclusion

This chapter presented the ISL model, which was developed by selecting the core aspects that emerged after a comparative analysis of ten spiritual leadership models. The model aims to promote the internal transformation of the spiritual leader and to inspire others to improve organisational performance. It comprises three core levels: the spiritual leadership, team, and organisational levels. These levels are interconnected and should be aligned if the organisation is to function optimally. The spiritual leadership level displays four key attributes: higher purpose and vision; core positive values; application of personal intelligences; and transformation from the inside out. The three core levels all influence individual, team and organisational outcomes by improving performance and employee wellbeing, leading to increased profit.

Unlike conventional leaders, it is argued that spiritual leaders are able to address 21st century organisational ailments related to ethical issues; concerns related to a loss of meaning and purpose; demotivation in the work place; and decreased productivity and profit due to a rise in stress-related diseases. Because spiritual leaders operate from a higher purpose and core positive values they are able to rise above adversity and resistance to change. A key benefit of the ISL model is that it can be used to transform individuals from inside out, and create a desired reality by changing beliefs. Because everything is interconnected, the spiritual leader can have a positive impact on the team, which in turn can have a positive effect on the organisation.

Endnotes

1. Transparency International, 2014, p. 6.
2. Runde, 2015.
3. White, 2016.
4. Howard & Welbourn, 2004, p. 17.
5. Skosana, 2014.
6. Fry & Slocum, 2008, p. 89.
7. Tsaenko and Tojib, 2012, p. 1121; Joseph & Sailakshmi, 2011, p. 21.
8. Morton et al. 2011, p. 2; Christians, 2015, p. 565.
9. Zohar & Marshall, 2004.
10. Fry, 2003, p. 706.
11. Cashman, 1998.
12. Fry & Slocum, 2008, p. 89.
13. Fry, Vitucci & Cedillo, 2005, p. 836; Fry, Matherly & Ouimet, 2010, p. 290.
14. Barrett, 2013.
15. Zohar & Marshall, 2004.
16. Spiritual Capital Foundation, 2014.
17. Keith, 2009, p. 1.
18. Sendjaya, Sarros & Santora, 2008, p. 403.
19. Burns, 1978, p. 20, cited in Covey, 2004, p. 355.
20. Sendjaya et al., 2008, p. 403.
21. Fry & Whittington, 2005a, p. 13.
22. Walumbwa et al., 2008; Klenke, 2007, p. 71.
23. Kalshoven, Den Hartog & De Hoogh, 2011, p. 52.
24. Brown, 2007, p. 151.
25. Fry & Whittington, 2005b, p. 193.
26. Fry & Whittington, 2005b, p. 191.
27. Fry & Whittington, 2005b, p. 184; Zohar & Marshall, 2004, p. 13.
28. Robbins et al., 2011.
29. Zohar & Marshall, 2004.
30. Cashman, 1998.
31. Covey, 2004.
32. Fairholm, 1998, p. 13.
33. Wolf, 2004, p. 24.
34. Ferguson & Milliman, 2008.
35. Fry, 2009.
36. Benefiel, 2005.
37. Parameshwar, 2005.
38. Wigglesworth, 2014.
39. Cashman, 1998, p. 64.
40. Cashman, 1998.
41. Frankl, 1985, p. 211.
42. Kuper, 2006, p. 17.
43. Ferguson & Milliman, 2008, p. 443.
44. Altman, 2010.
45. Fry & Kriger, 2009.
46. Caldwell & Dixon, 2010, p. 91.
47. Fry & Kriger, 2009, p. 1681.
48. Mangaliso, 2001, p. 26; Poovan, Du Toit & Engelbrecht, 2006, p. 17.
49. Patterson, 2003, p. 25.
50. Standifer, Evans & Dong, 2010, p. 138.
51. Fry & Kriger, 2009, p. 1681.
52. Wood, Joseph & Linley, 2007, p. 19.
53. Zohar & Marshall, 2004, p. 100.
54. Covey, 2004.
55. Zohar & Marshall, 2004.
56. De Klerk-Weyer & Le Roux, 2008, p. 111.
57. Ibid.
58. Zohar & Marshall, 2004.
59. Buzan, 2001, p. 7.
60. Goleman, 1998.
61. Cashman, 1998, p. 130.
62. De Klerk-Weyer & Le Roux, 2008.
63. Ibid.
64. Wigglesworth, 2006, p. 3.
65. Wigglesworth, 2006.
66. Miller, 2004, p. 20.
67. Cashman, 1998; Fry & Whittington, 2005b, p. 189.
68. Shapiro, 2005; Page & Hagenbach, 1999; Covey, 2004; Cashman, 1998.
69. Cooper, 2004, p. 21.
70. Ibid.
71. Kehoe, 2011, p. 31.
72. Kim, 2009, p. 33; Tipping, 2010.
73. Kim, 2009, p. 34; Kehoe, 2011, p. 12; Zohar & Marshall, 2004, p. 80.
74. Kehoe, 2011, p. 53.
75. Kehoe, 2011; Emoto, 2005.
76. Kehoe, 2011, p. 98.
77. Tipping, 2010, p. 83.
78. Tipping, 2010, p. 84.
79. Kehoe, 2011, p. 96.
80. Kehoe, 2011, p. 35.
81. Have et al., 2003, p. 138.
82. Ibid.

References

Altman, Y. 2010. 'In search of spiritual leadership: Making a connection with transcendence'. *Human Resource Management International Digest*, 18(6):35–38.

Barrett, R. 2013. *The values-driven organization: Unleashing human potential for performance and profit*. London, UK: Routledge.

Benefiel, M. 2005. 'The second half of the journey: Spiritual leadership for organizational transformation'. *The Leadership Quarterly*, 16(5):723–747.

Brown, ME. 2007. 'Misconceptions of ethical leadership: How to avoid potential pitfalls'. *Organizational Dynamics*, 36(2):140–155.

Burns, JM. 1978. *Leadership*. New York, NY: Harper and Row.

Buzan, T. 2001. *The power of spiritual intelligence*. London, UK: Thorsons.

Caldwell, C & Dixon, RD. 2010. 'Love, forgiveness, and trust: Critical values of the modern leader'. *Journal of Business Ethics*, 93(1):91–101.

Cashman, K. 1998. *Leadership from the inside out*. Minneapolis, MN: TCLG.

Christians, L-L. 2015. 'Ideologically oriented enterprises faced with reconfiguration of ethics and spiritual management'. *Brigham Young University Law Review*, 2014(3):565–584.

Cooper, D. 2004. *A little light on the spiritual laws*. London, UK: Hodder & Stoughton.

Covey, S. 2004. *The 8th habit: From effectiveness to greatness*. London, UK: Simon & Schuster.

De Klerk-Weyer, R & Le Roux, R. 2008. *Emotional intelligence: A workbook for your wellbeing*. Cape Town, South Africa: Human & Rousseau.

Emoto, M. 2005. *The true power of water: Healing and discovering ourselves*. London, UK: Simon & Schuster.

Fairholm, G. 1998. 'Leadership as an exercise in virtual reality'. *Leadership & Organization Development Journal*, 19(4):187–193.

Ferguson, J & Milliman, J. 2008. 'Creating effective core organizational values: A spiritual leadership approach'. *International Journal of Public Administration*, 31(4):439–459.

Frankl, V. 1985. *Man's search for meaning*. New York, NY: Pocket Books.

Fry, LW. 2003. 'Toward a theory of spiritual leadership'. *The Leadership Quarterly*, 14(6):693–727.

Fry, LWJ. 2009. 'Spiritual leadership as a model for student inner development'. *Journal of Leadership Studies*, 3(3):79–83.

Fry, L & Kriger, M. 2009. 'Towards a theory of of being-centred leadership: Multiple levels of being as context for effective leadership'. *Human Relations*, 61(11):1667–1696.

Fry, LW, Matherly, LL & Ouimet, JR. 2010. 'The spiritual leadership balanced scorecard business model: the case of the Cordon Bleu-Tomasso Corporation'. *Journal of Management, Spirituality & Religion*, 7(4):283–314.

Fry, LW & Slocum, JW. 2008. 'Maximizing the triple bottom line through spiritual leadership'. *Organizational Dynamics*, 37(1):86–96.

Fry, LW, Vitucci, S & Cedillo, M. 2005. 'Spiritual leadership and army transformation: Theory measurement, and establishing a baseline'. *The Leadership Quarterly*, 16(5):835–862.

Fry, LW & Whittington, JL. 2005a. *Spiritual leadership as a paradigm for organization transformation and development*. Paper presented at the National Academy of Management Meeting. Honolulu, Hawaii. 1–45.

Fry, LW & Whittington, JL. 2005b. 'In search of authenticity: Spiritual leadership theory as a source for future theory, research, and practice of authentic leadership'. In B Avolio, W Gardner & F Walumbwa. *Authentic leadership theory and practice: Origins, effects, and development*. Monographs in Leadership and Management Series, Vol. 3. 183–200.

Goleman, D. 1998. *Working with emotional intelligence*. London, UK: Bloomsbury.

Have, S, Have, W, Stevens, F & Van der Elst, M. 2003. *Key management model*. Harlow, UK: Pearson Education.

Howard, S & Welbourn, D. 2004. *The Spirit at work phenomenon*. London, UK: Azure.

Kalshoven, K, Den Hartog, DN & De Hoogh, AHB. 2011. 'Ethical leadership at work questionnaire (ELW): Development and validation of a multidimensional measure'. *The Leadership Quarterly*, 22(1):51–69.

Kehoe, J. 2011. *Quantum warrior: The future of the mind*. Vancouver, CAN: Zoetic.

Keith, KM. 2009. 'Servant-leaders are the best leaders during times of change'. *Branches Magazine*, 21(6):1–5, January–February.

Kim, L. 2009. 'Improving the workplace with spirituality: 1+1=5'. *The Journal for Quality and Participation*, 32(3):32–35.

Klenke, K. 2007. 'Authentic leadership: A self, leader, and spiritual identity perspective'. *International Journal of Leadership Studies*, 3(1):68–97.

Kuper, L. 2006. *Ethics: The leadership edge*. Paarl, ZA: Zebra Press.

Joseph, C & Sailakshmi, S. 2011. 'Spiritual intelligence at work'. *Journal of Soft Skills*, 5(4):21–30.

Mangaliso, MP. 2001. 'Building competitive advantage from ubuntu: Management lessons from South Africa'. *Academy of Management Executive*, 15(3):23–33.

Miller, W. 2004. 'Want to be a revolutionary leader?' *Management Next*, 20.

Morton, DM, Byrne, CJ, Dahling, JJ & Chau, SL. 2011. 'Spirituality, religion, and emotional labor in the workplace'. *Meeting Abstract Supplement*, 1–6. Academy of Management Annual Meeting Proceedings.

Page, C & Hagenbach, K. 1999. *Mind, body, spirit workbook: A handbook for health*. Essex, UK: Saffron Waldon.

Parameshwar, S. 2005. 'Spiritual leadership through ego-transcendence: Exceptional Responses to challenging circumstances'. *The Leadership Quarterly*, 16(5):689–772.

Patterson, KA. 2003. *Servant leadership: A theoretical model*. PhD thesis. Virginia Beach, VA: School of Leadership Studies, Regent University.

Poovan, N, Du Toit, MK & Engelbrecht, AS. 2006. 'The effect of social values of ubuntu on team effectiveness'. *South African Journal of Business Management*, 37(3):17–27.

Robbins, SP, Judge, TA, Odendaal, A & Roodt, G. 2011. *Organisational behaviour: Global and Southern African perspectives*. 2nd ed. Cape Town, ZA: Pearson.

Runde, D. 2015. *It's time to get serious about global corruption*. [Online]. Available: http://www.forbes.com/sites/danielrunde/2015/01/22/time-to-get-serious-global-corruption/#316dd2ec4fae. [Accessed 21 February 2016].

Sendjaya, S, Sarros, J & Santora, J. 2008. 'Defining and measuring servant leadership behaviour in organizations'. *Journal of Management Studies*, 45(2):402–424.

Shapiro, D. 2005. *Your body speaks your mind: Understand how your thoughts and emotions affect your health*. London, UK: Piatkus.

Skosana, I. 2014. 'Work absenteeism costs SA economy R16bn a year'. *Mail & Guardian*, 12 August. [Online]. Available: http://bhekisisa.org/article/2014-08-12-sa-losing-r16bn-a-year-due-to-absenteeism. [Accessed 22 May 2016].

Spiritual Capital Foundation. 2014. *The bottom line business benefits*. [Online]. Available: http://www.spiritual-capital.org/what-is-spiritual-capital-2/the-bottom-line-business-benefits/. [Accessed 23 May 2016].

Standifer, RL, Evans, KR & Dong, B. 2010. 'The influence of spirituality on buyer perception within business-to-business marketing relationships: A cross-cultural exploration and comparison'. *Journal of Relationship Marketing*, 9(3):132–160.

Tipping, CC. 2010. *Spiritual intelligence at work*. Marietta, GA: Global 13 Publications.

Transparency International. 2014. *Transparency in corporate reporting*. [Online]. Available: https://issuu.com/transparencyinternational/docs/2014_transparencyincorporatereporti?e=2496456/9997410. [Accessed 21 February y 2016].

Walumbwa, F, Avolio, B, Gardner, W, Wernsing, T & Peterson, S. 2008. 'Authentic leadership: Development and validation of theory-based measure'. *Journal of Management*, 34(1):89–126.

White, T. 2016. *Global economic crime survey 2016*. 5th South African edition, March 2016. [Online]. Available: https://www.pwc.co.za/en/assets/pdf/south-african-crime-survey-2016.pdf. [Accessed 29 May 2016].

Wigglesworth, C. 2006. 'Why Spiritual Intelligence Is Essential to Mature Leadership.' [Online]. Available: http://integralleadershipreview.com/5502-feature-article-why-spiritual-intelligence-is-essential-to-mature-leadership/? [Accessed 1 July 2016].

Wigglesworth, C. 2014. *SQ 21: The twenty-one skills of spiritual intelligence*. New York, NY: Select Books.

Wolf, EJ. 2004. 'Spiritual leadership: A new Model'. *Healthcare Executive*, 19(2):22–25.

Wood, A, Joseph, S & Linley, A. 2007. 'Gratitude: Parent of all virtues'. *The Psychologist*, 20(1):18–21.

Zohar, D & Marshall, I. 2004. *Spiritual capital*. London, UK: Bloomsbury.

Chapter 10

ETHICAL LEADERSHIP

Leon van Vuuren

It is assumed for the purpose of this chapter that organisational leaders are those people in organisations who have perceived and/or real power. They are in positions where they can influence others with whom they engage, are responsible for decisions with significant consequences, and act as role models. Not all leaders necessarily have a leadership competence; nor do they necessarily have an ethics competence.

The definition of ethics subscribed to by The Ethics Institute is that ethics concerns itself with what is good or right in human interaction. It revolves around three central concepts: 'self', 'good' and 'other', as depicted in Figure 10.1.[1]

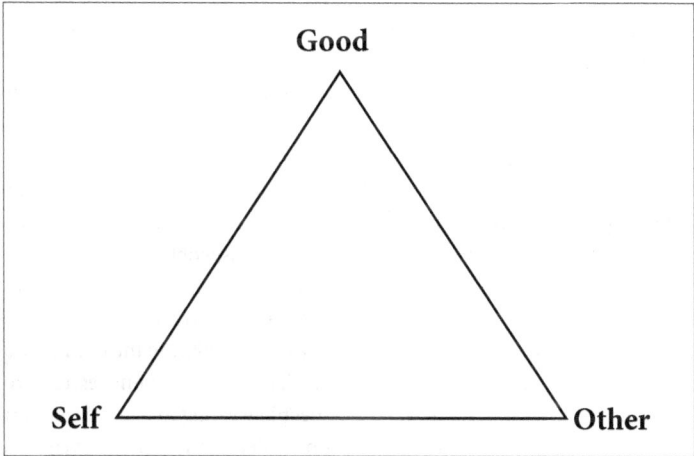

Figure 10.1: Central concepts in Ethics: Self, Good, Other

In terms of Figure 10.1, ethical behaviour results when one does not merely consider what is good for oneself but also what is good for others. Both the self and the other can refer to an individual, a group or an organisation. Organisational ethics is about a concept of what good qualities (values and standards) guide the organisation (self) in its interaction with the other (stakeholders) in a sustainable way.

Leaders are confronted on a daily basis with ethics challenges that call for explicit or implicit actions. Some of these challenges require a conscious awareness that the challenge is indeed of an ethical nature. Challenges that are, however, less overt in terms of tangible ethical consequences and call on a leader to deal subconsciously with them also occur. Irrespective of whether these challenges are dealt with consciously or subconsciously, they nevertheless need to be addressed to avoid immediate or delayed ethics fallout. This consequently raises the following questions:

- Why do ethically challenging situations occur?
- Why do leaders allow this to happen?
- What could they do, or what do they require, to pre-empt such situations and competently prepare themselves and their followers to deal with the challenge?

This chapter is structured by means of a realistic case study to be presented upfront. Thereafter the questions raised above will be dealt with in turn by continuous referral to the situation as described in the case study. International, organisational and individual contextual reasons for pressure to act unethically will first be presented. Secondly, potential reasons are examined for the frequently observed inadequacy of leaders to pre-empt ethical challenges and to deal effectively with these when they do occur. Lastly, an approach to leadership will be suggested that could potentially be utilised to address organisational ethical issues. This approach includes the respective potential contributions of ethics awareness, ethical behaviour, ethics management, and ethical decision-making to the formation of sustainable ethical organisational cultures.

Case Study: Go Big or Go Home[2]

Case description

You are the director of technology procurement of a large electricity supply organisation based in Johannesburg, South Africa, and you have just arrived at the international airport in Kinshasa (DRC). You have travelled via Nairobi from Singapore, where you attended an electrical engineering conference. The temperature inside the airport's arrivals hall is 40°C, and the humidity is in the 90s.

You are a key decision maker in a multimillion dollar capital equipment deal. You are due to meet with potential business partners from China and France later the same day. They will be in Kinshasa for one day only. Some of these businesspeople had travelled on the same flight as you had. Others had arrived earlier that morning from other destinations.

When going through passport control at Kinshasa Airport you are informed that the date of the inoculation as displayed on your yellow card is illegible to the immigration official. Yellow fever inoculation has a ten-year lifespan. Many African countries require proof of yellow fever inoculation by tourists and businesspeople wishing to enter the countries by air or ground transportation. Proof of inoculation is provided in the form of a yellow fever card, which is also yellow in colour. Immigration officials inspect travellers' yellow cards when they present their passports upon entering a country.

The French-speaking immigration official communicates with you in broken English. You are given the following choices: (a) to pay a 'yellow card fine' of US$300 to enter the DRC; (b) to return to Johannesburg on the next flight that leaves in an hour; or (c) to receive a yellow fever inoculation injection right there in the arrivals hall. Leaning over a table behind the uniformed immigration official is another official wearing a rather soiled white coat and a stethoscope around his neck. On the table are several syringes filled with an amber-coloured fluid and some cotton balls. You notice a speck of blood on one of the cotton balls. Some of the needles are not protected by the usual plastic cover. In despair you take your mobile phone from your pocket. There is no signal ... There are several heavily-armed Congolese policemen hovering in the arrivals hall. Since this situation is holding up the queue, some of your fellow passengers are peering over your shoulder to ascertain the source of the delay.

Chapter 10: Ethical leadership

Case analysis

Courses of action and implications

Does your interpretation resemble the following?

- You are probably quite desperate to be present and on time for the meeting arranged to construct the deal.
- You know that your yellow card is in order and has not yet expired.
- The immigration official is using a random ploy to solicit a bribe from you ('yellow card fine' was presented in inverted commas in the text above – no such thing exists and it is used as a euphemism for a bribe).
- You probably feel intimidated.
- The meeting is important to your career.
- The meeting is important to your employer – opportunities like these are rare and the deal could be extremely advantageous financially and even lead to the creation of several jobs.
- If you are delayed further at the airport and act defiantly there is no doubt that you'll miss your meeting.
- You cannot contact others via your mobile phone, to alert them that you could be late for the meeting or not attend at all.
- You have to rely on your own judgement and resources to make a decision.
- If you do pay a bribe, you cannot claim it as legitimate travel expenses (you will not get a receipt from the officer).
- You could hardly bribe the official without others knowing about it; for example, the passengers peering over your shoulder could be the very business partners that you will meet later that day.

Consider the following options and potential consequences:

	Option	Analysis and consequences
1	You decide to take your chances and agree to have the inoculation administered (after all, it does look like a qualified medical doctor or healthcare worker who is administering the injections).	Very few people would choose this option – the first ethical decision human beings make is to preserve their own life – receiving an injection under these circumstances could be life-threatening as you could contract a nasty disease from the unhygienic needles.

	Option	Analysis and consequences
2	You pay the official a cash bribe (for example, with three US$100 bills that you fold and tuck inside your passport when you hand it to him).	- This option is both illegal and unethical. - It could be a trap – you could be arrested and be locked up in a Kinshasa jail for some time until the matter is resolved. If the passengers peering over your shoulder are those with whom you will meet and they witness you bribing the official, a shadow could be cast over your integrity, or, alternatively, you could be perceived as 'bribeable'. - If your manager back at the office is a person of integrity you may lose your credibility in his/her eyes. - If your organisation has a strict anti-bribery policy, you could actually be dismissed should they find out about your action.
3	You decide to bribe and get on with, but negotiate an amount that is much less, as a 'minor' bribe would make you feel better.	Similar consequences to those in Option 2 above. Irrespective of the size of a bribe, it is both illegal and unethical.
4	You call his bluff and ask him to consult with others officials on the matter (in the hope that they are not corrupt or part of the 'scheme').	This is grasping at straws – other officials will probably concur with their colleague. You will merely 'delay the inevitable'. Besides, the language barrier will suddenly become more pronounced. You will still have to pay the 'fine' if you want to get to your meeting.
5	You politely refuse to pay the bribe and tell them that the date on your yellow card is legitimate and still within the ten-year timeframe. If your action is unsuccessful, you could probably decide to return home on the next flight.	This is the best option from both a legal and an ethical position. It is, however, unlikely that you will make him change his mind. It is not easy to do the right thing in such intimidating circumstances, though. As in Option 4 above, the language barrier will suddenly become more pronounced. Also, that implies that you will have to return home and therefore miss your meeting. Should your organisation turn a blind eye to situations like these and call bribes 'small routine' payments or 'facilitation payments', this could be seriously career limiting; you may even lose your job and have to face the consequences that come with such events.

Chapter 10: Ethical leadership

	Option	Analysis and consequences
6	You pay the bribe, but note down his name and badge number so that you can report him to his manager later.	Similar consequences to those in Option 2 above. The action would still be both illegal and unethical.
7	You confront him loudly and aggressively by giving him a lecture on why bribes are wrong and tell him in no uncertain terms that you will not pay the bribe.	This is most likely the worst course of action. The chances are good that you will be confronted by the armed security personnel and be arrested on a trumped-up charge, for example, for obstructing justice. Your initial 'fine' could then become a real one.
8	You plead with him to give you a chance and to let you go.	This is unlikely to have an effect – he is probably a seasoned campaigner in soliciting these types of 'fines' and will be adamant that you pay immediately. Again, the language barrier could come into play. You will still have to pay the 'fine' if you want to get to your meeting.
9	You ask him to allow you to go to your meeting and promise to return later to 'sort the whole thing out'.	It is a good option, but it is unlikely that your request will be granted. He will merely emphasise his initial take and say that your yellow card has expired and that you may not enter the country. You will still have to pay the 'fine' if you want to get to your meeting.
10	Any other?	?

What are the optimal options for this situation? A sound idea at this point would be to eliminate the options that could endanger your life or cause you potential harm. These are obviously Options 1, 4, 6 and 7.

You could then also eliminate other options that are founded in desperation and will most likely be ineffective in the situation. These would be Options 8 and 9: you plead with him to give you a chance and to let you go, or to come later to sort things out. Although Option 9 is a reasonable request, it is unlikely to succeed.

Option 5 is the option that is the only option that is courageous and both legal and ethical. The reality is, though, that the situation at the airport is intimidating, you are tired from flying, and you just want to get on with your life (and attend the meeting). Although most people agree that bribery is wrong, it is sometimes difficult to apply this value in trying situations.

The Ethical Challenge: Right, Wrong and Grey

An overwhelming majority of people in the world can distinguish between right and wrong. Most people and cultures will, for example know that 'treating others with respect' is right, good and just. The same people will agree that child molestation is wrong, bad and unjust. Employees in organisations know that keeping customer information confidential is right, and that stealing organisational property is wrong. The yellow-card scenario is actually an ethical dilemma or grey area. It causes uncertainty – if you pay the bribe, there will be negative consequences; if you refuse to fall for the official's effort to get you to bribe him, there could be negative consequences.

Not all ethics challenges are dilemmas, however. People mostly agree on the majority of things that are right and the majority of things that are wrong. In life, 99% of people in different societies and cultures know that taking innocent life is wrong. The same people know that preserving life is right. However, when societal ethical dilemmas such as abortion, the death penalty and euthanasia become topics of conversation, the same people will be divided in their opinions on right and wrong. Hence, grey areas are part of life as we know it.

By a similar token, not all ethics challenges in organisations are dilemmas. Employees all know that assaulting a manager because one did not agree with an instruction is bad and wrong. The same employees know that treating colleagues with respect is good and right. But then, different opinions on certain challenges emerge. As such, even the immigration official at Kinshasa Airport demands payment for a 'yellow card tax' rather than explicitly asking for a bribe – inherently he knows the difference between right and wrong and finds it difficult to use the word 'bribe'. Other examples of workplace ethical dilemmas are perceptions of whether accepting or receiving gifts is ethically sound behaviour; what types of behaviour actually constitute sexual harassment; under what circumstances conflicts of interest occur; and when employees actually perceive organisational demands on their time and resources as excessive and unfair.

We can now proceed to answer the questions posed in the introduction: Why do ethically challenging situations occur? Why do leaders allow this to happen? What could they do, or what do they require, to pre-empt such situations and competently prepare themselves and their followers to deal with the challenge? The questions will be dealt with under the headings: Reasons for pressure to act unethically; leadership ethics inadequacy; and a leadership approach to ethics. The case study will be referred to throughout.

Reasons for Pressure to Act Unethically

These reasons will be contextually categorised as international (cultural), organisational, and individual reasons.

International (cultural) context

The adage exists that it is quite acceptable to pay bribes or 'facilitation fees' in certain countries around the world, and particularly in Africa. The yellow card 'fine' would therefore be part of the 'way they do things in the DRC' and who are we to judge that? After all, that is how business is conducted in the DRC and elsewhere in Africa. Furthermore, the bribe is actually enabling a low-income earner, the immigration official, to survive in one of the poorest countries in the world.

The DRC is merely an example of a country marked by endemic corruption according to Transparency International's (TI) annual *Corruptions Perceptions Survey*.[3] The case study could have played out in many other countries.

The fact is that it is quite easy to get caught up in some countries' cultures of corruption when having to conduct business there or when dealing directly with their citizens. Although the majority of European countries are perceived to be corruption-free, until quite recently many of these countries perceived corruption to be acceptable and believed the myth 'when in Rome ...' when their organisations had to conduct business elsewhere in the world, and in the developing world in particular. Germany and France abolished the laws whereby organisations from these countries qualified for tax rebates after having had to pay bribes in other countries in order to ensure the acquisition of business deals, only in 1997 and 2001 respectively. Ironically, the said laws could not contain the word 'bribery' and its derivatives – therefore the euphemism 'facilitation fees' was coined. Organisations from these countries naturally fuelled corruption in Africa and elsewhere.

The question may be raised as to whether there was pernicious intent by such organisations. Since most people inherently know the difference between right and wrong, probably not. It could be surmised that these organisations and their members acted out of ignorance and have yet to interrogate the ill effects of corruption and bribery on the world's economy, and specifically how it is usually the poor who are affected most, and detrimentally so. The monetary gap between most countries' highest earners versus their lowest earners is actually globally on the increase. This may be ascribed to the failure of capitalism's 'invisible hand' to regulate the free market system through the assumed principle of fair distribution. However, it could also be the unreasonable greed of the rich and the subsequent disdain of the plight of the poor and vulnerable. Furthermore, the world of business may be viewed as an amoral one, where business and ethics cannot mix, and where dog can eat dog.

The evolution of ethics in business since approximately the late 1980s, and more vigorously in the post-Enron (2001) era, have brought a sense of rationality to business and how corruption is addressed. It could be that the onset and continual refinement of corporate governance guidelines and related legislation have been responses by society to protect vulnerable stakeholders while still encouraging business success – therefore enterprise with integrity. The 'when in Rome' justification of unethical behaviour as a result of the culture and customs of other countries has become an irrational cop-out. The unconditional acceptance of such practices has been replaced with defiance in many parts of the world. Many organisations are actually sending out clear signals about their ethical stance in certain international contexts – an example here is the recent withdrawal of the Dutch-based organisation Brunel and its €100 million annual contribution from Nigeria.

Organisational context

Culture

Should the apples (= employees) and barrels (= organisations) analogy be applied in business, the increased focus on the (ethical) state of the barrels is quite significant. The ethical state of the barrel is nothing but the ethical culture of the organisation. Whereas organisational culture could be practically described as "the way we do things here", the organisation's ethical culture could possibly be described as "the way we do things here even when no one is watching". Cultures shape values, beliefs and attitudes, and ultimately, behaviour.

Although organisations may survive for many years on *laissez-faire* approaches to ethics, truly sustainable organisations proactively build cultures marked by ethical leadership, ethics awareness, ethical decision-making, sustained ethical behaviour (= ethical action), and accountability for unethical behaviour. A truly ethical culture cannot be achieved in the short term, but requires sustained leadership commitment to ensure an ethical culture over time. As with any organisational culture-change exercise, the formation of an ethical culture could take years to reach maturity.

If one classifies people into three categories for the purpose of this discussion, one might say that (1) the minority of people are truly 'good' and will never compromise their ethics (= the good apples, or the unbendable); (2) a small number of people who are truly 'bad' (= bad apples, or the bent), such as those who cannot be rehabilitated or are recidivists. One could then perhaps speculate that the majority of people are (3) decent but dubious (in other words, they are bendable). The last category implies that people will do good or bad depending on their circumstances – in strong ethical cultures (= good barrels), such individuals will tend to remain 'decent'; but in ethically weak or unethical cultures (= bad barrels), the same people may veer in the 'wrong' direction. Examples of how ethical behaviour manifests in organisations that are in different states of ethics are shown in Table 10.1.[4]

Table 10.1: States of ethics in organisations

Amoral	Survival	Reactive	Compliance	Integrity	Totally aligned
Philosophy and practice exist that business and ethics cannot mix The free market system and taxes will bring balance Ethical consequences of business decisions ignored	Survival ethics (money before ethics) Lack of ethics awareness Many unethical practices, some even encouraged	Awareness of ethics risk Some ethical standards in place Blind eye turned to unethical behaviour	Prevent unethical behaviour People are told not to do bad things Rules-based	Promote ethical behaviour People do good things because they want to Values-based	Organisation's identity is distinctively ethical Ethics is embedded as strategic value Ethics is a way of life in the organisation

Source: *Adapted from Rossouw & van Vuuren, 2013*

Six states (or modes) of organisations' ethics are depicted in Table 10.1, namely amoral, survival, reactive, compliance, integrity, and totally aligned. Each state is characterised by collectively different perceptions of ethics in business and therefore different ethical cultures. Organisations in the *amoral* mode are devoid of an ethics mindset, while those in the *survival* mode are intentionally unethical, based on a dog-eat-dog mantra. The employees (= apples) in such organisations may experience anxiety resulting from cognitive dissonance, as their own values may be contradictory to those 'lived' in the organisational context. No overt ethical standards exist to guide them. Although ethically *reactive* organisations are aware of ethics risk and have adopted ethical standards, the latter exist purely for window-dressing purposes and are not necessarily enforced. The apples are confused as a result of inconsistencies between standards and behaviour.

Organisations, or barrels, in the *compliance* and *integrity* modes are serious about ethics. In the compliance mode there is zero tolerance for unethical behaviour as prescribed by numerous rules; while in the integrity mode, an ethics-mindedness is encouraged. However, the apples in the compliance barrel may try to get away with things that are not explicitly forbidden. Integrity-mode organisations probably still have some rules that act as a safety net and guide employees' behaviour. Ethics is undisputed and a way of life in the *totally aligned organisation* – the apples feel secure here and do the right thing naturally.

In essence, the modes of ethics as described above reflect the strength of ethical culture. Organisations in the survival mode may have no ethical culture. Those that are perhaps in the integrity mode may have a strongly developing ethical culture. An organisation that is totally aligned has ethical cultures that are core to the organisation's identity and seamlessly integrated with all organisational activities.

Application to case study

What would the way of thinking about the yellow card 'fine' be in each of these modes? It would be quite easy for the employees, even good apples, in amoral, survival or reactive organisations to pay the bribe and get the business done. Compliance barrels' apples might be punished for such behaviour. Employees in integrity barrels would cast shame on themselves and their organisations and dent their reputations. No apple in the totally aligned barrel would ever consider paying a bribe, unless, of course, they find themselves in a life-threatening situation. However, real life-threatening situations seldom occur, and we mostly have choices and time to decide on whether to do the right thing or not.

Since leadership is inextricably responsible for the development of organisational culture, and therefore also for organisational *ethical* culture, the leadership in each of these modes is directly responsible for the culturally induced behaviour of their followers. Should the 'big apples' be ethically negligent or reckless, their employees will pay bribes at airports and readily indulge in other forms of unethical behaviour. The converse applies, in that leaders in organisations that are ethically sound, be these organisations rules- or values-based, would frown upon such behaviour and address it assertively.

Rewards and incentives

Organisational reward and incentive systems are mostly structured more around 'what' performance is achieved than around 'how' it is achieved. Few organisations make provision for the extent to which targets are pursued in ethical ways in their performance management systems. When no ethics restrictions apply to performance criteria, employees chasing targets and bonuses often lose ethical perspective and pursue targets with an 'I have to win' mindset. Ethical behaviour and 'doing the right thing' are seldom rewarded.

Application to case study

It will be a rare occurrence if you are rewarded for walking away from the business in Kinshasa because you have integrity and refuse to pay bribes.

Punishment

Should organisations not have clear ethical standards or fail to communicate clearly expectations regarding the behaviour required by such standards, employees do not have ethics as a top-of-mind activity. Moreover, should organisations not assertively and consistently punish employees for ethics transgressions, the rest of the workforce become confused as to what the right thing to do is. Some potentially bad apples may even view absence of punishment practices as a licence to bend rules. Although punishment for unethical behaviour is a manifestation of the dark side of ethics management, and one would possibly do better in the long term to reward ethical behaviour, people do learn from observing others being punished for their mistakes. It is ironic that punishment as a deterrent prevents behavioural chaos in organisations in a negative way, as one would expect people to behave ethically because "it is the right thing to do" and not because they will refrain from doing wrong things out of fear of punishment.

Application to case study

The chances are good that you will lose your job if you dare to return from Kinshasa empty-handed. The best-case scenario is that your decision not to do the right thing will have career-limiting repercussions.

Individual context

The answer to the question as to why people do bad things is a relatively simple one. People could have acquired unethical habits due to groupthink or peer pressure, or they may react unethically in response to perceived unfair treatment. Ethical reasons are even sometimes used to justify unethical behaviour, for example, "I did it out of loyalty, for the good of the organisation". Or undesirable behaviour may be ascribed to under-developed cognitive ethical reasoning skills, for example, fear of punishment: "If I do not do as the manager says, I may be punished". It is also obvious that the ethical dimension of an organisation's culture may not be sufficiently powerful to guide employees ethically – in this scenario, employees may make ethical mistakes as a result of human fallibility.

Application to case study

In the DRC scenario, employees may justify unethical behaviour for 'the good' of their organisation. Or they may reason that "bribery is a natural part of the culture of the country and it is therefore acceptable within the context". They could, of course, fear retaliation from their organisation should they return without having concluded the deal. Should they know that the organisation has a zero tolerance policy for unethical behaviour, they may pay the $200 but tell no one about their action.

More perplexing, though, is why some individuals who are seemingly 'good', or above reproach, do bad things. Sportsmen or -women who have been banned for doping or match fixing, or businesspeople who have seriously transgressed ethically – the Enron, Ford and BP leadership cadres, for example – were surely not 'bad' people in their personal lives, and may even have lived 'clean' lives; they were perhaps pillars in their communities. It is suggested here that deviant behaviour may possibly be described as manifestations of psychological disorders such as psychopathy, narcissism, Machiavellianism, or borderline personality disorder.

These phenomena have a number of behavioural manifestations in common in that individuals afflicted in such a way are usually very intelligent, present charming and charismatic behaviour, and are quite likeable. Unfortunately they do, however, utilise these characteristics to manipulate others in order to get their own way. Since these disorders are not immediately obvious when new apples enter organisations, years could pass before the bad apples' wrongdoing is discovered and reacted to. The challenge for organisations is that such people are often in leadership positions where they are more likely to cause damage to the organisation in terms of reputation, financial losses, or otherwise, than if they had been in positions lower down the organisational hierarchy.

> **Application to case study**
>
> High-risk leaders as described in the previous paragraph may have no qualms in paying the bribe at the airport. Their ethical stance is usually marked by an exaggerated need to satisfy their self-interest, rather than the interest of the 'other'. Leaders such as these will also, at a minimum, turn a blind eye to their employees' unethical behaviour, or, in the extreme scenario, may even encourage and reward such behaviour. These leaders will probably punish ethics transgressors only if their own self-interest is under threat.

Leadership Ethics Inadequacy

Why do leaders sometimes act unethically and fail to deal with unethical behaviour that occurs in their organisations? In the following paragraphs, two potential explanations will be offered to the reader.

First explanation: Ignorance of the importance of ethics for organisations

This explanation relates to ignorance of the importance of ethics for organisations. It cannot be stated unequivocally that organisations who generally act ethically will financially be more successful or viable than those who do not. The fact is, there are many organisations which generally act unethically yet get away with such behaviour for many years. Ethical organisations may not necessarily be extremely financially successful in the short term. Over time, though, once they have built their credibility and secured the trust of all their stakeholders, the chances are excellent that they will enjoy long-term sustainable development.

Leaders who attempt to convince their organisations that ethical business is good business because "it is the right thing to do" may fail miserably. Organisational decision-makers would rather want to know whether being ethical will make or save them money. Leaders are far more susceptible to valid financial reasons as to why they should be ethical than to a call on their conscience. Typically such reasons would be: ethics prevents reputational risk, and inspires stakeholder trust and investor confidence. Other business case reasons may be that ethical organisations attract talented employees and customers and find it easier to retain them. It is, after all, much more cost effective for organisations to retain employees and customers than it is to recruit and acquire new ones.

At a cynical level, it can also be argued that organisations should consider the potential financial losses that may be incurred as a result of unethical behaviour. Although cynical in the sense that one should expect good barrels and good apples to act ethically because it is the right thing to do, fear of the potentially detrimental effects and huge costs (for example, through crippling fines imposed by regulatory authorities) associated with unethical behaviour may act as a 'cynical' type of deterrent (the fear-of-punishment mindset).

> *Application to case study*
>
> Should leaders or employees from whom bribes are solicited be unaware of the long-term value of ethical behaviour, they could easily succumb to the demands and manipulation of, for example, immigration officials, traffic police, and unscrupulous business partners and suppliers. An ignorance of the potentially detrimental effects of unethical behaviour could create an adage of "I didn't know that it was wrong". On the other hand, individuals who are highly risk-tolerant may readily reason that "as long as you don't get caught, it is fine". The latter reflects a blatant disregard for reasonable ethical rules and expectations.

Second explanation: Leaders have an ethics competence deficiency

Another explanation for a propensity to commit acts of unethical behaviour may be that leaders have an ethics competence deficiency. People who do wrong may not necessarily have evil intentions – it may just be that they do not have the experience or skills to deal with ethically challenging situations. Although human beings usually have a natural awareness of the difference between right and wrong, this is no guarantee that they will automatically do the right thing in testing situations. Nor does it mean that they have the knowledge and ability to make correct ethical decisions continually. It also does not imply that they have the wherewithal to manage successfully the ethical behaviour in and of their organisations.

It is suggested that leaders require ethics competence. This is not something that one could reasonably expect leaders to have, but it is something that can be learnt and cultivated. Rossouw proposes that ethics competence consists of three core competencies, each with a number of sub-competencies. The three core competencies are *cognitive, behavioural* and *managerial* competencies. The notion of ethical leadership competence is presented in Table 10.2 in terms of these core competencies and their sub-competencies respectively.[5]

Table 10.2: Dimensions of ethics (moral) competence[6]

Core competence	Features	Sub-competencies	Features
Cognitive	Acquiring intellectual knowledge and skills; identify, analyse, judge and evaluate ethical matters in business	Ethics awareness	Understanding the: 1. Moral obligations and responsibilities of business 2. Ethical issues and dilemmas
		Understanding ethics	Intellectual tools: 1. Theories, frameworks, models, concepts
		Ethical reasoning	Ability to: 1. Compare, evaluate different perspectives 2. Intellectual independence to make own assessment of ethical matters 3. Participate in critical ethics discourse

Core competence	Features	Sub-competencies	Features
Cognitive (continued)		Ethical decision-making	Understanding the: 1. Problems and processes around ethical decisions 2. Nature of ethical disputes and decision-making 3. Approaches, procedures, techniques available for decision-making
		Ethical tolerance	Ability to: 1. Endure ethical ambiguity 2. Tolerate other ethical perspectives 3. Continually search for ethical clarity
Behavioural	Cognitive competence alone does not imply ethics performance. Attention to affective, volitional and imaginative dimensions of ethics. A shift in focus from moral cognition to moral character	Ethical sensitivity	1. Caring about impact of business actions on affected parties 2. Minimising negative impact of behaviour 3. Empathy for those affected
		Ethical courage	1. Determination to improve the ethics of business behaviour 2. Acting on convictions 3. Leading by example
		Ethical imagination	1. Envisaging ethical alternatives 2. Imaging other, 'better' situations 3. Empowerment for the ethical transformation of situations
Managerial	Cognitive and behavioural competencies necessary, but not sufficient to deal with ethics in organisational settings. Managing ethics in a systemic and organisational fashion	Systemic ethics	1. Understanding ethics threats and opportunities 2. Discerning systemic implications of ethical behaviour

Core competence	Features	Sub-competencies	Features
Managerial (continued)		Ethics efficiency	1. Codifying and implementing ethical standards 2. Integrating ethics into the fibre of the business 3. Applying ethics knowledge to ethical matters
		Instrumental ethics	1. Ability to turn ethics into a strategic advantage for the business 2. Forsaking short-term gains for sustainability
		Ethical leadership	1. Ability to provide ethics vision and support to others 2. Awareness of a shared responsibility for ethics

Application to case study

It stands to reason that organisational leaders who find themselves in situations typical of the Kinshasa Airport example may pay the bribe should they have an underdeveloped ethical leadership competence. This holds particularly if they have (1) an *inadequate cognitive ethics competence* (an inability to recognise the potential ethical implications of situations and a lack of ethical decision-making skills) and (2) a *deficient behavioural ethics competence* (in other words, a failure to act on convictions, lead by example, and envisage ethical alternatives).

Employees who find themselves in organisations where the leaders lack *managerial ethics competence* may not have been exposed to or have learnt about ethics through ethics training, applying the organisation's code of ethics, and being aware of the potential consequences of unethical behaviour. Undesirable decisions may therefore consequently be the result.

A Leadership Approach to Ethics

Concerted and sound ethical leadership efforts are required to enable organisations to create sustainable ethical cultures. Concomitant with the acquisition of an ethical leadership competence, there may be a particular leadership approach to ethics. This approach could be that leadership should be anchored in strong values.

The values need to be demonstrated ('lived') through the following behaviour: *ethics awareness, ethical behaviour, ethics management,* and *ethical decision-making*. The application of these four dimensions could be seen to constitute an integrated ethical leadership approach. This integrated approach is depicted in Figure 10.2 below. The four different dimensions to the approach are thereafter discussed in turn.

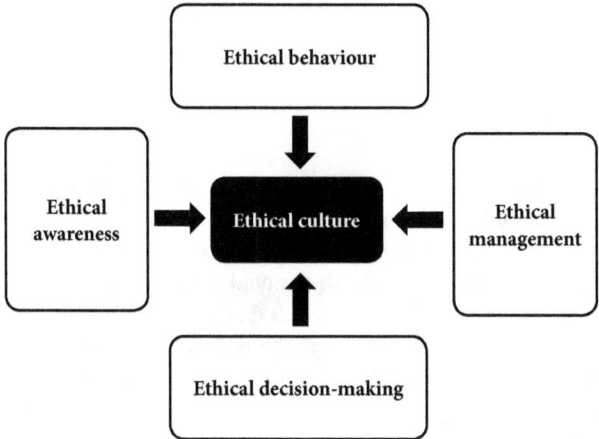

Figure 10.2: A leadership approach to ethical culture formation

Ethics awareness

Should leaders have moral blind-spots or have an amoral stance on ethics, is it highly unlikely that they will recognise ethical challenges within business situations or the ethical consequences of business decisions. They will also then be unable to influence their organisational environments to the extent that employees will be ethically sensitive and cognisant of the ethical implications of their actions. Organisational members become ethically aware when organisations constantly communicate their expectations of ethical behaviour, convey messages that endorse ethical behaviour, and stimulate awareness and utilisation of codes of ethics and ethics policies.

> **Application to case study**
>
> Ethically aware individuals would immediately have recognised the ethical challenge inherent in the yellow fever incident. As such, they would have known (1) that the 'yellow card tax' is in fact a bribe; (2) that bribery has dire consequences: (3) what their leaders would have wanted them to do in that situation; (4) that their codes of ethics and ethics policies could provide guidelines for appropriate behaviour under such conditions; and (5) that a legitimate, ethical decision-making process needs to be followed to avoid an over-reliance on gut feeling.

Ethical behaviour

It will prove difficult for leaders to expect their followers to conduct themselves ethically when the leadership is ethically dubious or inconsistent. Ethical leaders lead by example and walk and talk ethics. This means that their behaviour is ethically exemplary at all times and that they are prepared to verbalise their ethics expectations and openly talk about ethical challenges and grey areas. Ethical leaders take a firm stance on ethics and have the courage to communicate their stance when necessary. These leaders create environments where ethics talk is encouraged and decisions may be questioned. They are skilled at making ethical decisions and always do the right thing, unless, of course, the situation makes it extremely difficult for them to apply their ethical values. Employees view ethical leaders as role models – when ethical leadership pervades, employees are clear on what standards are expected of them, their environments become predictable, and this, in turn, gives them confidence and security.

> **Application to case study**
>
> Ethical individuals are skilled at making ethical decisions and generating different options when confronted with dilemmas. In other words, they use their ethical imagination. They invariably do the right thing, unless, of course, the situation makes it extremely difficult for them to apply their ethical values. They would therefore not bribe the immigration official, unless the circumstances were such that they perceived their physical wellbeing to be threatened. They would display the courage to refuse politely but firmly to pay the 'tax' and would persist in their stance until no longer able to do so. This requires ethical courage, though – which is described by Rossouw (2004)[7] as the resolve to act on moral convictions, even when it is not comfortable or self-serving to do so.

Ethics management

The philosophy of managing ethics is to apply the belief that ethics can indeed be managed in an organisation. Based on this assumption, the following five-step ethics management process could be implemented in organisations, as illustrated in Figure 10.3.

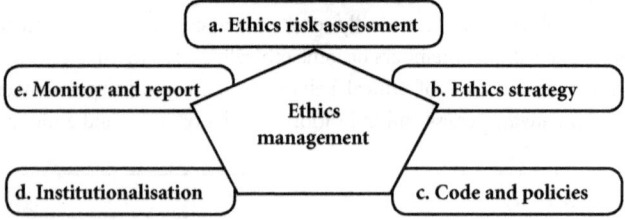

Figure 10.3: *The ethics management process*

Responsibility for the five-step ethics management process (see Figure 10.3) could be allocated to one or more of the following: an ethics management committee, an operational ethics committee, an ethics task team, a corporate ethics office staffed with designated ethics (integrity) officers (practitioners), and ethics champions.

The ethics-related roles and responsibilities of other organisational functions that should not only be represented in these structures, but should also integrate ethics management activities into their mandates, may include, but not be limited to, the complementary ethics risk-management role players mentioned earlier. Other functions actively involved in ethics management are internal audit, risk management, compliance, the company secretariat, procurement, and human resource management.

The ethics function and its practitioners actively manage ethics in the organisation, provide ethical guidance to the governing body (for example, the Board), senior management, and general staff on ethics-related issues; co-ordinate ethics risk and opportunity assessments; manage conflicts of interest; and develop and implement ethics awareness and other ethics training programmes, coupled with sound ethics management and anti-corruption measures. The five steps of the ethics management process are discussed below.

Step 1: Ethics risk assessment

An ethics opportunity and risk assessment is the indispensable first step in addressing the challenges of determining the *good* and striving for an optimal balance between the *self* and the *other*. The organisation should assess (in a structured way) what its ethics risks are. An ethics risk assessment culminates in an ethics risk profile and provides the organisation with a clear understanding of unethical behaviours and organisational practices that could put the organisation at risk. At the same time, an ethics risk assessment identifies the opportunities related to ethics that can be used by the organisation.

Step 2: Ethics strategy formulation

Once a risk assessment has been conducted, the organisation needs to decide on an ethics management strategy. This would, among others, depend on the perceived purpose of bringing ethics into the organisational domain, the current state of the ethics of the organisation, previous reputational damage incurred, the magnitude of identified risks, and the desired end-state at a point in the future. Once an organisation has determined its optimal ethics management strategy, it could design an ethics management plan that contains measurable objectives; assigns specific responsibilities, timeframes, and target dates; and allocates the human, financial, and other resources required to implement the strategy.

Step 3: Code of ethics and policies drafting

Once an organisation knows what its ethics risks and opportunities are, it can proceed to formulate (or revise) its code of conduct, code of ethics, and ethics-related policies. The risks identified inform the contents of these aspirational or prescriptive documents.

Step 4: Institutionalisation of ethics

Formulating a code of ethics and supporting policies is a necessary but insufficient step in making ethics an integral component of the organisation. Ethics needs to be institutionalised in the organisation – merely being able to demonstrate the existence of the code is not enough. Ethics management systems that complement the formation of an ethical culture, together with an ethics management strategy, need to be designed and implemented. Such systems are usually aimed at making ethics manifest throughout the organisation. Typical ethics management systems, among others, are:

- *Communication systems* (ethics awareness campaigns, ethics help-desks, and safe reporting/ whistle-blowing facilities)
- *Ethics training initiatives* (training on ethical standards and decision-making, providing line managers with the ethics competence they require to manage the ethics of their subordinates effectively)
- *Orientation/induction programmes* containing ethics as an important component
- *Performance assessments* including ethics as an indicator
- *Human resource management systems* that recruit, select, and retain employees with integrity
- *Disciplinary processes.*

Step 5: Monitoring and reporting

The ethics office should monitor the implementation of the ethics management plan, and report to the ethics committee on progress in this regard, as well as on the state of ethics in the organisation.

Application to case study

Leaders and representatives of organisations that pro-actively and openly manage their ethics will do the right thing in the DRC by refusing to pay the bribe. Bribery and facilitation payments would have been identified in ethics risk assessments. An organisation's ethics strategy, whether, for example, rules- or values-based, would be sufficiently explicit to pre-empt compromising situations; the code and policies would be clear on what employees should do in such situations; and in terms of ethics management systems, the following aspects would have been addressed:

- There would be a facility in the organisation where employees could obtain ethical advice or report observed ethics transgression by colleagues and other stakeholders – this would have informed them on the organisation's stance on bribery.
- Organisational members would have been trained on (1) applying the code of ethics and ethics-related policies (in the form of a section in the code that deals explicitly with bribery), and (2) making sound ethical decisions using heuristics provided by the organisation (for example, "Am I prepared to read about my decision in tomorrow's newspapers?").
- The human resources division would have made a structured effort to conduct integrity assessments during employees' selection processes (to keep out the bad apples who are likely to pay bribes).
- New employees would receive ethics training during their on-boarding programmes (for example, how to deal with situations where their integrity could be challenged, such as when crossing international borders).
- Employees would be rewarded for not paying bribes and would be punished when they did.

Ethical decision-making

Our ethical values are informed by a diversity of influences from birth, examples being laws; parental, societal and educational norms; the expectations of peers and colleagues; good and bad experiences; and many more. Individuals, however, have unique value systems that are comprised of different permutations of the diversity of influences as explained above. As such, no two individuals will reason about ethical challenges in exactly the same way or make identical decisions. Due to this diversity and human fallibility in this regard, it would stand organisations in good stead to provide employees with clear guidelines on how to recognise ethical challenges in different situations and respond to these in ethically appropriate ways.

The ethical dimension of situations that require decisions to be made is also not clearly obvious. Ethical challenges are often covert and may even lurk in unexpected consequences of decisions. It is useful to pay heed to common phrases used in business contexts that may provide clues to the presence of ethical challenges. Examples of such words and phrases are: 'unfair', 'we have to be careful here' (this is normally uttered in a whisper), 'shouldn't we get legal advice on this one?', 'you can make this decision, but I don't want my name attached', 'everyone else is doing it …' (when in Rome), 'we've always done it like this …', 'it's all about the bottom line', or 'it's not so serious'.

Organisations' ethics management functions could perhaps advise leaders and their followers to utilise structured decision-making heuristics (tools) when required to make ethically sound decisions. It is common practice to provide organisational members with a list of questions that they should consider when confronted with ethically compromising situations.

Figure 10.4 depicts four sequential questions that could be asked when ethics-laden situations arise. Those who find themselves challenged ethically should ask each question in turn. The decision-making process is terminated after any number of questions have been answered with a 'no'. Should all four questions provide acceptable or 'yes' responses, there is a solid likelihood that the decision-making process will culminate in an ethically justifiable decision.

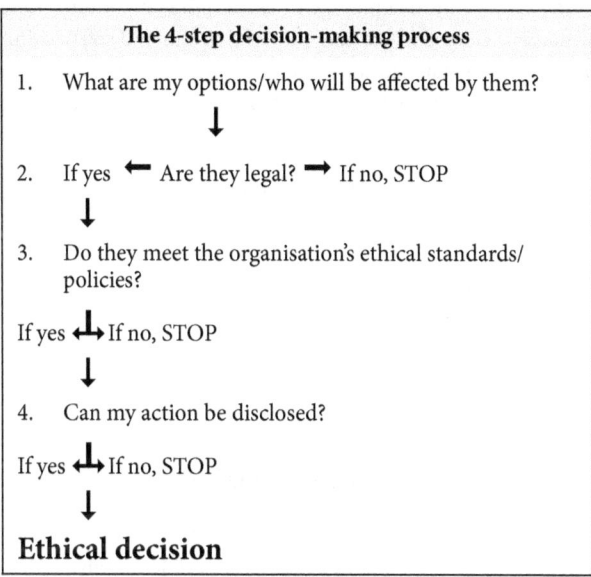

Figure 10.4: Ethical decision-making heuristic

Application to case study

Option: Pay a bribe to the immigration official

This option will not allow one to proceed beyond Question 2 (Is it legal?). Although bribery may go unpunished in many countries, the chances are very good that bribery is universally illegal. Such an action is also unlikely to pass Question 3, as most organisations, even those in the reactive mode, have some ethical standards. In terms of Question 4 (Can my action be disclosed?) – few individuals will be prepared to read about themselves, their affiliation to the organisation and their (un)ethical decision in a newspaper.

Option: Reluctantly pay the bribe, insist on a receipt and lay a charge of bribery against the immigration official the next day.

This may sound like a viable option at face value. As such, you may justify your decision by stating that you did it under duress; you knew the action was wrong; you did not have another choice; and you reported your action after the fact. You may pass Question 3 (alignment to the organisation's ethical standards), and perhaps even be prepared to read about your action in the media and therefore (only just) pass Question 4. It is, however, still illegal to pay the bribe (you fail at the Question 2 hurdle).

Conclusion

It should be clear that ethical organisational cultures can be established over time. This, however, requires sustainable leadership commitment to ethics. The need to account for ethics – in other words, the business case for ethics – needs to be clearly understood and articulated. The acquisition of leadership ethics competence should be encouraged by organisations and embraced and pursued by individuals. Leadership ethics awareness, behaviour and decision-making should be complimented by an investment in structured ethics management interventions.

This chapter is concluded with a question that needs to be answered at the discretion of the readers, based on the perceptions that may have been acquired by reading this chapter:

Many organisations succeed in creating powerful health and safety cultures (for example, in mining companies) that dictate attitudes and behaviour. Can an ethical culture not also be entrenched by adopting similar states of awareness, commitment and discipline utilised by organisations to create health and safety cultures?

Endnotes

1   Rossouw & Van Vuuren, 2013.
2   Rossouw & Van Vuuren, 2013.
3   Transparency International, 2016.
4   Rossouw & Van Vuuren, 2013.
5   Rossouw, 2004.
6   Integrated from Rossouw, 2004, pp. 37–41.
7   Rossouw, 2004.

References

Rossouw, D. 2004. *Developing business ethics as an academic field*. Johannesburg, ZA: BEN-Africa Book Series.
Rossouw, D & Van Vuuren, L. 2013. *Business ethics*.(5th ed.) Cape Town, ZA: Oxford University Press.
Transparency International 2016. Corruption perceptions index 2015. http://www.transparency.org/cpi2015#results-table [Accessed 26 August 2016].

SECTION 4
LEADERSHIP TYPES

Chapter 11

AFRICAN LEADERSHIP
Vusi Vilakati

African business leadership needs to be revisited and refocused. Current leadership paradigms often do not honour the essence of African human consciousness; do not create desired economic and developmental outcomes; and do not anticipate present and future shifts in the African setting. There is a need to identify and understand the historical and political legacies, structural and economic factors, including the impact of emerging economic players, and sociocultural influences that have shaped and are shaping Africa's Leadership Landscape and practice.[1] This understanding needs to be translated and integrated into evolving forms of leadership development and practice at individual, team and organisational levels.

Figure 11.1 provides an overview of how shaping political, economic and sociocultural shareholder and investor influences with the dynamic role of contextually-attuned and innovative leadership could facilitate Africa's human and economic advancement.

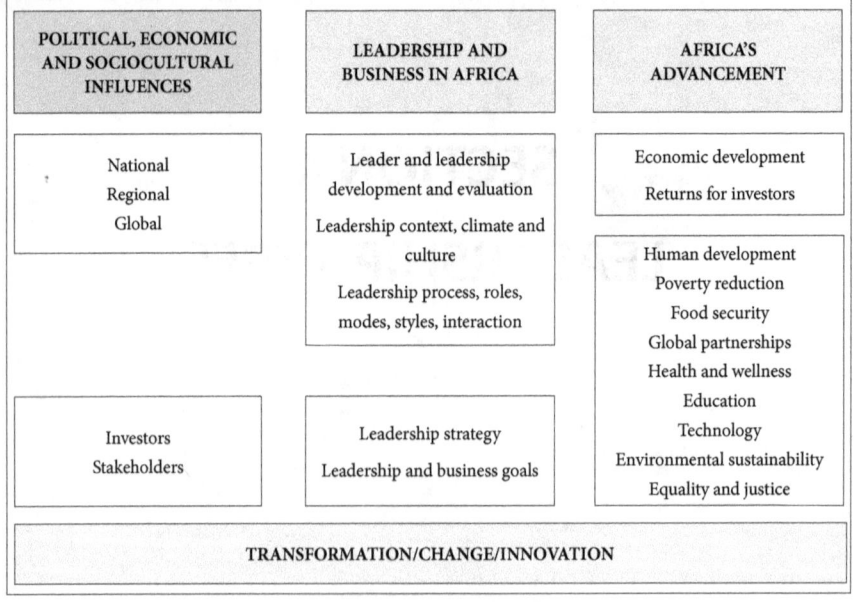

Figure 11.1: Context for business leadership for Africa's advancement

A key element to meeting Africa's future requirements for human and economic advancement is the need to reclaim collectively Africa's leadership wisdom (values, attitudes and behaviours) about the centrality of the human face of life and innovatively integrate it into leadership development and practice.

The purpose of this chapter is to discuss the need for and the features of Africa-fit leadership with its implications for organisational and leadership direction, practices and development. The story line of the chapter unfolds thematically as follows:

- **Theme 1: The *concept of African leadership*** has to take cognisance of Africa's historical and cultural roots, and not reflect a western perspective.

- **Theme 2:** The *rediscovery of a sense of humanity* through African leadership wisdom, in particular through the key value of Ubuntu.
- **Theme 3:** Refocusing the *future of African leadership* through a bottom-up, Africa-centred and adaptive leadership development strategy to harness the connectedness of human life as well as imaginatively liberating individual and collective creativity. Informed by African values, the outstanding African leader should exhibit a sense of rootedness, membership, belonging, and connectedness to an authentic community with a strong contextual responsiveness. From an African perspective, leadership must be broadly viewed as a dynamic collective, shared, and integrative system serving multiple stakeholders through multiple purposes, given the organisation's organic embeddedness in communities and society.

African Leadership in Context

Exploring the concept of African leadership is predicated on the recognition of Africa's historical and cultural roots, the vastness of the continent, and the national, tribal, ethnic and religious diversity, as well as the different economic development stages of individual countries. While it is true that the quest for a homogeneous or monolithic view regarding the continent fails to honour the multiplicity of epistemologies and the diversity of ontological understandings of African issues studied, the reality is that many commonalities exist which can be described within the entire African context.[2]

People searching for these commonalities often use prefixes such as African, Afro-centric, Africa, pan-African, African renaissance, African consciousness, and leadership in, within, for, or by Africans to describe in part the similarities they see. Many of these share a common pan-African search for a deepened awareness of the systemic leadership challenges facing Africa, the need to generate Africa-centred leadership knowledge and to systemise the study of leadership development and practice within the continent.[3]

Mindful of these diverse and complex geo-economic, political and sociocultural contours of the continent, African leadership knowledge has emerged as a confluence of small meandering streams from the fields of philosophy, political science, psychology and sociology. According to Fourie, van der Merwe and van der Merwe,[4] African leadership and management research over the last 50 years has concentrated heavily on political leadership issues, with a scattering of focus on leadership styles, management, gender, religion, development, African culture and values, liberation and transformational ideologies, succession, and local issues, including the role of education.

This quest for knowledge has extended into searches for the nature of adaptation and integration of African leadership wisdom and Africa-centred approaches into existing and emerging theories, including: transformational, charismatic, and transactional leadership; information processing, social exchange, and leader traits; cross-cultural power and influence; follower-centric, behavioural, and contingency-based competencies; strategic leadership, team leadership; contextual complexity and systems perspectives; leader emergence and development; ethics and morals; leadership creativity and innovation; and identity-based practices.[5] Each of these studies exhibits event, individual, dyad, group, organisation and/or context as levels of analysis.[6] It is important to note that similar searches are also shared by scholars and leaders in many other places throughout the world in their quest to bring advancement in the contexts they face in their daily world.

In a simplistic way, it is suggested that African leadership is intentionally Africa-centred and focused, and dynamically understands the complexity and connectedness of historical, current and future needs of the African context. In dealing with Africa's challenges and leveraging her advancement, it should innovatively integrate African humanism and leadership wisdom with international best practices for its leaders to be transformative, locally responsive and globally competent. It is anticipated that Africa's contribution to this leadership discourse could steer her away from persisting leadership dysfunctions, deficits and failures, restoring many human values of life by cultivating the foundations of peace, freedom, social cohesion and prosperity.[7]

Over the last half century, the description of African leadership often has been framed with activist and emancipatory tones against the denial, suppression and disfiguring of African humanity, rationality and knowledge through the superimpositions of western leadership scripts.[8] However, the evolving, reconstructing and refocusing of leadership patterns in Africa can be better facilitated through mapping their interaction with historical and political legacies, regional economic reform structures, and cultural renaissance.[9]

Historical and political legacy

A major portion of the colonial political history of Africa involved systematic entrenchment of western forms of knowledge and suppression of indigenous identities, values and cultures for an extended period of time.[10] While encouraging some forms of development, a major portion of this phase interrupted Africa's forward-looking developmental trajectory.[11] It also altered the political economy of most African countries, and disorientated production and trading patterns. Arising from this dislocation is the need to recover from the negative political, ideological, economic and cultural after-affects, encouraging pre-colonial wisdom that can inform the formation of evolved, authentic, modern African identities.[12]

Part of this recovery also involves the realisation that pre-colonial Africa was not a blank canvas waiting to be painted by colonialists. Post-colonial African scholars go to great lengths in criticising current neo-colonial market tendencies that continue to weaken Africa's global position.[13] Sadly, the transition from "Africa in the hands of the Europeans" to "Africa in the hands of Africans" over the last five decades has been littered with kleptocratic and predatory instincts of ruling elite who have used political and economic systems for their personal gain at all costs.[14] Some African countries continue to be described as irremediably corrupt, hopeless, criminal, ungovernable, or generally in chaos. The cause is often attributed to "inherent inadequacy of leadership and governance".[15]

Fortunately, some recent studies project an optimistic future for Africa with growing pockets of responsible, ethical and humane leadership that is forging democratic and transformative governance. These leaders are gradually replacing Africa's dictatorial regimes.[16] Through these efforts, poverty and inequality are falling; food productivity is rising; women are assuming positions of leadership; democracy and fair elections are strengthening; regional markets are developing; anti-corruption measures are gaining prominence; and Africa is becoming an important destination for foreign direct investment.[17] There is also a growing leadership focus on issues related to natural resources, globalisation, cross-cultural exchange, infrastructure development, scarce resources (such as energy and water), technological innovation, the influence of civil society, legislative frameworks, and consumer preferences.[18]

Economic and structural reform

As a consequence of these historical and political legacies, most African countries continue to confront economic and structural issues such as the fear of marginalisation or co-option by dominant economies; and being recipients of colonial economic baggage, neo-colonial tendencies, and the global economic apartheid caused by the international world's relative aloofness from Africa.[19] Added to these challenges is the entrance of emerging economic players such as Brazil, Russia, India, China and South Africa (BRICS) with their respective economic interests.[20]

African leadership's response to these challenges includes the development of institutions such as the New Partnership for Africa's Development (NEPAD), the African Union (AU), the Southern African Development Community (SADC), the Economic Community of West African States (ECOWAS), the Economic Community of Central African States (ECCAS), the East African Community (EAC), and the Common Market for Eastern and Southern Africa (COMESA).[21] These efforts are characterised by the determination to confront Africa's leadership deficit, the crisis of governance, its rising debt, the predatory instincts of its nation's elites, the corrupt appropriation of limited resources, and the conversion of political power into economic wealth.[22]

The determination by some African business leaders has also resulted in increasing levels of stability, economic growth and the incubation of positive economic frameworks that are opening doors to global business opportunities.[23] African business leaders are also assisting in regionalising and consolidating intra-African markets, developing urban environments, commercialising essential services, and developing capital markets. These positive trends are partly responsible for an increase of economic interest by potential investors in Africa and its markets.[24]

Sometimes overwhelmed by these impulses, mainly pivoted outside the continent, African leaders need to find new ways to incorporate the human face of life into business engagements with the view of redressing Africa's economic marginality and making globalisation a strengthening process.[25] Part of this should also include reconfiguring the economic interest of some African leaders who are primarily focused on profitability toward an orientation more centred on Africa's economic and human development.[26] For Africa to advance, she needs leaders who are able to map the historical and current economic trajectories as well as create an attractive business environment for both local and international investors.

Cultural renaissance

African cultural renaissance can be principally described as the focus on the rediscovery of an essential "essence" of African history and culture through a re-engagement with African cultural values, ethno-pedagogies, indigenous reference points and practices. It mostly is premised on the rejection of the assumption that Europe/the West is the universal standard or example of humanity.[27] Rectifying the impact of colonisation on Africa's destabilisation, erosion of African consciousness, African peoples' dehumanisation, denial of African agency, and subsequent fissures and cracks it created on African culture and personhood, all are embedded in the founding philosophy and goal of African renaissance.[28] In the current leadership development and cross-cultural management discourse, African renaissance manifests itself as the interdisciplinary quest for incorporating the most relevant and useful African traditional values into current leadership methodologies and practice.[29]

Many international studies comparing values and cultures, such as Hofstede (1980), Schwartz (1992), Trompenaars (1996), and GLOBE's (2004) cultural dimensions, have been criticised for their use of Western value scales which lead to a void of understanding of the embodiment of many non-Western indigenous values, especially African traditional values.[30] The reason often stated for this oversight is that the motivation for these studies is to more fully understand the link between these values and economic outcomes – a topic especially relevant in a western-orientated market economy.

These studies and the imported metrics used as benchmarks to understand culture and evaluate their application in leadership settings are not suited to capture fully the contextual fluidity of the needs of the African context. African leadership and management discourse over the last 40 years have sought in an essentialising tone to discover modified metrics and epistemologies that holistically capture the essence of African cultural evolution. An alternative relational, reflective and constructionist approach using inductive analogies has been suggested as a means of addressing and integrating culture into leadership development frameworks in order to forge new identities for African leaders.[31]

The growing interest in African markets and resources is creating new cultural interfaces. Business organisations are experiencing increased cultural convergences, divergences and cross-vergences that are evolving Africa into a "third cultural space" that integrates African traditional values and best international practices from the west and east.[32]

Cultural renaissance through the appropriation of relevant African traditional values has become urgent in light of the emerging "hybrid" nature of management and leadership practice in Africa. In a world where problems cross national, regional and continental borders, the task of cultural renaissance is to develop leaders who are firmly grounded in African values and also have suitable competiveness to function across those boundaries and cultures. As a consequence of the emerging business leadership context, cultural renaissance can redeem the cultural values of the past and give birth to authentic present expressions of cultural identities as well as foster cultural intelligence in a globalising world.

Africa's rebirth and resurgence necessitates the need for the continent to be recognised for its vibrancy, diversity, and energy rather than its poverty, instability and conflicts. Gumede[33] argues that in order to retrieve Africa from the peripheral position she occupies in the world order, business leadership development in the region needs to be characterised by: (i) *thought leadership* – the capacity to intellectually appropriate and prioritise Africa in the current global space; (ii) *thought liberation* – the cultivation of independent thinking devoid of the colonial baggage; and (iii) *critical consciousness* – deep levels of awareness that are not easily swayed by dominant thinking. An alternative consciousness linked to practical changes in the way leadership and business practice and goals are structured could also have an impact on advancing Africa.

Rediscovering the Humanity of African Leadership Wisdom

> "... The great powers of the world may have done wonders in giving the world an industrial and military look, but the great gift still has to come from Africa – giving the world a more human face." – Biko[34]

What comes through from Biko's acclaimed citation and the above discussion is the suppression of the wisdom and strengths of African humanity as it relates to leadership practice and human and economic advancement. The gaze often has been toward the West as a reference point for humanity, modernisation and leadership development. Africa must now recognise and implement the basic tenets of its own world view that inculcates the connectedness of people, resources and the world around in a way that enhances the natural creativity of individuals, communities and their leaders.

Sources of African leadership wisdom

Africa, referred to by many as "the cradle of humankind", has a rich history of community life and leadership wisdom that predates the colonial era. Historians argue that a substantial amount of Africa's leadership wisdom dates back to Africa's early empires such as West Sudan

(500 BC), Ghana (790 AD) and Mali (1230 AD).[35] To this day this wisdom exhibits itself in a very simple form in that most indigenous Africans have inherited "praise names" in addition to their surnames. These praises often trace the individual's clan history and honour their connectedness to family, their belonging to community and the environment, and their strengths and anticipated contributions to society.[36]

The current African leadership context

In the current context, the embodiment of these key values of African humanism include communal interdependence and belonging; caring and community; harmony and hospitality; dignity; empathy; co-operation, respect and responsiveness; custodianship of life and the shared way of being; and compassion and solidarity. Other attitudes associated with these values include humility; thoughtfulness; connectedness; consideration; understanding; and a focus on traditional wisdom, generosity, social sensitivity, reciprocity, sharing, and tolerance and regard for human virtues. Often the translation of these values and attitudes using the English language is inadequate to describe the concepts fully.[37]

These values and attitudes central to African humanism are embodied in a number of slightly varied philosophical concepts from across Africa. These include *Ubuntu, Botho, Bantu, Uhnu, Avandu, bunye* (Southern Africa); *Ujaama, Watu, umoja* (Eastern Africa); *Ngumtu, Kubuntu, Edubuntu* (Central Africa); and *Amani, Ogbara, ise* and *Ika* (West Africa).[38] These concepts are the unifying philosophical, anthropological, sociocultural premise for African thinking about human identity, consciousness, and relational ways of thinking, being and connecting with others and the environment in Africa.[39]

A widely discussed concept is *Ubuntu- (Zulu) Botho- (Sotho) Uhnu* (Shona) as derived from the southern African maxim *Umuntu ngumuntu ngabantu/Motho ke motho ka batho* (loosely translated as "a person is a person through other people"). It provides an integrative approach to studying African personhood, connectedness, and flourishing in a community. According to Tutu,[40] *Ubuntu-Botho-Uhnu* says "I am human because I belong. I participate, I share." Forster[41] synthesises the conception of Ubuntu philosophy in this manner:

> "The question 'who am I' (subjective) is intricately related to who you say that I am (objective), and who we are together (intersubjective). Instead of being a lone subject, or a quantifiable and containable object, we are all "intersubjects", fundamentally interwoven into a common cosmic identity and being that is run through with sacred dignity. It is not just me, it is not just you, it is not just the material reality, neither is it just the spiritual reality; true reality is a sacred interweaving of all these things – true reality is beyond one single quantifiable truth, it is generous. Identity, in this sense, is a dynamic engagement and discovery of mutual identity and shared dignity – that is, a generous ontology."

The term *Ubuntu-Botho-Uhnu* also comprises an extended understanding of African collective or communal conception of life and an ongoing connectedness to and fellowship with the living, the dead ("ancestors"), and the yet-to-be-born. There is an emphasis on the continuity of the past, present and future as all being one single point in present time. In other words, in our participation in the generation and the distribution of material and non-material resources, we are custodians of the past, present and future.[42]

Rediscovering and developing human-centred leadership can be achieved using responsive, reflective, relational, critical, and constructionist inquiry into the wisdom embedded in African community structures, lived experiences, and traditional thought, which is often expressed through language, idioms, stories, artwork, and spatial use of cues.[43] It is possible that rooted in Africa's world view are Africa's dreams and aspirations, novel ideas, inspiration, best practice, or theoretical insights that can inform leadership knowledge and practice.[44]

The current reality in Africa is that there is a heavy concentration on the national and business institutions that leaves substrata of weak individuals, families and communities. And yet at the foundation of the African human consciousness is the primacy of the development of strong and effective individuals and family. Families and communities can only be as strong as the individuals in them. In fact, the family creates the individual and the individual creates the family. This is a co-creation process that is central to African human consciousness and the way in which it is employed as a way of life in Africa.[45]

Rebuilding African humanity as a bottom-up process

Rebuilding African humanity should be a bottom-up process that begins from the foundation of individual and collective self-discovery and translates into the renewal of individual, family, and extended family relations, to action in the village community, local governments, and possibly in shaping business and national strategies.[46]

Fully integrating these fundamental principles of African human consciousness into the ethos of effective business team leadership has not been done sufficiently. Jackson[47] notes that the current key values that shape the dialogue and culture of teams in African business include sharing, deference to rank, sanctity of commitment, regard for compromise and consensus, and good social and personal relations. African leadership needs to evolve in order to embrace fully the African concept of consultative dialogue, planning, decision-making and consensus-building described in a number of southern African countries as *Indaba, Lekgotla, Dare, Tinkhundla* and *Imbizo*.

Some examples of efforts to translate African values into effective business and leadership practice within corporate and national settings have been documented. At a national level, Ubuntu has had an impact on South Africa's transition from apartheid, especially in the process of reconciliation and the inclusion of fundamental values of diversity, social democracy, dignity, equality, and social cohesion that underpin the new Constitution of 1996. In public and governance frameworks, Ubuntu has been applied as a *Batho pele- (people first)* philosophy to encourage more humane public services.[48] Newenham-Kahindi[49] uses cases of large South African corporations to demonstrate how Ubuntu has been integrated into their foreign operations. Another example is Ncube's work,[50] in which she uses many of the above Ubuntu elements to develop a leadership framework. It is not yet entirely clear how successful these efforts have been.

The application of the African leadership philosophy in organisational practice

While most of the values are positive, the application of the philosophy in organisational practice has revealed that it is susceptible to commodification, abuse and corruption, leading to discrimination, oppressive tendencies, and dictatorial management. Firstly, proponents of Ubuntu and related African human consciousness philosophies should guard against discouragement of individual initiative leading to "groupthink" and the reduction of humane competition. In reality, African human consciousness involves the commonality of interests instead of commonality of opinion. Secondly, they should also guard against the encouragement of patriarchal tendencies which lead to discrimination on the bases of age and sex.[51] They should also guard against the encouragement of nepotism that places the perceived interests of relatives and members of one's ethnic group, tribe, race, and political party first. African consciousness involves the ethical conscience of putting the common interests and advancement of community above all else.

Instead, African consciousness involves the encouragement of connectedness and equality in all social relations and the development of the individual. In its best form, African humanism should be viewed as a dynamic dialogical way of leadership and consensus building that should never regress to a static or archaic management imposition.[52] Its outcome should be holistic transformations that are responsive in adapting to continually changing developmental challenges.

One way to make the transition of African leadership from its political, economic and social legacies into an effective human-focused and holistic future advancement trajectory involves better integration of concepts from African consciousness and cultural wisdom into the development of individual leaders, teams and corporate practices.

Refocusing the Future of African Leadership

> *"If I had the opportunity of an informal chat with Afrikan government leaders, sitting in the shade of a tree in my village, I would say to them: 'Excuse me friends. The way I see it you are really trying to build the house backwards'."* – Rukuni[53]

The metaphor of "building a house backwards" is a criticism of the top-down manner in which government and business often approach leadership and investment in African communities. Carrying through his logic, Rukuni[54] argues that instead of increasing efforts to lay strong family and community foundations first, African leaders are "struggling to put a roof on the weak and crumbling walls and foundations of the nation state [creating] a dangerous disconnect between the…people on the ground…looking with suspicion at this 'roof' that is floating over them … an unidentified object filled with alien bureaucrats who do not know the needs of the community".

Transplanting this metaphor to the organisational context, the remaining challenge for Africa is to develop future-fit and contextually attuned leadership. It should start with individuals, moving to teams and organisations, so that all will act as innovative agents of transformation for African business and its constantly evolving society. This is a bottom-up, Africa-centred and adaptive leadership development strategy for harnessing the connectedness of human life as well as imaginatively liberating individual and collective creativity. If done with the recognition of our common existence and belonging as expressed in the African idiom *umuntu ngumuntu ngabantu*, it can help fulfil the aspirations of a peaceful, cohesive, and flourishing humanity.

Figure 11.2 provides a framework for how African leadership wisdom and values could be translated and integrated into leadership development and practice at individual, team and organisational levels so as to increase creativity and innovation in facilitating Africa's human and economic advancement.

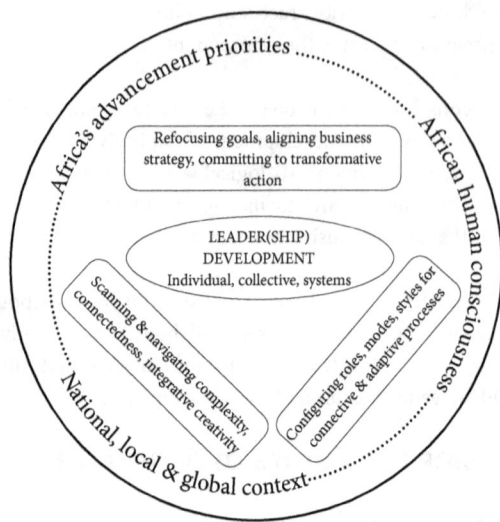

Figure 11.2: Developing leadership in the emerging African Leadership Landscape

African Leader of the Future

Informed by African values, the outstanding African leader should exhibit a sense of rootedness, membership, belonging, and connectedness to an authentic community. They should have strong contextual responsiveness, using a broad base of local and global knowledge to navigate creatively and innovatively the complex and constantly changing relationships among employee, team, community, business, investor, and stakeholder interests.

According to research conducted by Ashridge Business School,[55] business leadership in the emerging markets context requires three types of knowledge and skills: context, complexity and connectedness. With regard to context, the organisational leader needs to develop tools for scanning the horizon, especially in respect of connecting sociocultural and economic objectives with the financial goals of business. Complexity involves navigating situations resulting from the confluence of the many different business, economic, government, and political players. Connectedness involves building effective and lasting relationships with the communities served by each organisation, as well the emerging national, regional and global partnerships.

Added to these, research suggests that effective leaders across the world require three main types of desired leadership competencies:[56]

- *Core personal:* self-awareness, engagement in personal transformation, and inquisitiveness;
- *Adaptive cognitive and affective:* optimism, self-regulation, social judgement, empathy, motivation to work in national, regional and global environments, cognitive processing, and acceptance of complexity and its contradictions; and
- *Relational:* social and team building, networking, and cultural intelligence.

In the traditional African sense, leaders are custodians of the values and resources collectively held by their communities. They act as vessels of the developmental interests of the society, with responsibilities including to protect all, advance the general welfare, and cultivate social cohesion. In many African cultures, these roles are fulfilled by kings, chiefs, prophets and diviners, who are supposed to be responsible and accountable to ancestors as well as current and future generations.

Kets de Vries and Florent-Treacy[57] and Heames and Harvey[58] found that outstanding African leaders were thought to share many of the same characteristics as leaders from other parts of the world: excellent relational skills; curiosity; emotional intelligence; communication skills; energy and resiliency; high tolerance for ambiguity, frustration and uncertainty; capacity to learn and adapt; willingness to take risks; sense of humour; and the ability to envision a compelling future while empowering and energising staff members. As with other contexts, African leaders share the challenges of translating, implementing and aligning these skills with Africa's future requirements.

Current African leadership requires keener abilities for context scanning, navigating complexity, and effectively engaging the increased dynamism of the interaction between business and society.[59] Some of the requisite skills include cross-cultural adaptability and intelligence, social creativity and resourcefulness, global business savvy, perspective-taking, and problem-solving skills.[60] In applying these skills, leaders will need to steer away from a view of leadership as commanding, telling, persuading, influencing, and motivating towards a view of leadership as circular dialogue and sense-making in which all leaders, followers, stakeholders, and shareholders are engaged in a synergistic *Indaba*.[61] African leaders need to develop the courage to lead by having self-belief and self-confidence, being prepared, having passion, and taking action.[62]

The African value system gives us a framework in which all could potentially be agents whose solidarity and co-operation would lead to economic growth and development. In such a framework, one achieves one's humanity as a producer and a consumer, or a buyer and a seller, who responds not only to the forces of the market but also to both the material and spiritual needs of being human. This is the very meaning of African human consciousness, or the Ubuntu ecology of humanity.[63]

Business schools have a critical role in the development of this type of leader. In the holistic training of business leaders for this African context, several curriculum adjustments are needed to teach the skills which could help restore the practice of African human-ness.[64] These entail:

- Simultaneous and increased focus on the topics of *African history, politics, economics, social conditions and culture*, and *environmental development* so that a more holistic understanding of the interaction of business with African communities can be realised. This especially includes an increased focus on African indigenous knowledge, epistemologies and value systems.
- Increased focus on *eco-systemic approaches to leadership development* as espoused in ecological systems theory in order to help leaders to engage their micro, meso and macro aspects (such as those found in Ubuntu) effectively in developing all parts of their leadership.[65]
- Developing the leadership skills associated with *creativity and innovation in the context of effective and collaborative planning, consensus-building and decision-making*, such as those found in *Indaba*.

Developing Leadership Teams and Processes the African Way

Current leadership development literature makes a key distinction between leader development and leadership development.[66] Leader development refers to the development of the individual's capacity, self-management, social capabilities, and work facilitation.[67] Leadership development entails the "expansion of the organisation's capacity to enact the basic leadership tasks needed for collective work: setting direction, creating alignment, and maintaining commitment".[68] It is the interaction between individuals and teams with systemic processes of the organisation and context.[69]

Linked to the above distinction is the need to understand the shifts that have taken place in leadership theory and practice. Earlier understandings of leadership focused almost exclusively on traits, characteristics and capabilities of the individual leader – often focusing on one person sitting at the top of the organisation.[70] Currently there is a drive toward collective leadership – sometimes called shared leadership, connected leadership, collaborative leadership, or leadership community. Collective leadership focuses on processes, interactions, roles, interdependencies and the collective's ability to act upon a shared vision.[71] Leaders, by understanding leadership as a community of practice and as a simultaneous process, are better equipped to deal effectively with a more demanding and radically different context such as that found in Africa.[72]

From an African perspective, leadership is broadly viewed as a dynamic collective, shared and integrative system. This broadens the scope for leadership development practitioners and enables a holistic coverage of the full range and depth of leadership inputs, processes and outcomes.[73] Inputs include people, timing, and resources. Processes include roles, modes, styles, and longitudinal interaction of people and resources. Outcomes encompass the optimal levels of motivation and performance in relation to the leadership context, climate, and culture.[74] The resulting "community of practice" is an inductive, relational, reflective constructionist network of persons in an organisation who are guided and driven by shared goals, who interact on the basis of a shared strategic direction, and who continue to interact so as to build, support and develop the necessary knowledge base and skills for setting organisational direction.[75]

One specific form of this "community of practice" is *Indaba*, which is a circular, experiential learning and inclusive dialogical process of facilitating meetings, decision-making, conflict resolution, and building teams and organisational culture. In the development of individuals, teams and systems, this implies an integrative focus on the intra- and interpersonal content, leadership processes, multiple levels of analysis, longitudinal interaction of people and resources, and evaluation of leadership.[76]

Adopting a "community of practice" perspective for the emerging African context in developing leadership and aligning the overall organisational goals, aims, and mission will require an organisation to: (i) develop the relevant human capital through leadership development programmes, career development planning, succession planning, performance management, and competency frameworks; (ii) translate the value propositions embedded in the approach into its leadership culture and climate; and (iii) develop strategies for facilitating the transition into corporate protocols and culture.

Specific ways in which these can be achieved include encouraging the following behaviour at every level of the (business) organisation:[77]

- Collective ownership of responsibility, opportunities and challenges
- Focus on encouragement of contribution of new ideas from each person in the organisation
- Primacy of relationships: one becomes human only in the midst of others
- Harmony, humility and helpfulness as most desirable qualities and aims
- Spiritual guidance as natural in problem solving
- Consensus seeking as valued and taking time for it, without suppressing genuine differences in opinion
- Hierarchical status as recognised and respected as a core value.

Revisiting Business and Leadership Goals to Implement African Values

"Whenever money moves, it has an impact... Without a degree of forethought the impact is generally negative." – Bruce Herbert[78]

In light of these leadership challenges, it is important to explore whether business goals are structured in a way that translates Africa's economic growth into desired outcomes for Africa's social advancement responsive to the sociocultural context and future requirements. Applying the inherent values of solidarity, sharing, responsibility, custodianship and the holistic world emanating from African consciousness promises to close the existing gap between African leadership practice and Africa's developmental goals. This invites the exploration of potential hybrid forms of corporations that resonate with African leadership codes or values.

According to Carroll and Buchholtz,[79] the relationship between business and society has been characterised by increasing concern about sustainability. The envisaged partnership between business and society in Africa should not be the cause of social, environmental and economic problems, but should create shared value and promote positive short-term and long-term effects on employees, suppliers, customers, the public, and the environment.[80] Shared value in this regard means that societal needs, and not merely economic needs, must define markets.[81] To this extent, there is increasing demand on business and its leaders to depart from the traditional understanding that business goals are primarily about gaining profit, to focus on business becoming more responsible toward a greater collection of stakeholders, society, and the environment.[82]

Khoza,[83] basing his argument on the principles of African human consciousness, which includes integrative spirituality, community solidarity, and shared life and custodianship of shared resources, identifies six key values that need to be strengthened within the African context of business as well as public leadership: efficacy, ethics, personhood, governance, responsibility, and accountability. Recognised as intrinsic values at an individual and relational level from the African conception of reality, these are key to altering the culture of the business organisation towards creating a framework that makes economic growth and social development a product of the synergy of all stakeholders and actors: the state, the market, and the people.[84]

Of importance is specifically how business can make a positive impact on society through integrating social and environmental purposes into its goals and leadership development strategies. Using the 2015 UNDP projection of the Millennium Development Targets, these goals can be summarised as poverty reduction, food security, strengthening of global partnerships for the common good, improved health and wellness, improved education, access to technology, environmental sustainability and equality and justice.[85]

In order to cultivate these values at shareholder, strategic business and human resources levels of the business organisation, Ngambi[86] proposed the following focus areas:

- Leverage business and leadership goals that are responsive to Africa's social advancement and continental needs; and
- Identify leadership potential, build leadership capacity, utilise and export leadership excellence, and support leadership performance which serves to implement these goals.

Implying a wider and more flexible approach for business challenges our understanding of corporations and the goals of business and its leadership. The term "goal" is defined as the object or aim of action. Goals can be assigned, self-set, or set in a participative process.[87] They have the two attributes of content and intensity. Organisations set goals in order to heighten motivation, reduce discrepancy, align individuals, teams and systems, and set direction with the aim of increasing productivity and accelerating performance.[88] In a broader sense, goals relate to the fundamental purpose of business, and they shape the overall strategy of the corporation.[89]

The move towards business leadership implementing a multipurpose approach to addressing its markets shifts it from the traditional goals of creating wealth for shareholders, employees, customers and possibly society at large.[90] While profit remains important, corporations in the new context need to actively combine delivering optimum returns to shareholders with responsibility for social and environmental performance.[91] This modified understanding of business has been referred to as a flexible purpose approach.[92]

A flexible purpose approach to business goals involves creating a hybrid form of the corporation that has multiple and simultaneous goals to which the board of directors is held accountable.[93] It can elevate corporate social responsibility effort from a voluntary status to form part of the business core strategy. It allows a company to pursue profitability as well as social or environmental purpose.[94] Typical purposes include food production, education, health, alleviating poverty, and assisting the development of small business enterprises to promote community stability and security. Examples of this type of corporation include the California-based Benefit Corporation and Flexible Purpose Corporation.[95]

Comprehending business and leadership goals from a flexible purpose perspective is resonant with African human consciousness and related management concepts, including the values of Ubuntu which include caring and community, harmony and hospitality, respect and responsiveness.[96] This form of organisation needs no adaptation to be accepted by African communities, as it readily connects to the intrinsic values of African identity and how community is organised.

For African countries to benefit from economic growth, it is vital that leadership, stakeholders, and shareholders explore a flexible/multipurpose approach to business goals. If a new approach is not forged, business is likely to continue to support principles of wealth privatisation, which puts too much wealth into too few hands.[97] The growing disparity in income between the rich and the poor, along with the environmental tensions related to land, mining and minerals, are likely to persist unless solutions of this nature are implemented.

Conclusion: The Dance of African Leadership

> "In a circle holding hands, to the music and rhythm of drums and marimba, I danced with all, I danced in the centre for all to see, and then I danced with all. As the night went on, we all became alive, in a way we had never known, and our dance moved the mountains around to become one with us." [i]

Often Africa and its business have been viewed by outsiders as a "basket case" of poverty, corruption, social injustice and violence which can only sink into greater depth of misery. Yet at the core of Africa is a world-class perspective on humanity that many others can only hope to emulate. African leadership as a whole must now engage in its own dance with Africans to restore that practice of humanity.

Exactly how and when the realisation of Africa's future potential to transform itself into a modern and viable economic, political, social and cultural environment will become a reality yet remains unknown. However, it is certain that courageous and effective business leadership, focused on the goals of creating Africa as a holistic and connected people, economy, continent and environment, in a manner which draws on its culture of humanity, can greatly assist to propel this dream into reality.

---

i The author's metaphor, in which leadership is a circular African dance that affirms individual creativity while synergistically enhancing innovation, connectedness, multidimensional growth and organic solidarity.

Endnotes

1. Jayan, 2012; Jackson, 2002; McMahon, Barkhuizen & Schutte, 2014.
2. Nkomo, 2011; Kamoche, 2011a; Acquaah, 2007; Fourie, van der Merwe & van der Merwe, 2015; Iwowo, 2015.
3. Bolden & Kirk, 2009.
4. Fourie et al., 2015.
5. Dinh et al., 2014; Jack et al., 2011.
6. Dinh et al., 2014.
7. Jallow, 2014; Rukuni, 2009.
8. Sesanti, 2015.
9. Jackson, 2012.
10. Tabensky, 2008.
11. Buri Mboup, 2008.
12. Charles, 2014.
13. Ajulu, 2001.
14. Ibid.
15. Nkomo, 2011, p. 366.
16. Kiggundu, 2013.
17. French, 2015.
18. Jackson, Amaeshi & Yavuz, 2008; Jayan, 2012; Nkomo & Kriek, 2011; Walumbwa, Avolio & Aryee, 2011.
19. du Toit, 2008.
20. Jayan, 2012; Jackson, 2002; McMahon et al., 2014.
21. Buri Mboup, 2008; Desai, 2010; Jordaan, 2014.
22. Ajulu, 2001; Tsheola, 2002; Kuada, 2010.
23. Mataen, 2012.
24. Mataen, 2012.
25. Ajulu, 2001; Buri Mboup, 2008; Tsheola, 2002; Kuada, 2010; du Toit, 2008.
26. French, 2015.
27. Thomas & Thompson, 2013.
28. Ajulu, 2001; Buri Mboup, 2008.
29. Buri Mboup, 2008.
30. Steers & Nardon, 2009.
31. Bolden & Kirk, 2009; Kamoche, 2011; Tsheola, 2002.
32. Jackson, 2013; Minkes & Foster, 2011.
33. Gumede, 2014.
34. Biko, 1978, p. 46.
35. Gutto, 2013.
36. Rukuni, 2007.
37. Dalitso, 2010; Gade, 2012; Letseka, 2011.
38. Dalitso, 2010; Rukuni, 2007; Letseka, 2011.
39. Vilakati, 2012.
40. Tutu, 1999, pp. 34–35.
41. Forster, 2010.
42. Nafukho, 2006.
43. Bolden & Kirk, 2009; Vilakati, 2012.
44. Iwowo, 2015.
45. Rukuni, 2009, p. 50.
46. Rukuni, 2007.
47. Jackson, 2013.
48. Lutz, 2009.
49. Newenham-Kahindi, 2009.
50. Ncube, 2010.
51. Newenham-Kahindi, 2009.
52. Lutz, 2009.
53. Rukuni, 2009, p. 41.
54. Rukuni, 2009, pp. 41–42.
55. Ashridge Business School, 2009.
56. Jokinen, 2005.
57. Kets De Vries & Florent-Treacy, 2002.
58. Heames & Harvey, 2006.
59. Andreasson, 2009.
60. Drath et al., 2008.
61. Jackson, 2002; Newenham-Kahindi, 2009.
62. Rukuni, 2009.
63. Ntibagirirwa, 2009.
64. Nkomo, 2015.
65. Bronfenbrenner, 1979.
66. Day et al., 2014.
67. Day, 2001.
68. MacCauley & Van Velsor, 2004.
69. Day et al., 2014.
70. Walumbwa et al., 2011.
71. Liu et al., 2014.
72. Drath et al., 2008; Walumbwa et al., 2011.
73. Bolden & Kirk, 2009; Day et al., 2014; Iwowo, 2015.
74. Avolio, 2014; Dinh et al., 2014.
75. Veldsman, 2013; Drath et al., 2008.
76. Day et al., 2014; Gao et al., 2011; O'Connell, 2013.
77. Lutz, 2009; Newenham-Kahindi, 2009.
78. Herbert, 2012.
79. Carroll & Buchholtz, 2015.
80. Ajulu, 2001.
81. Porter & Kramer, 2011; Andreasson, 2009.
82. Maritz, Pretorius & Plant, 2011.
83. Khoza, 2012.
84. Ahlers et al., 2013.
85. UNDP, 2015.
86. Ngambi, 2011.
87. Porter & Kramer, 2011; Dufays & Huybrechts, 2015.
88. Locke & Latham, 2006.
89. Sastry, 2011.
90. Clarke, 2011; Haigh et al., 2015.
91. Sastry, 2011.
92. Clarke, 2011.
93. Haigh, Kennedy & Walker, 2015; Porter & Kramer, 2011.
94. Andreasson, 2009; Haigh et al., 2015.
95. Clarke, 2011.
96. Gade, 2012; Ntibagirirwa, 2009; Khoza, 2012; Bertsch, 2012.
97. Ajulu, 2001; Porter & Kramer, 2011.

References

Acquaah, M. 2007. 'Managerial social capital, strategic orientation, and organizational performance in an emerging economy'. *Strategic Management Journal*, 28(12):1235–1255.

Ahlers, T, Kato, H, Kohli, HS, Madavo, C & Sood, A. 2013. 'Africa 2050: Realizing the continent's full potential'. *Global Journal of Emerging Market Economies*, 5(3):153–213.

Ajulu, R. 2001. 'Thabo Mbeki's African renaissance in a globalising world economy: The struggle for the soul of the continent'. *Review of African Political Economy*, 28(87):27–42.

Andreasson, S. 2009. 'Understanding corporate governance reform in South Africa: Anglo-American divergence, the King Reports, and hybridization'. *Business & Society*, 50(4):647–673.

Ashridge Business School. 2009. *Developing the global leader of tomorrow*. [Online]. Available: http://www.unprme.org/resource-docs/developingthegloballeaderoftomorrowreport.pdf. [Accessed 8 February 2016].

Avolio, BJ. 2014. 'Examining leadership and organizational behavior across the boundaries of science'. *Consulting Psychology Journal: Practice and Research*, 66(4):288–292.

Bertsch, A. 2012. 'Updating American leadership practices by exploring the African philosophy of Ubuntu'. *Journal of Leadership, Accountability & Ethics*, 9(1):81–97.

Biko, S. 1978. *I write what I like*. Johannesburg, ZA: Heinemann.

Bolden, R & Kirk, P. 2009. 'African leadership: surfacing new understandings through leadership development'. *International Journal of Cross Cultural Management*, 9(1):69–86.

Bronfenbrenner, U. 1979. *The ecology of human development: experiments by nature and design*. Cambridge, MA: Harvard University Press.

Buri Mboup, S. 2008. 'Conflicting leadership paradigms in Africa: A need for an African Renaissance perspective 1'. *International Journal of African Renaissance Studies – Multi-, Inter- and Transdisciplinarity*, 3(1):94–112.

Carroll, AB & Buchholtz, AK. 2015. *Business and society: ethics, sustainability, and stakeholder management*. 9th ed. Stamford, CT: Cengage Learning.

Charles, A. 2014). 'The new scramble for Africa's resources: implications for its development'. *Africanus*. 44(2):1–14.

Clarke, C. 2011. 'California's Flexible Purpose Corporation: A step forward, a step back, or no step at all'. *Journal of Business, Entrepreneurship & the Law*, 5(2):301–328.

Dalitso, S. 2010. ' "I am because we are": Ubuntu as a cultural strategy for OD and change in sub-Saharan Africa'. *Organization Development Journal*, 28(4):41–51.

Day, DV. 2001. 'Leadership development: A Review in context'. *The Leadership Quarterly*, 11(4):581–613.

Day, DV, Fleenor, JW, Atwater, LE, Sturm, RE & McKee, RA. 2014. 'Advances in leader and leadership development: a review of 25 years of research and theory '. *The Leadership Quarterly*, 25(1):63–82.

Desai, N. 2010. 'India and Africa: A new engagement'. *India Quarterly: A Journal of International Affairs*, 65(4):413–429.

Dinh, JE, Lord, RG, Gardner, WL, Meuser, JD, Liden, RC & Hu, J. 2014. 'Leadership theory and research in the new millennium: current theoretical trends and changing perspectives'. *The Leadership Quarterly*, 25(1):36–62.

Drath, WH., McCauley, CD, Palus, CJ, Van Velsor, E, O'Connor, PMG & McGuire, JB. 2008. 'Direction, alignment, commitment: toward a more integrative ontology of leadership'. *The Leadership Quarterly*, 19(6):635–653.

Dufays, F & Huybrechts, B. 2015. 'Where do hybrids come from? Entrepreneurial team heterogeneity as an avenue for the emergence of hybrid organizations'. *International Small Business Journal*. doi: 10.1177/0266242615585152.

du Toit, C. 2008. 'Black consciousness as an expression of radical responsibility: Biko an African Bonhoeffer'. *Religion and Theology*, 15(1):28–52.

Forster, DA. 2010. 'A generous ontology: identity as a process of intersubjective discovery – an African theological contribution'. *HTS Teologiese Studies / Theological Studies*, 66(1):1–12.

Fourie, W, van der Merwe, SC & van der Merwe, B. 2015. 'Sixty years of research on leadership in Africa: A review of the literature'. *Leadership*. doi:10.1177/1742715015580665. [Online]. Available: http://0-reference.sabinet.co.za.ujlink.uj.ac.za/document/EJC125037. [Accessed 9 September 2015].

French, HW. 2015. *China's second continent: how a million migrants are building a new empire in Africa*. New York, NY: Vintage Books.

Gade, CBN. 2012. 'What is *ubuntu*? Different interpretations among South Africans of African descent'. *South African Journal of Philosophy*, 31(3):484–503.

Gao, J, Amulf, JK & Henning, K. 2011. 'Western leadership development and Chinese managers : Exploring the need for contextualization'. *Scandinavian Journal of Management*, 27(1):55–65.

Gumede, V. 2014 *Thought leadership, thought liberation, and critical consciousness for Africa's development and a just world*. Inaugural Professorial Lecture, 19 March, Senate Hall, Unisa.

Gutto, SBO. 2013. 'In search of real justice for Africa and Africans, and her/their descendants in a world of justice, injustices and impunity'. *International Journal of African Renaissance Studies – Multi-, Inter- and Transdisciplinarity*, 8(1):30–45.

Haigh, N, Kennedy, ED & Walker, J. 2015. 'Hybrid organizations as shape-shifters: Altering legal structure for strategic gain'. *California Management Review*, 57(3):59–82.

Haigh, N, Walker, J, Bacq, S & Kickul, J. 2015. 'Hybrid organizations: origins, strategies, impacts, and implications. *California Management Review*, 57(3):5–12.

Heames, JT & Harvey, M. 2006. ' The evolution of the concept of the "executive" from the 20th century manager to the 21st century global leader '. *Journal of Leadership & Organizational Studies*, 13(2):29–41.

Herbert, B. 2012. *Washington state tailors 'social purpose corporation' to sustainable business*. [Online]. Available: http://www.bloomberg.com/bw/articles/2012-03-16/washington-state-tailors-social-purpose-corporation-to-sustainable-business. [Accessed 8 February 2016].

Iwowo, V. 2015. 'Leadership in Africa: Rethinking development. *Personnel Review*, 44(3):408–429.

Jack, G, Westwood, R, Srinivas, N & Sardar, Z. 2011. 'Deepening, broadening and re-asserting a postcolonial interrogative space in organization studies'. *Organization*, 18(3):275–302.

Jackson, T. 2002. 'Reframing human resource management in Africa: A cross-cultural perspective'. *The International Journal of Human Resource Management*, 13(7):998–1018.

Jackson, T. 2012. 'Cross-cultural management and organizational knowledge in Africa: Postcolonial theory in the wake of China's presence'. *Organisation*, 19(2):181–204.

Jackson, T. 2013. 'Reconstructing the indigenous in African management research'. *Management International Review*, 53(1):13–38.

Jackson, T, Amaeshi, K & Yavuz, S. 2008. 'Untangling African indigenous management: multiple influences on the success of SMEs in Kenya'. *Journal of World Business*, 43(4):400–416.

Jallow, BG. 2014. *Leadership in postcolonial Africa trends transformed by independence*. New York, NY: Palgrave Macmillan.

Jayan, PA. 2012. 'BRICS: advancing cooperation and strengthening regionalism'. *India Quarterly: A Journal of International Affairs*, 68(4):363–384.

Jokinen, T. 2005. 'Global leadership competencies: A review and discussion'. *Journal of European Industrial Training*, 29(3):199–216.

Jordaan, AC. 2014. 'Regional integration in Africa versus higher levels of intra-Africa trade'. *Development Southern Africa*, 31(3):515–534.

Kamoche, K. 2011. 'Contemporary developments in the management of human resources in Africa'. *Journal of World Business*, 46(1):1–4.

Kets De Vries, MFR & Florent-Treacy, E. 2002. 'Global leadership from a to z: Creating high commitment organizations'. *Organizational Dynamics*, 30(4):295–309.

Khoza, RJ. 2012. *Attuned leadership: African humanism as compass*. New York, NY: Penguin Group.

Kiggundu, MN. 2013. 'Personal reflections on African management: looking in, looking out and looking ahead'. *African Journal of Economic and Management Studies*, 4(2):177–200.

Kuada, J. 2010. 'Culture and leadership in Africa: a conceptual model and research agenda'. *African Journal of Economic and Management Studies*, 1(1):9–24.

Letseka, M. 2011. 'In defence of ubuntu'. *Studies in Philosophy and Education*, 31(1):47–60.

Liu, S, Hu, J, Li, Y, Wang, Z & Lin, Z. 2014. 'Examining the cross-level relationship between shared leadership and learning in teams: Evidence from China'. *The Leadership Quarterly*, 25(2):282–295.

Locke, EA & Latham, GP. 2006. 'New directions in goal-setting theory'. *Current Directions in Psychological Science*, 15(5):265–268.

Lutz, DW. 2009. 'African ubuntu philosophy and global management'. *Journal of Business Ethics*, 84(S3):313–328.

Maritz, R, Pretorius, M & Plant, K. 2011. 'Exploring the interface between strategy-making and responsible leadership'. *Journal of Business Ethics*, 98(S1):101–113.

Mataen, D. 2012. *Africa – the ultimate frontier market: A guide to the business and investment opportunities in emerging Africa*. Petersfield, UK: Harriman House.

McCauley, CD & Van Velsor, E. 2004. *Handbook of leadership development*. 2nd ed. San Francisco, CA: Jossey-Bass.

McMahon, G, Barkhuizen, N & Schutte, N. 2014. 'The impact of globalisation on South African businesses: Some leadership thoughts'. *Mediterranean Journal of Social Sciences*, 5(9):215–220.

Minkes, AL & Foster, MJ. 2011. 'Cross-cultural divergence and convergence: With special reference to the family firm in southeast Asia and China'. *International Journal of Cross Cultural Management*, 11(2):153–166.

Nafukho, FM. 2006. 'Ubuntu worldview: A traditional African view of adult learning in the workplace'. *Advances in Developing Human Resources*, 8(3):408–415.

Ncube, LB. 2010. 'Ubuntu: A transformative leadership philosophy'. *Journal of Leadership Studies*, 4(3), 77–83.

Newenham-Kahindi, A. 2009. 'The transfer of ubuntu and indaba business models abroad: A case of South African multinational banks and telecommunication services in Tanzania'. *International Journal of Cross Cultural Management*, 9(1):87–108.

Ngambi, H. 2011. 'RARE leadership: An alternative leadership approach for Africa'. *International Journal of African Renaissance Studies – Multi-, Inter- and Transdisciplinarity*, 6(1):6–23.

Nkomo, SM. 2011. 'A postcolonial and anti-colonial reading of "African" leadership and management in organization studies: tensions, contradictions and possibilities'. *Organization*, 18(3):365–386.

Nkomo, SM. 2015. 'Challenges for management and business education in a "developmental" state'. *Academy of Management Learning & Education*, 14(2):242–258.

Nkomo, SM & Kriek, D. 2011. 'Leading organizational change in the "new" South Africa'. *Journal of Occupational and Organizational Psychology*, 84(3):453–470.

Ntibagirirwa, S. 2009. 'Cultural values, economic growth and development'. *Journal of Business Ethics*, 84(S3):297–311.

O'Connell, PK. 2013. 'A simplified framework for 21st century leader development'. *The Leadership Quarterly*, 25(2):183–203.

Porter, ME & Kramer, MR. 2011. 'Creating shared value'. *Harvard Business Review*, 89(1/2):62–77.

Rukuni, M. 2007. *Being Afrikan*. Johannesburg, ZA: Penguin Global.

Rukuni, M. 2009. *Leading Afrika*. Johannesburg, ZA: Penguin Global.

Sastry, T. 2011. 'Exploring the role of business in society'. *IIMB Management Review*, 23(4):246–256.

Sesanti, S. 2015. 'Teaching African philosophy in African institutions of higher learning: The implications for African renaissance'. *South African Journal of Philosophy*, 34(3):346–357.

Steers, RM & Nardon, L. 2009. 'The culture theory jungle: Divergence and convergence in models of national culture'. In RS Bhagat & RM Steers (eds). *Cambridge handbook of culture, organizations, and work*. New York, NY: Cambridge University Press. 3–22.

Tabensky, PA. 2008. 'The postcolonial heart of African philosophy'. *South African Journal of Philosophy*, 27(4):285–295.

Thomas, M & Thompson, A. 2013. 'Empire and globalisation: From "high imperialism" to decolonisation'. *The International History Review*, 36(1):142–170.

Tsheola, J. 2002. 'South Africa's form of globalisation: A continental posture paradox for insertion and dependence'. *Political Geography*, 21(6):789–811.

Tutu, D. 1999. *God has a dream: A vision of hope for our time*. New York, NY: Doubleday.

United Nations Development Paln (UNDP). 2015. *UNDP human development report 2015: Work for human development*. [Online]. Available: http://hdr.undp.org/sites/default/files/2015_human_development_report_0.pdf. [Accessed 8 February 2016].

Veldsman, TH. 2013. 'People professionals fit for emerging economies'. In S Bluen (ed). *Talent management in emerging markets*. Johannesburg, ZA: Knowres, 179–202.

Vilakati, MV. 2012. *African spiritual consciousness within the personal interpersonal and professional leadership perspective*. Master's thesis. Johannesburg, ZA: University of Johannesburg, Faculty of Management.

Walumbwa, FO, Avolio, BJ & Aryee, S. 2011. 'Leadership and management research in Africa: A synthesis and suggestions for future research.' *Journal of Occupational & Organizational Psychology*, 84(3):425–439.

Chapter 12

WOMEN IN LEADERSHIP
Mmasekgoa Masire-Mwamba

The volatile and uncertain world we live in calls for transformational leadership in all areas. Competence, vision and overall capability are prerequisites to lead effectively in our complex and ever-changing context. Specific requirements and demands for leadership will always differ depending on context. In political and elected office, for example, the demands of the political office often result in a high level of personal scrutiny and a need to be endorsed by a broad-based audience.

However, in business, for example, mastery of subject matter and experience may be key determinants for success. Notwithstanding these seemingly objective requirements, "gender is often the first prism though which women leaders are evaluated".[1] Perceptions about the ability of women and the readiness of women to undertake the rigorous scrutiny and to acquire the requisite experience are subjective and often rule them out of consideration.

Consider the following scenario: A young female engineer walks into the store with her assistant. Leaning across the counter is an enthusiastic clerk who leaps up, but does not address her, rather, smiles at her assistant and explains the technical options available. He is rather taken aback when he hears the words, "Well, don't explain to me, explain to her; she is my boss, she will decide." Variations on this theme have played out over several aspects of my professional and personal life. Invariably the supposition is that the woman should not be bothered. She is just not there, even as she stares right back at you. This is a stereotypical view that is under serious challenge in various aspects of our lives.

Women leaders bring advantages and disadvantages to the leadership role. "They are applauded for their ability to build consensus and team leadership while at the same time criticized for their lack of toughness. On the one hand, women's flexible approach to leadership, as opposed to the male command and control style, is critical in managing a culturally diverse workforce."[2] It can be argued that dictates of new world order (for example, globalisation, interconnectedness, terror threats, climate change, and other socio-contextual factors), which, coupled with the overall advantage of women in leadership, outweighs the real or perceived disadvantages. Ironically, the very skills and traits that women were once told have no place in the boardroom are the very same ones which now presumably give them a leadership advantage.[3]

Women also see leadership as a legitimate means of self-actualisation, and increasingly demand changes and an enabling framework for them to exercise their rights in this regard. Society is challenged to re-consider, in some cases, deeply-rooted culture, attitudes and norms. Every one of us is required to contribute new sets of skills, and bright ideas, and to offer better and more effective solutions in a more progressive and inclusive framework. Success and engagement of women in leadership will require a multifaceted approach for both men and women in order to address the enablers fully and create a context which readily provides for women to rise to positions of leadership in their chosen fields.

The purpose of this chapter is to address how the stakes can be transformed for women to realise their full potential as invaluable leaders. To this end, the following topics are addressed:

- The invaluable contributions of woman leaders.
- What has been achieved and happened to date?
- What does it take for woman leaders to succeed?
- What are the possible empowerment principles women can apply to transform the stakes?

The dominant perspective adopted will be of leadership by women in the political context. A review of women in politics gives us an opportunity to distil some of the conditions precedent for the success of woman leaders. We find that these women who wield enormous power have also experienced, to a lesser or greater extent, some of the common challenges faced by women in many other sectors. They too have had to overcome obstacles to get to the top. They have embraced the leadership challenge and made significant contributions to redress the prevailing imbalances. In modern-day society, the rise of the first female Prime Minister, Sirimavo Bandaranaike of Sri Lanka, in 1960, came after the assassination of her husband. Since then, many women have risen to political leadership, not always through a systematic development model, but rather through a range of unique and varied circumstances.

The Invaluable Contribution of Women Leaders

"Women have been leaders as queens of nations, tribal chiefs, and empresses throughout history".[4] This leadership has taken place during times of war and times of peace: "Women tend to wield power differently from men."[5] There is not yet a large enough number of women to define conclusively the 'difference' that women's leadership brings. Despite the relatively low numbers and slow pace of growth in this regard, research and experience have begun to confirm a real and beneficial value to society of women in leadership. Women have different points of view and values, informed and shaped by their unique life experiences, priorities and interests. The African Development Bank in its recent *Africa Gender Equality Index* concludes that "Investing in the human development of women generates important multiplier effects, enabling them to become champions of human development for their families and communities".[6] Combined with the men already at the power tables, there is a real opportunity for optimal utilisation of resources to address the challenges and offer humanity the best solutions from a shared responsibility.

Successive studies show that women traditionally lead by means of reconciliation, interrelations, and persuasion. Society has traditionally counted on women to keep the family together. Ironically, these developed and honed skills are among those considered to offer a better chance of success in responding to global challenges of the day. These skills are now gaining recognition as powerful ways to shore up traditional power.

"Women bring a different dynamic to leadership, one that's more instinctively team centred. They bring a female perspective to policy making. It is very important that women's voices are heard and represented"[7] in government, in business, and in civil society.

What has been Achieved, and What has Happened to Date?

The statistics

Although some progress has been made over the past few decades with respect to the number of women in leadership positions across the world, growth is slow and still falls short of the adopted 30% global target.

> "In 1995, at the Beijing Women's Conference, advancing women's participation in determining the shape of the future was recognised as a core means of enriching that future. The conference determined that the presence of 30% women in decision-making bodies as the tipping point to have women's ideas, values and approaches resonate." – Linda Tarr-Whelan[8]

For meaningful and sustained progress, a critical mass is required. We need to see the current global averages of women in senior leadership positions rise to the defined minimum of 30%. Having even a small number of women at power tables as role models is vital. However, there are seldom enough to change outcomes.

> "A sprinkling of women at the top, no matter how inspirational, is not enough to change how companies and governments operate. The weight of cultural inertia is too great." – Linda Tarr-Whelan[9]

International initiatives to bring more women into government

Since 1975, when the idea of a Women's Decade was mooted, there have been a number of high-level inclusive gatherings ranging from politicians, to policy makers, development agencies and civil society members across the world (see Figure 12.1). Global commitment and dialogue over the past few decades have encouraged greater participation through local and international consultations on women's rights and gender equality. The impact of these conferences has been to identify and remove barriers and to open up the space through dialogue and to review the progress made and lessons learnt. These approaches have sought to broaden existing participation and generate sustained participation at all levels. These fora also provide an opportunity to continue to review and to accelerate implementation of agreed global and regional commitments of gender equality and empowerment of women.

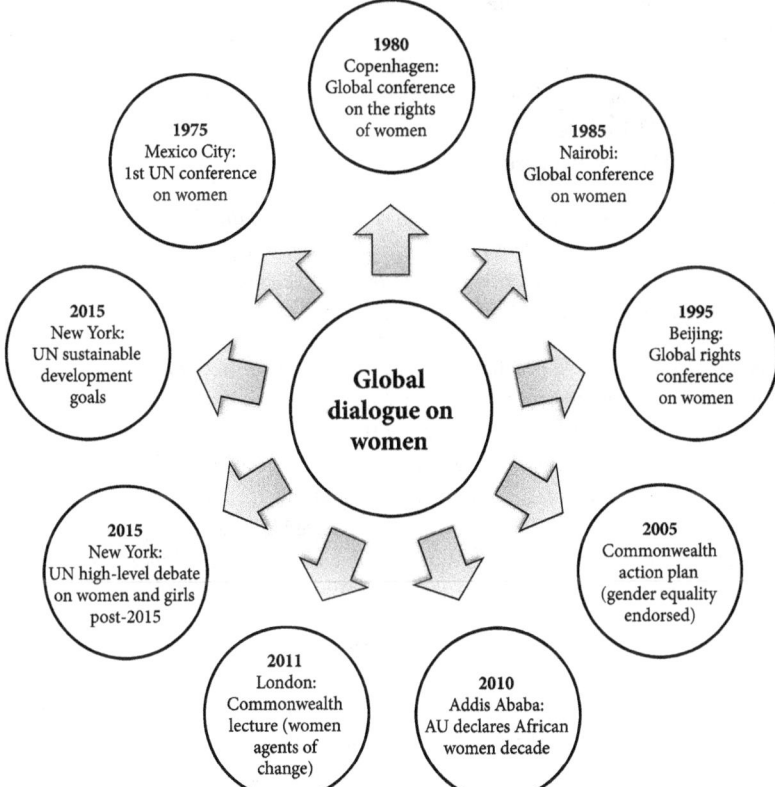

Figure 12.1: Global initiatives regarding women in recent years

There is a need to go beyond political rhetoric and declaratory statements. Dialogue and informed debate on gender equality advocate systemic and lasting change. Global resolutions and commitments to gender equality need to reach every young girl and every young woman, and to start to open up meaningful opportunities that create an enabling context for sustainable progress. "Social and cultural stereotypes are still amongst the most entrenched obstacles that many women in leadership have had to endure at some point; some of these are seemingly trivial and may be easy to overcome."[10] Others can present themselves as barriers to progress and hold women back. Women need to be proactive, not only to recognise the opportunity when it arises, but also to seek the opportunity actively and create one if none emerges.

In 2015, as one of the seventeen UN Sustainable Development goals, the goal of gender equality and empowering all women and girls – Goal five – was globally adopted. Leaders throughout these meetings have called for a zero tolerance policy on the structural causes of discrimination against women. Among the key challenges to leaders in achieving this goal are eliminating the laws and practices that perpetuate gender inequalities; and promoting equality in women's participation in public and private institutions.

The rise of African woman leadership

The African Development Bank's (ADB) *Africa Gender Equality Index 2015* assesses women's and men's equality in law and institutions.[11] Through this measure, African leaders are challenged to promote women's equality in order to enable both women and men to contribute to and benefit from social and economic development.

It is argued that promoting women's active citizenship, voice and leadership has the potential to make African societies more vibrant and its institutions more resilient and responsive. In assessing the current level of progress with respect to women's empowerment and engagement in development, the African Development Bank concluded that although some progress has been made, there was a lot that still needed to done.

> "We recognize that the status of women has deep cultural roots that are by nature slow to change. However, societies are asked to reflect on the gains made and areas that prevent women and girls from fulfilling their potential." – African Development Bank [12]

Some African countries have made important progress in promoting women's contribution to political life, primarily through quotas in their parliaments. There is no universal approval for adoption of quotas as a way of stimulating the increase of women in leadership. Among the reasons that both women (who could be advantaged through the quotas) and men (who could conversely be disadvantaged) argue against quotas is that they may not be an effective mechanism of ensuring that the best individuals are selected for leadership positions. Quotas and other forms of active compensatory measures can, however, be a useful means towards arriving at an outcome which is more equal.

> "Countries such as Rwanda and Tanzania have introduced constitutional requirements for their legislatures to include a minimum proportion of women. Rwanda is now a recognised global leader in this area — women make up over 60% of the national parliament. While it is still too early to assess the impact of these quotas, there is evidence of increased parliamentary attention to reform in areas like family land law and land rights, and a greater public acceptance of women as political leaders." – African Development Bank[13]

Supporters of quotas acknowledge the catalytic role and the positive impact of starting to build up a critical mass.

> "Even without quotas, women are taking on more leadership roles. In Liberia, Ellen Johnson-Sirleaf was the first woman to become president of an African nation, followed by Joyce Banda in Malawi and Catherine Samba-Panza in the Central African Republic. Today, women are represented in the cabinet of every single African country, and the overall proportion of women cabinet ministers has increased from 4% to 20%." – African Development Bank[14] [15]

Concrete steps and measures to address the inequalities have never been without controversy. Some women totally reject the notion of quotas:

> "To me, equality is the important thing, I don't want preferences, and I don't want to be preferred as a woman. But I want to acknowledge that I am a human being who has the capacity to do what I have to do, and it doesn't matter whether I was born a man or woman. The work will be done that way." – Eugenia Charles, former Prime Minister, Dominica[16]

Clearly, even without quotas, more women than ever are acceding to high political office. We now need to ensure that improved representation of women translates into real influence – in government, in business and in other spheres – so that women are in a position to make their full contribution to political, economic and social life.

What Will it Take for Women Leaders to Succeed?

Given that statistics indicate that women represent over half the global population, there is no doubt that humanity is not benefiting fully from the contribution women could make. The challenge remains how to improve the stakes to allow for a more significant role for women to assume in leadership. There is a real opportunity for optimal utilisation of women as invaluable partners. Women need to take up a seat at the table, to allow for their voice and their contribution to enhance and add value for holistic options and solutions by putting their heads together with the men already at the power tables, with the aim of offering humanity the best solutions from a shared responsibility.

In many different parts of the world, there have been practical efforts and consideration has been given to promoting and increasing women's participation. Consultations have included bringing in women from different political, social and cultural groups with a common agenda of addressing gender equality in various national, regional and international fora. New thinking and commitments to gender parity "stimulus measures" require shattering the barriers and increasing the numbers to achieve a critical mass.

The global focus on creating a conducive context to facilitate women in leadership has still not yielded the desired results, although legal policy and frameworks continue to be put in place. Only when leadership balance has become an important priority, have the results been real partnerships between women and men making important decisions for the future.

Many have referred to the "glass ceiling" as a way of describing how large pools of women who are doing well at the lower and middle levels of management and leadership do not seem to be able to break through to the higher levels. "Glass" is often adopted as a metaphor, given its transparent quality, which has often denoted gender barriers; its "invincible nature"; and also its sturdiness and the real barrier it creates. However, as easily as glass is shattered, the possibility of dismantling and shattering barriers for women in leadership is also concrete and real.

Other glass metaphors include the *"glass wall"*, denoting the symbolic invisible barrier that surrounds the inner sanctum of powerful senior male executives, resulting in the low number of women in executive positions (Klenke, 1997).[17] The *"glass cliff"* has been used to explain what sometimes may seem as women being set up to fail – for example, when promoted into companies in crisis, or set up for bad performance and thereby attracting negative attention. No matter how the barriers are denoted or explained, they are often complex and interrelated. Barriers can also be subtle and understated, and couched in tradition and culture. When women opt out or self-select out, rather than put themselves through a process, this may be yet another form of barrier, albeit an internal barrier.

In order to give our contributions effect and to progress beyond the apparent flickers of progress evidenced by the low number of women in leadership, there need to be supporting structures in place. On the one hand, concrete steps to overcome external forces imposed on the women may be required; while on the other hand, overcoming internal resistance may need to come from the women themselves. Women also need to embrace their power and to empower themselves to overcome whatever barriers they may face.

What are Some Possible Empowerment Principles that Women Could Apply in order to Transform the Stakes?

For women who wish to get to the top, passage is not always simple or direct. It may be full of twists and turns. Borrowing a metaphor from Greek mythology, Klenke (1997)[18] uses a labyrinth to capture women's journey as leaders. Because all labyrinths have a viable route to the centre, the metaphor acknowledges obstacles, but also possibilities. Women leaders in politics demonstrate how, for example, women have managed relations, accounting for their success, showing how they too have overcome barriers and made the necessary breakthroughs.

Women need to step out of the background and step up to embrace the power and success inherent in leadership. Ten empowering principles are able to transform the stakes in realising one's full potential as a woman leader. Though a political perspective, it is believed that these principles are applicable to women leaders in all contexts.

Principle 1: Understand the context with its associated expectations

> *Culture is the result of the dynamic relationship that exists between the context, society, and ourselves; how we are, affects society, while at the same time it influences us … we can decide to act as the prevailing culture or go against it."*
> – Chinchilla & Moragas[19]

Culture is probably the most dominant force in the justification for the pre-determined role that women will play in any society. It permeates the mindset, the expectations, and therefore the realities of both men and woman from a young age. We often derive comfort and certainty both at domestic and global level that things are the way they are supposed to be. Culture provides a systematic reinforcement, which ensures that the challenges encountered *en route* as barriers are explained away merely as a manifestation of a reality that is meant to be. However, culture is dynamic. It evolves to accommodate progress, and the proponents of women in leadership would argue that there is a growing awareness and now, the will and the power, to ensure that those evolutions take place at a much faster rate.

People have great expectations from women leaders. They think that when a woman leader comes to power, many problems will be solved quickly and easily. There is almost a sense that women must try harder and work harder than men. We are all very tolerant when men make mistakes, but I don't know of any society that is tolerant when women make mistakes. There is a tendency to say, "Well, she's a woman." Women still have the main responsibility for family, child rearing, and homemaking, and those are not shared in an equal and balanced way. Therefore, there is an additional need to be more assertive, or better, or more determined, to make more sacrifices, get up earlier, go to bed later, or whatever it may be.

Managing different contexts simultaneously also remains a major challenge for women leaders, because many of them function in more than one context, for example, family, workplace and community.

Principle 2: Seize the opportunity – you have to want it

> *"Your best chance to move forward is to seize opportunities as they come along. Success is never guaranteed, but if you do your best, there is no absolute failure."*
> – Harriett Woods[20]

Opportunities do not often arrive on the doorstep, neatly packaged and labelled, "at your convenience". There will always be difficult decisions and choices to make. The reality is that women leaders face more demands and scrutiny from their families, from their colleagues, and from the media; far more than their male counterparts. When I travelled to London, to the Commonwealth Secretariat, following my appointment as the Deputy Secretary General in 2007, there were a number of congratulatory calls, as the positon represented the most senior woman in the global body. However, when it became apparent that not all members of my family would immediately make the move with me, I received a number of rather pointed questions, bordering on admonition, in the midst of the congratulatory messages. It was clear that even as people around me wanted to support and encourage me, they also felt they needed to scrutinise the impact of my decision on my family a little further.

Principle 3: Have the courage to take risks

> *"Women's self-limiting attitudes and behaviour barriers may be part of the invisible barriers reinforced by culture and stereotypes."* – Author unknown[21]

Women can take risks because they are often underestimated and yet can demonstrate an inherent steel and resilience. Indira Gandhi, the first woman Prime Minister of India, in her presidential inauguration speech said: "We are the women of India, don't imagine us as flower-maidens, we are the sparks in the fire." – Katherine Frank[22]

Challenges and problems have been caused by the exclusion and under-representation of women. Women may be in a position to contribute their particular and unique values, opinions and solutions to complement and to assist in providing solutions and options for a way forward. As Indian political leader, Sonia Gandhi, observed in her Commonwealth Lecture: "Even a small investment in women has great economic, political and social reverberations." – The *Hindu* (18 March 2011)[23] It is only through an inclusion of a wider range of voices, points of view, life experiences, and ways of looking at life, that humanity can gain better insights into and options for development.

Principle 4: Claim your space at the table

"Naked ambition in a woman is problematic in the business world." – Betsy Stark[24]

The COO of Facebook, Sheryl Sandberg's, rallying call for women to *"Lean in"* and claim their place at the table in order to succeed in their careers has resonated with women in all spheres of life.[25] Political leadership and the general rise of women to decision-making levels have provided a range of strong, focused women. Women in the political sphere have been "leaning in" and making waves, leaving a significant trail in their wake.

Yet barriers for women in political leadership continue in varying degrees, creating a pronounced dearth of women in the political arena. Women entering politics and senior leadership positions face greater challenges; entry-level expectations are high and often shrouded in mystery, from selection processes, to capacity building and preparation. Even during their tenure, women leaders still cite the challenge of exclusion, awkward timings, and undermining in certain camps. A seat at the table does not therefore automatically translate to an easy ride. Women work hard at getting there, and sometimes even harder at staying there.

Principle 5: Learn, use and change the rules

> *"If you are a woman in a male world, you need to stand your ground and sometimes to assert yourself. Your integrity and professionalism should allow you to insist on the necessary improvements that help you and the institution deliver. That may require changing the rules of the game so they are more accommodating, more supportive and do not impose further barriers."* – Author unknown[26]

Significantly more women in leadership will assist in responding to the dominant culture evident in most leadership positions and institutions. Women, by lending their voices to position what their needs and wants are, can also open up the space for what they can offer: the differential impact of policies on women; and a gender lens to inform decisions, to establish what needs to be done differently and to help make progress toward creating an context which is ready to adapt to having more women at the power tables.

When Margaret Thatcher took up the position as Britain's first woman Prime Minister, as one of the few women in the House of Parliament, she quipped: *"The House itself was – still is – a very masculine place. This manifested itself above all, I found, in the sheer volume of noise."*[27]

- Men largely dominate the leadership arena; therefore, over time, they have formulated, developed and entrenched the rules.
- Performance measures and standards are often organised according to male norms and values, and in some cases even male lifestyles.
- Built-in practices and schedules have not necessarily been challenged to take into account the dual burden that women carry as the primary caregivers in most societies.

Women, like everyone else wanting to be taken seriously in an context in which they wish to participate, need to understand first how the system works. They need to invest in knowing and understanding what it will take to succeed in that specific context. The written rules and procedures are only a starting point; they will need to appreciate the traditions and the customs; the informal and the social norms. Networking and mentoring can be a useful way of understanding what is often referred to as, the 'old boys' network, be it in politics, business, or at any power table. Once women understand this, it will allow them to challenge from an informed position, and can also assist in making a breakthrough. They need to understand the politics, rules and biases inherent in the system in order to enhance their chances of adapting and/or lending their own blend.

Principle 6: Positioning for success – look as though you belong

Leading change for a new generation requires changing the look and feel of leadership. While competence comes first, clothing can enhance self-confidence and certainly plays a powerful role in how others perceive and receive you. Men seem to have narrowed down their selection to the power suit, which has become accepted as the symbol of confidence, control and assertiveness deemed appropriate in leadership positions. Women by their nature have far too many choices to make and there is no emerging single look that defines this for women. Many successful women dress to express their individuality, believing that it is not the looks, but the substance of leadership that matters. As Karren Brady remarks: *"Celebrate your uniqueness, be confident in your own values and own opinions and just because I work with men does not mean that I dress like one."*[28]

Dress in a way that makes the statement you want to make about yourself without taking away from your message. Senator Hillary Clinton, speaking to students at a commencement day, bemoaned the fact that her time at Law School had not prepared her for the attention that her hair got. She had been focusing on her dreams for the world when it would appear that the world was more interested in her hopes and dreams for her hair.[29]

Women have different forms of expression and the overriding consideration is always that they should feel confident and well presented, and that their clothes should not detract attention from the core message. Although choice of clothing is personal, many women have acknowledged that they do take particular care to ensure that it does not detract from their message. For Prime Minister of India, Indira Gandhi, *"clothes were always deeply important to her and ... she was never carelessly dressed."* – Katherine Frank[30] Women who have reached senior leadership positions do not adhere to any 'uniform', prescribed codes of dress. However, their choice of dress is constantly scrutinised and sometimes commented on more than the actual message they deliver.

Principle 7: Shoring up your confidence

> *"There's that kind of double bind that women find themselves in. On the one hand, yes, be smart, stand up for yourself. On the other hand, don't offend anybody, don't step on toes, or you'll become somebody that nobody likes because you're too assertive."* – Hillary Clinton[31]

Much of the bias against female competence is subtle and largely unintentional. But it does not mean it is trivial or inconsequential. Succeeding in any endeavour or field takes hard work, determination and patience. We gain confidence, when we push beyond our comfort zone. Women need to believe they can do it themselves, and should not ask for permission to lead, or wait to be asked to lead, but should take up the challenge in the knowledge that they can.

Media interest in women tends to be linked more to the person than to their politics, or their position. People start with the idea of questioning a woman's competence, whereas for a man, it's different. If he is elected to a senior position, it is readily assumed that it is because of his competence. Not only is the bar set higher for women, but also the burden of proof is on women to prove their competence in ways rarely required of men.

People need to have confidence in what you are saying:

- You have to have the confidence to convey your message clearly and competently.
- Whatever you do must be worthwhile, must resonate, and must make sense to you.
- You must be true to who you are.
- You must be able to articulate your thoughts, and to have and to express an opinion.

The places where women are most apt to feel incompetent and illegitimate are in the public spheres of power and authority. Since women do not have a long history of belonging in these spheres, especially at the highest levels, the feats of the great and powerful wizards seem to be downright mysterious.

Principle 8: Use women's power

"Being nice should never be perceived as being weak. It's not a sign of weakness, it's a sign of courtesy, manners, grace, a woman's ability to make everyone… feel at home, and it should never be construed as weakness. It does not mean women cannot be tough when necessary." – Edith Cresson[32]

"'Grace' is often associated with certain qualities of the feminine. It communicates attributes of flowing movement, delicate features and fragile beauty – sometimes used in this context to confine women to stereotypically weak roles. Sometimes we need to overcome what may initially seem impossible, this helps us gain an advantage, 'a silver lining' even in the midst of extreme stereotype."- Schaaf et al.[33]

Prime Minister Indira Gandhi indicated that it was easier for her to assume leadership after her father's passing, because, if she had been a man, her intentions and positioning would have been greatly analysed and steps could have been taken to block her progression. *"We need to encourage young women to open their minds to the possibility of what they can achieve – Playing to your strengths and using your skills in the best possible way."* – Karren Brady[34]

Mrs Gandhi was small in stature and frail looking; this apparently belied her ruthlessness and left many in awe. Her gender was generally considered as a weakness, allowing her to be able to strike firmly. She was not considered a threat; some had underestimated her, assuming that she would be a figurehead, a "malleable and token" leader. Others were convinced that somewhere lurking in the background was a man running the show. Even the press dismissed her as "the public pretty face". She invoked her womanhood as a source of strength and compassion, and presented herself as a great provider and reconciler. "This silk and steel woman had outmanoeuvred them all."[35]

When Hillary Clinton first applied to join a law firm, there was concern raised about how she would be introduced to clients and "what if she fell pregnant?". *"However, very soon, they were in awe of her talents, her intellect, and especially her tough mindedness"* (Bernstein, 2007).[36] On the other hand, Margaret Thatcher was thought of as too "doctrinaire and insensitive",[37] which led to mixed acceptance of her as a leader of the Conservative Party.

Former Prime Minister of Bangladesh, Begum Khaleda Zia, has been described as rather shy, but she believed her self-effacing style was welcomed by her people, because it contrasted with the style of past military dictators.[38]

Benazir Bhutto was challenged when she became pregnant while Prime Minster of Pakistan. It was argued that the Constitution did not provide for maternity leave at the level of Prime Minister. A constitutional crisis was looming in the minds of many. Wanting to shatter the glass ceiling for younger women, she was determined that the prospect of pregnancy would no longer be a barrier at any level. Therefore she arranged to go into hospital and had the baby delivered and was able to return to work the next day. She didn't want to encourage stereotypes that pregnancy interferes with performance, so she worked harder. It was a defining moment, proving a woman can work and have a baby in the highest and most challenging leadership position.[39]

Principle 9: Find a mentor

> "A person is a person through other persons ... I am human because I belong, I participate, and I share. A person with Ubuntu is open and available to others, affirming of others, does not feel threatened that others are able and good, for he or she has a proper self-assurance that comes from knowing that he or she belongs in a greater whole and is diminished when others are humiliated or diminished, when others are tortured or oppressed, or treated as if they were less than who they are." – Desmond Tutu[40]

Mentoring happens in one-on-one relationships, but it can help in women's circles around the kitchen table. We all need support, validation, mirroring and reflective listening in order to build confidence and stretch our leadership muscles. Mentoring is an opportunity to offer and receive that nurturing.

Women have plenty of experience being members of a minority. We are often a minority voice in discussion and decision-making, especially at the highest levels. Only in recent decades, with feminist movements, have these disparities been acknowledged and serious attention given to understanding the dynamics and consequences of marginalised women.

> "I think that the growing number of women as heads of state is work women have done themselves to promote women, to prove to the world that women are in no way inferior to men when it comes to having important posts. It has been a great struggle to prove that, and to know that half of the world doesn't know that yet."
> – Vigdis Finnbogadottir[41]

- Traits associated with women, such as empathy, sensitivity and thoughtfulness, are valuable traits; for example, empathy is one of the six traits cited as necessary to flourish in a new-world economy.
- There is a real and urgent need to extend the pipeline of women ready to embrace the opportunity of leadership. If meaningful change is to occur, we need all hands on deck.
- Regardless of whether women are considered a good fit in male-designed and male-dominated roles or choose be authentic and successful in their own way, it may be helpful to consider a few aspects of what a balanced leader is, and the tools required for success.

Principle 10: Find a male champion

An enabling context, a supportive context, and a celebratory context go a long way towards ensuring continued success, and the woman leader needs an adaptive and progressive context which allows for the growth and evolution of women to succeed as leaders.

"What you make of your destinies is up to you." – Benazir Bhutto's father, encouraging his daughter to stand up and fight against overwhelming odds (in Bhutto, 2007).[42]

Both Gandhi and Bhutto groomed their daughters for leadership. They imparted endurance, honour, and principles that prepared them to deal with the most challenging periods. Gandhi was groomed by her father and provided with practical coaching, including how to disguise failure and not let the opponent "read your face".[43] Strong women characters such as Joan of Arc were a constant reassurance that it was not only a few men who contribute to history, but that all people, regardless of their gender, who make up a country have the potential to contribute significantly. Margaret Thatcher's father taught her to read newspapers and discuss issues of the day. All three women often accompanied their fathers when they were carrying out their official duties. These fathers believed in educating their daughters.

Through customary rules governing marriage, inheritance, and property ownership, women's participation in society and the economy continues to be mediated in important ways by their husbands or other male relatives. Some of these practices are formally exempted from non-discrimination provisions in national constitutions, leaving little room for challenge or legal redress.

> "I have been influenced by some of the idealistic people – Gandhi, Martin Luther King, and Vaclav Havel – they would be the kind of people – they all happen to be men – who would influence me because they are emphasizing very important values for our time and for all time." – Mary Robinson[44]

Conclusion

The impact of women in leadership positions necessitates a redefinition of the role of women in society. As primary caregivers, it does not necessarily mean they will abdicate from their primary role, but what changes could be the "how" – the way in which they fulfil those obligations. There is a need for all of us to enable our boy children to take on greater domestic chores. We need to educate both boy children and girl children about respect and regard for the woman as a leader, as a provider, and as a contributor to the wellbeing and development of both their family and of humanity.

No one raises concerns about a man's ability to work and raise children at the same time. A struggling man at the helm is usually given the benefit of the doubt – it is not necessarily assumed that he is not up to the demands of the position. However, society is quick to sow these seeds of doubt about women. It is these doubts and biases which a woman faces that create difficult choices with regard to furthering her career at the expense of, not for the sake of, her family.

The inestimable value of the potential contribution of women's leadership is yet to be realised:

- Education, opportunity, and encouragement are among the key drivers to unlock the inestimable value of women's leadership to society at large.
- Women have different strengths that are needed to address the prevailing challenges to build better societies and better communities.
- Strengths of collaboration, co-operation, compassion, intuition, and emotional intelligence are among those identified for new leadership.
- A new way is needed of looking at what defines success in order to challenge stereotypes and to enable fulfilment for both men and women.

Ultimately, the ability – or inability – to lead will come from an individual's strengths and weaknesses, not their gender. After all, stereotypes can take one only so far.

The experience of Prime Minister Bhutto removed any remaining doubts that "even as Prime Minister, a woman can have a baby while holding down the highest position in the land".[45] As for the young man across the counter, I do not believe I have too many words, except maybe to point out to him that holding onto stereotypes may limit not just the potential of the women in his life, but his own as well!

Perhaps the most profound learning on my journey is that leadership is a choice I first had to make for myself, before others could play their part. You need to take ownership of your own path, and others will be there to help. Embracing the principles of empowerment is also a choice: "The road to success is nothing if not a series of choices."[46] It's not a recipe for success, but is an opportunity to reflect and draw on one's personal and others' experiences. Leadership is a humbling experience and one that allows for the self to continue to learn and grow. Successful leaders will not have all the answers, but will work with us to create a genuine partnership of leadership for enhanced results.

> "Imagine a world with women and men leaders who are vulnerable and powerful, empathetic and self-aware, rounded and connected leaders equipped to address enormous challenges of complexity, volatility and increasing pace of change."[47]

Endnotes

1. Klenke, 2011.
2. Ibid.
3. Ibid.
4. Schaaf et al., 2010.
5. Wong & Dawson, 2010.
6. African Development Bank, 2015
7. Wong & Dawson, 2010.
8. Tarr-Whelan, 2011.
9. Ibid.
10. Barsh et al., 2011.
11. African Development Bank, 2015.
12. Ibid.
13. Ibid.
14. Ibid.
15. Ibid.
16. Eugenia Charles, in Liswood, 1995.
17. Klenke, 2011.
18. Ibid.
19. Chinchilla & Moragas, 2008.
20. Woods, 2010.
21. Author unknown, nd.
22. Frank, 2001.
23. *The Hindu*, 2011.
24. Van Ogtrop, 2015.
25. Sandberg, 2013.
26. Author unknown, nd.
27. Thatcher, in Nunn, 2002.
28. Brady, 2013.
29. Clinton, 2003 (commencement speech.)
30. Frank, 2001.
31. Clinton, 2003.
32. Edith Cresson, in Liswood, 1995.
33. Schaaf et al., 2012.
34. Brady, 2013.
35. Bhutto, 2007.
36. Bernstein, 2007.
37. Thatcher, 1996.
38. Begum Khaleda Zia, in Liswood,1995.
39. Bhutto,2007.
40. Desmond Tutu, in Schaaf et al., 2012.
41. Finnbogadottir, in Liswood, 1995.
42. Bhutto, 2007.
43. Ibid.
44. Mary Robinson, in Liswood, 1995.
45. Bhutto, 2007.
46. Young, 2011.
47. Barsh et al., 2011.

References

African Development Bank. 2015. *Africa gender equality index 2015*. Abidjan, Civ: African Development Bank.

Barsh, J, Cranston, S & Lewis, G. 2011, *How remarkable women lead: The breakthrough model for work and life*. Reprint ed. New York, NY: Crown Business.

Bernstein, C. 2007. *A woman in charge. The Life of Hillary Rodham Clinton*. London, UK: Hutchinson Arrow Books.

Bhutto, B. 2007. *Daughter of the East: An autobiography*. 2nd ed. London, UK: Simon & Schuster.

Brady, K. 2013. *Strong woman: The truth about getting to the top*. London, UK: HarperCollins Publishers Ltd.

Chinchilla, N & Moragas, M. 2008. *Masters of our destiny*. Pamplona, SP (ESP): EUNSA.

Clinton, HR. 2003. *Living history*. London, UK: Headline Book Publishing, a division of Hodder Headline.

Frank, K. 2001. *Indira: The Life of Indira Nehru Gandhi*. Sydney, NSW, AUS: HarperCollins Books Australia.
The Hindu. 2011. *Women as agents of change: Sonia Gandhi's Commonwealth lecture*. 18 March. [Online]. Available: http://www.thehindu.com/news/resources/women-as-agents-of-change-sonia-gandhis-commonwealth-lecture/article1550685.ece. [Accessed 13 July 2016].
Klenke, K. 2011. *Women in leadership: Contextual dynamics and boundaries*. Bingley, UK: Emerald Group Publishing.
Liswood, L. 1995. *Women world leaders: Fifteen great politicians tell their stories*. London, UK: HarperCollins.
Nunn, H. 2002. *Thatcher, politics and fantasy: The political culture of gender and nation*. London, UK: Lawrence & Wishart.
Sandberg, S. 2013. *Lean in: Women, work and the will to lead*. New York, NY: Alfred A Knopf, a division of Random House, Inc., New York; and Toronto, CAN: Random House of Canada Limited.
Schaaf, K, Lindahl, K, Hurty, K & Cheen, Rev. G (eds). 2012. *Women, spirituality and transformative leadership: Where grace meets power*. Woodstock, VT: SkyLight Paths Publishing.
Tarr-Whelan, L. 2011. *Women lead the way: Your guide to stepping up to leadership and changing the world*. San Francisco, CA: Berrett-Koehler Publishers, Inc.
Thatcher, M. 1996. *The Path to power*. London, UK: HarperColllins.
Van Ogtrop, K. 2015. 'Why ambition isn't working for women'. *Time Magazine*, 8 October.
Wong, A & Dawson, R. 2010. *Secrets of powerful women: Leading change for a new generation*. New York, NY: Lifetime Entertainment series, Hyperion Books.
Woods, Harriett. 2010. *Stepping up to power: The political journey of American Women*. Boulder, CO: Westview Press.
Young, Valerie (ed). 2011. *The secret thoughts of successful women: Why capable people suffer from the impostor syndrome and how to thrive in spite of it*. New York, NY: Crown Business.

Additional Readings

International Institute for Democracy and Electoral Assistance (International IDEA). 2005. *Women in parliament: Beyond numbers. IDEA handbook*. Stockholm, SE (SWE): International IDEA.
Leimon, A, Moscovici, F & Goodier, H. 2011. *Coaching women to lead (Essential coaching skills and knowledge series)*. London, UK: Routledge.
Vagianos, A. 2014. 'The Hillary Clinton guide to being an empowered woman'. *The Huffington Post*, 3 April. Updated 07/22/2015.

Chapter 13

MULTI-GENERATIONAL LEADERSHIP
Graeme Codrington and Raymond de Villiers

"People resemble their times more than they resemble their parents." – Arab proverb

Each of us has a default setting. By this I assume that everyone else is like me, and that my views of the world are "normal", and even normative. If we did not know better, we would teach the way we learn; we would write the way we like to read; and we would lead in ways we prefer to be led. These are all natural to us. But they do not serve us well as leaders.

Good leaders adjust their leadership style and actions to suit their followers, taking into account a variety of factors including gender, culture, personality, education, social status, and age. This does not mean they are chameleons: shape-shifting to every whim and fancy of other people. Rather, they understand the delicate balance between being authentic ("being myself") and the need for connection and engagement with others. It is in this sweet spot that true influence takes place.

Therefore a key leadership competence is the ability to engage with difference. This requires both personal awareness and empathy towards others. This set of skills is often referred to as "emotional intelligence".[1] It starts with understanding a set of frameworks that make sense of the differences between people. Good leaders will select a number of these frameworks and use them to help anticipate and make sense of the actions and reactions of other people.

The choice of such frameworks depends largely on personal preference. Most of the best-known frameworks are equally valuable, each with its own slightly different approach. The most useful framework, though, is the one that is most often overlooked: it looks at age, life stage, and the era in which a person is born. It is generational theory.

The purpose of our chapter is to discuss how generational theory can be used by leaders to create that sweet spot of influence between the leader and different generations. To this end, the chapter proceeds by covering the following topics: the concept of "generation theory"; the leadership challenge of leading different generations; multi-generational implications for organisations; generations@work; organising and leading the next generation; and the evolution to the future world of work.

Generational Theory

Simply stated, generational theory explains that the era in which a person was born affects the development of their view of the world. Our value systems are shaped in the first two decades or so of our lives by our families, our friends, our communities, significant events, and the general era in which we are born. People who are born at the same time in history experience fairly similar forces at play, including everything from general political and economic realities all the way to popular culture, music, movies, and even school curricula.

In the past century, global forces, combined with the effects of international media and 24/7 news channels, communication technologies, and the growing interconnectedness of the world have meant that increasing numbers of people around the world are feeling the impact of the same defining events. Facing similar issues, with the same events having an impact on them, and sharing similar experiences, people of the same age are likely to have similar underlying value systems, regardless of their country or community of birth. These "value systems" are the drivers of behaviour and attitudes, and are good predictors of behaviour and expectations.

A "generation" tends to be about 20 years in length, representing roughly the time from the birth of a cohort (or group) of people to the time they come of age and start having their own children. Typically, generations are bound by significant events in the country or region being considered. This leads to slightly different dates in different areas, although defining global events in the last century tend to group quite remarkably around specific years.

Consider, for example the tumultuous year starting with the Tiananmen Square protests in China in June 1989; through to the tearing down of the Berlin Wall on 9 November 1989; the opening-up of eastern Europe; *Perestroika* in Russia; the release of Nelson Mandela in February 1990; and the end of Pinochet's Chilean dictatorship in March 1990. All around the world, these events affected people in similar ways, and mark a good boundary between generations.

The generally used labels for the currently living generations are: GI or Traditionalist (born 1900-1920s), Silent or Veteran (born 1929-1945), Boomers or Baby Boomers (born 1946-1960s), Generation X or Xers (born 1968-1989), the Millennials or Generation Y (born mid-1980s-2000s), and Generation Z, Digital Natives or iTouch Generation (born 2000s to the present).

There is overlap in the birth years of these generations as the boundaries between them are slightly fluid in different countries and regions. In addition, people born a few years before and after a key defining event may be on the "cusp" of a change of generations, and can exhibit the characteristics of two different generations.

Generational theory looks at the defining events and the prevailing cultural milieu of the era in which each generational cohort is born. It attempts to describe how these shaped the values of the young people at the time. Understanding these values allows us to predict how the different generations will approach each life stage they live through, and how they may act and react in different situations. Generational theory has been researched and verified in many different ways, and when used wisely, is a powerful profiling tool. [2, 3, 4, 5 & 6]

The Leadership Challenge: A Clash of Generations

The challenge for leaders comes from a *clash* of the generations: a collision of values, expectations, ambitions and attitudes of older and younger people. Each generation has a unique perspective on the world, as well as different preferences for acquiring, digesting, organising and applying information and skills. Dealing with this diversity of ages, values and worldviews can be a difficult job, and can affect everything from teamwork and motivation to customer care and sales strategies.

To understand and successfully interact with people from different generations, it is important to be familiar with what makes them tick. In the world of work at the moment, we have three main generations (Boomers, Xers and Millennials), with the Silent and Digital Native generations on the fringes as customers and background influencers (mainly as older parents being cared for, or children being raised).

A brief description is given of each generation from a work perspective.

General issue (or Traditionalist) generation: born 1900–1929

The oldest group of people still alive come from a generation that began at a time of great globalisation, which many people thought to be the pinnacle of development. Little did they know what awaited them in the 21st century, but they were shaped and formed during a time of great excitement and development for the future. Their title comes from the "General Issue" label applied to soldiers in World War I, and from the fact that they were born just as the modern age was beginning, and were a bridge between the old traditions of the past and the exciting new world which the Industrial Revolution had birthed. Many of this generation have lived long past their life expectancy (which was about 50 years at birth for most of them), with over 350 000 of them now past 100 years of age globally. Although some of this generation are still alive, they are unlikely to have an impact on the workplace, and we are therefore not going to consider them in the remainder of this chapter.

Silent generation: born 1929–1945

The Silent Generation was born before and during the Great Depression and World War II. It is no surprise that they are conservative, hard-working and structured, preferring rules, order and formal hierarchies. They believe in discipline and prefer consistency, predictability and stability rather than change. Their mantras include: "Get a good job in a big organisation, and stay there"; "Waste not, want not"; and "Young people should be seen and not heard".

They are founts of great wisdom, having lived through some of humanity's most profound change-moments in the last eight decades, but they are often slow to share this wisdom. They do their best to be self-sufficient, never asking for help, and are conservative in their approaches to life and work.

Baby boomers: born 1946–1960s

Baby Boomers are the post-war generation – the drugs, sex, and rock 'n roll set – who grew up during a time of grand visions. A man on the moon, civil rights, and the atom bomb were just a few. They are workaholics, putting in 60-hour-plus work weeks. Boomers are passionately concerned about participation in the workplace, motivated by vision and strategy, and care about creating a fair and level playing field for all.

They are idealists who believe that every problem has a solution. By working together we can do anything we put our minds to. They are image and status conscious, and practise conspicuous consumption. They are in more debt than any other generation ever. They are motivated by opportunities for personal growth and teamwork. They know every management technique in the book, and can be relied on to run regular visioning retreats. They are the driven, visionary leaders who have built the fast-paced, globalised world as we know it today.

Generation Xers: born 1968–1989

Generation Xers grew up as "latch-key kids" during the era of crises, from Watergate to South Africa's momentous events of 16 June 1976; through the energy crisis; to the collapse of communism. 'X' is the variable, the unknown. This generation certainly grew up during a time of chaos and change. They need options and flexibility. They dislike close supervision, preferring freedom and an output-driven system. They love change so much that they actually need it.

They are not great team players; they dislike rules, and do things their way. They build coalitions in an office, not pyramids. Therefore they are not at all concerned about hierarchies or authority. Xers strive for work-life integration, not just balance: they work to have a life. They do not live to work. They are pragmatic about the world.

Millennials/Generation Y: born mid-1980s–2000s

As some of the most protected children in history, this generation is confident – almost arrogant, they are so confident. It is actually just a veneer of confidence. They really need more help and assistance than they are prepared to ask for. They have unrealistic expectations of the workplace. Whereas the Silent and Boomers' attitude to work is "I have worked hard for 40 years, now I'd like to retire", the Xers' attitude is "I worked hard until lunchtime; now can I go home?"

Yet Millennials are the upcoming optimists, willing to co-operate, work and learn in the right setting. They need to be stretched and constantly developed. They want feedback regularly, not an annual review. They value diversity, often not even noticing it. They are altruistic, civic-minded, street smart and naïve all at the same time. They are growing up in a world that is creaking under the strain of our lifestyles, and they are daily made aware of the fragile environment. So it is no surprise that they are emerging as ethical consumers who want to change the world.

Eric Chester writes that the Millennials have, more than any other young generation, an ability to "filter out every command, every request and every instruction that is not bundled with acceptable rationale… they demand reasons and rationale, so the traditional 'because I said so' isn't going to cut it with them".[7]

Generation Z, digital natives or iTouch generation: born 2000s to the present

This generation is not yet in the workplace, but they are coming soon. Their values are important to consider now, as they are already having an influence on their parents and older siblings. The most important shift of values, attitudes and actions that will have an impact on the world of work is around communication and priorities.

They will not put work first, and will force us to take "work-life balance" to its logical conclusions with virtual teams, flexible working hours, on-demand workers, and remuneration for outputs rather than inputs. By way of communication, they will retire emails by 2030, replacing them with instant messaging and message board systems, and using virtual reality extensively in every part of their lives.

Multi-generational Implications for Organisations

The differences between the generations have many implications for organisations: specifically, how they have traditionally dealt with issues such as structure, hierarchy and authority, recruitment and career management, performance management, performance reviews and remuneration, training and development, succession planning, team dynamics, customer service, sales techniques, and so much more.

Here are some common scenarios that organisations with which we have worked are facing:

- Younger employees do not like email, preferring instant messages.
- Older people tend to manage by email, assuming that long, detailed emails are always read.
- Older employees tend to prefer meetings and face-to-face interactions as *their first choice* when dealing with important information and team issues, whereas younger people see these as a *last* resort.
- Younger employees want to work collaboratively and to be involved in decision-making, but their managers like being directive and making decisions themselves.

- In many professional organisations, the senior people may want to retire after a long working life with gruelling hours, but feel constrained because younger workers do not want the responsibility, long working hours, and commitment that are expected of a senior leader.
- Younger people are trying to create a healthy work-life balance, but can often appear to be lazy, uncommitted, or even distracted as they do so.
- Generation Y want to receive frequent feedback after every project. But their Generation X managers are too busy and do not have the same desire for feedback. They therefore do not prioritise this task, frustrating their Gen Y direct reports.
- Baby Boomers are motivated by career advancement, titles and perks. Younger people are more motivated by flexibility, freedom, and a sense of contribution.
- Older workers see information as power, believing that the more senior you are, the more access to information you should have. Younger people want all the information always available to everyone, and complete transparency.

These are just a few real-life examples of different generations' differing expectations of how the world of work should work. From the organisation's perspective, it can often be difficult to deal with these differences, because there are no "right" or "wrong" options. There are just differences in approach. Sometimes what one generation wants is also a really good option for the organisation as a whole, but often it is just an issue of style. Using a generational lens to look at organisational issues can help to evaluate and re-examine long-established policies and processes that need to change; or it can help people to understand why younger or older colleagues or clients act and react as they do.

The key to leading successfully in a multi-generational environment is awareness and understanding of the differences between generations so that the positives can be harnessed and the pitfalls avoided.

Generations@Work

With the theory established, albeit briefly, we can now consider two particularly valuable applications. The first is to understand how different generations approach a few key issues that most leaders consider essential to a well-functioning workplace. We will then focus our attention on the youngest generation in the workplace, who are currently causing many leaders significant concern.

Loyalty

The change in the contract between organisation and employee is the biggest generational shift of all in the workplace. The old contract was simple: an employee came into an organisation and accepted the values of the organisation; bought into the vision and mission; and sold the organisation's products/services to its customers, using the organisation's systems, vocabulary, methods, and processes. In other words, they made themselves virtually unmarketable anywhere else, which was not a problem, since the organisation offered employment as long as they wanted it. The employees paid their dues, working like slaves for a few years in order to be fast-tracked up the organisation structures. In return, the organisation guaranteed that there would be a management position available a few years from now. We are using hyperbole for effect, but this was the old contract of loyalty for security.

How many organisations can offer such security these days? Even if they did, would we believe them? If organisations cannot offer security, why are they still asking for loyalty? If they cannot give a long-term commitment, why are they still asking for it? There should be no surprise that organisations battle to get loyalty from staff, when actually they are offering nothing in return.

Yet, loyalty is still available. It must just be "purchased" with a different currency. That currency includes helping employees (and even customers) to develop generic skills and remain marketable; creating a setting that values fun, flexibility and freedom; and giving them constant, timely, honest feedback on everything they do. The interesting reality is that the more marketable and mobile your best employees feel, the more likely they are to stay with you. You have to help them to develop skills beyond their current job functions and ensure that they are continually developing in new ways. Even then, though, it is going to be tough. Loyalty is not something that younger generations give away easily. It may be easier just to build your organisation in such a way that you do not expect much loyalty to begin with.

Hard work

Different generations have different definitions of what hard work looks like. The Silents worked hard because it was "the right thing to do". Boomers were prepared to put in extra effort and to work long hours – and this is *their* definition of hard work – in order to secure promotions and bonuses, and be noticed. Gen Xers will work hard for shorter bursts of time in order to deliver on projects about which they are particularly passionate.

But Gen Y are not likely to do any of these things unless they have a very specific short-term balance for the hard work put in. If they work through a weekend to deliver on a deadline, they would like to take Monday morning off to recover, for example. If they put in a particularly impressive amount of work on a project, they would like a bonus as soon as the project is finished, rather than at the end of the financial year.

Gen Y also need to be told specifically that extra work, discretionary effort and things they do "over and above" their agreed contract are what is taken into account when considering promotions and advancement. At least, this is how Xers and Boomers see things. Many Gen Y employees want to be in management by 29, and partners by 35, simply by "doing their job" and not adding extra effort. This is an unrealistic expectation on their part. It is easily solved by explaining how things really work at the office.

Proactivity

Generation Y and the Digital Natives have spent almost every day of the first two decades of their lives in some kind of programme. From toddlers' groups to outcomes-based group work at school, their lives have been structured and nothing has been left to chance. They have been told where to be, what to do, and how to achieve their goals step-by-step throughout their lives. No wonder, then, that the biggest management complaint about today's younger people is that they lack initiative and proactivity. We are convinced that this must actually be taught and consciously developed in them when they arrive at the workplace.

Flexibility

Generation Xers and Ys value flexibility highly. They ask questions such as: "If I answer emails on a Saturday night, can I watch movies on a Tuesday morning?" and "If I take my work home, can I bring my family to the office?" We've known about telecommuting, virtual offices, remote management, flexitime and 'hot desking' – not having an allocated work desk – for many years now. Today's generation of young employees is just going to make sure we do something about it.

As customers, they are demanding more flexibility, too. No longer will they accept the excuse from your front-line staff that "the system won't allow it". They know that all systems can be changed, and overridden. They will continue to demand "mass customisation" from the organisations with which they interact.

Personal lives at work

Today's young workers do not understand why they must "leave their personal lives at home". They need a workplace that will allow them to make personal phone calls; send personal emails; and be flexible enough to let them take care of personal issues that must be dealt with during office hours. They would also be very attracted to workplaces that offered amenities such as gyms, "chill-out" spaces, crèches and day care centres, and areas for entertainment. We know of a call centre that built a skate park in the carpark for their employees, for example.

Oversight and supervision

The easiest way to stifle a Gen Xer is to micro-manage him/her. Xers like to be told what must be done, and then left alone to do it. In fact, at the heart of this desire is an understanding that people should be paid for their outputs, not their inputs. No longer should people be paid for just arriving at work. We need to make the transition to a world where people are rewarded for the quality and speed of their outputs. Generation Xers are ready for that world.

The flipside, though, is that Generation Xers often are given too *little* support. Boomers need more structure, more meetings and more formal agreement on tasks and outcomes before feeling comfortable. Gen Y and the Digital Natives need a lot more structure than they appear to, or will ever ask for. They like to know what tasks need to be done, and also *why* those tasks have to be done: why done by then, why done by them, why done that way, why done at all. It can be exhausting, but it is necessary to give this detail. Xers who are managers of younger or older people need to provide more information, more structure, and more support than they expect or feel comfortable with. People managing Xers need to back off more than they want to.

Rewards and recognition

Everybody responds well to public recognition of their contributions, but Boomers love this the most. Gen Xers are more concerned about being able to see the contribution they have made to the bigger picture and greater good. For Gen Y/Millennials, public recognition is not as important as the sense that they have contributed to the team and that their boss is pleased with them.

And the younger they are, the more personal accolades they need. Remember that this is a generation that received medals just for turning up. Participating was seen as just as significant as winning throughout their childhood and adolescence. Multiple opportunities for reward and recognition leverage this dynamic in the workplace, even if the rewards themselves are small and trivial.

Accountability

Do not misunderstand this list. Generation Ys understand that all these things come at a price. They are aware that with responsibility comes accountability. In fact, they expect to be held accountable for what they do, even brutally accountable. Any setting that allows too much slack – as opposed to flexibility and freedom – is one that they will want to leave quite quickly. They are prepared to put in serious effort as long as they know they will be rewarded and recognised for it, and not *next* year, either. But if the setting encourages – and even inadvertently rewards – loafing, then that is what you will get.

Focus versus experience

Today's young people want multiple job rotations, and a much broader scope of experiences early in their careers than any older generations would have dared hope for.

Technology and social networks

Giving younger generations good technology is not an optional extra for organisations. It is a base-level requirement. In fact, you need to go further, and tap into the bring-your-own-device trend, allowing your digital native employees to provide their own technology, where appropriate, to deliver tasks and functions in their jobs. You need to realise that they will be using their own technology to manage their social networks, whether you give them permission or not.

Making this a stressful hidden activity erodes their productivity and focus on the job. Rather, create time and space within their work day when they are freely able to connect with their network outside of the organisation. Remember, talented people have talented friends. Their social network is as much of an asset that you want to tap into as their brains and their professional abilities.

Organising and Leading the Next Generation

There are many other areas of organisational life with which generational theory can assist us. But for the sake of limited space in this chapter, we want now to focus our attention specifically on workplace and organisational design issues that specifically affect Gen Y/Millennials, and the soon-to-arrive Digital Natives.

When most leaders think of generational issues, they tend to think of the issues related to attracting, retaining and engaging the younger members of their teams. The key problem they find is that today's young people are not just younger versions of them. Millennials, and even more so, the Digital Natives, have values that are distinctly different from the conventional values that underpin the current workplace.

Many programmes that focus on talent development in organisations tend to be directed at moulding talent into a shape that fits comfortably with the existing organisational framework. Consequently, these programmes produce individuals who are very similar, if not the same, as people who are already working in the organisation; or they eject individuals who cannot or will not fit the mould. In the process, all effort is directed at making sure the individuals fit rather than looking at their specific, and unique, characteristics and the benefits they bring to the organisation. While there is some merit in this traditional approach to the leadership of talent, one could critically reflect that it generates groups of "Yes-persons", rather than a group of strong individuals who benefit from strong and effective leadership.

Leadership is not the ability to manage a group of like-minded individuals. Good leadership is evidenced in the ability to take a group of disparate individuals and get them moving in the same strategic direction. It may be that new approaches and even new structures are needed for a new generation.

Square-round pegs in round-square holes

Rather than trying to mould individuals to the organisation, the reality is that for an organisation to succeed in the future world of work, *the organisation needs to be moulded to fit the new type of individual who will be its employees.* When Generation X were rising through the ranks of organisations and having this very conversation with Baby Boomer management, it was a new and dynamic experience for the corporate world.

And yet, despite all the newness and the relative difficulty of this interaction, the resolution ended up being relatively simple: Baby Boomer executives developed concepts such as casual Fridays and flexitime to meet the demands and expectations of Generation X talent, who wanted a less formal environment and more flexibility in terms of their time.

Generation X is now having a similar interaction with Generation Y, and they are surprised that they cannot just maintain continuity from what the Baby Boomers put in place for them. The Generation X perspective so far has been that they are younger versions of us and need only a little bit of moulding and shaping to fit into the organisations we have created. Nothing could be further from the truth.

Who do they think they are?

When we were growing up and our parents asked us, "Who do you think you are?", they really did not mean it in a good way. But today's young people have been fed an almost constant diet of affirmation and encouragement. It is no surprise, then, that older members of the workforce are often frustrated with them when they arrive in our workplaces.

An additional reason for this disconnect is related to computer gaming. McGonigal[8] calculated that Millennials will spend about the same time in formal education as they do playing computer games. It is therefore a huge digital influencer. It has generated a worldview that new talent bring with them into adulthood, and into the workplace. It has formed and influenced their value system and worldview in different ways from the board games of Generation X and Baby Boomers. Beck and Wade[9] identified six values that this gaming generation had formed as a result of playing computer games: social, competitive, arrogant, flexible, multitasking, and insubordinate.

It is the last value that generates so much management frustration. What is seen as insubordination, when viewed through traditional lenses, is different when understood within the parameters of effective leadership in digital gaming. In a gaming community, the role of the Guild Master or leader is not to lead the group on every challenge or task. The role of the leader is to identify the best placed, or most qualified, individual on the team to lead the team to success. Once this individual is identified, they lead the challenge. The Guild Master's role is to make sure that they have all of the resources they need in order to be successful. At the end of the task the only thing that matters is: "Did we succeed or not?" Egos, titles, past experience, position in the social network, all function at a secondary level in making sure that the group succeeds.

Too many leaders in organisations lack this *ability to reframe and rethink their role and function from leading every task to identifying the right person to lead,* regardless of age or any other legacy criteria. As leaders, our task and responsibility is not to run everything. It is to make sure that we are successful at everything. But this is a very Gen Y/Digital Native mindset, not often supported by organisational structures or existing leaders.

In summary: based on our discussion, the following competencies point to potential success to lead effectively in a multi-generational context, as shown in Table 13.1.

Table 13.1: Key Inter-generational leadership competencies

Good leaders are good leaders in any generation	Each generation expects their leaders to know what they are doing in terms of both technical and people skills. They demand honesty and transparency. Care and growth.
Initiate conversations about generations	Getting generational judgements and preconceptions out into the open allows them to become less personalised and more generalised. They can then be more easily dealt with.
Everyone wants recognition and feedback, but in different ways	Our needs as people have not changed from one generation to another, but we fulfil these in different ways. Be deliberate about creating different approaches for different generations.
Do not let technology get in your way	Older generations need to learn to use technology better. Even ask younger colleagues to train you and help you get up to speed. Leaders must leverage technology, especially communication and productivity tools, to build the team.
Mentor and reverse-mentor	We all work with colleagues across a broader range of ages these days. Mentoring does not just go from old to young. Find ways to get younger team members to mentor and train the older ones, too.
Embrace diversity and offer options	Working successfully with a mix of generations requires offering as many choices as possible to suit the needs and preferences of your diverse team. The best multigenerational teams recognise the unique strengths of each individual and enable people to make a unique contribution, rather than just blending in with the team. Go beyond mere tolerance.
Ask questions	Leadership today is not so much about having good answers as it is about having good questions. We can project our own preferences onto others, especially across generations, and the only way to ensure we do not is to ask others what they are thinking and what they want.
Develop a collaborative approach	Younger managers of older colleagues would do well to involve them in decision-making more often.
Personalise and customise	Leaders of the future adapt and adjust their styles to match the people they are leading.
Engagement style	Boomers prefer to be team players, Gen Xers are best when treated as free agents, while Gen Y want to be supported as entrepreneurs/intrapreneurs.
Leverage the strengths of each generation	Understand that each generation has both strengths and weaknesses. Do not dwell on the weaknesses, but rather focus on the strengths and the best contributions that each can make.

All of this points to a required shift in organisational dynamics if we are to get the best out of a modern workforce building the workplace of the future.

Evolution to the Future World of Work

In his 2004 book, Thomas Malone[10] describes the social evolution of the workplace. This evolution is driven around the cost and effectiveness of communication. As communication becomes cheaper and more effective, it changes the way in which organisations are structured. He tracks the global economy from a world dominated by individualised small businesses, as would be seen in village-based life, through to the centralised corporate hierarchies of the late 20th century. He creates a compelling argument for a network structure as the next shift in organisational dynamics.

Though this book was written over a decade ago, it is useful to consider it in light of the rise of social media and social network technologies, none of which existed when the book was written. Digital Natives, because of their use and integration of social technology in their daily lives, live in a world that looks like the one Malone described in his 2004 book. The message for today's leaders is that in order to recruit or service Digital Native staff and customers effectively, we have to liberate ourselves from the historical hierarchical corporate view of organisations.

Malone looks at some examples of organisations he believed were making the transition. For our purposes, more practical structural insights are needed to enable us to build a modern business which functions successfully in this changing world.

Shifting from hierarchy to heterarchy

In a hierarchical structure, there is a very clear line of progression from the bottom to the top. The bottom layer of a hierarchy has many more elements that make it up. The higher up the hierarchy one moves, the fewer positions are available. This scarcity dynamic means that those functions or elements higher up in the hierarchy are viewed as more valuable, significant, and important, able to impose their desires on those lower down the structure. From a generational perspective, this was both the dominant structure of organisations *as well as* society for much of the lifetime of the Silent and Boomer generations. Society has shifted in the past few decades, and organisations need to shift, too.

Heterarchy is a structure that has seen more use in biology and information science than it has in organisational design. A heterarchy is a structure or system where all of the elements are unranked or non-hierarchical. Alternatively, the elements in the heterarchy are able to be ranked in a number of different ways rather than in just the single way of the hierarchical structure. In his 2006 book, Manfred Kets de Vries[11] argues that we should change our views of organisational structure from hierarchical to heterarchical.

He points out that in most organisations there are actually a number of hierarchical structures working in parallel to or in tandem with each other at any one time. Among the hierarchies present in an organisation are a professional hierarchy based on qualifications; a structural hierarchy based on job title; and a tactical or project hierarchy based on the specific requirements needed to deliver an outcome. It is possible for two individuals to occupy different positions relative to each other in these different structures at the same time. Individual A could have a PhD, operate in mid-management, and be leading a particular project. Individual B could have an undergraduate degree, be in senior management, and be a resource on the same project. Depending on the dynamic at the time, Individual A and Individual B will be shifting positions relative to each other.

Embracing heterarchy as a leadership and organisational model is an important shift in the leading of Millennials and Digital Natives. This is their natural organisational mindset. As young people entering the workforce, they are better qualified than anybody before, and have more experience of working in temporary teams and being judged and rewarded in groups. This has been entrenched in most education systems in the past two decades. It is possible that a young individual will be more qualified than his/her organisational superior. They may also be given responsibility to deliver projects based on this knowledge, where people with longer tenure in the business will be in reporting lines that are channelled toward the new talent.

Holacracy as the organisational leadership of the future

One particular system in which this new approach to organisation structure is being tested is called holacracy. It is a system, or structure, in which decision-making and authority are distributed through self-organising teams rather than invested in traditional management structures. It might be best visualised as flat, overlapping circles, rather than the traditional pyramid structure of the old hierarchies. Table 13.2 gives a comparison of traditional organisations to those following a holacracy.

Table 13.2: A comparison between traditional organisations and the holacracy

In Traditional Organisations	With Holacracy
Job descriptions	**Roles**
Each person has exactly one job. Job descriptions are imprecise, rarely updated, and often irrelevant.	Roles are defined around the work, not people, and are regularly updated. People fill several roles.
Delegated authority	**Distributed authority**
Managers loosely delegate authority. Ultimately, their decision always trumps.	Authority is truly distributed to team and roles. Decisions are made locally.
Big re-organisations	Rapid iterations
The organisational structure is rarely revisited or mandated from the top.	The organisational structure is regularly updated via small iterations. Every team self-organises.
Office politics	Transparent rules
Information is often kept back, and fails to filter down or up.	Information is widely shared and transparent.
Implicit rules slow down change and favour people "in the know".	**Everyone is bound by the same rules, CEO included. Rules are visible to all.**

Source: <http://www.holacracy.org (2016)

Zappos – owned by Amazon.com – has recently transformed its whole business into a holacratic structure, a strategic project that took 18 months to execute. There will be some missteps, and probably some mistakes, but there can be no doubt that the road they are on is a road that every organisation will have to journey down if it wants to connect effectively with younger generations. They have documented their journey for all to see. It a study of what they've done, and how they did it is a valuable exercise.[12]

Unfortunately, there are no quick fix answers, no "one size fits all" solutions. Simply making a few tweaks to your HR policy would not work. To adjust to a new generation in a new century requires a change of attitude, a mindset shift, and systemic changes in organisational design. The good news is that it is not as hard to do as you think. And if you do make the shift, you will open yourself up to such a leap forward in competitive advantage that the pain will be well worth it. Effective leadership in the new world of work for a generation of individuals who have grown up with very different values, expectations, and perspectives will require a rethinking of the way things have always been done.

Conclusion

A genuine appreciation and understanding of the needs of the different generations working side by side in an organisation will pave the way for smoother working relationships and getting the best out of staff and customers. But there is a danger in overstating the importance of these generational distinctions. Jennifer Deal makes this point best in her 2007 book,[13] in which she counsels us to use this framework carefully and wisely, and only after we have developed more understanding than can be imparted in a short chapter such as this. This is true of any of the profiling tools we may use to understand other people. Having said that, though, the benefits of using a generational lens should be apparent to anyone who has worked with a group of people of multiple ages.

At first glance, generational theory has an elegant simplicity to it. Unlike more complex segmentation tools, generational theory is immediately applicable. In the organisational setting it is often used to help front-line staff adjust the way in which they interact with clients: face to face, by phone, or in written formats. It is used by leaders to help them make decisions about team dynamics, whether managing younger or older people. Alongside other profiling tools, it can help us connect better with others and improve interactions that affect recruitment, engagement, reviews, motivation, incentives, and even workplace design. The attraction for the organisation is that just by knowing someone's age, one can adjust one's approach to them and have a greater chance of connecting with them, and therefore influencing them.

Of course, there are always exceptions to every profile "rule". There are many "young" old people in the world: people from the older generations who have adapted and changed their attitudes and outlooks to be more in line with younger generations. The same is true in reverse. There are young people who have the attitudes and expectations of much older generations. This can also be influenced by personality, gender, culture, and especially religion. All of these factors must be considered when trying to understand, predict and influence the behaviour of a particular individual. And it is clear that the more you actually know another person, the less you will need to use a profile tool to predict their behaviour or understand their attitudes.

Multi-generational leadership is an essential element in the toolkit of a 21st century leader. Hopefully this brief overview will inspire you to develop the skills needed to engage with older and younger people, and to use generational theory as a tool to help your teams engage more effectively with all forms of difference.

Endnotes

1. Goleman, 2006.
2. Strauss & Howe, 1991
3. Rainer & Rainer, 2011.
4. Zemke, Raines & Filipczak, 2000.
5. Tulgan, 2009.
6. Coats & Codrington, 2015.
7. Chester, 2002.
8. McGonigal, 2011.
9. Beck & Wade, 2004.
10. Malone, 2004.
11. Kets de Vries, 2006.
12. Zappos Insights, 2016.
13. Deal, 2007.

References

Beck, JC & Wade, M. 2004. *Got game: How the gamer generation is reshaping business forever.* Boston, MA: Harvard Business School Press.

Chester, E. 2002. *Employing generation why: Understanding, managing, and motivating your new workforce.* Lakewood, CO: Tucker House Books.

Coats, K & Codrington, G. 2015. *Leading in a changing world: Lessons for future-focused leaders.* TomorrowToday Global.

Deal, JJ. 2007. *Retiring the generation gap: How employees young and old can find common ground.* San Francisco, CA: Wiley.

Goleman, D. 2006. *Emotional intelligence.* New York, NY: Bantam Books.

Kets de Vries, MFR. 2006. *The leadership mystique: Leading behavior in the human enterprise.* Harlow, UK: Prentice Hall/Financial Times.

Malone, TW. 2004. *The future of work: How the new order of business will shape your organization, your management style, and your life.* Boston, MA: Harvard Business School Press.

McGonigal, J. 2011. *Reality is broken: Why games make us better and how they can change the world.* New York, NY: Penguin Press.

Rainer, TS & Rainer, JW. 2011. *The millennials: Connecting to America's largest generation.* Nashville, TN: B&H Publishing Group.

Strauss, W & Howe, N. 1991. *Generations.* New York, NY: William Morrow.

Tulgan, B. 2009. *Not everyone gets a trophy: How to manage generation y.* San Francisco, CA: Jossey-Bass.

Zappos Insights. 2016. *Holacracy and self-organization.* [Online] Available: https://www.zapposinsights.com/about/holacracy. [Accessed 24 May 2016].

Zemke, R, Raines, C & Filipczak, B. 2000. *Generations at work: Managing the clash of veterans, boomers, xers, and nexters in your workplace.* New York, NY: AMACOM.

Additional readings

Bush, N & Codrington, G. 2010. *Future-proof your child: Parenting the wired generation.* Parktown North, ZA: Penguin SA.

Codrington, G & Grant-Marshall, S. 2012. *Mind the gap: Own your past, know your generation, choose your future.* 3rd ed. Parktown North, ZA: Penguin SA.

DelCampo, RG, Haggerty, LA, Haney, MJ & Knippel, LA. 2011. *Managing the multi-generational workforce: From the GI generation to the millennials.* Farnham, UK: Gower Publishing.

Farrell, BF & Farrel, P. 2007. *Men are like waffles – Women are like spaghetti.* Eugene, OR: Harvest House.

Livermore, DA. 2010. *Leading with cultural Intelligence: The new secret to success.* New York, NY: American Management Association.

Prensky, M. 2012. *From digital natives to digital wisdom: Hopeful essays for 21st century learning.* Thousand Oaks, CA: Corwin.

Riso, DR & Hudson, R. 1999. *The wisdom of the enneagram: The complete guide to psychological and spiritual growth for the nine personality types.* New York, NY: Bantam Books.

Strauss, W & Howe, N. 1997. *The fourth turning: An American prophecy.* New York, NY: Broadway Books.

Strauss, W & Howe, N. 2000. *Millennials rising.* New York, NY: Vintage Books.

Chapter 14

DIVERSITY LEADERSHIP
Nene Molefi

Imagine leading an organisation where, at best, only half of the staff population are fully engaged and give their best. They feel valued and excited about working in that setting, but the other half feel disconnected, disengaged and excluded. What do you do as a leader?

In my years of consulting and engaging with leaders, practitioners and employees in both local and multinational organisations, I have come to realise that it is not just *words* or *actions* that are required from leaders to create an inclusive culture and workplace. To harness maximum potential for excellence, there are three important competencies required of leaders to lead inclusively in a diverse world: *the Knowing, the Being* and *the Doing*. While all three competencies are important for diversity leadership, it is the overall sum total that is likely to achieve world-class diversity leadership, rather than any one of them alone.

In this chapter I explore the attributes, values, and behaviours embedded within each of the Knowing, the Being and the Doing competencies. This is based on the firm belief that one of the most important roles of a future-fit and world-class leader is to create inclusive workplaces where diverse staff feel valued, appreciated, and able to give their best in order to help achieve the mission and vision of the organisation.

In his book *Leading in a Diverse and Conflicted World*, Fernandez argues that "the first step towards becoming a world-class leader is creating the right workplace environment".[1] Clearly the "right" workplace should be "right" for everyone and not advantage or disadvantage any sector of the employee population. And yet, unfortunately, in many organisations this is usually not the case.

All too often I have come across companies investing in expensive diversity initiatives with minimal or no returns. I have heard well-meaning CEOs say to their HR directors: "We have set targets for women and black people; why are we not making progress? You've been given the budget, just go and *get them*." On the other hand, I have heard line managers say: "We want to increase diversity but we just can't retain good talent." Others end up abandoning their diversity initiatives altogether, resulting in frustration and anger from employees about the concept of diversity and how organisations handle – or do not handle – it.

Thus, while many research studies have proven the value of diversity for organisations, opposing viewpoints also exist. Harvard political scientist Putnam conducted research that outlined the challenges and downsides of diversity in society, and has spurred some to reconsider the automatic "diversity is good" refrain.[2]

Yet I believe there is a lot more missing in current approaches to diversity leadership than meets the eye, and there is more at stake for those who are in leadership positions. As articulated by Heifetz and Linsky in *Leadership on the Line*:

> "To lead is to live dangerously because when leadership counts, when you lead people through difficult change, you challenge what people hold dear – their daily habits, tools, loyalties, and ways of thinking – with nothing more to offer than a possibility ... [but] that leadership, while perilous, is an enterprise worthy of the costs. Our communities, organisations, and societies need people, from wherever they work and live, to take up the challenges within reach rather than complain about the lack of leadership from on high, hold off until they receive a 'call' to action, or wait for their turn in the top job."[3]

So diversity leadership is not just about words, numbers or targets. It is also not about rushing to implement a weakly formulated strategy that will translate into throwing money into a bad plan. And it is also not about simply looking past differences in the hope that everyone can just "get along". Instead, true diversity leadership understands and taps into the critical interplay between the Head (intellectual buy-in and "the Knowing"), the Heart (emotional buy-in and "the Being") and the Hands (visible behaviour change and "the Doing").

Briefly, this chapter will start by looking at the *Knowing (= Head)*. A leader must know and understand his/her critical role in:

- Defining diversity and inclusion for themselves and for their employees and stakeholders;
- Developing a solid business case for diversity and inclusion;
- Continuous learning and exploring global perspectives and the changing landscape of diversity;
- Identifying misinformation and damaging narratives around diversity;
- Diagnosing the issues in the organisation, either through employee surveys or other measures;
- Developing a compelling vision for diversity and inclusion, e.g. what the ideal end state should look like; and
- Ensuring that diversity and inclusion are integral to the strategy of the organisation.

Secondly, this chapter will look at the *Being (= Heart)*. A leader must be willing to connect with his/her emotions and lead, for example, through:

- Investing emotionally in growing and developing talent instead of destroying talent;
- Confronting his/her own "baggage" and unconscious biases;
- Listening, engaging and communicating honestly and openly with employees and stakeholders;
- Creating a safe space for dialogue and emotional exchange; and
- Being willing to be vulnerable, make mistakes, recover, and come out as a better leader.

Finally, this chapter will explore the *Doing (= Hands)*. A leader must ensure that the intra- and inter-personal, systemic and stakeholder aspects of diversity and inclusion are integrated. To do this, they must:

- Outline a clear implementation plan for creating the desired culture, with clear mandates and guidelines for decision-makers at all levels;
- Put structures and support mechanisms in place in order to implement recommendations from stakeholder and employee engagement sessions;
- Use their rank and power to effect change in a practical way on a daily basis;
- Monitor progress through Key Performance Indicators (KPIs) or Key Performance Areas (KPAs), visibly acknowledging achievement and acting against non-compliance; and
- Communicate, through a clear communication strategy, that maps all stakeholders and outlines how key messages and decisions will be disseminated throughout the organisation.

The H3 Model for Diversity Leadership

While the concept of the Head, Heart and Hands is not new, how it relates to diversity leadership requires some new perspective. Popularised by Orr,[4] the H3 model has taken many shapes and forms in the workplace. As further explained by Singleton: "The model shows the holistic nature of transformative experience and relates the cognitive domain (head) to critical reflection, the affective domain (heart) to relational knowing and the psychomotor domain (hands) to engagement."[5]

So how can the H3 model help us move beyond the limitations of or failed attempts at diversity management? What does the ideal profile look like for leadership that effectively builds diverse and inclusive organisations?

Knowing: Head

Defining diversity and inclusion

The first important step in becoming competent in the Knowing (= *Head*) is to have a clear understanding and working definition of diversity and inclusion. There are too many complicated and academic definitions out there. Instead, Thomas defines diversity as "the collective mixture of differences and similarities, and related tensions and complexities that can characterise mixtures of any kind".[6] All too often differences are emphasised when discussing diversity. Or, in an attempt to be inclusive, leaders can swing to the opposite extreme and claim they do not recognise differences and believe everyone is the same. In contrast to both these pitfalls, leaders must find a balance between acknowledging similarities as well as differences.

Leaders must also be careful not to fall into the trap of associating diversity with only a few diversity markers, such as race and gender, for example. This is easy to do considering the fact that some diversity markers may need urgent attention; may be especially sensitive; or can trigger people more easily than others. Whenever differences are seen or experienced as a threat, leaders must be aware that the word "diversity" can be loaded, and then a broader definition becomes helpful – both conceptually and in practice.

I believe it is important for leaders to define diversity in the context of their national landscape. For example, in working with leadership teams in Africa, Asia and the USA, I frequently draw their attention to various pieces of legislation which (although similar in generic terms) contain nuances of each country or region. For example, the South African Constitution[7] (Chapter 2, Section 9) points to the broad scope of diversity and the responsibility of individuals and organisations to prevent unfair discrimination at a scale much wider than just race or gender.[i] The US Equal Employment Opportunity Commission (EEOC) also outlines a number of diversity markers, which need to be considered by employers in order to ensure a fair and inclusive workplace.[ii]

In contrast to diversity, which is a noun or descriptor of the differences and similarities in any team or group of people, inclusion requires action. It is the deliberate step of making someone or a group feel included where they were unfairly excluded or simply ignored and treated as if they did not exist. In the South African context, language exclusion is often experienced when a manager switches to speaking in another official language during a meeting despite the fact that other employees present in the meeting do not understand the language. Exclusion can also be experienced as a result of geographical location, where teams are spread across various continents and the organiser of the meeting does not make adequate effort to consider variations in time zones in setting up meetings; he/she may also tend to be biased in favour of the time zone most convenient to where the headquarters of the company are based.

---

i   The South African Constitution states: "No one may unfairly discriminate directly or indirectly against anyone on one or more grounds, including race, gender, sex, pregnancy, marital status, ethnic or social origin, colour, sexual orientation, age, disability, religion, conscience, belief, culture, language and birth."
ii Under the laws enforced by the EEOC, it is illegal to discriminate against someone (applicant or employee) because of that person's race, colour, religion, sex (including gender identity, sexual orientation and pregnancy), national origin, age (over 40 and older), disability or genetic information.

To cite another example, meetings are often arranged early in the morning, before official working hours, or after hours, causing serious inconvenience to those employees (especially women) who need to take children to school or to rush home to prepare a meal for the family. Inclusion is therefore about making everyone feel that they matter and are part of the team; where they feel listened to and their contributions are welcome and considered in important work deliberations. Ferdman asserts that "[i]nclusion involves how well organizations and their members fully connect with, engage, and utilize people across all types of differences ... the core of inclusion is how people experience it – the psychological experience of inclusion (and often collectively as well)".[8]

While the value of inclusion may sound universal and an obvious one for leaders to aspire to, the aspect of inclusion that is often neglected is the fact that it is a call to change. Change by its nature requires people to learn new behaviours or ways in which to manage unhealthy patterns of thought or behaviour. In contrast to corporate norms that often place the burden of assimilation or change on newcomers or minority groups, diversity leadership through inclusion means a shift or change in behaviour of those in the dominant group as well.

Building a business case

At the "Head" level, the second critical competency after defining diversity and inclusion is the ability to develop, articulate and gain buy-in through a solid business case for the desired change. Since change is uncomfortable and diversity and inclusion often do not come naturally, it is essential to know "why" diversity and inclusion are important. As noted by Ferdman: "Much of the focus in the field of diversity in organizations has been on reducing or eliminating undesirable, unfair, and illegal bias and discrimination and on increasing equity and social justice."[9]

In contrast, there has been less emphasis on the benefits and opportunities that diversity brings to individuals, groups, organisations and societies. What I have found most useful is for leaders to sit down with their teams and engage them in identifying the imperatives for diversity and inclusion in their organisation. The over-arching questions should be:

1. Do we, as leaders, believe inclusion is the right thing to do?
2. Do we see diversity as a value?
3. What are the internal and external benefits for creating an inclusive culture, and what are the risks and liabilities for not acting on this?

Although these questions can result in robust debate and differences of opinion, this process often leads to the recognition that diverse and inclusive teams are winning teams. When everyone in an organisation feels included, when people want to come to work because they are recognised and encouraged to be fully themselves, everyone is eager to get on with the business of the day. This starts with diversity leadership that clearly articulates why there is value in diversity and inclusion.

Identifying the narratives and diagnosing the issues

Once one has established a clear view on why diversity and inclusion are important, the next core competency for diversity leadership is the willingness to engage at the more granular level. This is the ability to answer the question: for what reason are we solving? To become competent in the Knowing, effective diversity leadership does not rely only on anecdotal evidence or the loudest voices or the opinions of individuals closest to leadership, but instead draws from a broad pool of knowledge. This can include a view on national statistics or industry trends, organisational employment data (for example, it is useful for Human Resources to track recruitment, promotion and retention trends by using a range of demographic variables), and engagement with employee concerns and experiences.

I have witnessed some organisations that try to skip this diagnostic step, either because the leadership think they already know what the issues are or do not want to invest financially in undertaking a survey. However, this is a big risk. Best practice in the field of diversity and inclusion suggests that diagnostics are critical to effective and sustainable diversity leadership.

I am one of the expert panellists of the Global Diversity and Inclusion Benchmarks (GDIB): Standards for Organizations around the World, developed by Richter, O'Mara, and 90 expert panellists around the world. The benchmarks, which have been made freely available by the authors and panellists, present "Assessment, Measurement and Research" as a key bridging component of global diversity leadership. This component defines multiple levels at which an organisation needs to check "the way D&I[10] is measured, whether the organization does research to support D&I strategies, and the organization's assessment processes around diversity, inclusion, and organizational culture."[11]

To give an example of best practice in action, I am currently working with a large and growing company in the financial services sector that has taken the time to engage with its senior management teams to identify the misinformation and damaging narratives around diversity that exist at that level. The executive team has been shocked by the results. Without this step they would have assumed that everyone was on the same page. In a much more informed manner, the executive leadership is now in the process of developing clear mandates and guidelines that will support the company's broader transformation and diversity vision.

Developing a vision and making sure diversity and inclusion (D&I) are integral to organisational strategy

So once leaders have diagnosed the problem areas, what can they do differently from what they have been doing all along? How will they know if they are achieving an ideal end state? And how do they ensure that measures are put in place to help foster diversity and inclusion, in a way that builds buy-in from both "in-groups" and "out-groups"? One of the most important competencies that falls in the "Knowing" category is not only the ability of leadership to define clearly the company's *vision* for diversity and inclusion, but also to articulate how this vision supports the company's broader strategic goals.

In South Africa, many corporates are faced with the complexity of holding as equally important the concepts of "shareholder value" versus "stakeholder expectations". In my experience, there is always a question posed as to whether a leader can drive business results while at the same time managing diversity and ensuring inclusion. The question arises because many decision makers (= Boards and Executive committees) still regard diversity and inclusion work as separate from the core business of the organisation. This separation implies that diversity and inclusion is a "nice to have", while core business is the primary means through which leaders can demonstrate shareholder returns. This is not only a South African phenomenon.

The surveys we have conducted have demonstrated that intangible, non-monetary benefits of diversity and inclusion cannot be overstated. Perceptions of unfair treatment, job dissatisfaction and unequal pay scales can lead to serious disruptions in operations which in turn affect productivity and delivery of service. What is often regarded as non-monetary risk can easily make the transition to hard numbers with regard to monetary loss.

Having a clear diversity and inclusion vision or statement of commitment helps to guide and remind leaders of its central importance in achieving broader strategic objectives. Some core questions to ask when developing a D&I vision and strategy include the following:

- What is your ideal end state with regard to diversity and inclusion?
- What is your big picture or aspiration with regard to diversity and inclusion?
- Does your organisation recognise diversity and inclusion as a part of their competency evaluation when selecting leaders?
- How do leaders learn to lead inclusively without losing focus of the purpose and fundamental mandate of the organisation?

One of the most important characteristics of the vision is that it must include the "why" – the driving reason or purpose behind the organisation's commitment to diversity and inclusion. The power of such a vision lies in its ability to unite the voices, outlook and intention of both leaders and employees.

Table 14.1 provides a summary of key "Knowing" (= Head) competencies.

Table 14.1: Key "Knowing" competencies for leading inclusively

1.	Willingness to broaden your understanding of diversity and inclusion
2.	Willingness to listen, engage in continuous dialogue and learning
3.	Desire to know why diversity and inclusion, are important for your organisation (=the imperatives), and willingness to take the risks that leadership demands
4.	Ability to identify the business case for diversity with both tangible and intangible benefits (=ROI) and risks
5.	Ability to take responsibility for educating yourself about your own and other's experiences of diversity and inclusion or exclusion
6.	Knowing where you are going and how you would like to get there: developing the D&I Vision

Being: Heart

Transitioning from the "Head" to the "Heart" is not easy. But it is one of the most important competencies for building a diverse and inclusive culture. How often have you seen powerful value statements hanging on the walls of corporations, on company websites, and even quoted by leaders in strategy sessions or company functions, yet see the opposite in terms of behaviour demonstrated by the same leaders?

Barrett maintains that "[c]orporations do not transform, people do. Corporate transformation is fundamentally about personal transformation. It will happen only if there is a willingness on the part of the leader and all those in authority to live according to values that are less focused on self-interest and more focused on common good".[12]

At the heart of the "Being" is how leaders make others "feel" in their presence. Sometimes there is not even a need to say anything. But it is the aura that some leaders create that makes those around them feel accepted and respected. I often ask my workshop participants to think of the best teacher that they have ever had, be it in primary school, high school or college. In almost all the cases, the answer I get is that of someone who made them "feel" valued, smart, seen, respected, important and/or special. Line managers often downplay "feelings", or refer to this as "airy fairy" stuff. But it is interesting how those very line managers would choose "feeling" words to describe why they thought their choice of teachers were the best.

Investing emotionally in growing and developing talent instead of destroying talent

When people feel that they "belong", and they are accepted and valued, they are more likely to give their best and reach their maximum potential in the workplace. As discussed by Wiseman and McKeown in their book *Multipliers: How the Best Leaders Make Everyone Smarter*, the role of a leader is to make everyone smarter, using five disciplines that distinguish multipliers from diminishers.[13] These are:

1. Attracting talented people and using them at their highest point of contribution.
2. Creating an intense workplace which requires people's best thinking and work.
3. Defining an opportunity that causes people to stretch.
4. Driving sound decisions through rigorous debate.
5. Giving other people ownership for the results and investing in their success.

The above disciplines describe an ideal diversity leadership setting, yet many leaders find it difficult to apply these when it comes to managing diverse teams. What could be the barrier?

Confronting our baggage, and unconscious bias

In my observation, the transition from the "Head" to the "Heart" is very difficult when it comes to diversity and inclusion. It challenges the core aspects of your identity, for example, your gender, sexual orientation, culture, age, race, language, and religion. When you have been brought up with a particular belief about your race group or your sexual orientation, accepting those who present an identity divergently opposite to yours can be a serious challenge.

We all have "baggage" – which I often refer to as an invisible "suitcase" we carry at all times – which is created through our early messages about those who are different from us and contains our biases, conscious or unconscious. These come into operation every time we interact with one another, each with our own "baggage". What is key is to recognise the existence of our individual baggage and to be on the look-out for possible triggers, and how to manage them while working towards eliminating them. Denying that one has baggage is counter-productive as it delays the onset of inner work. So the diversity and inclusion journey is as much your personal journey as it is for the people you are leading.

The importance of inner work

As is well articulated by Vince Lombardi, now owner of the Lombardi Packers American football team:

> "Leaders are made, they are not born. They are made by hard effort, which is the price which all of us must pay to achieve any goal that is worthwhile." – Vince Lombardi[14]

Inner work cannot begin unless there is an understanding and willingness on the part of leaders to "lead from the front". Leaders must show boldness in challenging their own and others' reluctance to change.

What some leaders often do not understand is that inviting diverse perspective does not mean you have to agree with all of them. Rather it provides a leader with a wider pool of options to select from when solving a problem or developing a new concept for improving business performance. Often the ego can stand in the way of a leader effectively engaging with someone who challenges their perspective or worldview, especially if they are junior to them.

Listening, engaging and communicating honestly and openly with employees and stakeholders

As a critical part of the "Being", I have found listening to be an underrated but critical competency of diversity leadership. One of the moments I remember most clearly from President Barak Obama's inauguration speech when he was first elected president of the USA was when he said, "I promise to listen to you, especially when we differ."

Jolles discusses the concept of trust and communication and believes that we communicate in three ways: (1) we listen, (2) we ask questions, or (3) we make statements. He further states that asking questions and listening are the driving forces behind trusting a person.[15] I have come across many instances where a new employee who has a different cultural background to the dominant (and relatively homogeneous) group, and whose traditions and practices are foreign to that group, joins the team and experiences exclusion and discrimination mainly because of lack of trust and fear of the unknown.

When we open the door and trust, as asserted by Katz and Miller, we:

- Are willing to give each other the benefit of the doubt.
- Expect to connect and gain something from our interactions.
- Listen more attentively and appreciatively to one another.
- Look for the value in what our colleagues say, and build on that.
- Show we are willing to act in spite of our discomfort, trusting our partners to have our backs.
- Let our partners know we have their backs and that they can trust us.
- Create a situation where team members are more likely to extend trust to us.[16]

Creating a safe space for dialogue and emotional exchange

So how should successful, inclusive, 21st century leaders *be*? How must they "show up" in the workplace? Based on my years of experience in the field, the key to inclusive leadership skills lies in continuous learning through engaging in dialogue with an open mind and an understanding that vulnerability is not a weakness but a means towards a useful end. This requires a few critical elements (which we describe using the acronym VETRO) in order to create safe and inclusive spaces:

- **Values-driven**: A leader must strive to narrow the gap between espoused values and lived values. Leaders dictate and influence the culture of an organisation, so values must not only reside on the company's website or annual report but must first reside in the hearts of the leaders.
- **Engaging**: A leader must show curiosity, engage employees, and encourage them to bring to the surface issues that they believe will get the company to a superior level of

performance where everyone can excel in their respective areas of responsibility. Inviting diverse perspectives will broaden the leader's horizon beyond one's homogeneous circles, and provide a rich canvas for innovation and problem solving.

- **Trusting**: A leader must lay the foundation for trust by listening and asking probing questions to get to know employees better and create solid relationships with as many diverse employees as possible. One example that comes up repeatedly is that of managers not greeting and just ignoring their employees. Those managers who have decided to adopt this practice have seen a marked improvement in trust levels and relations with employees. Those managers, and they are many, who argue that this is nonsensical and a "non-issue" have not yet realised the value of diversity leadership.
- **Reliable**: A leader must be dependable, consistent and honour his/her word. This is an extension of trust, because many leaders engage employees in dialogue sessions or surveys with the promise of addressing issues, but then a deafening silence follows. Instead, diagnostics must be followed by action.
- **Open**: A leader must demonstrate vulnerability and foster connections by encouraging a culture of giving and receiving feedback: a leader who admits mistakes; learns from criticism; and is not afraid to say 'I do not have all the answers'. This is a leader who is firm and deals with difficult situations like poor performance without hesitation.

Table 14.2 provides a summary of key "Being" (= Heart) competencies.

Table 14.2: Key "Being" competencies for leading inclusively

1.	Become a leader who seeks to make everyone smarter
2.	Understand that 'we all have baggage' and be willing to examine your own attitudes, stereotypes, and the limitations they place on your perspective
3.	Actively listen to and learn from others' experiences without trivialising their experiences
4.	Confront your own fears about challenging discrimination
5.	Make an effort to apply the VETRO principles
6.	Show acceptance of others once you have understood their world view
7.	Communicate, Communicate, Communicate

Doing: Hands

The "Head" (= Knowing) is about a leader understanding his/her critical role in diversity and inclusion, and gathering necessary information. The "Heart" (= Being) is about a leader's willingness to connect with their emotions and lead by example, which requires a certain disposition and preparedness. The "Hands" (= Doing) section is where everything culminates. It demands a total commitment to action and changing the status quo.

As stated by Ferdman and Deane: "Inclusion is grounded in **what we do** with that diversity when we value and appreciate people because of and not in spite of their differences."[17] It is all well and good to know your role and engage at an emotional level. However, what a leader does with the knowledge will ultimately distinguish theory and feelings from practice. All the feedback that was solicited during the dialogue sessions, and the analysis of quantitative data, will need to be translated into a tangible source of culture change with bias for action.

As a starting point, diversity leadership must outline a clear implementation plan for creating the desired culture with clear mandates and guidelines for decision-makers at all levels. In this regard, a structured approach to creating a culture of inclusion is highly recommended. Many leaders become frustrated when no roadmap exists to guide the process of implementation. In working with many organisations both in South Africa and abroad, I have observed two critical areas of action-based competency for effective change and creating an inclusive culture. These are attitudinal change and systemic change.

Actions for effecting attitudinal change

The baggage that was discussed above requires diversity and inclusion sensitisation and multiple interventions at both intra-personal and interpersonal levels. These interventions include individual diversity coaching, small group sessions, workshops, and team-building sessions with specific focus on addressing unconscious and conscious biases. Tools such as the Harvard Implicit Association Test (IAT) can be used as a pre- and post-intervention assessment. Other 360° leadership assessment tools can also be used to measure progress of individual leaders.

Small group sensitisation sessions and workshops need to be carefully designed to equip leaders with practical skills to deal with stereotypes, biases, and discrimination; and to establish high performance teams where everyone feels heard, understood and included. The most important aspect of attitudinal change is to link such interventions back to the workplace. All the dialogue and interventions should contain the "why". They must demonstrate how integral this work is for building effective teams and achieving organisational goals and objectives.

Actions for effecting systemic change

While exclusion, unfairness and discrimination need to be addressed at intra-personal and inter-personal levels, they can also be embedded in the policies, systems and procedures of the organisation. So what can a leader do differently to intervene at a systemic level? The best way to address exclusion at a systemic level is to implement changes at every step of an employee life cycle. For example, leaders must ask: "What are some of the barriers to inclusive leadership in:

- Recruitment and appointments?
- Allocating tasks, projects and responsibilities?
- Performance discussions and ratings?
- Promotion decisions and succession planning?
- Team meetings (who is invited, who is listened to, who leads)?"

Effective diversity leadership also means being aware that some of the "doing" is not in the big, obvious changes, but in the smaller engagements and interactions. These are called micro-messages or micro-aggressions versus micro-affirmations. Some useful questions for leaders to ask themselves are:

- **Do I solicit opinions?** Do I find opportunities to ask, "I'd like your opinion about…"?
- **Do I connect on a personal level?** Do I take a few minutes to engage in a non-business conversation with a colleague?
- **Do I ask open questions?** When I have a negative reaction to a colleague's statement or suggestion, do I lead my response with a question, not a statement?
- **Do I attribute/credit ideas?** Do I acknowledge, by name, the "owner" of an idea in a meeting?

- **Do I monitor facial expressions and body language?** Am I conscious of my facial expressions and body language while listening?
- **Do I actively listen?** Am I attentive to the speaker in order to enhance the quality of their message, or do I frequently interrupt or cut them off?
- **Do I draw in participation?** When addressing a group, do I actively encourage participation from everyone?
- **Do I monitor personal greetings?** Am I aware of who I greet and who I don't greet?
- **Do I respond constructively to differences?** When responding to someone's comment with which I disagree, do I show that I understand their perspective before I offer a different view?

For such awareness and action to be embedded within the organisation, leaders must be ready to monitor progress through KPIs or KPAs, visibly acknowledging achievement and acting against non-compliance; and providing ongoing communication about progress against set goals.

Table 14.3 provides a summary of key "Doing" (= Hands) competencies.

Table 14.3: Key "Doing" competencies for leading inclusively

1.	Develop a bias for action around issues of diversity and inclusion
2.	Implement plans to address both attitudinal and systemic aspects of diversity and inclusion
3.	Expect tension and conflict and learn to manage it
4.	Use language and behaviour that is non-biased and inclusive
5.	Work collectively with others and support efforts that combat prejudice, harassment, discrimination, exclusion, and oppression in all its forms
6.	Use your rank and privilege as a leader to address micro messaging and micro aggressions

Conclusion

In this day and age, organisations are becoming increasingly diverse and complex. At the same time they operating in a world where there are unrelenting instances of intolerance and exclusion. It has therefore become critically important more than ever for leadership to be characterised by the integration of the Head (= Knowing), Heart (= Being) and Hands (= Doing) when it comes to diversity and inclusion.

The profile of such leadership is relatively easy to recognise. But it requires courage, hard work, and dedication to achieve. As stated earlier in this chapter, I have observed over years of working with a wide range of organisations that each of the three competencies is important for diversity leadership, but it is really the sum of the total that is needed to achieve world-class diversity leadership. This is a leadership profile characterised by:

- A deep understanding and willingness to engage with the internal and external context in order to define a shared "why", and a clear business case for diversity and inclusion;
- A heart-level openness to engage in ongoing intra-personal and interpersonal work through listening, vulnerability and awareness of unconscious bias; and
- Unwavering commitment to creating inclusive spaces through visible action that includes both attitudinal and systemic change.

Such leadership will create organisations that not only bring out the best in all their employees, but will also be seen as beacons of hope and inspiration in a world that desperately needs the full-blown recognition of diversity and inclusion.

Endnotes

1. Fernandez, 2013.
2. Putnam, 2007.
3. Heifetz & Linsky, 2002.
4. Orr, 1992.
5. Singleton, 2015.
6. Thomas, 2010.
7. South Africa, 1996.
8. Ferdman, 2014.
9. Ibid.
10. D&I = Diversity and Inclusion.
11. O'Mara & Richter, 2015.
12. Barrett, 1998.
13. Wiseman & McKeown, 2013.
14. Maraniss, 1999.
15. Jolles, 2013.
16. Katz & Miller, 2013.
17. Ferdman & Deane, 2014.

References

Barrett, R. 1998. *Liberating the corporate soul: Building a visionary organization.* Woburn, MA: Butterworth Heinemann.

South Africa. 1996. *Constitution of the Republic of South Africa, 1996.* Pretoria, ZA: Government Printer. [Laws].

Ferdman, BM. 2014. 'The practice of inclusion in diverse organizations: Toward a systemic and inclusive framework'. In BM Ferdman & BR Deane (eds). *Diversity at work: The practice of inclusion.* San Francisco, CA: Jossey-Bass. 3–54.

Fernandez, P. 2013. *Leading in a diverse and conflicted world: Crucial lessons for the 21st century.* Philadelphia, PA: John Wiley & Sons.

Heifetz, R & Linsky, M. 2002. *Leadership on the line.* Boston, MA: Harvard Business School Press.

Jolles, R. 2013. *How to change minds: The art of influence without manipulation.* San Francisco, CA: Berrett-Koehler Publishers, Inc.

Katz, JH & Miller, FA. 2013. *Opening doors to teamwork and collaboration: 4 keys that change everything.* San Francisco, CA: Berrett-Koehler Publishers, Inc.

Maraniss, D. 1999. When pride still mattered: A life of Vince Lombardi. New York: Simon & Schuster, p. 405.

O'Mara, J & Richter, A. 2015. *Global diversity and inclusion benchmarks: Standards for organizations around the world.* [Online]. Available: http://diversitycollegium.org/gdib.php . [Accessed 25 July 2016].

Orr, D. 1992. *Ecological literacy: Education and the transition to a postmodern world.* New York, NY: SUNY Press.

Putnam, RD. 2007. '*E pluribus unum*: Diversity and community in the twenty-first century (the 2006 Johan Skytte prize lecture)'. *Scandinavian Political Studies*, 30(2):137–174.

Singleton, J. 2015. 'Head, heart and hands model for transformative learning: Place as context for changing sustainability values'. *The Journal of Sustainability Education*, 9, 16 March.

Thomas, RR. 2010. *World class diversity management: A strategic approach.* San Francisco, CA: Berrett-Koehler Publishers Inc.

Wiseman, L & McKeown, G. 2013. *Multipliers: How the best leaders make everyone smarter.* New York, NY: HarperCollins.

Additional Readings

Briskin, A, Erickson, S, Ott, J & Callanan, T. 2009. *The power of collective wisdom and the trap of collective folly.* San Francisco, CA: Berrett-Koehler Publishers, Inc.

Collins, J & Porras, J. 1996. 'Building your company's vision'. In *Harvard Business Review on Change*. Boston, MA: Harvard Business School Press.

Deloitte. 2015. *Global human capital trends 2015: Leading the new world of work.* Westlake, TX: Deloitte University Press.

Hubbard, E. 2004. *How to calculate diversity return on investment.* Petaluma, CA: Global Insights Publishing.

Patterson, K, Grenny, J, McMillan, R & Switzler, A. 2002. *Crucial conversations: Tools for talking when stakes are high.* New York, NY: McGraw-Hill.

Rowe, A & Stringer, D. 2014. *Making diversity and inclusion work: An integrative approach to culture change.* Workshop presented at Summer Institute for Intercultural Communication, 21–25 July.

Trompenaars, F & Hampden-Turner, C. 1998. *Riding the waves of culture: Understanding diversity in global business.* 2nd ed. New York, NY: McGraw-Hill.

Chapter 15

CHANGE LEADERSHIP
Sesh Paruk

> *"Transformation is the new type of change that has emerged and it is by far the most prevalent and complex type occurring in organisations today. Change management practitioners have attempted to provide solutions to overcome employee resistance and plan for better implementation. However, these components of change have not produced adequate positive results. It is now time to move beyond change management to conscious Change Leadership."* – Anderson & Ackerman Anderson[1]

Immediately, we are alerted to the importance of fully digesting the sheer magnitude and power underlying these words, before even attempting to comprehend the scale of change that the future will bring. There is little doubt that the rapid pace of change and the growing complexity we face demand very different paradigms, mental models, principles, values, attitudes, and behaviours by all of us. No doubt this has a direct bearing on leaders across the world, who now need to make the cognitive, emotional, spiritual and behavioural shifts necessary in order to fulfil their leadership mandates actively.

Leaders and those involved with leadership support need to absorb the full impact of the pace of global change rapidly and actively work on developing the mindsets, competencies and skills that enable leaders and their people to make the transition to new ways of living, working and interacting, if they are to be successful. Perhaps, at this point, we may refer to this emergent style of leadership as "Change Leadership".

> *"To accomplish great things we must first dream, then visualise, then plan ... believe ... act."* – Montapert[2]

> *"Change requires creating a new system, which in turn always demands leadership."* – Kotter[3]

When looking at these two quotes together, we have the underlying philosophy that speaks directly to the core of Change Leadership – the need to conceptualise fully, design/re-design, and configure our model of leadership, in order to emphasise Change Leadership. Underpinning these quotes is the ever-growing role of leadership in facilitating, enabling and guiding change, demanding new approaches and confirming the relevance of Change Leadership.

The purpose of my chapter is to argue the case for Change Leadership and what it takes competency-wise. This chapter will firstly contextualise the concept of Change Leadership by examining some of the critical drivers of change; outline the conceptual framework behind Change Leadership; and then look more pragmatically at the key competencies and skills that will be crucial if leaders are to evolve into effective Change Leaders. As such, I will aim to blend concept and technique, thereby igniting the reader's desire to grasp the framework and simultaneously providing practical areas that can be designed, tested and applied.

Why has Change Leadership Become so Important?

Having briefly introduced the concept of Change Leadership, it is useful to look more closely at the global conditions that demand it, now more than ever. To begin the conversation regarding the centrality of Change Leadership to leadership as a discipline and practice, let us look at global trends, patterns and themes. Global trends reflect accelerating and ongoing shifts linked to geopolitical and socio-economic dynamics. Close scrutiny of such dynamics reveal that they are intricately intertwined and influence multi- and bilateral power relations and alliances among countries and cultures. These drivers of change exert both overt and subtle influences on how change actually unfolds everywhere.

Toffler[4] has written extensively about the course of global human evolution and the pace of change that we can anticipate. In fact, his predictions have formed the foundation upon which significant first-world countries have based their national growth strategies. Toffler predicted critical global trends that influence how societies all over the world will function. Significant predictions include a phenomenon he calls the "Accelerative Thrust". The accelerative thrust refers to the increasingly rapid pace at which innovation, production and society in general will function. Toffler cites specific trends in order to assist leaders and strategists to understand the full impact of such rapid, widespread change.

A few notable trends include:

- The total output of goods and services in advanced countries doubles every 15 years, with doubling times shrinking.
- A growing teenager in society is surrounded by twice as much of everything man has made as his parents were when they were infants.
- With regard to technology and design, the time between the design of an original concept, its development and its practical use have been radically reduced.
- The speed of change is a psychological force, disturbing personal and group inner equilibrium. In other words, acceleration is experienced outside and around people, leading to acceleration within people.
- There will be increased transience and the emergence of what Toffler describes aptly as a "throwaway society". Such accelerated movement and transience will continue to have an impact on all facets of our relationships and lifestyles. Closely linked to this, our relationships will be of a shorter duration and be characterised by increased superficiality.
- The impact of change on people's personal lives will be greater. Toffler coined the term "fractured family syndrome", which describes the practical difficulties that would be experienced in maintaining conventional family relations and structures.

To summarise the essence of Toffler's predictions about how the future will unfold: the continuous accelerative pace of change will influence the fundamental principles and guiding values in society. For example, the emergence of "throwaway societal cultures" will directly influence the need for continuous novelty, new ideas, innovation, opportunities and challenges. This in turn will have a direct impact on people and organisations, who will need to become far more adaptable to cope with this rapid pace of change.

Understandably, such ever-increasing demands will lead and already are leading to widespread stress and strain at all levels of societal structures, almost as if the "future were arriving too soon". Predictably, mental and physical distress will increase as the sheer overload on people's physical and emotional adaptive systems increases exponentially.

Thus Toffler describes a very vivid picture of how global trends and patterns will unfold and permeate every intricate facet of life as we know it. Suffice it to say, cross-disciplinary research trends reflect that we have already started to experience the realisation of many of these predictions and scenarios. It will be useful now to look more closely now at the link between leadership, complexity, and the pace of change.

The Link between Leadership, Complexity, and the Pace of Change

Having described some of the demands the accelerated pace of change will have on all of us, it is useful to look at the impact it will have on leadership. Toffler foresees an increased reliance on leaders as a stabilising force and source of direction in a rapidly changing world; in other words, leading and managing how change is perceived, received and adapted to will be the key priority for all leaders.

Because the complexity and nature of change will be so vast, permeating every facet of life, people will increasingly turn to leaders to make sense of change and to guide them through such "turbulence". In order to do this, leaders will need to have an acute and heightened awareness of all the interwoven, intricate factors described above in order to lead people successfully through rapid change. Toffler refers to this leadership capability as "social futurism" which is the heighted responsibility that leaders should have towards their organisations and people.[5]

The pace of acceleration and its accompanying challenges therefore requires more intense and rapid change, momentum, adaptation and integration than conventional change efforts. This phenomenon presents a unique challenge and lays the foundations for what will be referred to as "Change Leadership". At this point we should start to clarify and define what Change Leadership actually entails.

Defining "Change Leadership"

"Change Leadership" is the ability to influence and arouse enthusiasm in others through personal advocacy, vision and drive, and to access resources in order to build a solid platform for change.[6] Anderson[7] defines Change Leadership as the ability of leaders to see the future and facilitate co-creation of the future with their people.

According to Kotter,[8] central to Change Leadership are the driving forces, visions and processes that fuel large-scale transformation. Change Leadership is associated with leaders being the "engine" to the whole change process: making the process of transition go faster, more smartly, more efficiently and more effectively. A greater sense of urgency is required by the Change Leader, coupled with an extraordinary ability to empower and energise people. It is people, after all, who are ultimately the key to the failure or success of change.

To further elaborate on the definition, Kotter predicts that *Change Leadership will be the most important challenge as we head into the future.* Kotter goes so far as to say that "the vast majority of organisations expect to achieve results by *managing* change, but ... more than 70% will fall short. The minority of leaders who do actually lead change equip themselves with the linchpin required for successful and sustainable change".[9]

Predictions about the centrality of Change Leadership within the broader ambit of leadership are unfolding already. We find an increasing focus in present-day leadership literature on the pivotal role played by leaders in facilitating large-scale transitions. An example of this emergent theme in global leadership studies is articulated by the American Management Association, who regard leadership as the ultimate key to driving change successfully.[10]

At this point we should explore what the key drivers were for this gravitation towards Change Leadership. What prompted it? What were the challenges leaders were facing that brought about this shift in their leadership needs and styles?

What Prompted Leaders to Recognise a Need for Change Leadership?

Anderson has delved into the history of Change Leadership and links the early origins to the dissatisfaction of leaders during the late 1980s and early 1990s with failed change efforts. Such change initiatives were based on creating and implementing changes in a top-down fashion.[11] Change was managed in a transactional manner despite the fact that transformations required by organisations were more complex and the stakes even higher. Challenges to leadership were similarly increasing.

Anderson describes the challenge of coping with this rapid pace of change as "capturing a river that keeps on flowing". However, change practitioners continued to focus on overcoming employee resistance and working on better implementation strategies. Although these are necessary components of a change process, leaders grew frustrated as they were still not achieving the results they desired. This growing dissatisfaction led to the ultimate evolution of the role of the Change Leader, who became accountable for the broader change process, particularly the side of change affecting and involving people.

Having briefly described the historical conditions leading to the emergence and evolution of the Change Leader, let us look at how we need to reconfigure leadership itself as a construct in order to produce the critical mass of Change Leaders the world so desperately requires.

Change Leaders: Reconfiguring Leadership

Ken Blanchard describes the process of Change Leadership as messy and chaotic.[12] He emphasises that Change Leadership involves designing, visualising and managing the "change journey", and that leaders usually do not focus sufficiently on this, but instead focus on the final destination. Linked to this, leaders need to have an expanded awareness of the subtle dynamics involved with change processes as it is these subtleties that will enhance or derail the broader change process.

This highlights a significant paradigm shift that will be required of leaders. Historically, leadership development has stressed a singular, almost linear, focus for leaders, namely the achievement of goals and targets. The so-called "softer aspects" of organisational life such as culture, climate, employee engagement, values, learning, and growth – that is, all the "people components" – have conventionally been relegated to support services such as Human Resources and OD. However, with the increasing complexity of a rapidly changing world and global competitiveness, leaders may no longer have such a linear focus. A fundamental paradigm shift needs to occur, accompanied by cognitive, attitudinal and behavioural changes. Ultimately, leaders need to acquire a new set of competencies and skills.

In keeping with leadership trends and requirements, writers such as Blanchard have emphasised the importance of leaders focusing on the actual "change journey". Underpinning this shift in focus is an alternate view of leaders playing a critical role in process issues versus a limited focus on organisational goals. Leaders are now required to focus on how people experience change itself, how they are likely to adapt to change, and to understand in depth what aspects of change will have the greatest impact on people.

Blanchard cites a significant study conducted at the US Department of Education.[13] This study postulates that people who are faced with change express six predictable concerns: informational; personal; implementation; impact; collaboration; and refinement concerns.

The study is very useful in outlining the range and nature of concerns people have when it comes to change, and these findings may be generalised across culture and context. The nature and extent of the concerns will, of course, be informed by the magnitude of the impending change.

The six areas of concern are a useful point of departure for Change Leaders, who can then re-orientate their focus accordingly. Change Leaders are able to attend to matters of process efficacy and efficiency and become sensitive to the concerns of people involved in a change process.

Further elaboration is provided by Richardson Sales Training and Effectiveness Solutions,[14] who emphasise Change Leadership as being a coherent leadership response to an urgent need for change. They conceptualise Change Leaders as innovative in describing how "change will look and feel" for the people affected.

To illustrate the impact of adjusting mindsets: in 1954 Roger Banister was the first person to run a mile in under four minutes. Until this achievement, the shared mental model was that it was impossible to run a mile in under four minutes. As soon as this "mental barrier" had been dismantled, the following month, 37 runners were able to achieve this goal. This example highlights how mental models can constrain vision and innovation. The Change Leader's role in *defining and clarifying the vision for the future and going beyond limited mental models* is thus a key success factor.

Closely linked to this *is the "will" of the Change Leader to empower people to create change themselves and participate in innovation during the change process.* This is a unique feature of Change Leadership, as leaders and managers have conventionally taken on the role of maintainers of the status quo. By default, leaders have inadvertently limited creativity and innovation in their organisations, often suppressing critical thinking and the birthing of novel ideas. Creativity, innovation and decision-making have mistakenly been restricted to a small, select group of people – usually at the top of the leadership chain. Unlocking organisation-wide creativity and innovation linked to the change process is therefore a courageous and necessary role of the Change Leader.

An interesting point linked to power relations is highlighted by Greg Satell.[15] He alerts leaders to the tendency to overestimate the power of their authority in driving change. In facilitating large-scale change, actual leadership ability/competence is far more important than authority. He goes on to challenge common associations between authority, power and control, viewing control as an illusion. In relinquishing false notions regarding power and control, Satell emphasises the need for leaders to facilitate true empowerment of people. This is a marked shift from the temptation all leaders face, namely to "bully" or "coerce" people into submission. This supports the point made earlier regarding Change Leadership having a different focus and thrust from conventional leadership styles. Conventional leadership styles often regard innovation as risky and therefore restrict idea generation and decision-making to a limited small group.

A key differentiator between leadership in general and Change Leadership is therefore the paradigm within which the Change Leader functions.

Critical Paradigm Shifts Required by Change Leaders

The Change Leadership paradigm necessitates the following fundamental shifts in the mental models used by leaders in order for them to be effective Change Leaders. There are four overarching paradigm shifts that are needed, discussed below:

A move from diagnostic-driven problem-solving to a dialogic organisational change paradigm as a new frame of reference

Diagnostic-driven, problem-solving organisational change emerged in the 1950s–1970s with the aim of improving the functioning of overly formalised, standardised, hierarchical organisations – the typical command-and-control organisations – by re-conceiving them as living, open systems that require the (re-)alignment of their components within the environment in which they are embedded. The approach was one of increasing awareness through conducting accurate diagnosis, then engaging organisational members in formulating changes in order to solve problems based on the new awareness brought about by the diagnostic findings. It was about incremental change: how to make the current system better at what it already is and does. It focused on the present in a linear, programmatic way.

Dialogic OD emerged as a paradigmatic shift in practice long before it was recognised in theoretical circles. It was formalised in a 2009 article by Bushe and Marshak.[16] This approach views organisations as dialogic systems. Individual, group, and organisational actions result from socially constructed realities created and sustained by the ruling narratives, stories, metaphors, and conversations that people use to make sense of and give meaning to their (organisational) experiences. Organisational change results from transforming the conversations shaping everyday thinking and action by involving more and different voices in order to alter which people engage with each other in making sense and giving meaning, and how they do so; and by stimulating alternative (or generative images) to reframe how people think about things, and act with regard to them. The aim is to induce new ways of thinking by altering the ongoing organisational conversations that in an ongoing, real-time way create, re-create, and frame understanding and action. Dialogic organisational development/change is future-focused and possibility-centric.[17]

The implication of the above paradigmatic shift for Change Leadership is to move away from a diagnostic driven, problem solving to a dialogic organisational change vantage point, by rather viewing their change role as one of shaping and transforming organisational conversations.

Discarding archaic, superficial notions regarding control and power

In order to do this, Change Leaders need to have a deeper, more intricate understanding of human behaviour (both individual and group dynamics) and its link to systemic change. Narrow, linear models of causality have become increasingly inadequate, along with mechanistic views of how people and organisations function. Models that emphasise the organic nature of organisations and emergence have far greater relevance to the role of the Change Leader.

The capacity to be effective in rapidly changing contexts

Another paradigm shift that the Change Leader needs to grapple with is the ability to conceptualise change as an ongoing process with periods of rapid transition. This is a distinct departure from most models of change which are based on the following process: "Unfreezing" the organisational environment, along with its leadership styles, people practices, and culture; then applying a "Change" process in a programmatic/project-based approach; and finally "refreezing" and institutionalising the changes in this new context.

However, analysis of global organisational trends and predictions of scenario planners strongly suggest a need for us to conceptualise growth patterns in a different way. These emerging growth patterns and trends emphasise the dynamic, evolutionary and emergent nature of change. They point to a more cyclical, continuous process that unfolds.

The implication of this alternate conceptualisation of change requires the Change Leader to have a far deeper understanding of and acceptance of the fluidity of context and the interconnectedness of seemingly disconnected systems. In the absence of this deep understanding of continuous, evolutionary change, the leaders themselves may experience change as destabilising and will not be able to perform a critical function that is inherent to their role, namely, contextualising change and thereby making it meaningful for the people on whom it will have an impact.

The will to involve and mobilise people genuinely in decision-making, design, and implementation of change processes

Closely linked to the capacity to handle rapid change, the ability to mobilise and engage people is paramount to the Change Leader. Mobilisation is defined as a *process* that accelerates the achievement of organisational vision through harnessing and unleashing individual and collective energies and talents. It involves the ability to align individual and collective performance by deeply linking individuals and groups to planned outcomes.

Involving people requires continuous transparent communication based on the understanding of how critical it is for people to feel safe during transitions. Such deep involvement and engagement of people in the process of change is usually overlooked or underrated by leaders, which explains the frequent failure of organisational change processes. The Change Leader, however, subscribes to a paradigm in which people are central to driving change. Former CEO of IBM, Thomas J Watson captured this well when he said:

> *"I believe the real difference between success and failure in a corporation can very often be traced to the question of how well the organisation brings out the energies and talents of its people."* – Watson[18]

Bearing this in mind, it becomes clear how adopting and functioning from a Change Leadership paradigm will have an impact on every facet of the leader's approach to his/her role. Similarly, Change Leadership brings with it a deep awareness that if people's concerns are not addressed, contained, or channelled appropriately, the Change Leader actually runs the risk of sabotaging the broader change process.

In summary, focusing on "the journey", or process, requires leaders to have a heightened sensitivity towards the experiences and emotions of people on whom the change will have an impact. Addressing the fears and emotions of people who have felt the impact of change leads to increased trust relations in organisations, which has a positive impact on how change unfolds, and its sustainability.

Specific Competencies Required by Change Leaders

Having looked at the overall paradigm within which the Change Leader positions his/her role, we can now focus on some of the specific competencies required. Competence is defined as a cluster of related abilities, commitments, knowledge and skills that enable a person to act effectively in a job or situation. Competence indicates sufficiency of knowledge and skills to enable someone to act in a wide variety of situations. It is important to examine the specific competencies that enable Change Leaders to be maximally effective. These competencies are outlined and explained below.

Clarity of purpose

While many methods may be used to facilitate change, it is critical that the Change Leader should have the utmost clarity on the outcomes that need to be achieved. People on whom change has an impact experience the process more positively when the leader has a clear sense of purpose and directionality. A lack of clarity of purpose by the leader has the potential to make the change process unnecessarily unstable and fearsome for people. This then causes resistance, which hinders forward movement and may even sabotage the whole change process.

Ability to cope with high degrees of complexity

In addition to clarity, the Change Leader needs to be able to grapple with a high level of complexity and uncertainty: global geopolitics, socio-economic dynamics, and the rapid pace of change have caused the world to become increasingly competitive and complex. Such complexity has a direct bearing on organisations, which are then bombarded by a multitude of external and internal forces. Needless to say, this has a direct impact on leaders, organisational dynamics, and people.

Change Leaders need to effect and drive change within such complex systems. It is therefore critical that they are able firstly to understand and contextualise the dynamics underpinning such complexity; "buffer/shield" the organisation from any negative impact of such complexity; and concurrently lead the change processes that are aimed at enhancing the organisation's efficiency and efficacy.

Change Leaders need to understand and contextualise such complexity, yet "unpack" complexity by continually striving towards simple, achievable outcomes. Tom Peters captures this well when he refers to great leaders being brilliant on the basics and keeping things simple in a complex world.[19] Fitzgerald succinctly captures the Change Leader's role in handling complexity when he says: "The test of a first rate intelligence is the ability to hold two opposed ideas in mind at the same time and still retain the ability to function."[20]

Possess sound diagnostic and predictive abilities

Clarity and the ability to make sense of complexity are two of the fundamental competencies required by Change Leaders. Blanchard adds a further competency to this role, namely, the ability to spot organisational patterns and diagnose organisational trends accurately. Accurate organisational diagnosis enables the Change Leader to manage the emotional climate in the organisation and in turn provide interventions that are needed to assist people through difficult transitions. Such interventions could range from the amount and quality of information provided to employee engagement programmes, all aimed at minimising resistance and allowing for smoother transitions.

The Change Leader needs to be adept at gauging the appropriate timing for specific interventions and sensitive to unspoken organisational and behavioural patterns. Blanchard emphasises that people are usually at different levels of readiness for change in organisations and sensitivity, so where "people are at" is crucial for Change Leaders. Resistance to change often occurs as a result of people being complacent or comfortable with the status quo and denying that the reasons for change are real. This is often linked to poor organisational trust relations, leading to a deep fear of what change will bring. Such deeply rooted fear may be exacerbated by rumours or misinformation.[21]

To counter such resistance, the Change Leader would need to be cognisant of the underlying reasons for resistance, and allay fears in the most appropriate, authentic way. This could include continuous reinforcement of the benefits of change; thoroughly explaining why the change is necessary; recognising and rewarding people's efforts; and, when necessary, providing appropriate training for new skills that may be required.

An authentic, credible, developmental leadership style

In general, leadership competence goes beyond technical skills or intellectual ability. It requires personal congruence with the role the leader holds. Such congruence emerges when there is synthesis of technical ability, personal maturity, emotional intelligence, and a deep understanding of human dynamics and power relations. Leaders inadvertently set the cognitive, emotional and behavioural tone in the organisation.

It should be clear that an authentic approach to leadership is critical to effective Change Leadership. The authenticity and credibility of the Change Leader is a long-term investment in the organisation as it leads to robust trust relations between the leader and the people. Ultimately, it is the trust people have in the Change Leader that determines their willingness to participate genuinely in change and experiment with novel ways of working.

Being an authentic and credible leader necessitates that the Change Leader be personally confident and resilient, with sound emotional intelligence and introspective capacity. The reason for this is that the emotional task of the Change Leader is the ability to act as the group's emotional guide or compass. The Change Leader has maximal power to sway people's emotions, and a key competence is thus driving the collective emotions of people in a positive direction. Unfortunately, containing and channelling people's emotions is often not emphasised as a vital component of sound Change Leadership.

Similarly, the role of Change Leaders in transforming the organisation into a safe setting for development, learning and growth is usually underplayed. This is perhaps linked to outdated command-and-control models of leadership, which do not focus sufficiently on human factors and group dynamics. A sincere concern for people's emotions during change is key to the credibility of the Change Leader and although delving into emotions within the work context may be uncomfortable, if left uncontained, people's emotions present a far greater risk to the change process.

The acceleration of the pace of change will demand a high level of personal grounding on the part of Change Leaders along with a strong and stable inner core. The ability to draw on such internal reserves of strength and stability leads to resilience and the capacity to cope with unpredicted challenges/barriers during the change process. This capacity is particularly important to the people being led through the change process, who need assurance that changes will lead to an improved context and that new ways of working will in fact enhance their experience of work.

Accompanying authenticity, enhanced emotional intelligence, and personal grounding is the Change Leader's developmental approach to leading people. As a result of organic, emergent approaches to change, it will often be necessary for people to experiment with new ways of working and to acquire new skills. How this is managed is critical, as it involves consciously shifting people out of their comfort zones. A developmental approach to people assists the Change Leader to adopt the roles of mentor and coach naturally, as required. This then transforms the organisation into a learning context where people feel safe to experiment with new ways of working.

Consciously understand and focus on culture building

An authentic, credible, developmental leadership style enables the Change Leader to focus on organisational culture. According to Senge, an organisation's culture can be seen as its members' collective mental models, shared values and norms of behaviour. He goes on to say that "[b]uilding learning-oriented cultures is hard work in any setting. It takes months and years – indeed it is a never-ending journey. It is fraught with risks, either of failing to realise true cultural change, or of succeeding in doing so and thus becoming a threat to those who want to keep things as they are. Building learning-oriented cultures is demanding because learning stretches us personally, and it is always easier to stay in our comfort zones."[22]

So essentially organisational culture is made up of the unspoken codes of conduct, approaches to problem solving, and communication styles within the organisation. Organisational culture is significantly influenced by leadership style and the values that underpin how work is done in the organisation. The all-pervasiveness of organisational culture has direct impact on how the organisation and its people respond to change. Understanding and influencing organisational culture is thus inherently connected to the role of the Change Leader.

In order to ensure sustainable change and embed a culture of continuous learning and openness to new paradigms and ways of working, the Change Leader needs to connect, engage and involve people actively. The Change Leader harnesses creativity and innovation by understanding that when people are involved in problem solving, their commitment to making solutions work increases exponentially.[23] To facilitate such deep emotions, the Change Leader needs to have integrating and synthesising competencies.

In summary, it becomes clear that Change Leadership requires a paradigm shift and competencies beyond the norm of ordinary leadership. I have attempted to outline the underlying paradigm that characterises Change Leaders and analysed key competencies that are critical to Change Leadership. The role of making change meaningful to people is the fundamental challenge to the Change Leader.

Conclusion

This chapter has clarified the alternate paradigm within which Change Leaders need to function and the competencies they need in order to lead change effectively. Leadership trends and the complex requirements of an ever-changing world suggest that the need for Change Leadership is rapidly growing.

Change Leadership requires a special brand of leadership that is distinguished by mental models, approaches to people, and development, along with the capacity to function effectively in complex systems. Closely linked to these competencies is the ability to involve people in the change process actively through sensitivity to their fears and concerns, the ability to reframe change so that it becomes meaningful to people, encouraging innovation, and consciously building a flexible and adaptable organisational culture of continuous learning.

Change is the result of various behaviours of many different people. The Change Leader energises, integrates and synchronises changes in order to catalyse forward movement for the organisation. The key challenges to Change Leadership are succinctly captured in the following quotations, which confirm that Change Leadership is no longer a "nice to have", but is instead an indicator of organisational success:

"There is nothing more difficult to take in hand, more perilous to conduct, or more uncertain in its success, than to take the lead in the introduction of a new order of things." – Machiavelli[24]

"The rate of change is not going to slow down anytime soon. If anything, competition in most industries will probably speed up even more in the next few decades." – Kotter[25]

Endnotes

1. Anderson & Ackerman Anderson, 2010.
2. Montapert, 1970.
3. Kotter, 1996.
4. Toffler, 1970.
5. Toffler, 1970.
6. Higgs & Rowland, 2000.
7. Anderson & Ackerman Anderson, 2010.
8. Kotter, 1996.
9. Kotter, 1996.
10. American Management Association (AMA), 1994.
11. Anderson & Ackerman Anderson, 2010.
12. Blanchard, 2007.
13. Blanchard, 2007.
14. Richardson Sales Training and Effectiveness Solutions, 2014.
15. Satell, 2014.
16. Bushe & Marshak, 2009.
17. See Marshak & Bushe, 2013, Bushe, 2013 and Bushe & Marshak, 2015 for expositions of this shift and Dialogic OD in detail.
18. Watson, n.d.
19. Peters & Waterman, 1982.
20. Fitzgerald, 2008.
21. Blanchard, 2007.
22. Senge, 1994.
23. Peters & Waterman, 1982.
24. Machiavelli, 1532.
25. Kotter, 1996.

References

American Management Association (AMA). 1994. *1994 AMA survey of downsizing: Summary of key findings.* New York, NY: American Management Association (AMA) [An American leadership Consulting Company established in 1923]. [Online]. Available: http://www.amanet.org/ [Accessed 25 May 2016].

Anderson, D & Ackerman Anderson, LS. 2010. *Beyond change management: How to achieve breakthrough results through conscious change leadership.* San Francisco, CA: Pfeiffer.

Blanchard, KH. 2007. *Leading at a higher level: Blanchard on leadership and creating high performing organizations.* Upper Saddle River, NJ: Pearson/Prentice Hall.

Bushe, GR. 2013. 'Dialogic OD: A theory of practice'. *Journal of the Organization Development Network,* 45(1):11–17

Bushe, GR & Marshak, RJ. 2015. *Dialogic organization development: The theory and practice of transformational change.* Oakland, CA: Berrett-Koehler Publishers, Inc.

Fitzgerald, FS. 2008. 'The crack-up'. [Online]. Available: http://www.esquire.com/news-politics/a4310/the-crack-up/. [Accessed 25 May 2016].

Higgs, M & Rowland, D. 2000. 'Building change leadership capability: "The quest for change competence"'. *Journal of Change Management,* 1(2):116–130.

Kotter, JP. 1996. *Leading change.* Boston, MA: Harvard Business School Press.

Machiavelli, N. 1532. *The prince.* [Trans. WK Marriott]. [1950 edition published by Heritage Cross Classics]. [Re-published 2010]. Lewiston, NY: CreateSpace Independent Publishing Platform.

Marshak, RJ & Bushe, GR. 2013. 'An introduction to advances in dialogic organization development'. *Journal of the Organization Development Network,* 45(1):1–4.

Montapert, AA. 1970. *The supreme philosophy of man; the laws of life.* Englewood Cliffs, NJ: Prentice-Hall.

Peters, TJ & Waterman, RH. 1982. *In search of excellence: Lessons from America's best-run companies.* New York, NY: Harper & Row.

Richardson Sales Training and Effectiveness Solutions. 2014. *Leading and managing change.* Philadelphia, PA: Richardson Sales Training and Effectiveness Solutions. [Online]. Available: https://(www.richardson.com). [Accessed 23 July 2016].

Satell, G. 2014. 'To create change, leadership is more important than authority'. *Harvard Business Review,* 21 April. [Online]. Available: https://hbr.org/2014/04/to-create-change-leadership-is-more-important-than-authority/. [Accessed 25 May 2016].

Senge, PM. 1994. *The fifth discipline fieldbook: Strategies and tools for building a learning organization*. New York, NY: Currency, Doubleday.

Toffler, A. 1970. *Future shock*. New York, NY: Random House.

Watson, TJ, Jr. 1963. *A business and its beliefs: The ideas that helped build IBM*. New York, NY: McGraw-Hill: A Division of The McGraw-Hill Companies. © 1963 Trustees of Columbia University, City of New York; © 2003 McGraw-Hill. [Online]. Available: http://www.leadershipnow.com/managementquotes.html; http://perspective-power.com/i-believe-the-real-difference-between-success-and-failure-in-a-corporation-can-be-very-often-traced-to-the-question-of-how-well-the-organization-brings-out-the-great-energies-and-talents-of-its-peop/. [Accessed 23 July 2016].

SECTION 5
LEADERSHIP SETTINGS

Chapter 16

TEAM LEADERSHIP

Drikus Kriek

One can hardly deny the critical role that teams play in 21st century organisations. The use of teams can rightly be regarded as one of the most significant characteristics of modern organisational life. Therefore, it has become crucial for leaders to optimise the use of teams in their organisations. However, any leader of a team is sure to know that there is no "one solution", "magic wand" or "*n*-step magic" that is sufficient to act as a "paint-by-numbers" solution to all potential challenges in a team. The dynamics of interpersonal interaction, idiosyncratic demands of various teams, and challenges of individual organisations render such simplistic solutions impossible.

This chapter offers a framework to increase understanding of teams and to assist in handling, facilitating or leading teams to increased performance. The following topics are covered: what is team leadership?; introduction of the available frameworks for understanding teams; and then addressing the seven focus areas, the 7 Fs, that leaders need to consider in leading teams to higher performance, namely Frame, Foundation, Functioning, Field, Force, Flow and Fitness.

What is Team Leadership?

A group of people becomes a team when its individual members join together to pursue some aim they all desire; it may be to raise funds, or to design a new automobile, or to climb Everest, or to win the rugby World Cup. However, while the use of teams seems to be ubiquitous and a variety of factors can be identified on why they are used, one needs to ask what a team is. In this chapter we will regard a team as follows:

> Embedded in and aligned with its context, a team is a type of social system whose members communicate and work interdependently together in roles and with a shared sense of purpose in order to reach its targets in and/or on time.

Team leadership is the process of facilitating the team's development processes and dynamics to reach these targets and therefore to "become" a team.[1]

Frameworks for Understanding Teams

To understand the prevalence and ubiquitous nature of teams it comes as no surprise that a variety of ideas exists about what teams are and ways to understand them. This has led to a number of different frameworks or theories on how to understand teams; each of these provides valuable insights and illuminates elements of teams. A selection of such frameworks can be identified and are mentioned briefly.

Development frameworks

These conceptualisations focus on the development of teams in time. They stress that teams develop through different stages from start to finish with the famous forming, storming, norming and performing stages of Bruce Tuckman[2] as the most famous example.

Component frameworks

These frameworks identify various elements that make up teams. For example, components such as composition, goals, climate, tasks, inputs and many more have been identified.[3]

Roles

Theories focusing on roles identify different role preferences that individuals enact in team settings with those of Belbin[4] and the roles of the Team Management Profile identified by Margerison and McCann[5] being classical examples.

Systems framework

The influence of input, process and output from the world of systems thinking dominates this view of teams.

Psychological frameworks

The emphasis in these models is on the unconscious psychological drives and needs of individuals and teams, with the most influential of these being those of the Tavistock Institute and later proponents such as Kets de Vries.[6]

In an effort to integrate findings from these various perspective, this chapter highlights seven focus areas that leaders need to consider in leading teams to higher performance, namely Frame; Foundation; Functioning; Field; Force; Flow and Fitness. Figure 16.1 illustrates these key foci of teams.

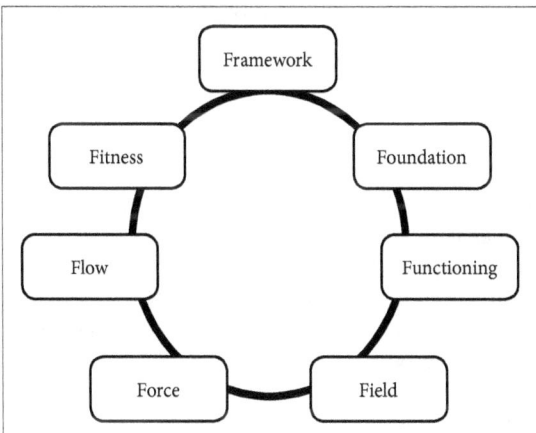

Figure 16.1: Key foci of teams

Each one of these focus areas is subsequently discussed in more detail and examples of how they manifest are provided to assist leaders of teams.

Frame: The Bigger Context

Every team, irrespective of the dynamics thereof, is situated within larger systems and operates in a given historical context. On a larger scale, what is happening in the economy, social trends and political decisions is constantly present in the manner in which the team conducts itself. Thus, the team interacts with elements from its context and environment or, as Kozlowski and Ilgen[7] state, a "dynamic, shifting, and complex environment creates commensurate team task demands that members have to resolve…". What is happening in this context influences the dynamics of the team.

The context of a team can be divided into four distinguishable types.

Ecological context

This refers to the larger systems of which the group forms a part, and it represents all the interactions that the team has with its environment. The remote context includes larger trends and societal processes that influence each individual in one way or another. It is, of course, impossible to identify all trends or to map the total impact of trends on a team's behaviour. It is also not necessarily true that a particular trend will have an impact on each individual member of the team or on all teams in a similar way. However, it is important to realise that aspects within the remote context can have an impact on the functioning of a team and they therefore form a critical component. Aspects of the remote context that are distinguished include the so-called PESTLE factors, namely political, economic, sociological, technological, legal, and environmental issues.

Organisational context

This context includes the cultural context of the organisational and the operational context (including the resources made available to the team) it provides. As a consequence of these influences, a team's effectiveness is determined by the reciprocity between team and organisational effectiveness. This entails that the effectiveness of the entire organisation may influence the output of the team, and conversely, the organisation may be influenced by the performance of the team. The main organisational contextual influences on a team are the organisational strategy, culture and operational systems.

Team context

This context is unique to the specific team and includes the type of team, its levels of authority within the organisation, and the actualised context created by the team. Aspects to look for include the use of teams in the organisation, and the development of the team. It can be a newly-formed team or a team that has been part of team development exercises before, having experience and knowledge that members of teams of this nature acquire. A further element is the type of team where teams can be differentiated as to whether they are production, creative, management, or virtual, among others.

Individual context

This refers to the members who constitute the team and includes what each member brings to the team from his or her environment.

Implications for team leadership

The Frame of a team is key to the leader as it provides the backdrop to what is happening in the team. Alternatively put, it identifies the constraints under which the team has to operate. For example, if a team is operating in a very hierarchical and autocratic organisational context, one should consider the potential impact of such factors on how a team of that type should be led.

While the impact of each potential influence of the context cannot be predicted or determined, leaders should be aware of contextual influences on the team as a social system. It is therefore important for a leader to understand these contextual influences and acknowledge how they can enhance or impede the team's functioning. It is particularly valuable to use contextual efforts to determine the influence the context has on the foundation of the team. This will be discussed next.

Foundation: Thrust, Structure and Targets

The foundation of the team is made up of its thrust, structure and targets.

Thrust

The thrust of the team is the "heart and soul" of the team and provides the driving force of the team. It consists of the vision and values of the team and forms the gel that glues the team members together. The vision includes the reason why the team exists and presents the desired outcome propelling the team to the future.[8] It may be generated from within the team (self-directed work team) or (more likely) it can come from outside the team (for example, provided by the organisation). The values are the cornerstone of behaviour and present beliefs about what is good or bad and what is important or not. They determine the performance ethic of the team and serve as a generating factor in specifying behaviour in the team. The function of thrust provides commitment of the team to common goals, unconscious elements that bind the team together (for example, shared mental models), and its energy.

Structure

The structure represents the actual physical embodiment of the team as it is made up through the diversity of its members; it is thus the "make-up" of the team. It refers to the composition of the members (for example, the demographic composition of a team, or the personality facets of its members) as well as the team composition, including the size, roles, stability and balance of the team. In a team, as in a social system, this refers to the people who make up the team; they therefore form the talent pool of the team. The different characteristics, dispositions and traits of the team's individual members therefore influence the team. It is impossible to provide a complete list of all demographic characteristics that differentiate between individuals, and it is not inevitable that each or any of these demographic differences will have a direct impact on the processes of the team. However, some that could be considered include:

- *Capability:* This component refers to the knowledge, skills and ability (KSA) a team needs in order to be effective and to complete the tasks it has to accomplish in delivering on its vision. Knowledge or skills levels include levels of education, functional knowledge, information or expertise, training, experience, and abilities.
- *Personality:* An important part of personality is that it is unique to each individual and that it sets us apart from others. It is generally understood to be a developing process whereby stable, core elements and fluid, peripheral elements are patterned by the individual and his or her context to form a personality.
- *Team composition:* The team composition refers to elements of structure that relate to the team as a whole and include its size, balance and stability. The size of the team forms part of the structural architecture of the team and therefore can contribute to the performance of the team. As a general rule it can be stated that the optimum size of a team is the minimum

- number of people required to ensure effective and efficient delivery of the team's tasks.
- **Roles** in teams play a critical part and operate unconsciously as well as formally in determining the manner in which teams operate.[9]

Targets

The targets of a team provide the link with the contextual demands and concretise the journey towards attaining its vision. Every team must have the following four components[10] of performance covered to ensure that its targets are reached, namely:

- *Production output:* Every team delivers on a particular outcome and one can argue that that is probably the most important element of the target.
- *Individual member growth and satisfaction:* The consequences a group has for its members and the benefits each member finds in being part of the group should form part of the target of the team. Examples could be that the individuals view their membership of and participation in the activities of the team as assisting in career opportunities, contributing to personal satisfaction, and/or developing or satisfying personal needs and motives.
- *Team development:* This refers to the viability of the team, which must ensure that it has the required elements in place to make the team sustainable and capable of reaching its targets. A team should act to ensure its longer-term viability and sustainability, and create a sense of belonging and cohesion for its members.
- *Organisational alignment and benefit:* A team can be successful only once it meets key demands of individuals, the team and the organisation. These demands are related to performance and viability, and they ensure that satisfaction and learning/growth are key elements of the team's operation.

Implications for team leadership

Team leaders play a critical part in assisting the team to clarify its Foundation. In particular, the task of articulating and/or clarifying the vision of the team is a key leadership task. Leaders also have the responsibility of constituting the team in terms of the key compositional aspects of the team and by ensuring that the team is balanced and stable. Since it is the key reason of existence for all teams in reaching their vision, the manner in which the targets of the team are shaped by the leader is key to ensuring its success. It is therefore vitally important to leaders of teams to ensure that the foundation of a team is in place as it provides the basic building blocks of its success.

Functioning: Communication, Task-work and Teamwork

Three elements interact to ensure that a team functions optimally. These can be identified as communication, task-work and teamwork.

Communication

Communication serves to share information, energise and motivate members, manage behaviour, and facilitate interpersonal interaction. Fundamentally, communication is used in teams to facilitate three things, namely:

- To assist in co-ordinating its task-work – communication is needed to help the team to complete its tasks and to coordinate those tasks;
- To help with co-operation through teamwork: the teamwork a team completes is dependent on communication; and
- To foster understanding of the purpose of the team: the mutually shared understanding of what the purpose of the team is as it relates to its vision and targets needs to be conveyed through the team's communication processes.

In particular, leaders have to ensure that the following communication tasks are successfully implemented:[11]

- Every member talks and listens in equal measure.
- Contributions are short and to the point.
- Face-to-face interaction facilitates energetic conversation.
- Members connect directly with one another and not only with or "through" the leader.
- Communication and conversation outside the team's formal meetings happen and are useful.
- Members periodically explore outside the team and bring the information into the team. Through clear communication efforts, leaders are able to ensure that key idiosyncratic and generic tasks that the team has to complete are delivered and that the required interdependent teamwork activities are in place.

Task-work

It goes without saying that each individual has to perform certain tasks in the team.[12] This is to ensure that the team functions successfully and that it meets its aims. The tasks of a team represent the interaction the team has with its environment, resources and systems. The "task-work" of a team is therefore the "what" a team does to meet and complete its targets. Idiosyncratic tasks of teams include the activities each team has to complete in order to ensure effective performance levels, but from the perspective of the unique outputs of each member. What a team member does therefore has an impact on the performance of a team in general.

Generic tasks refer to universal tasks each team has to complete to remain optimal. In this regard the work of Margerison and McCann assists as they identify:

- *Advising*: to gather and report information and data
- *Innovating*: to create ideas, alternatives and experiment with them
- *Promoting*: to explore and present opportunities
- *Developing*: to assess and test the applicability of new ideas
- *Organising*: to establish and implement ways to get things done
- *Producing*: to deliver outputs
- *Inspecting*: to control and audit systems
- *Maintaining*: to uphold and safeguard processes.[13]

Teamwork

Members in teams do not only complete tasks. The interaction of activities ensures flow of work and products and is what teamwork consists of.[14] It can be defined as the interdependent acts that convert inputs to outcomes when team members do the tasks assigned to each of them. This includes monitoring, backup behaviour, co-ordination, and optimisation of processes including conflict management and creative problem-solving procedures.[15]

Implications for team leadership

The Functioning of a team consists of its communication, task-work and teamwork, and the leader and team leaders devote a lot of attention to these critical elements.

Field: Alignment with Contextual Systems

Once a team leader has ensured that the team is optimally configured (in other words, the Foundation and Functioning of the team are in place), the next key leadership role is to ensure that the team is aligned with its contextual systems. In this regard, the following need to be in place.

- *Performance management system* **(PMS):** The team's targets are dependent on the PMS that the organisation employs and must line up with the individual effort and the performance management system in order to ensure alignment.
- *Operation systems:* Any team functions in a particular organisational context that is made up of an operational context and a culture. In enabling the context of the team and facilitating optimum performance, the team leader has to align team behaviour with the organisational culture and operational demands. In particular, operational systems and procedures need to be in place and the resources required to perform optimally need to be provided.
- *Communication system:* The next level of alignment required of the organisation is to provide an information system that assists the team to find the information required to do their work.
- *Talent management system:* The leader of the team should align its training, development and recruiting systems to such a degree that a team is able to have the required skills, knowledge and abilities available when needed. This means that the organisation must provide the team with the talent pool required to deliver on its promises; alignment of this aspect is therefore critical to keep in pace with developments. Individual members of the team are required to provide their skills, knowledge and abilities and ensure that they are used optimally so that the team can succeed.

Implications for team leadership

The alignment of the various elements of the organisational context and that of the members of the team allow the leader to create the context in which the team's goal can be pursued. It provides the supporting context that helps members to understand the value and meaning of their own individual contributions to the greater goal. Once this contribution is individualised and measurable, the leader's role in maintaining the field becomes focused on providing the requisite resources, reward and motivation.

The leader therefore aligns the performance management system according to individual and contextual demands in order to ensure performance. The leader aligns operational and cultural contexts with individual behaviour to enable operation and a good fit with culture to ensure operational efficiency. The information system should be optimised by the leader to engage in communication and to empower talent. The resourcing, development and training of the team members should be aligned with the systems of the organisation. The last level of alignment refers to the thrust of the team and the requirements of organisation and individual alike to align with the team's vision, values and potency. Thus, a team leader considers each of the constituent elements and facilitates alignment of each with the corresponding organisational and individual contextual element. These are the alignment tasks a leader needs to fulfil to ensure that the Field of the team is used optimally.

Forces: Unconscious and Conscious Interactions

While the Field of a team relates to the alignment of individuals with the organisational culture, it is focused more on the "harder", tangible and operational interactions. For example, what are the required tools I need to do my job? By contrast, the Force of a team relates to the unconscious and psychological forces that stem from human interaction.

It has two components, the first of which comprises the unconscious drives and needs that influence individual behaviour "from the bottom up". The team's operations (since it is a social system as well) are influenced by these unconscious forces. The second component, as the team performs its daily activities, is the interaction between members (including the unconscious forces accompanying individual behaviour). This influences the emotional and cognitive mindset of the team, and a collective state emerges. This can be regarded as the "feel" or "climate" of the team and acts as a cloud hovering above the operation of the team. It simultaneously influences the interactions and operations of the team while also being influenced and affected by the same interactions and operations. These so-called "emergent states" will be discussed first.

Emergent states

Emergent states[16] consist of the psychological and emotional activity within members, within a team and between members. As the levels of interaction and engagement between members of the team occur, members are affected by the impact they have on one another. This influences the manner in which they interact, although they may not be aware of the dynamics, energy and influence of the forces at a deeper level having an impact on their behaviour and emotional and cognitive states.

Behavioural emergent states emerge as teams have collective mental maps about their own ability to complete the task at hand, which is collective distribution of information and knowledge. They therefore do things with the knowledge that team mates will reciprocate in a particular manner.

Similarly, teams also share emotional emergent states that develop and emerge collectively. Sometimes a team can be excited and happy because of a success or a positive development in the team. Alternatively, the team can feel depressed, despondent or negative because of perceived frustrations with leadership, organisation, interpersonal relations, or a number of other antecedents to emotional and mood states. The cognitive emergent states operative in a team can be seen as the mental models or mindmaps influencing the team's behaviour patterns.

While these are individually generated, a "shared, collective" mental map emerges as members work in teams. This consists of words, images and stories that occupy the thinking processes in a team. For example, it can refer to the collective sense of what is required to "get the deal" or to "visualise" the successful completion of a project or product.

These emergent states (behavioural, emotional and cognitive states) allow for a climate to develop, for cohesion between members to enhance, and for identity as well as trust/security to develop. Cohesion is the collective sense of belonging that exists within the team. It refers to a sense of rapport, camaraderie or "we-ness". It is the invisible binding ingredient that contributes to the team's solidarity, sense of community, and fellow-feeling.

The team is in constant interaction with its environment (= the context of the team). However, the team needs to create a boundary in order to define itself from this environment (in other words, assert its identity). It needs to determine its limits and identify what makes it unique in its environment. This allows the team to determine how it wants to relate to the context and enables it to facilitate its interaction with the environment. Of specific importance to teams is the state of security and trust that develops as teams grow cohesive. As trust increases between members of a team it creates a safe environment in which to operate, and each member is given an opportunity to participate in the team. Trust is the confidence that a member has in another individual or the team that commitments made to the member will be honoured.

Unconscious forces

The second element of the Force of a team is the role the unconscious plays in a team's operations. These unconscious elements exist because teams are social systems consisting of individuals bringing personal dynamics to the team. This perspective on teams require us to expand our notion of human behaviour to acknowledge that it is more than merely rational and logical, but that human interaction is also characterised by anxiety, fantasy, wishes, drives, needs, and conflicts that go beyond rational comprehension – especially since these are sometimes conscious but are often also unconscious.[17]

As teams consist of human beings, they also operate in teams with their individual "psyches", and the content of the unconscious and the manner in which this operates influence team behaviour as well. This is so because the unconscious influences behaviour even though the individual member may not be aware of its operation. For example, some of these influences relate to:

- *Dependence*, which asserts that as during childhood where the child is dependent on the parent (or parental figure), team members project needs for dependency on the team and its leadership.
- The *"fight-or-flight" assumption* contends that team members use either fight or flight behaviour to manage the assumed anxiety-producing environment. Fight assumptions manifest in teams through constant conflict, aggression, jealousy, team rivalry, in-fighting, competition, and jostling for position. On the other hand, flight assumptions manifest through behaviour such as avoidance, absenteeism, and distancing issues from the self.
- *Pairing* focuses on mechanisms members put in place to avoid anxiety and alienation. Members pair with perceived powerful team members or sub-groups to create a sense of security and safety. The members can also try to split up the team to form smaller subsystems in which they can feel safe and secure, and belong.

Implications for team leadership

Thus the Force of a team has an emergent state element (= behavioural, emotional and cognitive states) and an unconscious component. The task of the leader is to activate and channel the forces – both unconscious and emergent states – to assist the team in its operations. For example, it is key for the leader to facilitate a sense of belonging and cohesion as it influences the behaviour of a team. Failing that, the roles that members play in a team need to be optimised.

The leader also has to channel unconscious forces and should understand and optimise how team members' dependence, fight-or-flight and pairing assumptions have an impact on the team's performance. Thus, the examples indicate that the role of the leader should be focused on both parts of the forces – the unconscious forcing upwards and, as the emergent states develop, their influence "downwards" on the team's operations and interaction.

Flow: Life Span of Team over Time

The next element that must be considered is that teams develop over time. This refers to the life span of the team and how changes occur in the life of a team. Thus, as time passes and a team develops there could be potential changes occurring in the development of a team. A number of different conceptualisations of this flow in time have been proposed and two of them – linear and the punctuated equilibrium framework – are presented here to illustrate the role of development in time.

Linear

This type of framework assumes progression of a team to a higher, more efficient stage as the team develops in time, thus it proposes teams develop progressively and linearly "up" – think of climbing a long flight of stairs from the bottom to the top. As time passes and a team develops, certain stages or phases are completed in order to enable this linear progress. These stages are viewed as fixed in sequence and length and occur independently of context or type of team.

The framework of Tuckman[18] in the late sixties (and the adjustment thereof by Tuckman and Jensen[19] a decade later) is arguably the most widely cited example of this nature. It provides a step-wise progression of a team through the well-known stages of forming, storming, norming, performing, and adjourning. A major problem with the linear view of team development is the notion that it is pre-determined and that teams can't "regress" to revisit earlier stages once they have progressed beyond a particular stage. Furthermore, it assumes that teams spend equal time in these stages and that the sequential order is fixed.

Midpoint transition

The midpoint transition framework (also known as the punctuated equilibrium framework) proposed by Gersick[20] challenges the progressive and linear nature of teams. It focuses on three main stages in the development of a team.

At first it suggests a set of behaviours, assumptions about what is required, and scrutiny of the membership of the team that emerge very early in the team's existence. The first phase sets the tone for the rest of the development of the team and influences a team's approach to its project. The team employs that framework throughout the first half of its life as it sets out in earnest to complete its task.

This manner of operation and pattern of behaviour remain intact until the calendar midpoint of the team. During this "midpoint", a transition or paradigmatic shift occurs that allows the team to take stock of the learning that has taken place during the first phase. During the midpoint phase members find that old perspectives are no longer viable, and they start to explore new ideas to use during completion of the team's work. At this point the team realises its time is limited and it offers an opportunity to the team to calibrate its actions and to move forward. The team opens up for external influences to its operations and external resources, and benchmarks are used to re-chart its progress.

After this midpoint transition, a second phase of relative inertial movement follows that is informed by the events of the first phase and influenced by the team's expectations regarding requirements of the last phase. Shortly before completion of its tasks, the team "launche[s] into a final burst of activity".[21] In an effort to satisfy outside expectation, the team experiences the positive and negative consequences of decisions it has taken during its operational life cycle.

Implications for team leadership

The flow of the team (that is, its development in time) provides opportunity for leaders to interject and ensure optimum performance aligned with the particular stage. At the start of the team's operation, an initial period ensues with focus on benefits to members and on the tasks of the team. The first task is to provide the background to the team's existence and to provide clarity on its strategy. The leader also assists the team to interact and to learn about one another during interaction. Although the team may be familiar with one another and some members may even know one another well, it remains a key part of the team's operation to allow opportunity for the team to link their interactions and knowledge about each other around the vision of the team.

As the team develops, the role of the leader focuses on clarifying the various roles and tasks each member has to complete. The leader directs and co-ordinates the flow of work and helps to grow the identity of the team by clarifying norms and values. Through the initial period of operation, the leader should keep the focus of the team on its performance and monitor the allocation of roles, tasks, and the attainment of goals. Hackman and Wageman[22] call this the motivational task of leaders, which is complete once the team enters its midpoint transition stage.

The leadership task during the midpoint transition of the team is to allow stock taking and evaluation of operations. The team experiences a heightened sense of urgency to complete the project deliverables, and the leader drives the team to complete its tasks. The role of the leader during this time of turbulence is large and strategic,[23] and positions the team for its next phase. After the team has re-calibrated its processes and aligned its interaction, a sense of urgency and determined action towards the deliverables of the team ensues. The team sets out to answer: "Do we deliver?"

During this (second) phase of relative inertial movement, the team drives its operation with renewed rigour and synergy. This is the final phase of a team's operation, where the team evaluates the completion of its purpose and terminates its activities. The stage is characterised by the team taking a more reflective and contemplative stance. The responsibility of the leader is to focus on the educational aspect of the operation and how learning and lessons from the project can be used to improve future performance.[24]

Fitness: Optimal Performance

Lastly, the team needs to stay "fit" to ensure optimal performance. In this regard team building is used and various team management tools and techniques need to be employed.

The first of these, team building, comes in a variety of forms, and the following can help the team leader:

- **Role-definition:** The aim of this approach is "to clarify each individual's role expectations, the norms of the group as a whole and the shared responsibilities of the different group members".[25]
- **Problem-solving approach:** This is a more general model of team building based on problem solving. According to this approach team members identify major problems, generate relevant information, engage in problem solving and action planning, and implement and evaluate action plans.
- **Cohesion building approach:** The aim of this approach is to "foster a sense of team spirit and build the interpersonal connections among team members" and to create "a sense of unity and belonging, a climate of mutual understanding, and a sense of pride in the team".[26]
- **Psychodynamic approach:** Behaviour in teams (that is, behaviour driven by dependency

needs and, fight-or-flight, as well as pairing-drives) manifests in a team context through anxiety, taking up a role, dependencies, boundaries, and helping teams to understand the dynamics thereof can be useful team development activities.[27]

- *Adventure programming:* The use of adventure or outdoor learning approaches to facilitate team-building interventions can become "increasingly popular" as it focuses on *emotional intensity, psychological safety, consequentiality, use of metaphors, unpredictability* and *focus on transfer*.[28]
- *Assessment approaches:* These approaches include climate assessment, personality preferences, and role indicators.[29]

When considering team management tools, the efficiency and effectiveness of a team on its performance journey must be mapped and measured. The deliverables of the team determine the processes that need to be followed, the resources required, and the metrics that need to be achieved in order to ensure performance. In this regard, the measurements help to create understanding, to drive behaviour, and ultimately, to facilitate results.

Implications for team leadership

The last task of a leader is to ensure that the team stays Fit, that is, that it maintains its optimum performance and that it fulfils its vision. To sustain the performance efforts of the team, the team leader has to ensure that the team stays motivated and performs and executes its tasks efficiently and effectively. For this, the leader employs effective team-building initiatives according to the needs of the team. Furthermore, the leader needs to manage and lead the team with appropriate management techniques to facilitate efficiency and effectiveness.

Conclusion

The "seven Fs" provided in this chapter gives a framework for leaders to utilise and assist them in understanding:

- *Frame:* The environmental context of the team that includes the larger societal influences and the organisational and individual contexts, as well as the type of team.
- *Foundation:* The core of any team is determined by its goal and the members that constitute the team. The manner in which the targets of the team operationalise the vision and motivate the members forms part of the foundation of the team.
- *Functioning:* Once the foundational elements are in place, the team's functioning can be conceptualised as the communication in the team, as well as its task-work and teamwork.
- *Field:* The manner in which the leader is responsible for facilitating a context in which a team can excel through aligning the organisational and individual contexts constitutes the field of a team.
- *Forces:* The operations of a team are influenced by unconscious needs and forces, while at the same time, the interactions in the team and the influence of these psychodynamic forces create a "cloud" that has an impact on the operations thereof.
- *Flow:* As the team operates, in time it develops through identifiable stages during which the team completes developmental tasks in order to optimise its operations.
- *Fitness:* The leader has the responsibility for monitoring the team's operation through the phases and has to ensure the "fitness" thereof through team-building activities, team coaching, and performance measures.

Thus, to lead a team, the leader has to understand the demands of the context (Frame); put the building blocks for success in place (Foundation); ensure optimal operations (Functioning); create an aligned context for performance (Field); optimise the drives, needs and climate of the team (Force); lead the team in time (Flow); and ensure its Fitness as it succeeds in delivering its mandate.

Endnotes

1. Northouse, 2013.
2. Tuckman, 1965.
3. Lencioni, 2006; LaFasto & Larson, 2001.
4. Belbin, 2004.
5. Margerison & McCann, 1985.
6. Kets de Vries, 2011.
7. Kozlowski & Ilgen, 2006, p. 78.
8. Hackman, 2002.
9. Belbin, 2004; Margerison & McCann, 1985.
10. Thompson, 2007.
11. Pentland, 2012.
12. Thompson, 2007.
13. Margerison & McCann, 1985.
14. Salas, Sims & Burke, 2005.
15. Salas, Burke & Cannon-Bowers, 2000.
16. Kozlowski & Ilgen, 2006.
17. Kets de Vries, 2011.
18. Tuckman, 1965.
19. Tuckman & Jenson, 1977.
20. Gersick, 1988, 1989, 1991.
21. Ibid.
22. Hackman & Wageman, 2005.
23. Ibid.
24. Ibid.
25. Hayes, 2002, p. 60.
26. Levi, 2007.
27. Kets de Vries, 2011.
28. Ibid.
29. Ibid.

References

Belbin, R. 2004. *Management teams: Why they succeed or fail*. 2nd ed. Oxford, UK: Elsevier Butterworth-Heineman.

Gersick, CJG. 1988. 'Time and transition in work teams: Toward a new model of group development'. *Academy of Management Journal*, 31(1):9–41.

Gersick, CJG. 1989. 'Marking time: Predictable transitions in task groups'. *Academy of Management Journal*, 32(2):274–309.

Gersick, CJG. 1991. 'Revolutionary change theories: A multilevel exploration of the punctuated equilibrium paradigm'. *The Academy of Management Review*, 16(1):10–36.

Hackman, JR & Wageman, R. 2005. 'A theory of team coaching'. *Academy of Mangement Review*, 30(2):269–287.

Hackman, JR. 2002. 'Leading teams: Setting the stage for great performances'. Boston, MA: Harvard Business School Publishing Corporation.

Hayes, N. 2002. *Managing Teams: A Strategy for Success*, 2nd Edition. London: Thomson Learning, p 60.

Kets de Vries, MFR. 2011. *The hedgehog effect: The secrets of building high performance teams*. San Francisco, CA: Jossey-Bass.

Kozlowski, S & Ilgen, D. 2006. 'Enhancing the effectiveness of work groups and teams'. *Psychological Science in the Public Interest*, 7(3):77–88.

LaFasto, F & Larson, C. 2001. *When teams work best*. Los Angeles, CA: Sage Publications.

Lencioni, P. 2006. The five dysfunctions of a team: A leadership fable. Mumbai, IN: Wiley-India.

Levi, D. 2007. *Group dynamics for teams*. 2nd ed. Thousand Oaks, CA: Sage Publications, Inc.

Margerison, C & McCann, D. 1985. 'Team management profiles: Their use in managerial development'. *Journal of Management Development*, 4(2):34–37.

Northouse, P. 2013. *Leadership: Theory and practice*. 6th ed. Los Angeles, CA: Sage Publications.

Pentland, A. 2012. 'The new science of building great teams'. *Harvard Business Review*, 10 April.

Salas, E, Burke, C & Cannon-Bowers, J. 2000. 'Teamwork: Emerging principles'. *International Journal of Management Reviews*, 2(4):339–356.

Salas, E, Sims, DE & Burke, CS. 2005. 'Is there a "big five" in teamwork?' *Small Group Research*, 36(5):555–599.

Thompson, LL. 2007. *Making the team: A guide for managers*. Upper Saddle River, NJ: Pearson Prentice-Hall.

Tuckman, B. 1965. 'Developmental sequence in small groups'. *Psychological Bulletin*, 63(6):384–399.

Tuckman, B & Jensen, M. 1977. 'Stages of small-group development revisited'. *Group & Organization Management*, 2(4):419–427.

Chapter 17

ENTREPRENEURIAL LEADERSHIP
Boris Urban

This chapter aims to provide an overview of the interconnectedness between leadership and entrepreneurship. The chapter starts by examining how entrepreneurial leaders in a corporate setting need to adopt an entrepreneurial mindset. The entrepreneurial economy is then discussed in the context of corporates creating a conducive context that facilitates entrepreneurship. Several measures, outcomes and guidelines are suggested based on best practices and illuminated through practitioner profiles. The chapter ends by examining the future of entrepreneurial leadership, which includes focusing on both economic and social elements.

Connection between Entrepreneurship and Leadership

Entrepreneurial ventures and small businesses contribute about 2.5 times more innovations per employee than do large corporates. They are responsible for most of the major innovations in the economy. Innovation is central to the development of new businesses and wealth. Even though large corporates have the resources and skills to manage innovations, their ability to create innovative breakthroughs is limited. Many of the important innovations in the last two centuries have come from individual entrepreneurs.[1] What gives individual entrepreneurs a radical innovation advantage? One may be that opportunities to innovate depend more on individual knowledge, risk-taking and proactiveness and less on organisational processes.

Bearing in mind the advantages of the small, adaptable and flexible venture, one should not underestimate the contributions of routine innovations by large corporates. These can contribute greatly to growth, sometimes more than radical innovations. Though each improvement may be relatively small, added together, they can become quite impressive.[2]

The relationship between the entrepreneurial innovator and the corporate innovator is explained via entrepreneurial leadership. Entrepreneurial leaders in a corporate setting do more than the traditional product and service innovations. Their innovation is in processes, value chains, business models, and across different functions of management. Entrepreneurial leaders are motivated, flexible, have a sense of urgency, and are prepared to take advantage of new business opportunities when they arise.[3]

We need to understand the links between entrepreneurship and leadership. Leadership is close to management. It is mainly concerned with leading and managing existing resources. However, entrepreneurial leadership is mainly concerned with the discovery of new opportunities. It requires the ability to anticipate the future, be flexible, and to think strategically, while working with others to use opportunities and make changes that will create a sustainable organisation. This requires a different set of skills from those of leading, planning, and co-ordinating existing resources, associated with the late stages of organisational development.

Entrepreneurial leaders understand that they must produce results through acquiring and managing resources. Managing existing resources is what happens in traditional management. Acquiring or making new resources is what entrepreneurship is about. Entrepreneurship pursues opportunities that will create value regardless of the resources currently controlled. Schumpeter (the father of entrepreneurship) defines the entrepreneur as an innovator who tries new combinations of economic development, which are new goods, a new methods of production, new markets, new sources of raw materials, or a new organisational form. The entrepreneur co-ordinates production and is an agent of change that brings about creative destruction.[4]

The Unique Nature and Mindset of Entrepreneurial Leadership

The true value of entrepreneurship as a leadership concept lies in how much it helps organisations to create sustainable competitive advantage. Even though traditional corporates may be considered to be at odds with entrepreneurial practices, considering their focus on economies of scale and maintaining the status quo, it is increasingly recognised that sustainable competitive advantage can be achieved only through continuous innovation and the creation of new ideas.

A corporate's competitive advantage often depends on identifying new and emerging opportunities in the marketplace where traditional strategic thinking based on stable industries has long ceased to be as effective. Entrepreneurial leaders can increase an organisation's adaptability and innovation through its entrepreneurship champions. They must encourage managers to help employees to get their work done, remove obstacles, and make innovation easy. Most importantly, they must make exploitation of opportunities seem highly desirable.[5]

Entrepreneurial leaders are also more tolerant of risk, mistakes and failures, and allow employees to experiment. They know how important it is to share risks and rewards with employees, as this is how the entrepreneurial vision is shared. In large and mature organisations, entrepreneurial leadership is fast becoming a weapon of choice for many corporates because it uses the mindset and skills demonstrated by start-up entrepreneurs, and merges this with the culture and activities of the organisation. Entrepreneurial leadership is the antidote to big business staleness, laziness, and an absence of creativity.

Even though corporates have focused on efficiencies in general for the last few decades, for both leaders and entrepreneurs this is not enough. Most entrepreneurial leaders are visionaries who create unique businesses by giving them a sense of purpose and identity. They do more than cost-cutting or re-engineering exercises. They are adaptable and able to gather resources and exploit opportunities. There is evidence of strong links between the levels of entrepreneurship in an organisation and many performance outcomes.[6]

Leading in an Entrepreneurial Economy

Many writers today are talking about the entrepreneurial economy. This type of economy is based on the input of knowledge and ideas, and not so much on the traditional inputs of natural resources, labour and capital. Looking at the complexity and uncertainty of the 21st century business context, organisations today are no longer certain what products should be produced; how they should be produced; and who should produce them. This uncertainty increases the difficulty of selecting the correct outcomes and the likelihood that the wrong market and industry may be targeted.[7]

Corporations realise that knowledge is a different input into the production process from machinery or workers who serve as parts of an assembly line. New ideas are uncertain. The trial-and-error process, which is part of the entrepreneurial process, is not welcomed in established organisations. Large corporates do not tolerate risk or failure. The status quo is maintained at all costs.

In what has been termed *The Age of Uncertainty*,[8] the business policy is to target those inputs involved in the creation and commercialisation of knowledge. The entrepreneurial economy calls for corporates to create a context that facilitates just that. Such innovative activity by corporates is essential. It requires entrepreneurship to achieve commercial success. Entrepreneurship and innovation are not restricted to the early stages of a new business. Rather they are active and holistic processes. Entrepreneurial and innovative organisations are discussed in the following section.

Corporate Entrepreneurship and Leadership

Entrepreneurship is not found only in small businesses. Corporates of all sizes and in all markets can engage in entrepreneurial activities and they look to entrepreneurship as a means to prevent the lethargy, bureaucracy and cultural lock-ins experienced.

Entrepreneurship in corporations has been labelled in many different ways. It started with the terms "entrepreneurship", "innovation" and "management". It now includes terms such as "intrapreneurship", "venture entrepreneurship", "strategic entrepreneurial posture", and "internal corporate venturing". Corporate entrepreneurship refers to an organisation's commitment to pursue new opportunities; create new units or businesses; innovate in terms of products, services and processes; and perform strategic self-renewal, constructive risk-taking, and proactiveness.[9]

Leaders are responsible for putting into place "pro-entrepreneurship" organisations, where the workplace provides structural, cultural, resource, and system attributes that encourage entrepreneurial behaviour, both individually and collectively. There is a philosophical component to corporate entrepreneurship as well, which is represented by an entrepreneurial strategic vision that defends the need for a pro-entrepreneurial organisational architecture.

Entrepreneurial leadership requires more than a decision, act, or event. It needs agreement between the entrepreneurial vision of the organisation's leaders and the entrepreneurial actions of those at all levels of the organisation. This means that corporate entrepreneurship represents the organisation that has creative strategic processes throughout the entire organisation. This is why entrepreneurial leadership is essential: the message must flow from the top.

For corporates to become more dynamic and innovative they must adopt an entrepreneurial orientation (EO). EO incorporates organisational processes, practices, and decision-making styles where entrepreneurial behavioural patterns recur. The theoretical roots of EO lie in its three elements: innovativeness, risk taking, and proactiveness. These elements and the relationship between EO and organisational performance has been debated and extensively recorded for several decades. There are many reports of a positive relationship between EO and firm profitability: corporates with higher levels of EO tend to out-perform other similar organisations with less EO.[10]

Entrepreneurial Leadership Measures and Outcomes

Entrepreneurial leadership is not just another management trend or fad. It has significant consequences if properly adopted and practised, mainly because entrepreneurial leadership helps the organisation to reinvent and invigorate itself continuously. Entrepreneurial leadership has been linked with strategic and organisational change, including restructuring, re-engineering, business-model changes, and the introduction of system-wide changes to increase the levels of entrepreneurship.

The scope of entrepreneurial leadership is widening. Organisations that were not previously recognised as entrepreneurial are adopting entrepreneurship so that they can survive and succeed in competitive and financially constrained contexts. For instance, the banking sector in South Africa has faced a great deal of change and volatility in recent years, yet FNB has become known in the industry as a leader in banking innovation. When Jordaan took over the reins in 2004, he took innovation to a new level through the Innovators Campaign.

Entrepreneurial leaders realise they must provide appropriate reward systems, support, explicit goals and appropriate organisational values which show that entrepreneurial behaviour and action is expected from every employee. Adrian Gore, CEO of Discovery, instils in all employees that they must have innovation, business astuteness, and prudence as part of their values. Through extensive innovation on many fronts such as service delivery; the Discovery Life loyalty programme; their creative distribution systems; and scientific breakthroughs, Discovery remains a top hub of corporate entrepreneurship in Africa and globally.

Several measures of entrepreneurial leadership can be traced back to generic forms of entrepreneurial behaviour: (1) strategic orientation, (2) a commitment to opportunity, (3) a commitment of resources and control of resources, (4) management structure, (5) reward philosophy, (6) entrepreneurial culture, and (7) a growth orientation. Entrepreneurial leaders understand that concentrating on noticeable measures, and relying on entrepreneurial strategies and actions, will help to build other elements of the organisation such as strategy, management style, and structure.[11]

To track the efficacy of corporate entrepreneurship activities, a number of measures are used: inputs (such as the number of hours devoted to innovative projects); throughputs (such as the number of feasible new ideas in the innovation pipeline); and outputs (such as the profit and cost advantages gained from innovative breakthroughs). Here, organisations are judged according to how the firm uses technology and innovation to achieve objectives, such as maximising profits, gaining market share, creating niche markets, or adding value for stakeholders.

Although in established corporates, innovative activities are carefully designed to prevent unwelcome surprises and to keep risks to a minimum, large firms sometimes try to unleash their employees engaged in innovative activity by following a set of guidelines, which are discussed below.

Guidelines for Sustainable Entrepreneurial Leadership

On a practical level, leaders often find themselves with no guidelines on how to direct entrepreneurship in an organisation. As with any evolving field, it is often practices that generate principles, which then serve as generic guidelines. Although guidelines exist, it is important to remember that entrepreneurial leadership differs with every situation. In other words, what may have worked at a particular time and in a particular context may not be suitable under different circumstances. That is why adaptability is important.

Some key guidelines are offered below that are illustrated with examples from the First National Bank (FNB) Innovators Campaign:

- Entrepreneurial leaders must establish a *culture tolerant of risks, mistakes and failure* by allowing employees to take calculated risks and experiment in the workplace. At FNB, fostering a culture of innovation depended on a number of critical success factors of which FNB saw its owner–manager business model as one of its key differentiating factors in the market. A culture of empowerment and entrepreneurship created a powerful competitive advantage and a differentiated strategy for this business.
- They should create imperatives so that employees perceive innovativeness, proactiveness and risk taking as *strategic requisites* to avoid organisational complacency and inactivity. While FNB had actively engaged in innovation initiatives and campaigns since the early 2000s, it was during former CEO Jordaan's tenure that innovation had been formally entrenched in the company's overarching strategy. Innovation became the way in which FNB conducted business. Innovation was seen as part of a growing, vibrant business in a thriving owner–manager culture. Innovation was seen as the task of every FNB employee.
- Entrepreneurial leaders must design a *network-orientated structure* that encourages entrepreneurial initiatives. Lean or flat structures allow for employee empowerment, experimentation, and a learning context which is more receptive to failure. During the early days of the FNB Innovators Campaign, people would often come up with ideas for other departments. This was a bit of a mess, according to Jordaan, because you would have someone with no knowledge of another area coming up with an idea that was not practical. There would be so much explaining to be done that people grew disillusioned.

Subsequently, as part of the strategic model to integrate innovation throughout FNB, each business unit and segment was assigned an innovation "champion", who was tasked with processing ideas that were logged.

Entrepreneurial Leadership in Practice: Profiles

Entrepreneurial leadership in practice starts with vision. Two brief profiles demonstrate this core principal of entrepreneurial leadership. Both individuals illustrate how entrepreneurial leaders move beyond building traditional organisations to pioneering entrepreneurial businesses.

First, Adrian Gore founded Discovery in 1992 with a simple vision: to enable people to live healthier lives. Gore did not believe that he fitted the mould of a "typical entrepreneur". In fact, he did not see entrepreneurs as necessarily belonging to a different category of people. More than making money, his desire was to make a positive impact on society. So when Gore started Discovery, he had building an empire in mind. "I was never a trader. I'm an institutional entrepreneur," he said. "I had a clear view when Discovery started that I wanted to build the kind of company that I grew up in." Today Discovery Ltd is an integrated financial services organisation that operates in health insurance, life assurance, investment, and health- and wellness-markets. The company operates in South Africa, the United Kingdom, and the United States.

Second, Herman Mashaba, the founder of revolutionary hair-care brand "Black Like Me", is one of South Africa's most interesting business visionaries. Beginning from the humblest of backgrounds, he started out in business by selling various products from the boot of his car. His company was the first black-owned hair-care company in the country. Mashaba is now one of South Africa's most prominent entrepreneurs. He was executive chairperson of Lephatsi Investments, a broad-based BEE company with investments in financial services, mining, transport and logistics, and construction.

The Future: Combining Economic and Social Elements

According to Porter (the famous Harvard Business School Professor of Strategy), the authenticity levels of business have fallen because of the short-term focus of financial markets and the narrow-minded thinking of management. Despite this, Porter states that not all capitalism or profits are equal. Profits involving a social purpose represent a higher form of capitalism, one that will enable societies to advance more rapidly while simultaneously allowing corporates to prosper.

Porter's starting point is that shared value will unlock the next wave of business innovation and growth. It can connect company and society success in ways that have been lost within narrow management approaches. The principle of shared value involves creating economic value in a way that also creates value for society by identifying opportunities and recognising the potential of new markets that traditionally have been overlooked.[12]

Even though corporates are at times seen as pariahs of society, the role of corporates as powerful instruments of progress, innovation, and development is often forgotten. An inclusive business sector lies at the heart of good society. It is easier to see the destructive side of capitalism rather than its creative side, but it is far more creative than destructive. In its direct impact, business changes individual lives and empowers national development. Corporates can be a vehicle for both growth and inclusive development.

Additionally, and linked to the notion of transforming the face of business, there is a new movement in business today. This movement knows that innovative management and efficient operations may ensure financial sustainability but they do not drive social change. The potential to achieve a new, or more just, social balance has led to the current interest in social business and social entrepreneurial leadership.

Conclusion

Leadership requires an entrepreneurial vision from the organisation's leaders and entrepreneurial actions by all at all levels of the organisation. Entrepreneurial leaders are constant innovators, more tolerant of risk, mistakes and failures, and allow employees to experiment. They know how important it is to share risks and rewards with employees, as this is how the entrepreneurial culture is created. Entrepreneurial leaders in the 21st century understand that creating a sustainable competitive advantage is more than looking at only the economic domain. They recognise the need to understand the entrepreneurial economy as well social elements of business so that they can contribute to an increase in the overall wealth standard of the country.

Endnotes

1. Baumol, 2006, pp. 33–56.
2. Marvel & Lumpkin, 2007.
3. Kuratko, 2014.
4. Schumpeter, 1947.
5. Phan et al., 2009.
6. Kuratko, Ireland & Hornsby, 2001.
7. Audretsch & Thurik, 2000.
8. Krugman, 1994.
9. Morris, Kuratko & Covin, 2011.
10. Covin & Lumpkin, 2011.
11. Kuratko & Audretsch, 2009.
12. Porter & Kramer, 2011.

References

Audretsch, DB & Thurik, AR. 2000. 'Capitalism and democracy in the 21st century: From the managed to the entrepreneurial economy'. *Journal of Evolutionary Economics*, 10(1):17–34.
Baumol, WJ. 2006. 'Education for innovation: Entrepreneurial breakthroughs versus corporate incremental improvements'. Working Paper 10578, in *NBER Innovation Policy and the Economy (Vol. 5)*. 33–56.
Covin, JG & Lumpkin, G. 2011. 'Entrepreneurial orientation theory and research: Reflections on a needed construct'. *Entrepreneurship Theory and Practice*, 35(5):855–872.
Krugman, P. 1994. *The age of uncertainty*. Cambridge, MA: MIT Press.
Kuratko, DF. 2014. *Introduction to entrepreneurship*. 9th ed. Canada: South-Western Cengage Learning.
Kuratko, DF & Audretsch, DB. 2009. 'Strategic entrepreneurship: Exploring different perspectives of an emerging concept'. *Entrepreneurship Theory and Practice*, 33(1):1–17.
Kuratko, DF, Ireland, RD & Hornsby, JS. 2001. 'Improving firm performance through entrepreneurial actions: Acordia's corporate entrepreneurship strategy'. *Academy of Management*, 15(4):60–71.
Marvel, MR & Lumpkin, GT. 2007. 'Technology entrepreneurs' human capital and its effects on innovation radicalness'. *Entrepreneurship Theory and Practice*, 31(6):807–828.
Morris, MH, Kuratko, DF & Covin, JC. 2011. *Corporate entrepreneurship and innovation*. 3rd ed. Mason, OH: Thomson/South-western Publishing.
Phan, PH, Wright, M, Ucbasaran, D & Tan, W-L. 2009. 'Corporate entrepreneurship: Current research and future directions'. *Journal of Business Venturing*, 24(3):197–205.
Porter, ME & Kramer, MR. 2011. 'Creating shared value: How to reinvent capitalism – and unleash a wave of innovation and growth'. *Harvard Business Review*, 1–17, Jan–Feb.
Schumpeter, JA. 1947. 'The creative response in economic history'. *Journal of Economic History*, 7(2):149–159.

Chapter 18

BOARD LEADERSHIP
Carmen Le Grange

The traditional role of the Board has been one of stewardship and to provide oversight in order to ensure a company's profitability. These days Boards are more concerned with how the company creates and enhances value within the context of ensuring sustainable business into the future. There is a "new capitalism". Boards have orienated themselves toward a longer-term governance focus instead of short-termism.

In this chapter, I will focus on:

- Why is there a need for more responsible and accountable Board leadership?
- What is on the agenda of high-performing Boards today?
- What is the typical profile of a high-performing Board?
- What are the key attributes required of directors in order to be successful in the current context of "business unusual", and as we move towards the Fourth Industrial Revolution (Industry 4.0)?[1] And finally:
- What are the developments and disciplines globally that can make a Board successful?

Why is a New Approach to Board Leadership Necessary?

A new approach to Board leadership is required because the emerging world requires (1) business as "unusual" in this changing world; (2) new business responses to risk and opportunities; (3) more demanding stakeholders; and (4) shifts in international and (5) SA corporate governance codes. Each of these requirements is discussed below.

The emerging world is demanding "business unusual"

The need for transparency and accountability and the rising influence of social media which allows people all over the world to connect real-time on a digital platform and interact with online content, means business operates under a new normal. It is "business unusual".[2]

The 2008–2009 financial crisis heralded unprecedented turmoil and change in the financial markets. Since the failure and collapse of Enron and WorldCom and the corporate scandals of Lehman Brothers, British Petroleum and the Royal Bank of Scotland, to name but a few, the world has seen a proliferation of legislation, for example, the Sarbanes-Oxley Act 2002 (SOX). We have also witnessed the introduction of various *Codes of Corporate Governance*, including the *NYSE Listed Company Manual* (US), the *UK Corporate Governance Code* (UK), *Corporate Governance Principles and Recommendations* (Australia), and the *OECD Principles of Corporate Governance*, in an effort to control business behaviour.

But in spite of this, public trust in large business has fallen dramatically. In fact, while we see a recovery in some countries in Western Europe and North America, in the United States a little more than a third (38%) of respondents and in the United Kingdom 42% of respondents actually trust business leaders to tell the truth. The fact is that the wealth of many international companies is greater than the GDP of many countries, enabling them to wield significant global influence and control. As a result, Boards have become dominant and powerful institutions with the power to influence and shape the economies of the countries they operate in.[3]

The world is changing. With a growth in population and finite resources, business operates in a society that poses greater risks but also significant opportunities. Global mega-trends are reshaping the world.[4] These include:

- **Technological breakthroughs:** Technology is increasing productive potential and opening up new investment opportunities. If Facebook were a country, it would be the second most populous in the world after China.
- **Shifts in global economic power:** A few years ago we spoke about the rise of the BRICS (Brazil, Russia, India, China and South Africa). Today we are talking about Colombia, South Korea, Vietnam and Indonesia.[5]
- **Accelerated urbanisation:** Growth in the urban population will increase dramatically in the coming decades. By 2050, the world's urban population will have increased by some 72%. The number of people living in urban slums since 1990 has increased by 33%.[6]
- **Demographic shifts:** Explosive population growth is taking place in some areas against declines in others. For example, ageing populations in the western world versus a growing population in emerging economies is giving rise to a vibrant middle class. Fifty per cent of the world's population growth between now and 2050 is expected to come from Africa. More than 50% of women graduate from universities and enter the workforce, resulting in approximately 70% of women controlling household budgets. This is leading to shifts in economic power, resource scarcity, and changes in societal norms.[7]
- **Climate change and resource scarcity.** Scarcity of resources and the impact of climate change are of growing concern. The demand for energy is forecast to increase by as much as 50% by 2030, and water withdrawals by 40%.[8]

Finding new business responses to the mega trends in reflecting on risks and looking at opportunities

- *Reflecting on risks:* In PwC's 18th Annual Global CEO Survey released in January 2015, more than 75% of global CEOs continue to see regulatory complexity as an area of concern, followed by data security and privacy and then, cost pressures.[9] In PwC's 19th Annual Global CEO Survey released in January 2016, 70% of global CEOs cited over-regulation as the number one risk, followed by geopolitical uncertainty at 74% and exchange rate volatility at 73%. This comes at a time when terror attacks are increasing on a global scale, many linked to the conflict in Iraq and Syria, and in Africa, to the activities of Boko Haram.[10]
- *Looking at opportunities:* Changing consumer behaviour was the top-rated market opportunity in the survey. This has dramatically escalated in business impact, especially with the rise in social media, digital and mobile channels that are being used to enhance the customer experience. New threats such as cybercrime are requiring new and improved controls. In response to external forces, companies are rethinking and redesigning their entire business models, product and service portfolios, go-to-market strategies, back-office support and supply chains.

Looking ahead, global CEOs are less optimistic about prospects for the global economy than they were in 2015 but do see the USA, China and to a lesser extent, Germany and the UK as top overseas growth markets. On emerging economies, Mexico and the United Arab Emirates (UAE) in the Middle East claim top spots as economies with significant growth and development potential.

Stakeholders are demanding more transparency, accountability and equity from business: the Panama Papers case study

The leak from the database of the world's fourth largest offshore law firm, Mossack Fonseca, based in Panama, highlights recent public reactions to companies shifting profit for tax purposes to jurisdictions other than where they have their customer base and business and operational activities. The escalating tax debate highlights that the payment of taxes is a matter that is now linked to good corporate citizenship and the reputation of a company. It is no longer acceptable for companies to shift their assets to safe tax havens and to exploit mismatches in the tax regimes of different tax jurisdictions, albeit that these may be done within legal parameters. However, at the same time, shareholders have a legitimate expectation that cost, including taxes, will be kept to a minimum.

Because of the complexity and the high risk that the activities above now pose, the Board has a responsibility to ensure that the company's tax strategy is aligned with good corporate citizenship and takes account of its reputation in society. All stakeholders are now being required to play their role in ensuring proper governance and accountability, be they compliance officers, regulators, tax authorities, and even financial institutions. The Panama Papers scandal further contributes to the debate on whether the current financial system requires re-engineering, given how an array of bankers, lawyers, accountants, broker dealers and other regulated entities may have played a role in protecting the assets of unscrupulous investors, as funds have over many years been moved to tax havens, without proper risk assessments and due diligence processes taking place. What should the Board consider when providing oversight and guidance on investments in different legal jurisdictions?

Developments with regard to international corporate governance codes

Corporate governance is a vital mechanism through which business ensures that the behaviours of their workforce are aligned to the organisation's purpose and principles. It also serves to ensure that corporate goals and values are translated into the organisation's people's decisions and actions.

A comparative analysis of *King III*[11] and the following international prescripts on corporate governance were reviewed: *NYSE Listed Company Manual*, the Australian Code, the UK Code, the OECD Code and the Canadian Code, to obtain a sense of how South Africa's state of corporate governance compares. Over and above this, we also referenced a study released in February 2016 on *"The State of Corporate Governance in Africa: An Overview of 13 Countries"*, produced by the New Economic Partnership for Africa Development (NEPAD),[12] through its African Corporate Governance Network (ACGN), together with Ernst and Young. This study documents a high-level overview of the current state of corporate governance frameworks and systems in 13 countries in Africa, including Egypt, Ghana, Kenya, Malawi, Mauritius, Mozambique, Nigeria, South Africa, Tanzania, Tunisia, Uganda, Zambia and Zimbabwe. The report highlights how the different countries are navigating their economies and business communities through their individual in-country corporate governance development journeys. NEPAD's mission is to promote sustainable economic development in Africa through the private sector.

The challenges facing corporate governance reform in Africa include, among others, corruption, political instability, regulatory issues, inactive shareholders, state-owned enterprises, a one-size-fits-all governance code, and a lack of institutional capacity. Against this context, we submit that South Africa is truly at the forefront of thinking and development in corporate governance practices on the African continent and, indeed, globally.

Developments in corporate governance in South Africa and King IV[13]

In South Africa the *King III Report on Corporate Governance* provides guidance on leading governance practices. It has been internationally acclaimed as one of the most advanced *Governance Codes* globally. The draft *King IV Report on Corporate Governance for South Africa* was made available to the public for comment in March 2016.

The King IV definition of corporate governance

The following outcomes (or benefits) are considered to encapsulate what sound corporate governance should accomplish:

- A company with an ethical culture;
- Performance that constitutes the sustainable creation of value;
- Balancing driving the company forward while exercising effective control; and
- Stakeholder relationships that build legitimacy, reputation and trust.

Shifts from King III to King IV

The three shifts from *King III* to *King IV* are:

1. **From financial capitalism to an inclusive capitalism:** There is recognition of the fact that a singular focus on the employment, transformation, and provision of financial resources or capital represents only a fraction of the activities of a company. Instead, an inclusive approach takes account of the employment, transformation and the provision of all sources of capital.
2. **From short-termism to long-term sustainability:** This shift arises from the need for sustainable development. Companies and investors alike, as well as all other stakeholders, have to take a longer-term view so that the capital market system is enabled to incentivise and reward long-term decision-making in the interest of a more sustainable model of development to the benefit of all.
3. **From silo reporting to integrated reporting:** The move from silo reporting to integrated reporting has been given impetus by the increased appreciation of the triple-bottom line reporting with the introduction of integrated reporting and the move towards integrated thinking.

Corporate governance is therefore defined in King et al.[14] as

> "... *the exercise of leadership by the Board towards the outcomes of an ethical culture, sustainable value-creation, effective control and building legitimacy, reputation and trust through relationships with stakeholders. Leadership encompasses providing strategic direction, approving policy to put strategy into effect, providing effective oversight of implementation culminating in disclosure.*"[15]

What is on the Agenda of High-performing Boards?

There are a number of governance issues for Boards to consider in 2016. In a recent guidance paper issued by the Institute of Directors' Corporate Governance Network, these issues included, in no particular order of importance: cyber security, emerging technologies, Board skills, composition and diversity, shareholder activism, compensation and the pay gap, risk oversight, crisis management, corporate and integrated reporting, value creation and strategy, over-legislated and regulated landscapes, social media, and sustainability.

Out of this list of issues, I will address five critical agenda items that I believe need to be considered by a high-performing Board, in no particular order of importance: risk oversight; technological innovation; regulatory compliance; stakeholder activism; and sustainability.

Agenda item 1: Risk oversight

There are many definitions of corporate governance. For some, it is about legal structures. For others, it is mainly about business controls and the checks and balances on how people carry out their work. However, for still others, it is a much wider concept. It encompasses the way in which a business is led and managed. In September 2014, the Financial Reporting Council revised the UK *Corporate Governance Code* for UK listed companies. The key message that emerged is that *risk awareness is the bedrock of good corporate governance*.[16] The FRC emphasised the importance of risk appetite and risk culture and the role this will play in building resilient organisations post the financial crisis.

Risk is at the heart of corporate governance

Managing risk and being accountable for doing this effectively is central to the Board's role. The right focus on identifying and owning risks equips the Board to understand, analyse, prioritise and manage all risk types. From setting the right "tone from the top" to maintaining and monitoring business controls; and from rewarding the right behaviours to communicating openly and transparently with all stakeholders, the Board plays a pivotal role in all aspects of corporate governance. These activities can sometimes be disconnected. So it is the Board's role to apply the right risk lens to every decision and action. For this to be a success, organisations need to have the right people on the Board: challenging, experienced, enquiring, and with the time to understand both the risk landscape and their legal and ethical responsibilities.

However, Boards are becoming risk averse due to the volatile economic conditions, increasing regulatory complexity, and geopolitical risk. If we are to progress, informed and strategic risks need to be taken for growth and developmental purposes. Are Boards focused on tracking the right risks around new political dynamics such as geopolitical uncertainty, regulatory complexity and cyber security as they replace concerns related to coping with the financial crisis?

Risks are on the rise

In a PwC survey publication issued in August 2015,[17] entitled *Africa Risk in Review*, it was revealed that Africa's executives were increasingly concerned that risks to their companies are on the rise. Across the continent, ongoing political, economic and social developments are raising concerns among African businesses.[18] The basic lack of infrastructure; concerns over access to healthcare; food security; and the effects of climate change are accelerating significantly. Technology continues to disrupt, through innovations such as cloud computing, social media, and the Internet of Things. There also is an increase in awareness by African businesses with regard to managing cybercrime and cyber-terrorism.

Risks are increasing: CEOs are seeing more opportunities and more risks today than three years ago. A high percentage of survey respondents (89%) expect business transformation to have some impact or a significant impact on their businesses in the short to medium term. This impact was anticipated across all sectors. Over-regulation and compliance is increasingly becoming a concern for doing business in Africa.

In South Africa we also see the impact of geopolitical uncertainty on the growth and development of the economy. Commodity-related prices, which make up the bulk of our exports, have plummeted as a result of labour unrest. There has been a decline of the mining industry on which our economy is largely based. The effect of the drought on agricultural production and a rising rate of inflation have seen a rise in food prices. The devaluation of the Rand, given the political events of 9/12,[19] as well as the increasing public perceptions of corruption and cronyism in the public sector, are expected to result in rising interest rates. All these factors have had an impact on economic growth.

With the rating agency, Moody's, rating South Africa two notches above "junk bond" status, the risk of the country being downgraded to the "junk bond" category, could result in overseas institutional investors (made up predominantly of pension funds) having to sell/dump billions of Rands' worth of investment. In this context, Boards are concerned about whether they can navigate through this complexity and uncertainty, while still ensuring a decent Return on Investment (ROI) in the short term and value creation in the medium to long term.

The main lesson learned from the global financial crisis was that risk has become more systemic owing to globalisation and increased connectivity. This calls for a shift from a financial capital model to a more inclusive capital market system. The oversight of risk management must include emerging and complex risks, within the context of how these will have an impact on company performance in the medium to long term.

Adopting a new perspective of risk and risk governance

In 2007 the author Nassim Taleb[20] put forward the concept of "black swans": unforeseen risk events that have a major impact. Notable examples of these are the 11 September 2001 attacks in the USA; the Indian Ocean tsunami of December 2004; and the 2015 student uprisings which sparked the #FeesMustFall debate at South African tertiary institutions. This concept has rapidly taken hold, and has been applied to recent events ranging from the credit crunch, to BP's Deepwater Horizon Oil Spill, to the Arab Spring. Today, "black swan" events like these are regarded as one of three types of risks that an organisation can face:

- **Known risks:** These are risks that companies can identify and plan for, in an effort to avoid or mitigate them.
- **Emerging risks:** These are risks that have come on to the radar, but whose full extent and implications are not yet completely clear.
- **Black swans:** These risks hit business, and even society, as a whole without warning – they cannot be predicted or avoided. By their nature, black swan events should occur only at unpredictable intervals. Yet recent experience suggests that events that fit the definition of black swans are happening more and more frequently. So black swans are actually turning grey! Risks are changing, and today's fast-changing world creates more uncertainty for organisations. It makes it harder for them to understand where new risks are going to come from. Understanding which risks are becoming more prevalent, and the risk mitigation strategies being used to manage them better, is becoming key.

Agenda item 2: Technological innovation

Industrial manufacturing companies plan to invest 5% of annual revenue in digital operations solutions over the next five years. Companies in general are setting ambitious targets for the level of digitisation and integration that can be achieved. Many companies are already producing machines to deliver on the vision of the connected factory, using the power of the Internet to link machines, sensors, computers, and humans in order to enable new levels of information monitoring, collection, processing, and analysis.

This is adding to the products/services that companies can offer their customers, helping them work in collaborative ways in the design of future machines and their digital environment in order to boost performance. The rate of adoption of Industry 4.0 technologies by industrial manufacturing companies is accelerating fast. The digitisation, integration and automation opportunities offered enable companies to collaborate both internally and across their value chains in ways that can provide a steep change in productivity as well as design and build quality.[21]

Mobile connectivity and social media in particular have become fundamental ways to get information and buy products and services. The "Uberisation" of a growing number of sectors offering quick, simple and dynamic ways to access goods and services, using mobile applications, is an important trend. It is changing customer perceptions of value. Directors must be asking whether their organisations are preparing to face non-traditional competitors, now and in the future, and also whether their innovation efforts are geared towards generating products/services that meet big societal needs and generate good long-term ROI.

As big data, cloud computing, and the "Internet of Things" become even more important in modern business, the role that technology plays is more pervasive than ever before. Not being a "digital native" will no longer be an excuse. Board members must not only be able to engage as technology transforms existing business and operating models, but must also be able to oversee the management of cyber-security risks and the ethical, responsible use of technology and information.

Agenda item 3: Regulatory compliance

Companies today are faced with many onerous laws and regulatory requirements. Corporate governance practices should cater for how directors can ensure compliance with laws and regulations so that their companies are not exposed to the risk of fines and penalties, and ultimately losing their licence to operate. A key attribute of directors in the future will depend not only on how to create value within this context, but also being able to influence (or facilitate) engagement with government and the regulators to achieve common goals for compliance.

Agenda item 4: Shareholder activism

An analysis of the registers of shareholders of the major companies listed on the Johannesburg Stock Exchange (JSE) shows that they are now mostly comprised of institutional investors, both foreign and local. These institutional investors – consisting mostly of pension and retirement funds – have fiduciary duties towards the individual members who contribute to these funds and their dependants.

The individuals contributing to these funds have become the ultimate beneficiaries of the companies in which institutional investors invest. This is a worldwide trend. This is one way in which companies are now more closely associated with societies. In an effort to address the responsibilities of institutional investors for responsible investment policies and practices in South

Africa, the *Code for Responsible Investing in South Africa* (CRISA) was issued in 2011.[22] CRISA encourages all role players in the investment chain to become aware of their duties. It places accountability for responsible investing on the owner of the equity who has the responsibility to regulate and monitor application of CRISA via its mandate with its service providers. It is anticipated that as shareholders become more educated, this is an area that will start to receive more attention. The director of the future will be required to build competencies around how to engage various shareholders.

Agenda item 5: Sustainability

Sustainability is no longer peripheral. It is core to business strategy and risks. The Sustainable Development Goals (SDGs) are what governments will be using in the next 15 years to set their regulatory and compliance regimens.[23] Hence directors must be able to oversee how their companies are able to identify, quantify and report on the impact they have in society.

What is interesting to note is that when one contrasts the things CEOs say will define business success in the 21st century with the issues that are on the Board agendas of large companies, there is a high correlation between the two. Business is becoming more responsible and transparent about the impacts that they measure, report on and communicate to their stakeholders. The good news is that this is more than merely the financial reporting of profits to shareholders!

What Does a High-impact Board Focus On?

When it comes to corporate governance requirements and leading practice, organisations often fall into a trap of trying to implement actions that are far more than may be required of them by legislation. This is often done to be able to claim that they have implemented "best practice" or that they are "fully compliant". However, a compliance regimen for governance is often extremely cumbersome and costly to implement and maintain.

Each organisation should therefore consider the applicability of the principles and then look at the most efficient and practical approach to implementation. Key to developing "fit-for-purpose" governance frameworks includes looking at the Board structure and composition; Board effectiveness and operation; strategy planning and monitoring; risk management and compliance; transparency and disclosure; and corporate citizenship, which includes influencing the tone at the top through a Code of Conduct managing business ethics and social responsibilities.

Perhaps one of the simplest models of Board governance is PwC's Board Evaluation Model, which guides the evaluation of Board performance and effectiveness. It has four key building blocks which assess the impact of the Board, illustrated in Figure 18.1:

1. *Foundations* – Purpose, Composition, Role Clarity and Relationships
2. *Board Focus* – Strategy, Performance and Monitoring, Risks and Finance
3. *Board in Action* – Agenda, Information, Challenge and Decision-making
4. *Engaging and Improving* – Stakeholder Engagement, Individual and Whole Board Development and Succession Planning

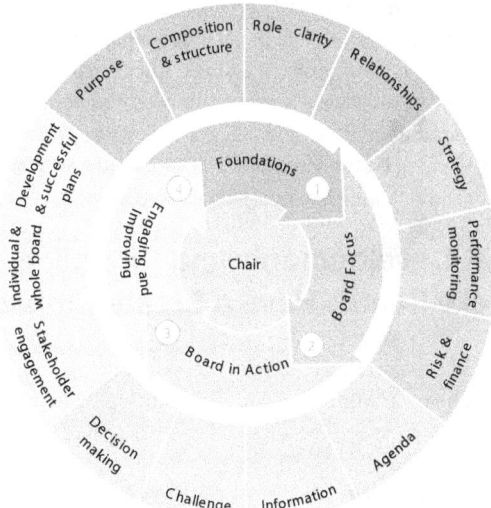

Figure 18.1: The PwC Board Evaluation Assessment Model

By contrast, the Institute of Directors in South Africa categorises assessment questions for Board performance and effectiveness across six broad areas: Board composition, Board responsibilities, Board Committees, Relationship with shareholders and stakeholders, Relationship with management, and Board meetings.

In 2013 McKinsey conducted an online survey of more than 770 directors from public and private companies across industries around the world and from non-profit organisations.[24] They garnered responses from 772 corporate directors, 34% of them chairpersons. The research found that Boards that have a low to moderate impact focused on getting "the basics" right by ensuring compliance, reviewing financial reports, and assessing portfolio diversification. Boards that have high impact focused their attention on matters of strategy and mergers and acquisitions (M&A), as well as performance, risk, and talent management.[25]

- **Strategy.** This is an area where there is often a disconnect between the value the Board believes it contributes and what executives think. There are a number of issues that Boards grapple with: from analysing what drives value, to debating alternatives on strategy such as adjusting strategy to changing conditions, or assessing whether strategy stays ahead of trends, evaluating the allocation of resources and engaging on innovation.
- **Value add.** More engaged Boards are becoming even more introspective about the area of value add. Through the Board evaluation process, many directors are, in fact, becoming more mindful about how the Board contributes to the business in a more sustainable way, as a collective. Here, they are focused on the time directors spent in preparing for meetings; the time spent discussing strategic matters; and the quality of the deliberations and interaction with the executive team.
- **Time spent.** A high-impact Board spends 40 days per annum in meetings contrasted with a lower impact Board's average of 19 days per annum.[26] It is predicted that in the next five years a single Board meeting could last up to at least three days. Key to this is the quality of the information provided by management to the directors. In preparing for meetings, directors must apply a mindset of "trust but verify" as they distil the critical issues so that they can provide effective oversight.

- ***Board "refreshment" practices.*** Board composition, director succession planning, Board evaluation processes, and director skill sets are important drivers for effective Board leadership. In recruiting new board members, chemistry is key: being able to work with fellow directors in a collegial way that does not stifle debate is important. Being knowledgeable about the industry in which the company operates and staying up to date through ongoing learning is also critical for directors. And finally, staggered rotation is also key for continuity and retaining institutional knowledge.

What Developments and Disciplines will Make Boards Have a Greater Impact?

In this section I would like to cover three developments and disciplines that I believe will make Boards more impactful: being a "Mindful Board"; introducing Board coaching; and Board self-evaluations and assessment of the performance and contribution of Directors.

Being a "Mindful Board"

Boards are evolving as the world becomes fraught with intensity, stress and complexity. In addition to focusing on financial profitability, Boards are having to view the world intentionally through multiple windows: technology, politics, sociology, environment, and economics. According to Charlotte Roberts and Martha Summerville,[27] Boards evolve along a developmental path in terms of which they can choose to move as their external and internal contexts change, and to assess what impact they can make as corporate challenges become more complex. This is graphically depicted in Figure 18.2.

As boards evolve toward the mindful state, they develop the ability to expand their consciousness and have a greater impact

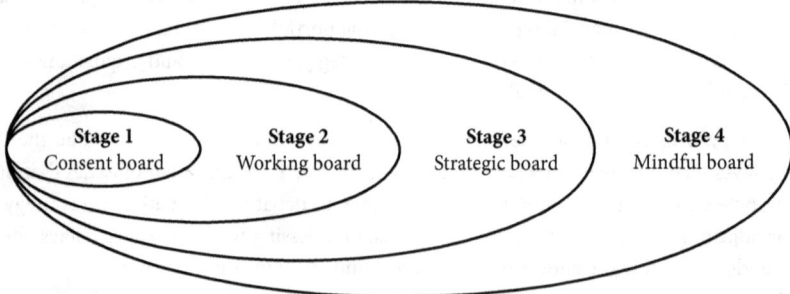

Figure 18.2: Evolution of the Board Species[28]

Table 18.1 gives definitions of the different stages 1 to 3 species of Boards given in Figure 18.2.

Table 18.1: Definitions of species of Boards

Stage 1: Consent Board
The consent Board is the traditional model of governance. Engagement is minimal as members focus on fiduciary oversight responsibilities and supporting the agenda set by the CEO. At its best, the consent Board is efficient and tightly managed. Open dissent is discouraged. Monitoring officers' actions is regarded as poor form. The limitations of this stage are evident when poor governance spills out into public view, as happened with the Enron and WorldCom implosions in 2001 and the 2008 serial banking debacles.

Stage 2: Working Board

Through its committee structure and in partnership with officers, this Board builds a greater understanding of operations and performance in key markets. It connects operational performance to competitive advantage. Although the Board's agenda remains driven primarily by the CEO and the Board chair, the members have an expanded view of operations and the business model. Yet that view does not increase the Board's likelihood of detecting broader issues and potential strategies that may move beyond senior management's analysis.

Stage 3: Strategic Board

This Board understands the organisation's wider reaches in its regional, national, and international contexts. It takes a longer-term view of the organisation's business success and potential impact on the community and society. It seeks wider and longer perspectives, sometimes by turning to outside expertise. It distinguishes itself through systems thinking, seeing both the interdependencies among the constituent parts and the whole organisation in the context of larger systems. But this Board is constrained by its focus on one industry/sector. When they are faced with a profound challenge, or when significant changes occur in society, technology, or economies outside the industry, the Board members may fail to identify risks and opportunities. This Board looks out through a variety of windows – all facing the same direction.

The definition of Stage 4: Mindful Board goes far beyond personal mindfulness practices. Mindfulness in the Board room refers to "the capacity of a group of people to think in a deep way together".[29] In assessing a current challenge, the Mindful Board looks at the past, present, and future. Deliberations encompass the impact of a decision not only on the enterprise, but on the industry, society, and the planet. The Mindful Board considers how the decision will play out in both the short term and the very long term. This is seen as the Board's mandate. To leverage this, members of a Mindful Board hone their individual capabilities while practising three interdependent disciplines as a governing body: leadership by the group; expanded consciousness; and fearless engagement. Table 18.2 shows a structured process that Mindful Boards can embark on using a value system to arrive at a set of outcomes.

Table 18.2: Building mindful boards[30]

Obstacles and resistance	Strategies
Process	• Design board meetings to allot more time to strategic issues, guided by questions that engage members in mindful questions. • Get started with a simple tool: Use tent name cards and print three or four provocative questions about the context "beyond the walls" on the back so each participant is facing the questions during all deliberations.
Values	• Use board retreats as the time and place to set mutual expectations and board goals that pull the board toward mindfulness. • Work directly with the CEO on how the board's transformation and evolution may affect the leadership of the CEO and senior officers, and how they may stay aligned.
Capabilities	• Engage the governance committee of the board to design learning conversations about how leadership by the group, expanded consciousness and fearless engagement benefit the organisation. External facilitators or members of the board can serve as discussion leaders. • Track and report examples of when these capabilities were actively used successfully and what the concrete outcome was – new strategic moves, positive changes in business metrics, public relations reports, etc.

Given that the Mindful Board concept is still in its infancy, no information is available to provide a quantitative assessment of the productivity and returns generated by a Mindful Board in comparison with the other species of Boards: the Consent Working Board and the Strategic Board.

In fact, many Boards operate in some form or other, and even as hybrids, but this is certainly a topic for future research. In South Africa there are a number of examples of how the Boards of state-owned companies are already having to apply the principles of a Mindful Board, being forced to consider socio-economic and development issues as they plan for and contribute to how the country's key industries will look in years to come.

Introducing board coaching

Board coaching is becoming a popular mechanism to help Boards collectively determine sustainable outcomes for the companies they oversee. Given the premise that coaching Boards is different from coaching teams, Hawkins[31] describes the five disciplines of a high-performing Board:

1. **Commissioning:** Ensuring governance facilitates effective and prudent entrepreneurial management to deliver shareholder and stakeholder value
2. **Clarifying**: Thinking through their roles and responsibilities and what value must be delivered as a Board member and the collective
3. **Co-creating:** Challenging the executive team to push the boundaries by promoting a culture of collaboration and shared accountability
4. **Connecting**: Engaging meaningfully with stakeholder groups in the spirit of transparency and openness about the company's long-term goals
5. **Core learning**: Carrying out regular reviews of Board performance that are not limited to structural and process issues but also to reflecting on personal and behavioural elements of how the Board functions

Board self-evaluations and the assessment of the performance and contribution of Directors

High-performing Boards assess their own effectiveness, as well as the performance and contribution of individual directors. They use the annual Board and committee self-evaluation processes to examine their performance and look for areas for improvement. Principle 2.22 of the *King Code on Corporate Governance* requires that the evaluation of the Board, its committees and individual directors should be performed at least annually.

An effective self-evaluation requires strong leadership and the willingness to have potentially difficult conversations about peer performance. The vast majority of directors view their Board's self-evaluations favourably. Over 90% believe their processes are at least somewhat effective and 86% find Board leadership at least somewhat effective in leading the process. However, the majority of directors have a difficult time speaking their minds. Seventy percent believe it is at least somewhat difficult to be frank in their self-evaluations. Nearly one in five think it is very difficult. Almost two-thirds of directors believe self-evaluations are at least somewhat of a "check-the-box" exercise. In fact, most self-evaluations are really focused on whether the Board is executing on its mandate/charter. The self-reports seem to suffer from a high degree of social desirability and getting a good score.

Most leading Boards prefer external independent assessments. This typically involves supplementing the questionnaire process with an interview process during which directors are encouraged to speak openly (but on a confidential basis) to share their views about the Board processes and performance, its committees, and fellow directors with the third party performing the assessment.

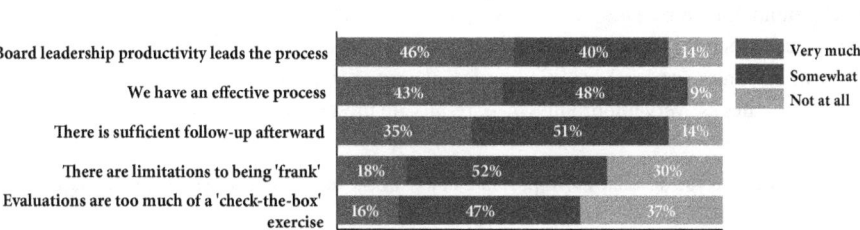

Figure 18.4: Board/committee self-evaluations

The bar for what is acceptable Board performance continues to rise. In the August 2015 PwC Corporate Directors Survey,[32] directors expressed increasing levels of dissatisfaction with their fellow directors, with members expecting better performance from their peers. Directors continue to cite diminished performance as a result of ageing; unpreparedness for meetings; and a lack of expertise as the top reasons for their dissatisfaction with peer performance. Overall, director criticism of peers may indicate recognition that changes to Board composition are necessary to promote long-term value creation.

Compared to prior years, a smaller percentage of directors say changes are being made as a result of their self-evaluation processes. Only half of the directors say they made changes in 2014 compared to two-thirds who said they did just two years ago. This could be because a greater percentage of Boards are more satisfied with their overall composition and processes. The most common changes are adding additional expertise to the Board; changing committee composition; and providing counsel to one or more Board members.

What are the Critical Attributes of a Director and a Typical Board Profile to Meet the Specific Needs of the Emerging Context of Business as Unusual?

I will now address the most desirable, generic attributes for a Director to meet the needs of the emerging context of business as unusual, but then zero in on the director attributes required by the Fourth Industrial Revolution.

Most desirable generic Board attributes

Board composition is under pressure to evolve. In the survey, the most desirable director attributes continue to be financial expertise (91% describe it as very important), industry expertise (70%), operational expertise (66%), and risk management expertise (62%). These areas are crucial to Board service as they provide the foundations for overseeing the business. International experience was also considered an important attribute.

The percentage of directors who think Board diversity is an important attribute increased: 39% now consider gender diversity very important compared to only 37% in 2014. Thirty percent now consider racial diversity very important, up from 28% last year. What was interesting from the survey was that females assessed diversity and race as more important than their male counterparts did.

Given the climate around cyber-breaches, it is not surprising that 87% of directors find Board expertise in this area to be at least "somewhat" important. But it is surprising that directors rate IT strategy expertise as a higher priority than having a director with a cyber-risk background. The importance of cyber security has certainly been recognised, but directors are strategically focused when it comes to IT, understanding how critical it is to long-term success. Human resources and legal expertise are less sought after, only one in five directors describing these attributes as "very important". These results are presented in Figure 18.5.

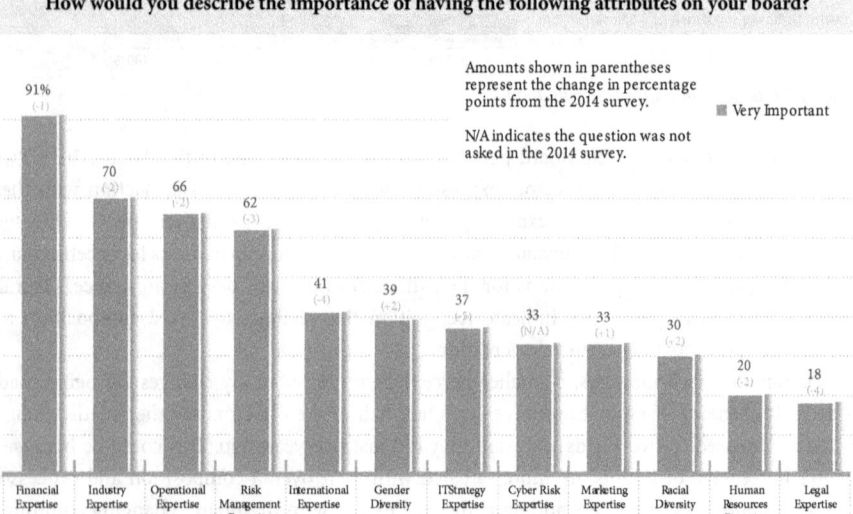

Figure 18.5: Important director attributes
Source: *PwC's 2015 Annual Corporate Directors Survey*[33]

Desired board attributes for the Fourth Industrial Revolution

While the above attributes and skills requirements for a Board are important today, what will be required for future directors to thrive in the Fourth Industrial Revolution? A World Economic Forum (WEF) Report[34] states that five years from now, over one-third of the skills (35%) that are considered important in today's workforce will have changed. By 2020, the Fourth Industrial Revolution will have brought us advanced robotics, artificial intelligence and machine learning, advanced materials, biotechnology and genomics, transforming the way we live and work. Consequently skill sets of the workforce will change.

According to a survey done by the WEF's Global Agenda Council on the Future of Software and Society by 2026,[35] people will expect artificial intelligence machines to also be part of the company's Board of Directors. Disruption in the industry will require complex problem solving, critical thinking and creativity as the top three skills, followed by people management, co-ordinating with others, emotional intelligence, judgement and decision-making, service orientation, negotiation, and cognitive flexibility. With mobile Internet and cloud technology already having an impact on the way we work, technological literacy will be high on the list of skills directors must have, and Boards will be expected to demonstrate that they are composed of directors who are properly qualified, experienced, and skilled in the relevant competencies.

Conclusion

We live in an era where trust in business is at a premium. Scrutiny from stakeholders is more intense. Now more than ever before, it is important that organisations behave in accordance with their core purpose and values in order to protect their reputations and engender trust. The profit-centric business model is becoming a thing of the past with 82% of global CEOs saying they prioritise long-term profitability over short-term. Seventy-six percent of CEOs saying that business success in the 21st century is about more than just financial profit. CEOs are starting to take accountability for impacts beyond the financials as they exert tighter control on a wider set of risks.

At a time when the role of business in society is coming under the spotlight, businesses are moving away from the era of shareholder value towards an era of stakeholder value. Boards are powerful institutions with the ability to influence not only the financial outcomes but also the social, economic and environmental impacts of their company. It is a new normal, and the Board as a collective must mindfully apply itself to lead the company it governs in a responsible, accountable and transparent manner.

Individual directors must develop competencies and skill sets that will assist the companies they govern by spending sufficient time on Board matters. They need to focus on the right risks to gain competitive advantage. They need to leverage their individual strengths. They must hold each other accountable for effective performance through mindful engagement and ongoing evaluation. This must not only lead to high-impact performance, but also result in refreshing Board leadership in ways that will deliver sustainable business relevant to the Fourth Industrial Revolution.

Endnotes

1. PwC, 2016a.
2. Mennie, 2015.
3. Haley, 2016.
4. PwC, 2013.
5. Ibid.
6. Ibid.
7. Ibid.
8. Ibid.
9. PwC, 2015a.
10. PwC, 2016b.
11. Institute of Directors in Southern Africa, 2009.
12. African Corporate Governance Network (ACGN), 2016.
13. Institute of Directors in Southern Africa (IoDSA), 2016.
14. King, van Wyk & Kuper, 2015.
15. Institute of Directors in Southern Africa, 2016.
16. Financial Reporting Council, 2011.
17. PwC, 2015a.
18. Ibid.
19. 9 December 2015, when President Zuma fired Finance Minister Nhlanhla Nene and precipitated a major economic and financial crisis.
20. Taleb, 2007.
21. PwC, 2016c.
22. Institute of Directors in Southern Africa, 2011.
23. See *Global trends 2030: Alternative worlds* (National Intelligence Council, 2012).
24. McKinsey & Company, 2013.
25. Ibid.
26. Ibid.
27. Roberts & Summerville, 2016.
28. Ibid.
29. Ibid.
30. Ibid.
31. Hawkins & Hogan, 2014.
32. PwC, 2015a.
33. PwC, 2015b.
34. World Economic Forum, 2016.
35. World Economic Forum, 2015.

References

African Corporate Governance Network (ACGN). 2016. *State of Corporate governance in Africa: An overview of 13 countries*. February 2016. [Online]. Available: http://www.afcgn.org/wp-content/uploads/2016/03/ACGN-Corporate-Governance-Report-Feb-2016.pdf. [Accessed 2 June 2016].

Financial Reporting Council. 2011. *Guidance on board effectiveness*. [Online]. Available: https://www.frc.org.uk/Our-Work/Publications/Corporate-Governance/Guidance-on-Board-Effectiveness.pdf. [Accessed 2 June 2016].

Haley, JA. 2016. *The new age of uncertainty: Notes from the margins of the IMF spring meeting*. CIGI, 18 April 2016. [Online]. Available: https://www.cigionline.org/blogs/new-age-of-uncertainty. [Accessed 2 June 2016].

Hawkins, P & Hogan, A. 2014. 'Coaching the board: How coaching boards is different from coaching executive teams, with case samples from the private, public and voluntary sectors', in P Hawkins (ed.). *Leadership team coaching in practice: Developing high-performing teams*. London, UK | Philadelphia, PA: Kogan Page Limited. 171–186.

Institute of Directors Southern Africa. 2009. *King code of governance for South Africa 2009 (King III)*. [Online]. Available: http://www.ngopulse.org/sites/default/files/king_code_of_governance_for_sa_2009_updated_june_2012.pdf. [Accessed 8 June 2016].

Institute of Directors Southern Africa. 2011. *CRISA Code for Responsible Investing in South Africa 2011*. [Online]. Available: https://www.icgn.org/sites/default/files/South%20African_Code.pdf. [Accessed 8 June 2016].

Institute of Directors in Southern Africa (IoDSA). 2016. *The King IV report on corporate governance in South Africa (Draft King IV)*. Johannesburg, ZA: The Institute of Directors in Southern Africa.

King, ME, van Wyk, A & Kuper, MD. 2015. *The corporate report: Facilitating business in South Africa, Volume 5 – Issue 2*. Cape Town, ZA: Juta & Company.

McKinsey & Company. 2013. *Improving board governance: McKinsey global survey results*. August. [Online]. Available: http://www.mckinsey.com/business-functions/strategy-and-corporate-finance/our-insights/improving-board-governance-mckinsey-global-survey-results. [Accessed 2 June 2016].

Mennie, P. 2015. *Social media risk and governance: Managing enterprise risk*. 1st ed. London, UK, Philadelphia, PA: Kogan Page Limited.

National Intelligence Council (US). 2012. *Global trends 2030: Alternative worlds*. [Online]. Available: https://www.dni.gov/index.php/about/organization/global-trends-2030. [Accessed 2 June 2016].

PwC. 2013. *Five megatrends and possible implications*. November. [Online]. Available: http://www.pwc.com/us/en/faculty-resource/assets/symposium/2014-megatrends-overview.pdf. [Accessed 2 June 2016].

PwC. 2015a. *Africa risk in review 2015*. August. [Online]. Available: https://www.pwc.co.za/en/assets/pdf/africa-risk-7-resilience.pdf. [Accessed 2 June 2016].

PwC. 2015b. 'Governing for the long-term: Board composition and diversity'. *PwC's 2015 annual corporate directors survey*. [Online]. Available: https://www.pwc.com/us/en/governance-insights-center/annual-corporate-directors-survey/assets/pwc-2015-acds-module-board-composition-and-diversity.pdf. [Accessed 9 June 2016].

PwC. 2016a. *2016 global industry 4.0 survey: Industry 4.0: Building the digital enterprise*. [Online]. Available: https://www.pwc.com/industry40. [Accessed 2 June 2016].

PwC. 2016b. *Redefining business success in a changing world: CEO survey*. January. [Online]. Available: https://www.pwc.com/gx/en/ceo-survey/2016/landing-page/pwc-19th-annual-global-ceo-survey.pdf. [Accessed 2 June 2016].

PwC. 2016c. *Industry 4.0: Building the digital enterprise: Industrial manufacturing key findings*. May. [Online]. Available: https://www.pwc.com/gx/en/industries/industries-4.0/landing-page/industry-4.0-building-your-digital-enterprise-april-2016.pdf. [Accessed 2 June 2016].

Roberts, CM & Summerville, MW. 2016. *The mindful board*. January. [Online]. Available: http://www.strategy-business.com/article/The-Mindful-Board?gko=97a18. [Accessed 2 June 2016].

Taleb, NN. 2007. *The black swan: The impact of the highly improbable*. New York, NY: Random House.

World Economic Forum. 2015. *Deep Shift Technology Tipping Points and Scietal Impact*. Global Agenda Council on the Future of Software & Society [Online]. September 2015. Available: http://www3.weforum.org/docs/WEF_GAC15_Technological_Tipping_Points_report_2015.pdf. [Accessed 2 June 2016].

World Economic Forum. 2016. *The 10 skills you need to thrive in the fourth industrial revolution*. [Online]. Available: https://www.weforum.org/agenda/2016/01/the-10-skills-you-need-to-thrive-in-the-fourth-industrial-revolution/. [Accessed 2 June 2016].

SECTION 6
LEADERSHIP OUTCOMES AND IMPACT

Chapter 19

LEADERSHIP EXCELLENCE MEASUREMENT

Anton Verwey, Steven Teasdale, Marzanne de Klerk and Francois du Plessis

Any conversation on the impact of leadership, or as in the case of this chapter, the measurement of the outcomes of leadership excellence, has to consider a number of perspectives. Among others, these include:

- Are the outcomes and measures at the level of the individual leader or the level of a leadership community?
- Are these measures short or long term?
- Are the measures quantitative, qualitative or both?
- Who do we ask to provide the evidence?

As we will show in this chapter, the traditional perspective of measuring something like or similar to return on investment may simply not be a robust enough measure to provide a true reflection on the impact of leadership effectiveness.[i]

In this chapter, the following topics are covered:

- Evidence of leadership excellence;
- Achievement of leadership excellence;
- The components of building leadership excellence;
- The outcomes of implementing a process of building leadership excellence;
- Leadership capability maturity;
- Practical application of the principles and processes; and
- Case studies to illustrate how this type of work has been done in practice.

As initial point of departure, we would like to define leadership excellence as an organisational capacity to ensure, through effective and efficient leadership at all levels, the achievement of business benefits aligned to the strategic intent of the organisation.

What is the Evidence for Leadership Excellence?

Leadership excellence has traditionally been viewed from two perspectives: (i) organisational and (ii) personal perspectives. Typical measures of leadership excellence at the organisational level include increased team performance, improved communications, motivation, and better decision-making. At the individual level, the measures utilised range from improved leadership style to personal productivity. These are simply measures of leadership excellence and do not talk to the actual evidence of leadership excellence.

Although the literature is filled with research on the measures of the leader, leadership and leadership excellence, very little is being written on the actual evidence of such leadership excellence. We have become so obsessed with measuring the leader and leadership that we have forgotten that leaders and leadership must benefit the teams and organisations in which they

---

[i] When reading this chapter, the reader may want to refer also to the following sections:
- Section 2: Leadership Excellence and Branding;
- Section 8: Looking Ahead.

serve and work.[1] So how does one know that leadership has an impact?

The inavit iQ Business Value Model© utilises the following reversed logic:

The realisation of specific business benefits (i.e. operating profit, top line revenue and market share) is dependent on the creation of

- Customer delight (loyal and satisfied customers)
- Which is a direct result of the delivery of value-added products/services by
- High-performing people; who work in an
- Optimised work environment (organisation capacity in terms of process, structure, people, technology and culture), whose people are
- Led by capable, competent and credible leadership
- Towards a common goal and strategy.

The inavit iQ Business Value Model© is graphically represented as follows:

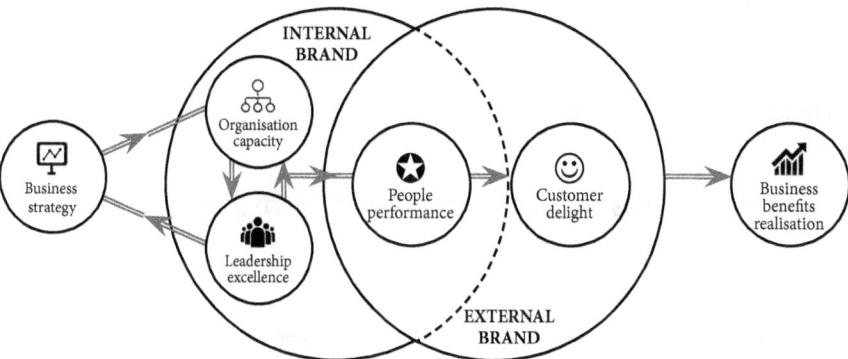

Figure 19.1: inavit iQ Business Value Model©

From the Business Value Model© [ii] perspective, it is obvious that the ultimate evidence of leadership excellence lies in the achievement and realisation of business benefits.[iii] However, it is important to note that business benefits realisation in the form of financial results is not the only evidence and that leadership excellence has a much broader (across the organisation) and deeper (within the organisation) impact. Leadership impact and example evidence are summarised in Table 19.1.

---

ii The reader will notice a similarity between the BVM™ and the Modified Service Profit Chain Expanded diagram used in chapter 3 on Leadership Excellence Dimensions. The intention with the development of the BVM™ was in fact to simplify the process of measuring the impact of leadership excellence, and the two diagrams should therefore be viewed as complementary rather than different.

iii Note: We use the term "business benefit" to mean the value added by the organisation to its key stakeholders.

Table 19.1: Leadership impact and example evidence

Leadership Impact	Example Evidence
Strategic	- Strong external brand reputation among customers and competitors alike; - Strong internal brand reputation: brand ambassadorship among employees; and - Investor confidence.
Tactical	- Brand loyalty; - Culture of inclusion and collaboration; - Innovation and renewal: new ideas being generated; and - EBITDA and EBITDA margin growth.
Operational	- Customer experience and satisfaction; and - Employee retention, engagement and performance.

In the next section of this chapter, we will explore ways the organisation may think about and approach the creation of leadership excellence.

The Process of Achieving Leadership Excellence

Simplistically, the literature reviewed seems to suggest that the purpose with the measurement of leadership impact broadly has two points of departure. On the one hand there is the approach that attempts to determine to what degree leadership development processes and programs have some demonstrable "value". The typical and well known approaches of Kirkpatrick and Philips[2] are examples of this approach, both of which at some point in their models move to the second approach, which is to move the focus away from development *per se* and towards the actual business benefits realised.

The following highlights the salient points of these two approaches:

- *Kirkpatrick 4 level model*

    o   Reaction of student – what they thought and felt about the training
    o   Learning – the resulting increase in knowledge or capability
    o   Behaviour – extent of behaviour and capability improvement and implementation/application
    o   Results – the effects on the business or environment resulting from the trainee's performance.

- *Phillips*

    o   Reaction, satisfaction, and planned action:
        - Measures participant reaction to and satisfaction with the training programme and participant's plans for action.
    o   Learning:
        - Measures skills and knowledge gains.
    o   Application and implementation:

- - Measures changes in on-the-job application, behaviour change, and implementation.
  - Business Impact:
    - Measures business impact.
  - Return on Investment (ROI):
    - Compares the monetary value of the business outcomes with the costs of the training programme.

The inherent assumptions of both approaches are:

- They measure TRAINING impact;
- The unit of measure remains INDIVIDUAL skill; and
- There is a direct relationship between skills acquired and job/organisation impact.

While there may be some broad consensus on how the "value" of leadership development may be calculated, there is significantly less clarity and consensus on how the business benefit of leadership itself may be determined. The reason for this lack of clarity is that the answer depends on what the question is we are asking, and of whom. The following examples will illustrate the point:

- Whose growth should we be measuring – the individual's? Or that of the function or business unit? Who should be considered the beneficiary?
- What are the benefits we should be looking to measure? Should we also measure benefits that are unplanned?
- What if the person had had an "AHA!" experience a few years after the class she had taken? Would that still be counted as a successful outcome of that class?
- If there are unintended learning outcomes, are these to be accounted for in measuring ROI?
- Who should be counting the return on investment: The organisation? The employee's manager? The individual?
- Who should the organisation invest in – the select few high potentials or the poor performers? The return will obviously be much higher if the base is smaller.
- Is the Return on Investment a measure of the teaching skill of the facilitator, or does it reflect the learning ability of the employee? Or should the credit go to the instructional design team?

The literature (both academic and corporate) contains a variety of models positioning leadership impact in slightly different ways. Some of these will be shared here.

Leadership brand

Figure 19.2 positions leadership within the context of organisational leadership branding.

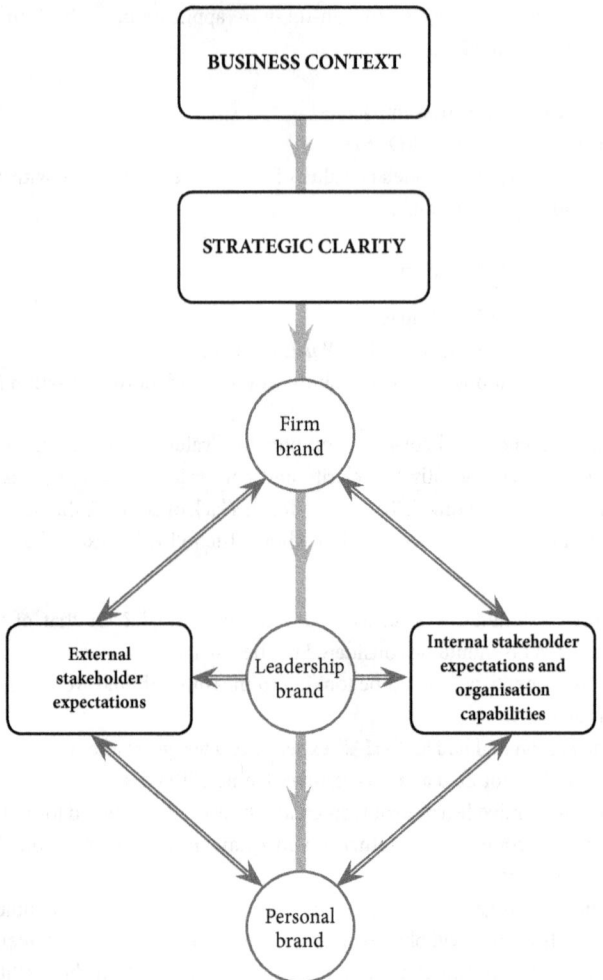

Figure 19.2: Leadership branding[3]

This model clearly positions leadership at a strategic level. Additionally, it implies that to a large extent, the ability to build and leverage such a leadership brand also requires alignment of the personal brands of individual leaders to the desired corporate leadership brand.

Integrated leadership strategy model

The following model is an integration of the approaches articulated by institutions such as the Corporate Leadership Council,[4] DDI,[5] and Center for Creative Leadership,[6] as well as more academic or research-based approaches described by, among others, authors such as Ulrich & Smallwood.[7]

The common themes through all of the approaches identified through our literature review are that:

1. Leadership impact begins with a leadership strategy clearly linked to the overall business strategy;

2. An outcome of the leadership strategy is a clearly defined set of behavioural expectations of leadership. Sometimes this is also called a leadership brand or a leadership culture
3. Against which current and potential leaders are assessed and then developed
4. Which should serve to create a Leadership Landscape: for example, capacity, style, demographics; and
5. This should serve to create measureable value[8] linked to the business strategy.

This logical flow is presented in Figure 19.3.

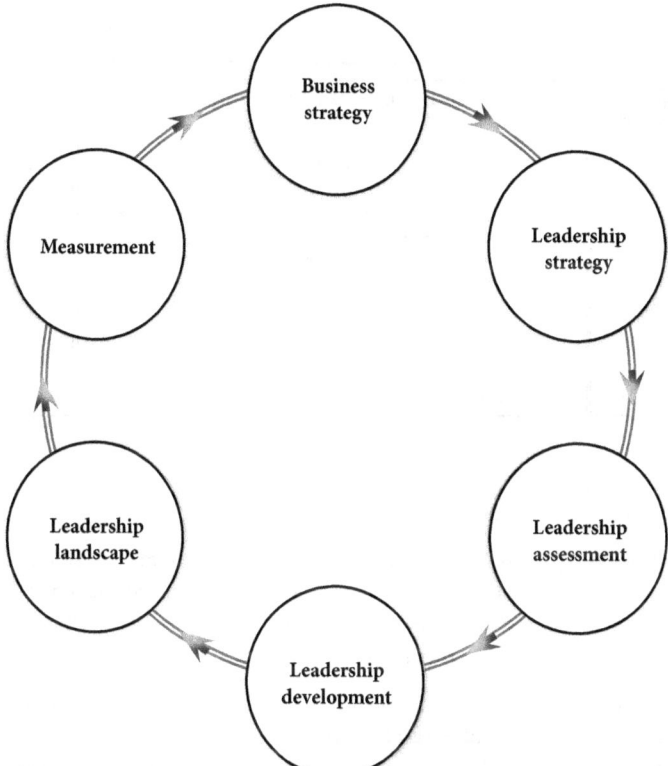

Figure 19.3: Integrated Leadership Framework

Our own sense, however, is that measurement should not be reserved for later in the process, but may in fact be introduced at each phase of the process. A more complete representation of the inputs from various models and approaches is therefore presented in the following diagram.

Conceptual leadership excellence dashboard

Given the preceding discussion, as well as the model for impact measurement developed for a number of organisations in South Africa, the model proposed in Figure 19.4 provides a good compromise between what organisations typically already have in place in terms of thinking and the insights gained through more recent research and publications, as discussed in this chapter.

Leadership Excellence

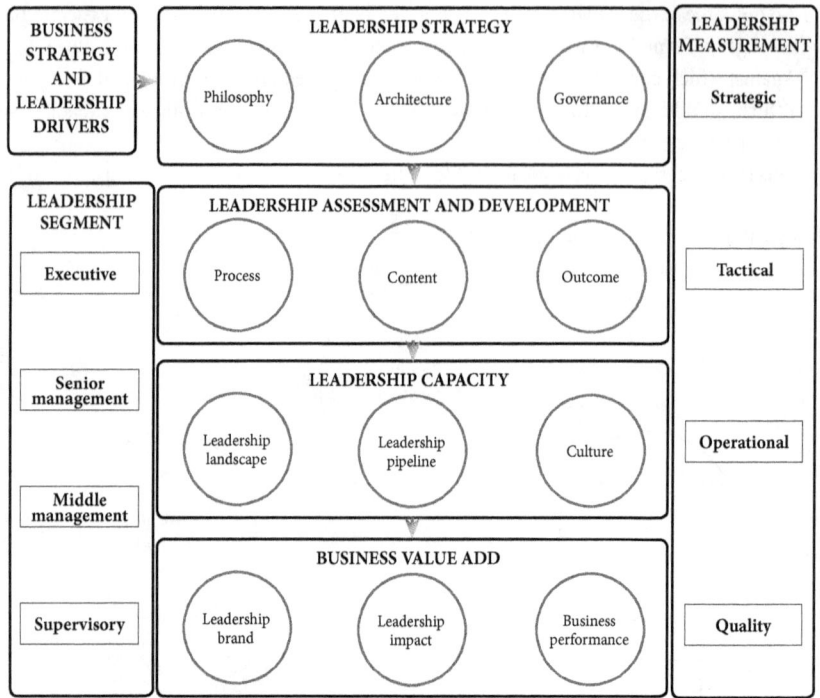

Figure 19.4: Conceptual leadership excellence measurement model

The features of the proposed model as given in Figure 19.4 are:

1. Leadership strategy should be defined within the context of the overall business strategy, which should as a matter of course include an assessment and articulation of the leadership drivers inherent to or assumed by such a business strategy. A leadership strategy in turn should be explicit about aspects such as:
   a. The desired leadership philosophy (or brand) including the desired leadership behaviours at different levels of leadership;
   b. Architecture, meaning how do we segment leadership levels, how do we allocate resources to the leadership strategy, how do we structure both interventions and delivery channels; and
   c. Governance such as budgets, participation rules, accountabilities, etc.
2. Leadership assessment and development (= leadership practices) should be based on the desired leadership brand, and specifically should consider:
   a. The assessment and development processes;
   b. Definition of the appropriate assessment and development content (= interventions and technologies); and
   c. Clearly defined outcomes of assessment and development. From a development perspective, this clearly is where the traditional thinking about evaluation of learning, such as through the Kirkpatrick and Philips models, comes into its own.
3. Leadership capacity which is the level at which one would finally like to see the actual impact (or benefits realisation) of the entire leadership strategy. It would typically include aspects such as:

a. Leadership landscape – the degree to which the organisation has enough leaders at the various levels with the requisite capability and competence to perform to expectations;
b. Pipeline – succession for key roles and/or people, the nurturing of high-potential individuals, leader mobility and risk cover; and
c. Leadership culture – the experience of internal stakeholders of the desired leadership brand. It therefore extends beyond employee engagement and will by definition include aspects such as leadership community.

4. For each of these domains of measurement, specific measures and/or metrics may exist at the strategic, tactical, operational and quality levels. These "levels" of measurements can loosely be seen as being related to the principles of Levels of Work or the Matrix of Working Relationships as defined by Elliot Jacques and others.[9]

5. For each of the measures and/or metrics, one would also need to establish their specific relevance to and definition for each of the different leadership segments (executive, management, supervisory) as the assumption cannot be made *ab initio* that they are identical.

Outcomes Across the Leadership Excellence Crafting Process

Contemporary academic and industry literature currently accepts that there is a relationship between the use of corporate storytelling and heightened employee engagement.[10] Corporate storytelling is the practice of using narration from within the organisation relating to its people, practices, policies and visions to effectively engage with staff. A Leadership Dashboard story will be used to communicate not only the purpose of leadership development, but also the organisational Leadership Journey, thereby linking past leadership practices to the desired future leadership brand.

Figure 19.4 represents the way one may think about the leadership story within the organisation:

- Investment in leadership excellence must lead to demonstrable[11] business *benefits*;
- In order for this investment to do so, we have to ensure that specific *deliverables* are achieved;
- This means that our leadership assessment and development practices[12] must be relevant to our intent with leadership;
- Which means we have to be clear and aligned on our thinking about leadership.[13]

Given the preceding, a framework for a Leadership Dashboard is proposed in Figure 19.5.

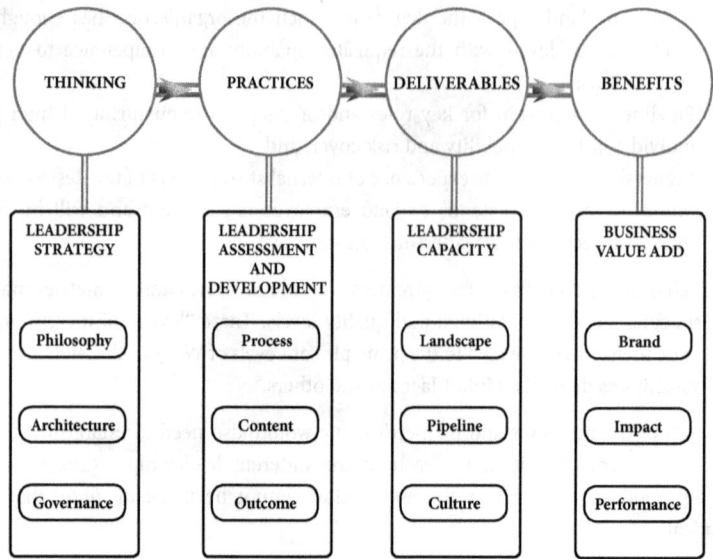

Figure 19.5: Leadership dashboard framework

As is shown in Figure 19.5 this approach has some specific implications:

- There is an implied and specific sequence to the dimensions and elements of the leadership measurement model: a lead and lag effect;
- For each of these elements, one or more specific measures/metrics may be defined;
- Each of the measures/metrics may be of a strategic, tactical, operational or quality type;
- The measurement model may exist for various subgroups:
    o Operating Units; and
    o Leadership Segments.

Each dimension of the Leadership Dashboard also has a specific meaning, and consists of related elements:

1. *Leadership Strategy*
    - The high level plan of action designed to drive the achievement of the long-term aspirations for the organisation through effective leadership.
    - The evidence for a clearly defined leadership strategy is:
        o Leadership Philosophy: the organisation has a clearly defined approach to leadership excellence, including clear expectations in terms of a Leadership Framework, leadership brand behaviours and Leadership Competency Model
        o Architecture: the organisation has a clearly defined process for the identification and development of leadership talent, including alignment to our overall business strategy
        o Governance: the organisation has a clear set of roles and accountabilities for leadership talent identification and development, including planning, budgeting and monitoring systems and processes

2. *Leadership Assessment and Development*
    - The dimension of Leadership Assessment and Development refers to the required processes, content and outcomes to create leadership capacity.

- The evidence for appropriate practices is:
    - *Processes:* The organisation has a clearly defined process for the assessment and development of leadership
    - *Content:* Leadership assessment and development interventions are clearly and deliberately linked to the organisation's leadership strategy
    - *Outcomes:* Leadership development processes lead to a perceptible improvement in leadership behaviour (skill) including an alignment to our leadership philosophy

3. *Leadership Capacity*
    - The dimension of Leadership Capacity refers to the Leadership Landscape, organisational culture and leadership pipeline which will drive ultimate business value add.
    - The evidence for leadership practices delivering capacity is:
        - Leadership Landscape: Our Leadership Landscape enables leadership to be effective as a collective and reflects high levels of trust and trustworthiness
        - Pipeline: The organisation has adequate cover, now and in the future, for leadership in all key and high risk roles
        - Culture: The leadership brand is lived consistently internally

4. *Business Value Add*
    - Business Value Add refers to the longer-term benefit realisation of leadership brand, leadership impact or effectiveness and business performance.
    - The evidence for leadership deliverables adding business value is:
        - *Brand:* The leadership philosophy is lived consistently externally and our leaders are respected by external stakeholders
        - *Impact:* Leaders have the capability and competence to be effective in their roles
        - *Performance:* Leaders are aligned to the overall business and leadership strategy and drive performance to achieve these

Leadership Capability Maturity

Given the preceding content, readers may come to the conclusion that measurement of leadership effectiveness and impact is only for organisations very advanced in their leadership talent development processes. Our own perspective is that this is not the case, and that one of the first decisions to be taken is on the degree of "maturity" the organisation: (i) requires from a strategic perspective; and (ii) is capable of introducing given its resources.

As a point of departure, we used the People Capability Maturity Model (P-CMM) framework that focuses on continuously improving the management and development of the human assets of an organisation. The maturity model consists of five maturity levels that establish successive foundations for continuously improving individual competencies, developing effective teams, motivating improved performance, and shaping the workforce the organisation needs to accomplish its future business plans. Each maturity level is a well-defined evolutionary plateau that institutionalises new capabilities for developing the organisation's workforce. By following the maturity framework, an organisation can avoid introducing workforce practices that its employees are unprepared to implement effectively, or that are simply inappropriate for its own phase of development.

Based on this approach, we constructed a maturity model specific to leadership talent processes, as outlined in Figure 19.6.

Table 19.6: Leadership Capability Maturity Model

Dimension	Element	Maturity Level				
		Nothing in Place – leadership does not feature in business, nor in business conversation	Fads and Fashions – what is the flavour of the month	Fragmented – good, stand alone building blocks, but no systemic thinking regarding leadership	Internal Coherence – leadership building blocks and framework aligned, integrated and systemic, but with no strategic business context – the leadership specialists rule	External Coherence – leadership framework aligned to business strategy with a Strategic Leadership Framework that is an inherent part of ongoing strategic-tactical business conversation
Leadership Strategy	Philosophy	There is no formal and unified approach to leadership in terms of a Leadership Strategy, Leadership Brand Behaviours and Leadership Framework	The Leadership Strategy, Leadership Brand Behaviours and Leadership Framework are defined but not consistently applied	The company has a clearly defined approach to leadership excellence, including clear expectations in terms of a Leadership Strategy, Leadership Brand Behaviours and Leadership Framework	The Leadership Strategy, Leadership Brand Behaviours and Leadership Framework are aligned across the organisation, with a common awareness and understanding of them throughout	The shared leadership thinking in terms of Leadership Strategy, Leadership Brand Behaviours and Leadership Framework are aligned with the future intent and growth path of the company
	Architecture	There is no formal and unified approach to leadership talent assessment and development	The leadership talent practices defined are a "one size fits all"	The company has a clearly defined approach to leadership talent assessment and development. Development processes (formal and informal) are specific to different leadership segments and are all based on an integrated perspective on leadership capacity.	The company has a clearly defined approach to leadership talent assessment and development, and it is entrenched and integrated with other organisational practices and processes	The approach to leadership talent assessment and development are geared towards enhancing the external brand reputation of the company
	Governance	Roles, accountabilities and governance mechanisms around leadership practices are non-existent	Roles, accountabilities and governance mechanisms around leadership practices are based on the view of some individuals, implemented inconsistently	The company has a clear set of roles, accountabilities and governance mechanisms for leadership talent identification, development and integration	Efficiency and effectiveness metrics are used to make decisions about how to improve alignment to leadership roles, accountabilities and governance mechanisms	Alignment to leadership roles, accountabilities and governance mechanisms is second nature across all leadership segments and operating divisions

Table 19.6: Leadership Capability Maturity Model (continued)

Dimension	Element	\multicolumn{5}{c}{Maturity Level}
		Nothing in Place – leadership does not feature in business, nor in business conversation	Fads and Fashions – what is the flavour of the month	Fragmented – good, stand alone building blocks, but no systemic thinking regarding leadership	Internal Coherence – leadership building blocks and framework aligned, integrated and systemic, but with no strategic business context – the leadership specialists rule	External Coherence – leadership framework aligned to business strategy with a Strategic Leadership Framework that is an inherent part of ongoing strategic-tactical business conversation
Leadership Assessment & Development	Process	There is no defined process for the assessment and development of leadership	The process for the assessment and development of leadership within the company is based on practices copied from other organisations/institutions	The company has a clearly defined process for the assessment and development of leadership	The process for the assessment and development of leadership is aligned and consistently integrated with other organisational practices and processes	The company's process for the assessment and development of leadership are in place and actively used to improve leadership capacity in line with the future intent of the organisation
	Content	There is no "golden thread" between the content of leadership assessment and development practices and the leadership framework or philosophy	Leadership assessment and development interventions are aligned with a dedicated theme, however they are not integrated and aligned to a larger framework or philosophy	The content of the company's leadership assessment and development practices are clearly and deliberately defined, however in isolation (does not relate to business)	Leadership assessment and development interventions are clearly and deliberately linked to the company's Leadership Strategy, Framework, Brand Pillars and Competence Models	The content of leadership assessment and development interventions is also reflected in ongoing strategic-tactical business conversation
	Outcome	Leadership development interventions lead to no real improvement on leadership competence (knowledge and skills) and behaviour	Leadership development interventions lead some improvement in leadership competence (knowledge and skills) and behaviour	Leadership development interventions improve leadership competence (knowledge and skills), however there is no explicit change in leadership behaviour	Leadership development interventions lead to a perceivable improvement in leadership competence (knowledge and skills) and behaviour, aligned to the the company leadership philosophy	The company leadership development interventions are regarded as best in class, and have created the required future leadership capacity across all leadership segments

Table 19.6: Leadership Capability Maturity Model (continued)

Dimension	Element	Maturity Level				
		Nothing in Place – leadership does not feature in business, nor in business conversation	Fads and Fashions – what is the flavour of the month	Fragmented – good, stand alone building blocks, but no systemic thinking regarding leadership	Internal Coherence – leadership building blocks and framework aligned, integrated and systemic, but with no strategic business context – the leadership specialists rule	External Coherence – leadership framework aligned to business strategy with a Strategic Leadership Framework that is an inherent part of ongoing strategic-tactical business conversation
Leadership Capacity	Leadership Landscape	There is no evidence of an the company leadership community	Some individual leaders are trusted and seen to actively drive leadership excellence within their areas of responsibility	The company leadership is regarded as a leadership community geared towards creating leadership excellence	The the company leadership community enables leadership to be effective as a collective and reflects high levels of trust and trustworthiness	The the company leadership community is regarded as trustworthy, and is able to create collective alignment and focus across the company, its shareholder and external stakeholders
	Culture	The company leadership does not live / display the the company values	Some leadership segments emphasise, and actively drive the desired internal organisational culture	The company leadership actively role models the desired company values	The company leadership brand is lived consistently internally which creates the desired internal organisational culture	The internal organisational culture is enabling successful implementation of the the company strategy
	Leadership Pipeline	The company does not have the leadership capacity required to successfully execute on strategy	There is some leadership capacity to leverage, however significant gaps remain in key and critical roles	There is sufficient cover for most key and critical leadership roles	The company has adequate cover, now and in the future, for leadership in all key and critical roles	The company has adequate leadership capacity, now and for the future, and also has an external talent pool to leverage from
Business Value Add	Leadership Brand	The company leadership does not live / display the the company brand behaviours	Some leadership segments emphasise, and actively drive the desired brand behaviours	The company leadership actively role models the desired company brand behaviours	The company leadership brand is recognised by external stakeholders	The company leadership philosophy is lived consistently and our leaders are recognised and respected by external stakeholders
	Business Performance	There is no consistent or repeatable level of performance within the company	The company leadership has a common understanding of the goals and objectives to be achieved	The company leadership is aligned on goals and objectives, and collectively work together to achieve these	The company leaders are aligned to the overall business strategy, goals and objectives, and perform to achieve these	The company leadership is regarded as achieving exceptional business results

Given this framework, the organisation can:

1. Assess its current level of maturity of leadership capability;
2. Decide what level of maturity is appropriate and achievable; and
3. Based on the gaps between (1) and (2), plan specific leadership talent development processes and interventions.

Using this fairly simple framework will therefore allow the organisation to be specific about the leadership processes and interventions to be introduced, and, perhaps more importantly, also to be specific about the expectations of the impact of such processes and interventions.

Experience and Application

In the application and implementation of a leadership excellence measurement framework, specifically by means of a comprehensive scorecard, the following key experiences or lessons learnt became evident and may be important for other practitioners to take into account in future:

- Try to find existing measures in the organisation that are fit for purpose, rather than inventing new ones.
- Do not automate straight away, but definitely automate after a few iterations. The manual process allows the practitioners of the scorecard to understand fully the measures and associated relationships involved.
- Ensure that you can drill down to a senior leader's area of accountability (for example, provision of Divisional results). This helps with the engagement of specific leaders on their direct areas in influence.
- Create a strong storyline upfront that clearly illustrates the key purpose and logic around the scorecard when sharing it with various stakeholders.
- Make sure all those in your leadership development unit understand how they influence the measurements.
- Make a point of developing different ways to communicate results from the scorecard at the requisite level of complexity.
- To ensure alignment to best practice and to remain "honest" regarding the purpose of the scorecard, allow external thought leader(s) to audit and provide recommendations for enhancement on an annuals basis if possible.
- Always be open to new measures and don't protect ones that merely exist.
- Avoid the temptation to try to crystallise leadership excellence into one score; it will ultimately dilute to robustness of the scorecard and its purpose.
- Understand the logic of the scorecard and the limitations; the complexity of the wider context will generally influence the results.
- Set the long-term desired leadership results in line with your leadership strategy, and track interim progress against a defined path on your leadership capability maturity model. This can be flexible in relation to the context that the organisation finds itself in at a particular point in time.

Case Studies

Perhaps the best way to explain the impact (and evidence) of leadership excellence is by means of a case study. We will utilise the inavit iQ Business Value Model© (see Figure 19.1) as a thinking framework for the case studies, all from different industries, being presented. It should be noted that a narrow definition of business benefits (EBITDA and EBITDA margin) is used to simplify the message from these cases. Table 19.2 provides a profile of the case study organisations.

Table 19.2: Case study company profiles

	Case Study 1	Case Study 2	Case Study 3
Industry	Retail	Financial Services	Manufacturing
Location	Southern Africa	Southern Africa	Africa
Employees	16 000+	2 500+	3 500+
Listed Company	Yes	No	No
Leadership Strategy	Yes	Yes	No
Period under Review	36 months	24 months	24 months

Case Studies 1 and 2: Positive leadership impact

When confronted with shifting market demands these organisations repositioned themselves through an integrated market demand and growth strategy. From the outset, leadership and people was identified as a key pillar to the success of the respective business strategies.

Through an inclusive and collaborative process the organisations developed a formal leadership development strategy in support of the business strategy, the purpose of which was the development of the requisite leadership capacity (= competence and capability). The leadership development strategy was executed through both formal and informal leadership processes to ensure deliberate and consistent alignment of the leadership community.

Figures 53.7 and 53.8 illustrate the positive impact over time that improvement on leadership excellence had on both employee engagement and ultimately EBITDA.

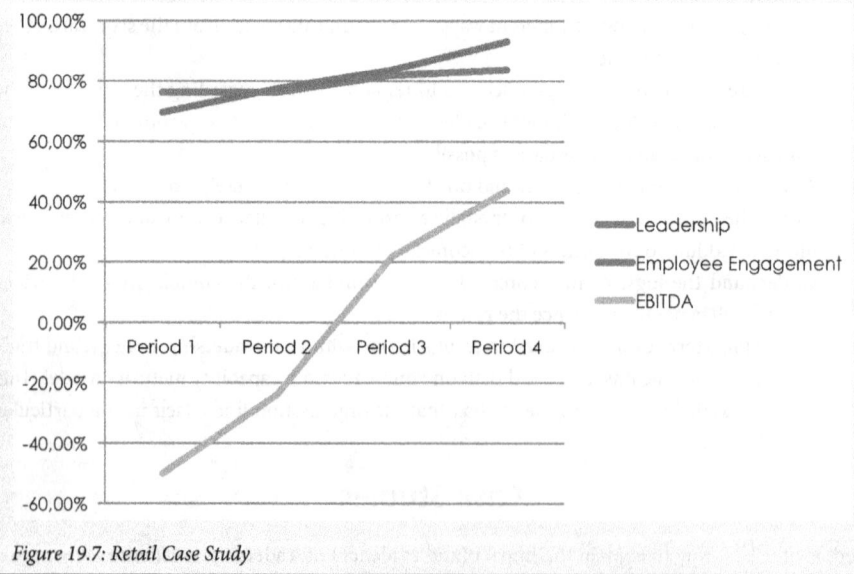

Figure 19.7: Retail Case Study

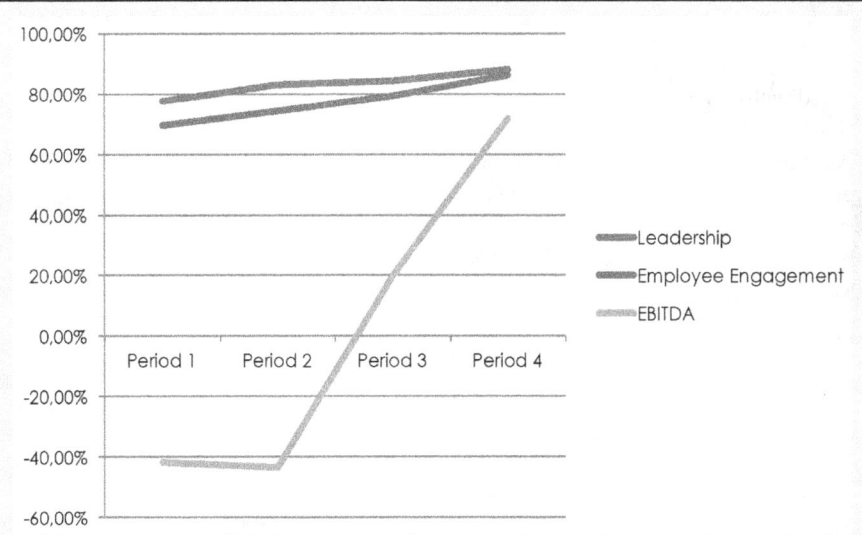

Figure 19.8: Consumer Finance Case Study

Leadership strategy: In both cases requisite leadership is seen as an integral part of the business strategy and as such enjoys executive sponsorship and support. Leadership practices and processes are also planned carefully and the organisations are clear about what must be achieved through a healthier leadership community.

Employee engagement: In both cases the organisations have seen an increase in levels of employee engagement since Period 1. By actively working on the levels of engagement through development, a clearly defined EVP and leadership development, the organisation has seen (and is set to see in future) an increase in engagement.

Customer satisfaction: Customer satisfaction (with products and service) showed an increase from Period 1 to Period 4 and is set to increase in future. In both the retail and consumer finance sectors customer satisfaction is (in large part) a function of the service provided by employees. The organisations successfully use employee engagement levels as a leading indicator of customer satisfaction levels.

Business results: Business results are both a result of the external and internal environment. In this case EBITDA was used as the measure of impact. What is clear (and supported by the research in the inavit iQ Business Value Model©) is that an increase in employee engagement (even slightly) may have a direct and indirect impact on business indicators as is confirmed in these case studies.

Case Study 3: Negative Leadership Impact

Faced with changes in the competitive landscape and pressure from shareholders about financial performance the organisation decided to build the strategy around customer centricity. The departure point for the new strategy was repositioning of the external brand and a strong focus on customer satisfaction. The new strategy was driven mostly through the marketing and sales departments.

Figure 19.9 illustrates the negative impact over time that a decline in leadership excellence had on employee engagement, customer satisfaction, and ultimately EBITDA.

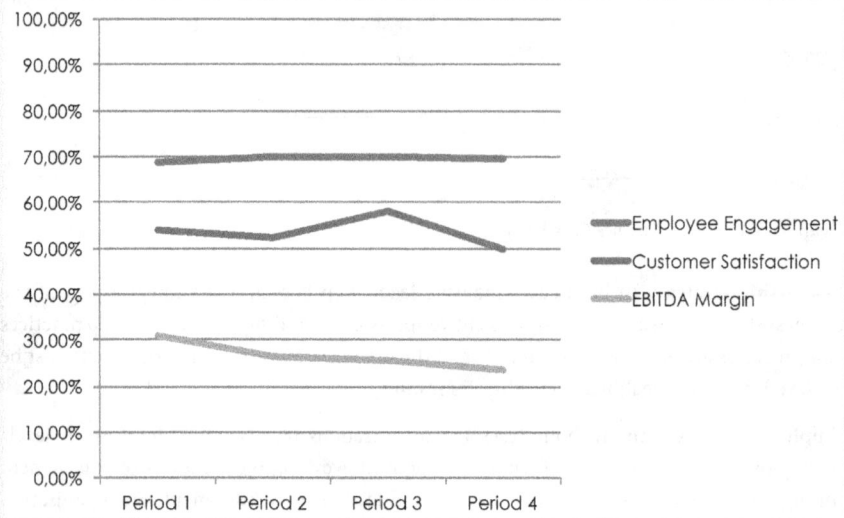

Figure 19.9: Manufacturing case study

Leadership strategy: In this case the organisation did nothing formally on the alignment of leadership, people and the organisation to the changes in strategy. Rather the strategy was driven through various marketing and sales campaigns.

Employee engagement: The organisation has seen an incremental drop in employee engagement since Period 1. Since Period 1 employee engagement has reached a "plateau" and shows a slight decrease in Period 4.

Customer satisfaction: Based on the data, customer satisfaction is decreasing and may even further decrease in future (based on current levels of engagement).

Business results: The EBITDA margin is also a good indicator to use as it takes the impact of operations into account. What is clear (and supported by the research in the inavit iQ Business Value Model®) is that a drop in employee engagement (even slightly) will have an impact on business indicators as is confirmed in this case study.

Reflections on our experience with clients

Our experience with clients over many years and across a variety of industries has shown us that most if not all clients find that the inherent logic of the Business Value Model™ really resonates with them. The realisation of business benefits is dependent on the creation of customer delight (= loyal and satisfied customers). This is a direct result of the delivery of value-added products / services by high-performing people who work in an optimised work environment (= organisation capacity in terms of process, structure, people and technology). These high-performing people perform even better when managed by capable, competent and credible leadership, towards a common goal and strategy.

From a leadership impact perspective, the logic allows them to think through the specific impact they wish to see on issues such as employee commitment and engagement, people performance, and customer delight. The ability to demonstrate these relationships with clients, using their own data, has also led to the consequence that few, if any, of these clients ask about the "ROI on Leadership Development". In our view, this is a significant shift in mind-set where there is a much better grasp of the simple fact that leadership capacity-building processes demonstrate their value and impact over time.

Conclusion

In this chapter, a very specific approach was taken to the measurement of leadership effectiveness and outcomes. The key learning points, in no particular order, may be summarised as follows:

1. Every organisation needs to start by deciding what level of leadership capability maturity the really need to aspire to, and whether or not this is in fact achievable (see Leadership Capability Maturity);
2. The next step would be to take a process perspective on the development of leadership capacity (outlined in Outcomes across the process); and
3. The organisation then has to decide what the specific measures and metrics could be used to demonstrate the impact of leadership outcomes (see Experience and Application; Case Studies).

Our chapter also adopted the approach of measuring leadership impact at the level of leadership as an organisational capability, and not the impact of an individual leader. We also hope to have made clear that the measurement of leadership impact is not only or even in the first instance about financial returns, but that a much broader and systemic perspective should ideally be taken.

End notes

1. Kanji & Moura e Sá, 2010.
2. Collins, 2002.
3. Ulrich & Smallwood, 2008.
4. Ellehuus, 2010.
5. Osterman, 2005.
6. Martineau & Steed, 2004.
7. Ulrich & Smallwood, 2009, pp. 32–35.
8. Jackson, 2011.
9. Dai, Tang & De Meuse, 2011.
10. Gill, 2011.
11. McGurk, 2010.
12. Coverdale Global, 2011.
13. Acharya, 2010.

References

Acharya, TK. 2010. *Anatomy of an effective leadership development strategy*. Arlington, VA: Corporate Leadership Council.

Collins, DB. 2002. *The effectiveness of managerial leadership development programs: A meta-analysis of studies from 1982-2001*. Doctoral dissertation, Graduate Faculty, Louisiana State University.

Coverdale Global. 2011. *What is the ROI of leadership development?* [Online]. Available: http://us.coverdale.he-hosting.de/news/what-roi-leadership-development?destination=news. [Accessed 7 August 2016].

Dai, G, Tang, KY & De Meuse, KP. 2011. 'Leadership competencies across organizational levels: A test of the pipeline model'. *Journal of Management Development*, 30(4):366–380.

Ellehuus, C. 2010. 'Improving returns on leadership investments'. *Strategic HR Review*, 10(6). Emerald Group Publishing Limited. [Online]. Available: http://www.emeraldinsight.com/doi/abs/10.1108/shr.2011.37210faa.002?journalCode=shr. [Accessed 7 August 2016].

Gill, R. 2011. 'An integrative review of storytelling: Using corporate stories to strengthen employee engagement and internal and external reputation'. *Prism*, 8(1):1–16.

Jackson, J. 2011. 'Leader development yields ROI'. *Plastics News*, 22 February. Toronto, CAN: Jackson Leadership Systems Inc. [Online]. Available: http://www.plasticsnews.com/article/20110211/OPINION02/302119998. [Accessed 7 August 2016].

Kanji, GK & Moura e Sá, P. 2010. 'Measuring leadership excellence'. *Total Quality Management*, 12(6):701–718.

Martineau, JW & Steed, JL. 2004. *Measuring the impact of leadership development: How can it best be accomplished?* Paper presented at the 19th Annual Conference of the Society for Industrial and Organizational Psychology, 3 April, Chicago. Chicago, IL: Center for Creative Leadership.

McGurk, P. 2010. 'Outcomes of management and leadership development'. *Journal of Management Development*, 29(5):457–470.

Osterman, B. 2005. 'Measuring your leadership effectiveness… One conversation at a time'. *Business Strategies Magazine*, June. Pittsford, NY: Human Solutions LLC. [Online]. Available: http://www.humansolutionsllc.com/articles/measuring-your-leadership-effectiveness/. [Accessed 7 August 2016].

Ulrich, D & Smallwood, N. 2008. 'Aligning firm, leadership, and personal brand'. *Leader to Leader*, 47:24–32.

Ulrich, D & Smallwood, N. 2009. *Leadership development that delivers results*. Chief Learning Officer, 8(3):32–35, March.

SECTION 7
LEADERSHIP STORIES

Chapter 20

LEADERSHIP STORIES

Introduction

In its very essence, the organisation is a dialogical network of interpersonal interconnections based on conversations, expressed in the form of stories. Stories are naturally-occurring phenomena in organisations through which information, shared experiences, expectations, culture, and identity are passed on. Stories are the very fabric of organisational life. They add a psychological dimension to organisational life through its feeling and experiencing dimension in the form of sense-making, meaning-giving, as well as emotional attachment and involvement which rational, empirical information and lack of knowledge cannot provide.

Storytelling infuses the whole Strategic Leadership Value Chain. It is persuasive leadership-in-action. A story as a form of conversation is capable of representing and transferring complex, multidimensional organisational realities to listeners in a simple and effortless way in order to make sense of, and give meaning and purpose to, organisational reality.

At its most basic level, storytelling as a conversation (or dialogue) refers to what is being said and listened to between people. The word 'dialogue' stems from two Greek roots, "*dia*" and "*logos*", jointly suggesting the sense of "meaning flowing through". Stories help organisational members to make sense of who they are, where they come from and fit in, and what they want to be. They help reduce organisational uncertainty, complexity and ambiguity by quickly and coherently disseminating information; they frame organisational events through their value-laden features; and they promote organisational culture and identification by establishing a context for organisational members.

Using stories is one of the best ways to:

- make abstract concepts meaningful;
- help connect people and ideas;
- inspire imagination and motivate action;
- give "breathing space" in the frenetic and merciless task-driven nature of the organisation;
- allow different perspectives to emerge;
- create sense, coherence, and meaning;
- develop value-centric descriptions of situations, allowing knowledge to be applied and solutions to be found;
- convey organisational values and culture;
- communicate complex messages simply;
- connect people into a shared frame of reference; and
- inspire change.

In the *first instance* leaders are, and have to be, storytellers about themselves: from where they have come; who they are; what they stand for; what they believe in; what they want to achieve and how; and what they want to leave behind as a legacy. The character, competence, connectedness, caring and commitment of leaders are manifested *inter alia* in how well they understand, and are able and willing to share, their personal journeys as leaders: from the past, through the present, into the future. It is a most powerful way in which to connect with others.

In the *second instance*, leaders have to be able to tell the story of the organisation they are currently involved in: the identity and ideology of the organisation; where the organisation has come from; its desired future destination and legacy; the journey travelled to date by the organisation; the journey still to be travelled; and how things are done and not done in the organisation.

This Section provides examples of the first kind of leadership stories: leaders' stories about themselves as leaders.

The accompanying box gives a list of the leaders whose stories follow – with their respective core themes – are included in this Section.

LEADER'S STORY	THEME OF STORY
Thuli Madonsela	*Leadership as the giant leap necessary for an inclusive, prosperous and peaceful future*
Shameel Joosub	*Creating movement as a leader in a constantly evolving and changing environment*
Mohammad Karaan	*Intuition, silence, giants and the cattle herder*
Dave Macready	*Leadership built on vision, belief and passion*
Hendrik du Toit	*Good leaders stand or fall by their principles*
Ian Donald	*Being an authentic and confident leader*

References

Boje, D. 2008. *Storytelling organizations*. Thousand Oaks, CA: Sage.

Boyce, M.E. 1996. 'Organisational story and storytelling: A critical review.' *Journal of Organisational Change Management*, 9(5):5-26.

Christie, P. 2009. *Every leader a story teller – storytelling skills for personal leadership*. Johannesburg, ZA: Knowres.

Denning, S. 2011. *The leader's guide to storytelling*, San Francisco, CA: Jossey-Bass

Gabriel, Y. 2000). *Storytelling in organisations: Facts, fictions and fantasies*. New York, NY: Oxford University Press.

Ibarra, H & Lineback, K. 2005. 'What's your story?' *Harvard Business Review*, 1–7, January.

Veldsman, D & May, M. S. 2012. 'The stories that leaders tell during organisational change: The search for meaning during organisational transformation'. Unpublished Masters thesis, University of South Africa, Pretoria, South Africa.

Leadership as the giant leap necessary for an inclusive, prosperous and peaceful future

Thuli Madonsela

Introduction

A book on leadership is a timely contribution as South Africa reflects on two decades of transitioning from its dark past in search of catalysts to accelerate progress towards the constitutional promise of a prosperous and peaceful future, where everyone's humanity is affirmed, potential freed and life improved in a strong constitutional democracy anchored in the rule of law.

Why leadership?

Leadership is critical for the future of people, organisations, communities and society. Inspired by a vision of a better future, true leadership conceives, actualises and leaves a sustainable future for all, to the benefit of all. However, leadership is not tied to a single person – the 'messiah' – or a position. It cannot be overemphasised that for groups to achieve the futures they desire, the burden of leadership must be borne by all members with each playing differentiated but complementary leadership roles. No one needs a title to lead. In fact, a person who is not leading without a title cannot lead with a title. Instead she/he will diminish the authority of the title.

Since the test of leadership is followership, anyone can and many do lead unconsciously through the things they do or say that influence and inspire others to do the same or act in a particular way or achieve a desired future. The crucial difference is conscious and purpose-driven leadership, which is at the core of true leadership. True leadership, which is effective leadership, is about consciously influencing others to embrace and resolutely pursue a cause or desired outcome. True leadership requires purpose-driven actions by persons seeking to make a difference through influencing themselves and others to act in congruence with the outcomes they seek.

True leadership is accordingly different from unconscious leadership. The latter often translates into what is often referred to as 'misleading'. An unconscious leader may not even realise they are responsible for others going astray. Accordingly, it is true leadership that is required for impactful peer influence and the success of families, organisations, communities and global quests.

A true leader's leadership is an inside-out conscious exercise that starts with leading oneself to do the right thing or that which must be done to achieve a desired end. He/she is not a whiner but a purpose- and principle-driven problem-solver who identifies or creates opportunities for him/herself and others to achieve desired outcomes when an opportunity presents itself or by creating the opportunity him/herself. The strength of an organisation, community and society is where there is an unstoppable, pervasive desire by everyone to be a leader.

What difference must leadership make?

To my mind, the difference a leader has to make is threefold. *Firstly*, a leader has to be *purpose-driven*. He/she must be driven by a quest to make difference, fully conscious of their role and responsibility regarding the achievement of the desired future or outcome for the collective he/she serves.

Secondly, a leader needs to be *vision-driven*, which requires a clear sense of the desired future or ideal world that the collective desires to achieve. He or she need not be the originator of that vision but must play a role in helping the collective to develop or embrace the vision of the future end state they want.

Thirdly, leadership is about *service* to one's collective and humanity. For sustained followership, a leader's impact should be improvement in the lives of followers and others. When leadership ceases to be about service, the privilege of being followed is lost. The mantra of leaders should be: 'Do all the good you can do wherever you can, and with all the people you can work with.'

What are the features of leadership who make a lasting, worthy difference?

I believe such leaders have five critical differentiating characteristics: Firstly, they live out uncompromisingly and with *integrity* their values, regardless of the persons, institutions and circumstances involved. They do the right things for the right reasons for the right outcomes, regardless of the level of resistance and critique. Secondly, they are *authentic* as a person in all they do. They are true to themselves, and what they stand for. Thirdly, they are *service focused, selfless and people centric*. They reach out to others from the premise that everyone is trying to do the best they can. And if they knew better, they would do even better. The leader must strive to create win–win situations.

Fourthly, these leaders apply *systemic, big-picture thinking* linked to their *values and principles*. They seek to understand the impact of their daily, transactional actions on the goals and vision they are endeavouring to achieve. These leaders always begin with the end in mind and stay with the end in mind throughout the path they are following towards their vision. Fifthly, such leaders are *resilient by* doggedly sticking to what they have set out to achieve, again regardless of persons and circumstances.

How should leaders go about making a real difference?

My firm belief is that true leaders do things differently. First, in achieving their goals and vision – as informed by their life purpose – these leaders realise that *leadership starts with themselves as persons* in the first instance. One cannot lead others if one cannot lead oneself and those dearest to oneself, like being a true parent to one's children. Second, these leaders *lead from the perspective of being servants*. He/she seeks to find the challenge, issue or problem they were 'born' to solve to the benefit of all, in this way adding value for all. It is not about themselves and their personal interests and benefits. The 'Me' is subservient to the 'Us'.

Third, to make a difference, these leaders infuse everything they do with *passion and dedication* in the way that they want to make the best of whatever area or situation they are entrusted with as a leader, regardless of the resistance and critique. Fourth, such a leader always seeks, as a starting point, to *understand others*, their world views, and circumstances before pushing to be understood as a leader. This requires active listening by the leader, and one-on-one, quiet conversations. In particular, the leader seeks to uncover the unsaid, the undiscussables, what is skirted around, or avoided. She/he realises that she/he may also be hampered by her/his own blind spots. Regardless of what a leader asks her/his followers to do, they will start doing things based on how the leader interacts with them as opposed to what the leader tells them to do.

Fifth, difference-making leaders ensure at all times that their *day-to-day transactional decisions and actions are tied to their overall purpose and vision*. Sixth, these leaders allow *followers to influence* them regarding the vision, the path to the vision, and the pace at which to move towards the vision. Seventh, they *communicate* on an ongoing basis to all concerned parties to keep them informed, and are *personally visible* where it matters. Eighth, though they have 'hard' power which they have the full right to apply, they seek primarily to use their 'soft' power: *engaging people* by appealing to their aspirations, hopes, ideals, needs and dreams.

Ninth, they engender *teaming and team work*: 'We are in this together, and are all needed to realise the vision.' Tenth, they act as inspirational *role models* by setting the example. Eleventh, they are *good followers* which is reflected in assisting fellow leaders to achieve common goals. Twelfth, replicate leadership by building the *next generation of leaders*, especially amongst the upcoming youth, realising that they want to be part of building a new world. With or without leadership's permission, they will play that role.

The future

Many of the ideas I have raised above are explored at great length throughout *Leadership Excellence*. It is my wish that this book, in exploring the key topic of leadership, will enable you as a leader, organisations and institutions, leadership teachers and researchers, to go and make that sorely needed difference. I also hope the book will assist our leaders, particularly our young and corporate leaders, to enable our country to make the much-needed and desired giant leap into the inclusive, prosperous and peaceful future we all yearn for so passionately.

> Thulisile Madonsela was South Africa's Public Protector. She is also a Human Rights Lawyer and Equality Expert. Madonsela is one of the 11 technical experts who helped the Constitutional Assembly draft the final constitution in 1994 and 1995. Previously, she was a member of a Task Team that prepared constitutional inputs for the Gauteng Province of the African National Congress. She presented the final document at the African National Congress' Gauteng Constitutional Conference in 1995.

Creating Team Movement in a Constantly Evolving and Changing Environment

Shameel Joosub

Interview conducted during February 2013 by Adriaan Groenewald of Leadership Platform. Used with permission

In describing myself as a leader and my leadership, it is first and foremost about the team. You need to have the right people around you to be able to deliver. If you have the wrong people, things are not going to happen. So yes, more emphasis on the quality of the team, and making sure we have the right people one level down, two levels down. Our ability to execute really comes down to the quality of the people as far down as possible. And then removing oneself from the detail and rather playing the role of coaching, guiding. You actually do not have the time to get into the detail even if you wanted to.

Also, a big change in the CEO role now is the whole investor relations. So on one side you are operationally involved, guiding, and so on, and then on the other side it is the investor relations, government relations, all the different stakeholder relations. You need to find a happy balance.

Sitting and looking at Vodacom from the CEO chair, firstly and obviously, the competitive environment has changed. I would say that South Africa lags by about 18 months. So having been seconded to Spain as Vodaphone's CEO for 18 month it was very good to see what the trends were, what to do and what not to do. For example, one area we have to improve in would be Customer Value Management. South Africa was quite advanced in what we would call Customer Relationship Management. But the world has moved on into Customer Value Management which is all about the systems and processes that ensure you are managing the value of a customer – one is the loyalty part; how you manage your most valuable customers, all those type of programmes.

I have been in the telecommunications industry already for 20 years. But what keeps me interested about the industry is the beauty that it is constantly evolving, constantly changing. There is always a new trend, there is always something new you are busy with. And that keeps it exciting. The nature of the industry provides so many opportunities as you go forward, and ones we have not even thought of yet.

Just to give one example. Oxford University reckons that the average person will have 16 SIM cards by 2020. All the technology, everything that we need to develop, to evolve, to create the different eco-systems and everything necessary for that to happen. It is going to be the world of connected devices. This puts you into a world where you walk into a store and you swipe your phone to pay for your purchases. All your loyalty cards, everything is in your phone. The reality is the technology is there now. It has already been developed. Now we have to create the eco-systems to take it to its full potential.

To put it in perspective, we have almost 14 million people accessing the internet via their cell phones just in South Africa. When we look at the fixed line penetration to access the internet we have via your desktop computer, this is what's happening on the mobile. It is huge. And every quarter when we look at the numbers, the amount of growth, and how much people are using – data grew by 40% in terms of usage per customer – you are starting to see more and more of that.

As leader it is crucial to be able to absorb intense competition: "The environment is quite competitive so yes, we have to look after our customer base and customers. What's more important is that you don't get fazed by competition no matter where that competition comes from, that you're executing on your own strategy, that's what's important – you have to have your own plan. You can't react to everything that competitors do. There will be times when you will need to react but what's more important is that you have your own plan and strategy that you're executing."

What is essential is to have a clear plan and strategy and everyone knowing exactly what is expected of them, with clear targets that are cascaded down and used to measure people. So they have clearly set targets with five priorities for each person three levels down, to make sure everyone is aligned. Every quarter they review the priorities and set new ones. Joosub believes this "helps to create common goals, common purpose, and common vision. That's extremely important – to know that the different teams within the company are pulling in the same direction."

Leadership is about creating movement. Over the last year, what has positively moved in Vodacom? "Firstly, from an international perspective, we have now cracked the international model – into Africa, and we are doing exceptionally well. Growth is coming from Africa where South Africa started to slow down a bit – that has created some great movement. It's also made us more confident as a team. In coming back one of the things that I've been pushing is a growth agenda. Why? Part of my role is to ensure the future success of the company, not just the current success of the company."

Other things that I think have evolved are our approach to what we are doing with the technology in the different countries. Also our approach to enterprise and the business, and what we started three years ago and how that has evolved. And then trends have changed, and that has forced us to make some evolutions. The other thing is that there has been some movement in people as well – making sure that we have the right skills to be able to deliver. That also plays a big role.

In keeping my mind and awareness sharp and to remain leadership fit as the CEO, a couple of things are important. Firstly, the exposure to Vodaphone as our international majority shareholder and, secondly, the different development programmes that they run. They do not allow you to become leadership-unfit. They run leadership development programmes a couple of times a year to help keep you abreast of trends and so on. Then things like being part of the strategy, being part of the bigger decisions, and playing a role. So you are getting constant feedback and seeing where the world is going and so on. Then I think one needs to stay abreast of technological advancements: what is happening; feedback from your own teams; reading extensively. All of these things I think help you to evolve yourself in terms of making sure you stay leadership fit.

Vodacom's role in making a difference in South Africa is to clearly align ourselves with government in every country in which we operate and help government to achieve its objectives. There is a strong association between access to mobile telecommunications and GDP growth. I think Vodacom has a key role to play in helping deliver those objectives. From a telecoms perspective in South Africa there is a policy that says we want to have access in every home – mobile access – by 2020. So the discussions I have been having with the President, the Deputy President, the Ministers and so on, is to say we can help you to deliver that strategy. We can and we will help you to deliver that strategy.

Shameel has been the Chief Executive Officer of Vodacom Group Limited since September 2012. He also has served as CEO of Vodafone Spain, one of the top 5 companies in the Vodafone Group between April 2011 August 2012. He holds a MBA.

Intuition, Silence, Giants and the Cattle Herder

Mohammad Karaan

*Article published in Sake Beeld on 1 October 2015.
Translated from Afrikaans. Used with permission*

My approach to leadership can be summarised in twenty principles.

1. *Share the future.* An open hand and open systems will better serve you than selfishness and closed systems. To prosper, grow and foster positivity, the benefits of knowledge and wealth must be shared in a conscious manner. Those who are blessed with great vision, carry a greater burden of responsibility.
2. *Find a different path.* Conforming to convention is not how you prosper – the way to do it is to forge a new or different path. Amongst any population group there are a select few who intuitively strive to be different, and leaders are amongst their number.
3. *Intuition first, then logic.* Logic can be misleading. Leaders trust their intuition and their sixth sense, even if it is subjective. Logic is shaped by personal experience and the viewpoints of others. Each being grows from, and is connected to, a bigger truth. Learn to trust this truth.
4. *Channel energy.* Leaders understand that goals are achieved by channelling energy in a certain direction. Inspiration unleashes energy.
5. *Trust swarm intelligence.* The birds and bees do not hold meetings. Lions instinctively know how to hunt. Thanks to swarm intelligence, every animal understands its role. Leaders build organisations in which employees' instincts and innate understanding of their individual critical roles determine the company's language, relations and operations. So that there is no need to be guided by hierarchies or await instructions.
6. *Seeing around corners.* Leaders see the future long before others do, and lead them towards it without necessarily knowing the destination. The future is an uncharted land with unknown challenges, many of which will be revealed in due course. A leader can see around corners.
7. *Actively pursue blessings.* No one can predict the outcome of events with any measure of certainty, and many of our actions are largely dependent on luck. Happiness is a blessing. We create blessings through the goodwill of others. Good leaders surround themselves with people who bless them with their care, protection and nurturing.
8. *Giants and dwarves.* Leaders build their organisations on the shoulders of giants and continuously involve those who are greater than themselves. Growth comes from appointing people who are 'greater than' you are. Conversely, appointing those who are 'lesser than', diminishes you.
9. *All people are the same.* Yes, diversity is a reality which leaders can use to their advantage. But at their core, people are the same regardless of ethnicity. True leaders can lead regardless of the circumstances, even if that means leading groups who are different from them.
10. *Doubt and faith.* Leaders are not hobbled by doubts, but are impelled to act by the strength of their convictions and their unwavering faith in the future. This keeps them on track as their peers run out of steam.
11. *Savour the silence.* Many leaders are loners because they tend to live in a world of their own that is nurtured by a wellspring of silence from within. Silence is synonymous with peace.

Contact with a greater Truth allows you to replenish your energy. Leaders know how to savour the silence.

12. *Avoid fools.* Fools not only derail you, their foolishness expends your energy unnecessarily. Leaders avoid fools by keeping the peace and leaving the foolish on their road to nowhere. Yes, leaders are often confronted by angry people, and know that their anger stems from a siege mentality. Man is just a different breed of animal. A threatened animal becomes aggressive. Leaders handle aggression by identifying the root cause and addressing it in a subtle way.
13. *Speak less, listen more.* Leaders know that it is much more important to listen than it is to speak. They also know that sometimes contemplation is more valuable than speaking out. Not everything you know needs to be shared. The right word at the right time is far more effective than an uninterrupted flow of opinions.
14. *Tread lightly on this earth.* True leaders do not threaten, they lure. They tread lightly, knowing that they are but a small part of a much greater and more powerful whole. Their aim is not to take, but to give.
15. *Walk a mile in someone else's shoes.* Many great leaders had difficult childhoods, but knew how to turn this to their advantage. That experience allows them to see life from a different perspective, thanks to the benefits of insight and wisdom.
16. *The further you look into the past, the further you can see into the future.* Today was created yesterday, tomorrow will be created today. The future is uncertain because you are still constructing it today. Leaders are not intimidated by the uncertainty and mystery of the future. They know that because the future is shaped by the past, they need to understand the past. The past is still the best predictor of the future.
17. *Your scars tell a story of who you are.* Many great leaders and prophets grew up in single-parent households. Many successful individuals have reported how their difficult childhoods inspired them to face difficult challenges later in life. Use those tough lessons of your youth to your advantage.
18. *Friends, heroes and travelling companions.* Success is not the preserve of the sage or the slave. It largely depends on the quality of the people with whom you surround yourself. Be discerning and clever in choosing your sidekicks. On the road to success, make sure you choose the right travelling companions when they cross your path.
19. *The truth shall set you free.* The essence of good leadership is to strive for the truth in all things, no matter the risk.
20. *The cattle herder's creed.* Many great leaders learned valuable lessons while working as cattle herders. First, in the morning the cattle herder leads the herd to green pastures, leading the way from the front. Second, once in pasture he keeps a watchful eye on them, praising good behaviour and punishing transgressions. Third, at dusk, when they return to the camp, he walks behind the herd to ensure that there are no stragglers because the cattle already know their end destination.

Prof Mohammad Karaan is an Agricultural Economist and Dean of the Faculty of Agrisciences at Stellenbosch University. He served on the National Planning Commission, was Chairman of the National Agricultural Marketing Board and worked as an economist at the Development Bank of Southern Africa. He is the Director of Pioneer Foods, as well as several other companies.

Leadership Built on Vision, Belief and Passion

Dave Macready

Article published in Sake Beeld on 20 August 2015.
Translated from Afrikaans. Used with permission

When I am asked about leadership, I immediately think of the great leaders I have known who have exuded vision, belief and passion. Our own Madiba embodied all three of these qualities, shining a light in the dark for all of us to follow and creating a passionate, contagious belief in a better, more sustainable future for all South Africans. He demonstrated that by inspiring the inner core of those he led, a great leader can define a new reality and make possible what was previously impossible or unimaginable.

Leaders with vision often come to the fore in a time of crisis, when their ability to see the bigger picture is most needed. Leaders need to see around corners and look beyond current realities to envisage a new future. They must be able to change mindsets and create belief – faith without evidence – in a better future that doesn't exist yet. All boats rise with a tide. Leadership is only really challenged when the tide goes out. It is in this empty space – a void etched with dark spaces where everyone looks around at everyone else and there are no obvious answers, only questions – that great leaders emerge.

As important as vision is belief. Belief in self, belief in those being led and belief in a better tomorrow. Rudy Giuliani, the mayor of New York at the time of the 9/11 attacks, immediately understood this. Instinctively he knew that what a city reeling with shock needed more than anything was a unifying force: a strong, resolute, resourceful leader confident about finding solutions. He swung into immediate action to address basic needs, both physical and emotional, steering New Yorkers away from fear, grief and despair to a shared belief in their ability to overcome the crisis.

Reinforcing every great leader's vision and belief is passion. Passion is everything. It stems from a feeling, a feeling of being part of something, something you believe in, something bigger than yourself. Years ago I watched a movie called *Any Given Sunday* in which Al Pacino played a coach who had only a few minutes in which to motivate his exhausted team to persevere and succeed. Few things I have watched have been as simply passionate or powerful as the 'Inch by Inch' speech he delivered. With deep commitment and raw honesty, he reignited his team's belief in their winning skills and got them to summon all their strength, passion and fire to achieve their goal, literally in this case.

That scene struck a chord with me because of the basic truth it captures. Great leaders must connect and identify with those they lead to unleash the full power of passion, tenacity and perseverance. That connection needs to be built on reciprocal trust: every leader must engender the absolute conviction that he or she has the team's best interests at heart, and at the same time convey the belief that the team has what it takes to deliver excellence.

Of course, vision, belief and passion alone do not guarantee moral, ethical or servant leadership, as despots and tyrants from Hitler to Pol Pot have proved. Fine leadership, leadership that is for the greater good, requires the essential qualities of integrity, courage, humility and humanity. I think Madiba again. I think Mahatma Gandhi. I think Thuli Madonsela.

Fine leaders do the right thing even when nobody is watching. They have the courage to make hard, but necessary decisions; the courage to abandon the past; the willingness to learn, unlearn and relearn; as well as the courage to be the change they want to see against all odds. Part of fine leadership may be inherent, but part is acquired through life's brutal lessons in wisdom. It cannot be taught in a classroom or lecture hall.

Abraham Lincoln, one of the wisest Presidents of the United States, achieved great things by creating an exceptional culture of learning, thinking and debating. Those he surrounded himself with were the best and brightest he could find, even if their opinions diverged from his own. Importantly, he had the courage to challenge the conventions of previous generations, and to abandon them where they fell short of the principles he stood for.

South Africa is under enormous political and economic pressures and faces significant challenges at this critical juncture in our history. We are a country calling out for inspiring and effective leadership in business, in labour, in government. We are a country desperate for leaders to have the courage to engage, shift perspectives and abandon our well-entrenched vested positions. Leaders who are prepared to invest in a new trust equation that brings business, labour and political leadership together to better serve the interests of a more sustainable, more inclusive South Africa. Leaders who selflessly put *all* South Africans' interests at the centre of the agenda.

> Dave Macready is the recently appointed CEO of Old Mutual South Africa. He is a chartered accountant and a former partner at Deloitte in Cape Town and London. After choosing to return to South Africa in 1999, he held senior executive leadership positions in Syfrets, Nedcor Investment Bank and the Nedbank Group Executive before joining Old Mutual in May.

Good Leaders Stand or Fall by Their Principles

Hendrik du Toit

Article published in Sake Beeld on 17 September 2015.
Translated from Afrikaans. Used with permission

The current era is characterised by a paucity of political leaders, both nationally and internationally. It seems apt to label this the 'post-Mandela' era. Could this perhaps be attributed to social media, or the spineless politics of 'opinion polls'? Locally, citizens are faced with a surplus of Party apparatchiks in positions of power, and very few inspiring leaders. Europe has a surfeit of bureaucrats and professional politicians, but very few leaders.

What can we learn from leaders who make a difference? Ordinary people across Europe are frustrated by the handling of the economic melt-down in Greece, the volatile situation in the Ukraine and the chaos of the migrant crisis in the Mediterranean. Pope Francis, President Xi Jinping of China and Premier Narendra Modi of India offer glimmers of hope, but their respective tenures have thus far not been lengthy enough to merit a considered opinion.

Despite widespread optimism at the start of his historical election to the most powerful position on earth, President Barack Obama has not managed to sway America from its destructive path of petty politics, and has failed to pave the way for international cooperation in the post-Bush era. He was overly ambitious, and sadly did little to form the right coalitions. Leadership is about much more than making rousing speeches.

What can we learn from those leaders who truly made a difference through the ages? What do Alexander the Great, Admiral Nelson, Mohandas Gandhi, Winston Churchill, Deng Xiaoping, and our own Albert Luthuli, Nelson Mandela and FW de Klerk have in common?

Leadership is the ability to make a real difference by motivating people, rather than forcing them to work together towards a common goal. The concept of single-mindedness explains why certain leaders were so successful. Good leadership is not a popularity contest. In fact, Churchill was extremely unpopular when he vetoed any form of compromise with Hitler. Gandhi and Mandela were incarcerated; De Klerk was branded a traitor.

Good leaders do not change their tune at the drop of a hat. The have faith in the courage of their convictions, follow their own path and act in a consistent manner. They stand and fall by what they believe in. They are authentic, rather than the creations of spin-doctors. They step up to the plate in high-pressure situations. Cricket supporters who saw cricketer Clive Rice in action in his heyday will recall many instances where he shouldered the burden of responsibility, rather than expecting his team to follow instructions. Richie McCaw did the same during a game at Ellis Park, against the Springboks, where his unorthodox line-out calls soon swung the game in the All Blacks' favour.

True leaders are credible, be they politicians, businessmen or sporting heroes, because they are goal-oriented in their approach and have a clear vision. Why else would people walk through fire for them? Most successful leaders are authentic because they are comfortable in their own skins. That is one aspect of leadership which nobody can teach you.

Although leadership can be defined quite narrowly, leadership styles tend to be divergent. I usually encourage leaders to adopt the leadership style they are comfortable with. The literature outlines and analyses numerous leadership styles, but in my view those theories are not as important as this basic truth: no movement or organisation that works towards a common goal, can effectively channel the energy and talents of its people, without effective leadership at all levels. Those who underestimate the impact of good leadership or leadership development, do so at their peril.

Hendrik du Toit is Executive Head of Investec Asset Management and a Director of Investec plc and Investec Ltd. In 1991 he joined the group as Portfolio Manager and founding member of Investec Asset Management, before leading the company to become a multinational specialist asset management firm with assets in excess of R1 400 billion. In 2008 he was named *Global Investor's* Asset Manager of the Year. In 2011 *Financial News* named him one of the world's ten most influential asset managers. In 2012 he was *Financial News'* Executive Head of the Year.

Being an Authentic and Confident Leader

Ian Donald

*Interviewed on 30 October 2014 by Adriaan Groenewald of
Leadership Platform. Used with permission*

Every now and then I meet a leader that comes across as truly authentic with a healthy confidence. Ian Donald, the newly appointed CEO of Nestle SA is such a leader. He has lead in Philippines, Nestle Ice Cream SA, Pakistan together with war-torn Afghanistan and East Africa that includes 21 countries. And now he is back in South Africa to create movement in his motherland.

Authentic and confident leaders have a track record of having created successful movement over and over. Donald has done this in several diverse geographical locations, which is part of why he projects confidence. In fact because of this track record, his reputation and respect for him precedes him. Confidence is "trusting processes that work", and this is the same for leadership. To be a confident leader one must learn to trust leadership processes that work, which presupposes doing it over and over.

The mere announcement that Donald is coming to a country, division or branch triggers movement, action and people anticipating what he wants or expects of them. This is a powerful position to be in, which is part and parcel of an authentic and confident leader. Unfortunately in a world of "immediacy" where leaders want career progression now, and where movement from one position to the next happens fast, together with overall societal change that happens at breakneck pace, these kinds of leaders may become rarer.

Authentic and confident leaders possess the courage to make themselves vulnerable, probably because they have learnt to manage or destruct their ego. They really believe that they are still learning. They admit when they do not know something or when they have made a mistake. While it may not be easy, they accept when others point to their incongruent behaviour; and they are comfortable with engaging staff on all levels. If leaders would only check their egos at the door, the world would be a better place.

Donald says: "I'm now sixty-three but still believe in this principle of learning all the time. I am conscious of what I learn. So going to Pakistan for example, I hope I made a contribution, but boy did I learn, and did I grow as an individual." And he adds: "I find the biggest journey I have been on all my life is knowing myself. And that's still the journey I am on most." This attitude manifests in his everyday behaviour, like walking around, wanting to connect with the people.

Authentic and confident leaders buy into the truth that human beings are driven by deep-rooted values. So they fanatically drive values inside their business, while striving to remain true to their own. They work with the big picture of matching individual needs and values with the organisations, and even broader society. As Donald comments: "It comes back to values all the time – the importance of respect, and the importance of understanding other people, other cultures." He has had to apologise because a staff member challenged his behaviour as being incongruent with values.

Authentic and confident leaders achieve greatness because they usually care relatively little about what others think of them. They are driven by what is right, rather than by how others perceive them. They do not act for approval but for successful movement as leader as required by a particular situation. Because of a tamed ego they do not just change things around them for the sake of changing. They move in, listen, and do what needs to be done. If the situation requires radical change, they do it. If the situation requires them to merely build on what has been achieved, they make this happen as well.

When Donald moved into Pakistan he did not just change everything. At the time he commented: "The correct approach in a business that did not require turnaround but merely wasn't living up to its full potential was not to change everything. In fact, coming in and changing everything, especially as an expat, sends out a clear message that what was done up until then was not respected." He was conscious of showing appreciation for the past and building on it.

Authentic and confident leaders understand that all of the above and more are important, but none of it matters if the business is not profitable and sustainable. "You can't get away from the fact that at the base of it all is to create a sustainable, long-term, growing, profitable business. Otherwise you can't do anything; it all falls apart," explains Donald.

At Nestle they speak of "shared value rather than social responsibility". They feel that to survive in a long-term sustainable way they have to add value all the way through the value chain from beginning to end: from the farmer that provides raw material to the end consumer. Everyone in the value chain must be successful. And then follows the responsibility to add value to broader societal issues like gas emissions, water pollution and so on, which Nestle is very involved with.

The future changes every day. There is so much happening around one that is unexpected and beyond your control. So one has to be prepared to adapt. According to Donald: "Watching the scenery and keeping yourself aware is very critical." For example, the Ebola outbreak is already impacting their business on cocoa supplies for chocolate. "You have got to be aware and cannot be fixed in a vision and direction blindly," says Donald. And so, an authentic and confident leader is very aware of the big picture and uses this to create meaning, purpose.

> At the time of going to print, Ian Donald was the newly appointed CEO of Nestle SA. He has led Nestle Organisations across many countries, mostly in emerging economies.

SECTION 8
THE FUTURE OF LEADERSHIP

Chapter 21

LOOKING AHEAD

The Future of Leadership
Andrew J Johnson and Theo H Veldsman

In closing our brief excursion into *Leadership Excellence* it is worthwhile repeating some key assertions we made in the opening chapter:

- leadership is under severe scrutiny, and;
- leadership is in the overheating crucible of a reframed/reframing world that is in the throes of fundamental and radical transformation, hence; and
- the search is on for better and different leadership, in the present and going into the future.

Going into the future, the need for organisations to have an ongoing, deliberate, comprehensive and in-depth conversation about leadership is an imperative if they want not merely to survive but also to thrive sustainably.

In this chapter we would like to gaze into the crystal ball by posing the question: If there is a need for better and different leadership going into the future, what would it look like with the conditions attached to such future-fit leadership?

To this end we explore the features of the growing crisis around leadership; the unfolding, future contextual leadership challenges; profiling the "context fit" leadership of the future; effective leadership engagement with the future context through Skilful Improvisation; and finally, the implications of Skilful Improvisation for growing and developing future-fit leadership.

Features of the Growing Leadership Crisis

Some of the important features of the growing leadership crisis that will have a significant impact on future leadership are:

- *Leadership no longer has any place to hide*. Leaders are in the public eye and under public scrutiny constantly because of the power of social media, and more stringent and expanding corporate governance requirements and demands.
- *Accelerating mistrust, anger towards, suspicion of, disillusionment in, and sense of alienation from, institutional leadership*, whether in business, the public sector, or in politics. There is a growing general public perception that "they are in it for themselves and their own enrichment. People and institutions are merely the means to satisfy their ego-centric needs, wants and purposes."
- *Greater and unrealistic expectations for "leadership on steroids"*. There is little patience with new leaders taking time to settle into and acclimatise to their new roles. The pressure is for instant delivery from the word "go", often against unreasonable deliverables, goals and standards. In many instances, the leadership role expectations from stakeholders are unclear and ambiguous, resulting in decreasing leadership tenures, and higher frequencies of derailment and burnout.
- The *emergence of more spontaneous leadership* in more places, at more times and by more people, the growing trend of "leaderless revolutions". These revolutions are fuelled

by the multiplication and mobilisation power of social media in the hands of everyone, everywhere, anytime. The spontaneous revolutions are blossoming around issues regarding globalisation, climatic warming, technological innovation, religious "holy wars", and demographic displacements like the European refugee crisis. Recent examples of such "leaderless" movements include the #arabspring movements of the Middle East; the #occupy movements in North America and Europe; and #mustfall movements in the South African higher education sector.

- The *growing cancer of toxic leaders, followers and organisations* because of the fanatical worshipping of unfettered individualism and egocentricity to the detriment of the pursuit common good; the rampant growth in personal self-interest and self-love (in other words, narcissism); putting "Me Pty Ltd" at the centre; the weakening of the overarching authority of commonly accepted ethical values and norms, also because of value clashes resulting from increasing multicultural settings; and weak followers unable and unwilling to challenge toxic leadership courageously and fiercely.

Unfolding Future Leadership Contextual Challenges

Against the backdrop of the above features of the growing leadership crisis, what are the most apparent unfolding future contextual leadership challenges? We would like to explore these challenges in terms of the conceptual framework given in Figure 21.1, constructed around the relationships in which a leader is embedded.

Figure 21.1 Leadership in relationship with the World, Organisation, Others and Self

According to the framework given in Figure 21.1, the leader's success resides in successfully connecting, nurturing and maintaining four interdependent, critical relationships – each with their unique interacting leadership challenges, demands and requirements – with the World; one's Organisation; Others; and Self. Each of the four relationship of leadership will be discussed in turn from a futuristic perspective. Though discussed separately and sequentially, the four relationships form an organic, systemic whole; are in constant reciprocal interaction; and form dynamic patterns, whether vicious or virtuous.

World

Much has been written and spoken about the VUCA World context of Volatility, Uncertainty, Complexity and Ambiguity, expanded here by ourselves to VICCAS: a World of increasing Variety, Interdependence (that is, connectivity), Complexity, Change, Ambiguity, Seamlessness and Sustainability. The counter, "dark" side of the above VICCAS features must also be considered: Over-standardisation, Over-dependency, Over-simplification, Over-formalisation, Over-control, Over-specialisation and Over-concentration. Going forward, the expectation is that the VICCAS Context will intensify.

The key challenges of the VICCAS Context are:

- Pressures arising from *macro destructive and threatening global, socio-economic dynamics invading the global village*, such as wealth concentration in the hands of a few "Haves"; the significantly growing income gap; the relative impoverishment of the middle class; growing structural unemployment because of the Fourth Industrial Revolution (see below); and population displacement because of climatic change and value clashes (see below). The sensitive, interwoven fabric and tapestry of the World – the playing field of leadership – is being torn apart.
- Social media *fragmenting the world into "e-suburbs" of vast global (radicalised) interest groups* talking only to themselves in self-referential ways in self-created echo chambers; radical group recruitment via the Internet; the global tsunami waves of fads and fashions, uninformed opinions and views engulfing the world; the snowballing generation of vast amounts of unvalidated data, information and knowledge feeding and swaying public opinion; parochial, selective views fed by search engines, for example, Google's search engines defining siloed realities for people. Those who have to be led are "disappearing" and becoming faceless in cyberspace through virtualisation and digitisation.
- *Vast technological innovation*, characterised by an exponential rate of change in and merging of multiple technologies across diverse domains such as the physical, digital, and biological manifested in, for example, Artificial Intelligence (AI), robotics, DNA sequencing, the Internet of Things (iot), driverless vehicles, 3D-printing, nanotechnology, biotechnology, big data, materials science, energy storage, and quantum computing. Digitisation and emails are replacing direct face-to-face leadership. It is believed that machines and systems are taking over, replacing people. Against the backdrop of keeping up with technological innovation, future leadership will have to align effectively in real-time technology, people, and working mode continuously relative to the strategic intent they are pursuing.
- Global fundamental *value system clashes and tensions* creating deep fault lines and schisms in communities, organisations and societies. Future leadership will need to build common, shared value spaces enabling diverse people to collaborate for the benefit and common good of all.
- The increasing *untrammelled power of big global corporates* – some bigger than states – leveraged from their control over vast resources globally, pressurising governments, institutions and stakeholders to "toe their line" in order to suit their parochial, narrow, corporate interests. The resources can be moved at the click of a mouse. The challenge to leadership is to move beyond narrow corporate self-interest and adopt a corporate social investment, common good, and a perspective infusing all of the corporate's thinking, decisions and actions.
- The growing *mismatch of global institutions* such as the United Nations (UN), World Bank, IMF, the International Court of Justice, International Criminal Court, and Interpol to

oversee and deal in globally representative ways with the increasing contextual complexity of the World. Increasingly these institutions are becoming too simple for, and too unrepresentative of, the complexifying World. The leadership challenge is the re-creation of the existing, and the setting up of newly conceived, institutions matched to the requisite contextual complexity of the VICCAS Context.

Organisation

Against the features of the VICCAS Context, organisations (including institutions) to be led in the future will be facing at least the following challenges:

- The heightened *vulnerability of the organisation's reputation and brand* to social media used for mobilisation against organisations by lobby/interest/pressure groups. Future leadership will have to be a master of the social media, and dominate this communication in space-time.
- The *disruption of traditional business models* because of virtualisation and digitalisation, for example, Amazon, e-Bay, and the on-demand economy driven by the emergence of applications (apps)-based organisations, for example, Uber and airbnb. Future leadership will have to question their existing business model on a continuous basis from first principles.
- The *deconstruction of big corporates* into smaller, highly autonomous, network-based business units in order to instil corporates with nimbleness, agility, client centricity, and responsiveness. The leadership of the future will have to be a networker and alliance and partner builder. He/she will have to be outstanding at building deep and robust relationships.
- Increasing pressure for *demographic representivity* regarding race, gender and culture at all leadership levels from board-level down the organisation, reflective of the organisation's chosen operating arena. Diversity sensitivity will be essential for future leadership.
- Globalisation, enabled by digitisation and virtualisation, will force organisations and leadership to adopt a *global mindset* manifested in thinking globally but acting locally.
- Organisations and their leadership will need to be *future centric* by visiting the future in order to create previously unimaginable, desirable futures. They will then have to return to the present to realise that future. Merely extrapolating from the present into the future, and applying past success recipes, will be a cause of certain extinction for organisations.
- *Disruptive innovation* because of the Fourth Industrial Revolution will necessitate the ongoing re-invention of organisations in terms of client needs, products/services, markets, and modes of delivery. Organisations will be in a constant state of flux. Future leadership will have to be relentless innovators, entrepreneurs and risk takers.
- The *increasing "algorithmisation" of professional knowledge, expertise and decision-making*, enabling para-professionals and users to take over work previously reserved for and claimed by professionals such as medical doctors, lawyers, chartered accounts, and psychologists.
- The *global demand for talent* appropriate to the VICCAS Context will lead to quicker promotion of leaders, resulting in less "intelligent" and mature leaders (see below) in senior and executive positions.
- The VICCAS Context will impose the imperative to shift from *the all-knowing, all-powerful single leader* to *shared (or distributive) leadership and the creation of leadership communities* in organisations, operating beyond hierarchy and function. This will enable the organisation to address more effectively the "wicked" challenges, problems and issues of the VICCAS Context.

Others

Some of the more important future challenges with respect to others are:

- The **range and diversity of stakeholders** of organisations and leaders will grow by leaps and bounds, also because of some of the above discussed trends and leadership challenges, such as the power of social media. Leadership will have to be knowledgeable about the diverse and conflicting needs of multiple stakeholders, including shareholders, the board, employees, suppliers, customers, regulators, competitors and the communities in which they operate, as well as the dynamics infusing each and among one another.
- In the VICCAS context there will be a **growing sense of disempowerment among stakeholders**, and consequently growing feelings among them of being helpless, threatened, anxious and angry. There will be a fervent, mounting, search for "the leader who can save us", creating the potential for followers to be vulnerable to leader exploitation and toxicity.
- The growing ambiguity with regard to **commonly accepted ethical values and norms**, also because of value clashes arising out of the growth in multicultural settings, giving rise to a greater need for value-based leadership, and to build on the "should" and "right". This leadership will need to focus not only on ethical leadership but also on creating a better society and world for present and future generations. Future leadership will have to be imbued by a moral consciousness, compass and courage leveraged from a transcendental leadership stance, namely "why?" leadership.
- The **growing power of public opinion**, solicited by ongoing surveys and referenda, and resulting in the **rise of opportunistic leadership** playing to the grandstand without a firm point of view, and acting without integrity. The need would be for future leadership acting with integrity from a clearly selected position.
- The employee base of organisations shifting to a **significant number of temporary/part time/contract workers** – many merely linked to the organisation through the Internet or an app – who have no real stake in and long-term commitment to the organisation. The challenge to future leadership would be how to engender high levels of engagement from these employees who in many cases have highly sought-after specialist skills.

Self

The challenges emerging from the above will require the future leader to dig much deeper into him-/herself, even though already being overstretched. Specific to the leader, at least the following major future challenges can be distinguished:

- The **constant onslaught on the leader's identity**: who and what am I?; what do I stand for?; what do I want to achieve?; to what end, and for whose benefit?
- The **rapid unlearning of a fixation on past success recipes**; being seduced by transient fads and fashions, and/or the fervent search for "silver bullets" propagated by snake-oil salespersons.
- More **frequent and widespread leadership transitions** requiring constant transitional adjustments by the leader. Leaders will have to be equipped with strong transition strategies and capabilities.
- A **tuned-in-ness to the vulnerability to succumb to toxic leadership**, arising out of the worshipping of individualism and giving rise to self-love; unclear, ambiguous, and conflicting values; the greying of ethics; and toxic friendly followers.
- Leaders running the risk of falling into the trap of **self-protective, "spin-doctoring" conduct** to protect themselves against relentless, merciless public exposure.

- A significantly greater likelihood and frequency of **burnout and organisational derailment** because of contextual pressures and unclear/unrealistic leadership expectations and demands by stakeholders. Leadership resilience will be a key future capability.

"Context Fit"-Leadership for the Future

A cursory scan of the contextual challenges discussed above, highlights the sizeable and seemingly overwhelming contextual demands on leaders going into the future. Leading in this unfolding new world is somewhat, in the words of Hixonia Nyasulu, Chairman of the women-controlled Ayavuna Women's Investments, "like playing tennis in the dark with unknown opponents, unexpected balls, unclear tennis court lines, and unpredictable weather". Equally, there are the possibly bewildering myriad leadership capabilities seemingly necessary to navigate and lead in the VICCAS Context, as elucidated above.

This situation could potentially leave an existing and/or aspiring leader deeply discouraged, with the natural, spontaneous response to withdraw, succumb or fight, instead of engaging positively. Going into the future, we submit that what is required is not a "silver bullet" set of specific capabilities, all needed at the same time in order to produce the "super" leader, able to be fully in charge at all times and under all circumstances; instead, the need will be rather to appreciate situation-specific leadership requirements and in this way identify, grow and develop context-fit leadership. Additionally, a community of leaders should be established, people who are able to lead effectively in a given/expected context through complementary, shared leadership, supplying collectively all of the necessary capabilities within and across situations.

Furthermore, in going into the future, a long-term, complex, and not short-term, mechanistic, vantage point to leadership should be adopted. Such a vantage point will enable us to re-imagine in a holistic, organic, integrated and dynamic way at a truly deep level a leader as a whole person embedded in his/her fourfold relationships with the World, Organisation, Others and Self, which will have to be dynamically and simultaneously aligned in real time.

Going Wide: Future-fit Leadership Capabilities Domains

Based on the above "design criteria", we would like to submit that contextual future-fit leadership will consist of five interdependent capability domains:
- *Able:* The hard and soft capabilities necessary to perform competently relative to contextual demands. The deployment of the required capabilities needs to be infused with the necessary qualities that will bring about hope, passion, caring, harmony, faith, confidence efficacy, courage and perseverance among followers, the psychosocial capital essential for followers to deal with the VICCAS Context effectively.
- *Intelligent:* Leadership who can observe, think, judge, act, learn and reflect with a growing understanding as they engage – conceptually and practically – with the VICCAS Context through converting experiences into information, information into knowledge, and knowledge into wisdom. The total "intelligence" (or meta-intelligence) of an excellent leader will consist of the five interdependent intelligence modes of Intra- and Interpersonal, Systemic, Ideation, Action, and Contextual Intelligence.
- *Mature:* Leadership able to engage consistently in relevant, productive, meaningful and constructive and uplifting ways with Self, Others, the Organisation, and the World.
- *Ethical:* Leaders and leadership who do the right thing for the right reasons in the right way in the right place and the right time with the right persons, that is, the "Should Do", the "Right thing".

- **Authentic:** Leaders and leadership which nurture and affirm the dignity, worth and efficacy of an individual(s), concurrently creating enabling, empowering, and meaningful work experiences.

Specific Future-fit Leadership Capabilities

Given the need for able, intelligent, mature, ethical and authentic leadership, required by the VICCAS Context, Figure 21.2 provides summarised clusters of suggested, more important capabilities ("Can Dos") for future-fit leadership, as per the leadership relationship dimensions discussed above – World, Organisation, Others, and Self. All of these capabilities are infused by the five capability domains of ability, intelligence, maturity, ethics and authenticity, as outlined above.

Figure 21.2 Clusters of suggested, more important capabilities for future-fit leadership

Effective Leadership Engagement with the Future Context through Skilful Improvisation

It should be clear that even when one distils the future-fit capabilities required by leaders – as per Figure 21.2 – to respond effectively to the VICCAS challenges, the list is daunting and intimidating. Therefore, as suggested earlier, one should rather adopt a situational appreciation for the contextual, relevant application of particular capabilities. Such an approach may then lead one to think of effective leadership as an act of "Skilful Improvisation". Perhaps as the futurist, Alvin Toffler, points out, a "new" type of leader is called for, one who depends less on his/her intellectual and technical skills, and is instead one who is open to learning new things, unlearning old things that no longer serve, and relearning some things of value that have been forgotten. In this case, "effectiveness" can be defined as the extent to which a leader is able to achieve his/her intended consequences in a certain context. If leadership is action, it implies that such action can be effective or ineffective relative to the context concerned. Skilful Improvisation entails enabling and empowering leadership to re-invent him-/herself continuously in real time as contextual leadership challenges, demands and requirements shift, expectedly and unexpectedly.

Conceiving of leadership as Skilful Improvisation accepts certain future-fit capabilities will be required to lead effectively in the unfolding Context. In order to do so, leadership will have to develop – holistically and organically – deep capabilities with regard to all of the relationships he/she is embedded in across the five critical capability domains discussed above: ability, intelligence, maturity, ethics, and authenticity. The development of such deep capabilities will require fundamentally deep self-introspection and reflection because the barriers to true leadership effectiveness, organisational change, and excellence reside fundamentally inside the individual leader.

We contend that the VICCAS Context faced by leadership we have sketched in *Leadership Excellence* will only become worse. It is quite possible that by the time we have developed our leaders in what we consider the "necessary" capabilities, they will already have become outdated. Skilful Improvisation appears to be best suited to address the chaotic VICCAS Context adequately: the insight and will to be able to "read" the situation as a leader correctly; to exercise the right judgement; to choose from a set of capabilities such as those given in Figure 21.2 those that are situationally relevant skills as demanded by the task, people, organisational and contextual requirements; reflecting-in-action both on his/her own state of mind and the backtalk[1] of the situation, in order to perform effectively.

Impossible? Then perhaps leadership growth and development should be informed by the approach of artists. The above is precisely what jazz artists do so well.[2] Leaders know very well that life more often than not does not turn out in the way one has planned it. What if our thinking and doing are agile enough to bend with what we get served, analogous to the way in which jazz artists think and act. The jazz band may be playing a piece that they have rehearsed well, then unexpectedly someone makes a mistake. Now what if the thinking in that moment is: "There are no mistakes"; certainly not a "mistake" by someone else. Only the "mistake" of an inadequate in-the-moment response to the backtalk of the situation.[3]

Implications of Skilful Improvisation for Growing and Developing Future-fit Leadership

Skilful improvisation requires very deep personal development. Because leaders have little control over their external (chaotic) context, and quite likely become drained by its demands, it stands to reason that leaders will have to find resources internally in themselves. Such growth and development will include capacity growth and development in respect of the capability range indicated earlier (see Figure 21.2) but first and foremost in his/her relationship to him-/herself.

Going deep

This is essential because there is a blindness in all human beings through years of socialisation that necessitates that such growth and development drill deeper into the deepest layers of leaders' lived world if they are to be capacitated for the intensifying VICCAS Context. Figure 21.3 depicts the respective layers making up the leader's lived world, from "deep" to "shallow".

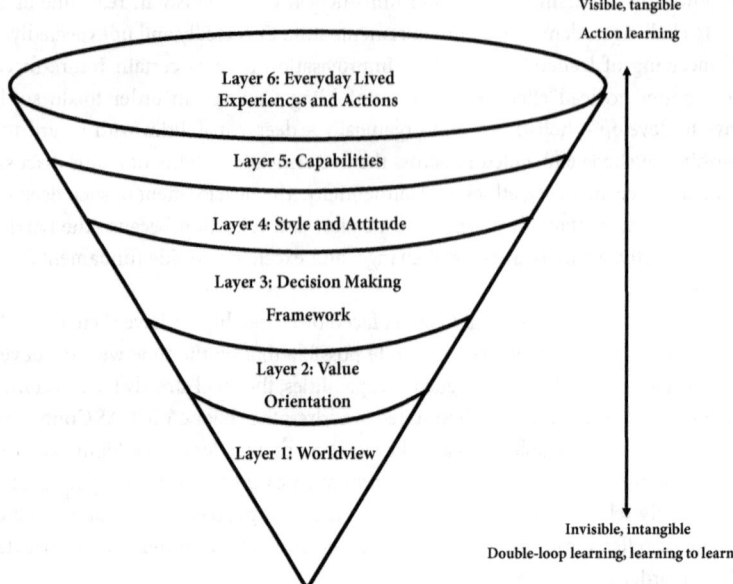

Figure 21.3 Layers making up the leader's lived world

Analogous to the building of a house, future-fit leadership growth and development have to commence with the deep Layer 1: Worldview (or Mental Model), and then proceed progressively to the more shallow layers in a "building onto" manner. Learning in this way will help the leader to bring his socially programmed blindness to conscious reflection, and develop new pathways towards effective leadership, including purposefulness: an authentic balanced disposition to the needs of others (= all stakeholders), the organisation, and the world. Learning approaches and methods will have to be employed by organisations that elicit valid information and knowledge about what individuals think and do at deep layers, because the default pattern of individuals is to employ defensive reasoning. We espouse leadership effectiveness, but as human beings we lack the ability to produce such holistic inside-out development. In addition, we are unaware of this serious, future-compromising limitation.

Bringing about deep learning

How do we effect this deep learning? As indicated earlier, one cannot simply focus on changing Layers 6: Everyday lived experiences and 5: Capabilities (see Figure 21.3). Layers 5 and 6 learning tend to break down when people experience stress because stress triggers default conduct. One has to change the underlying layers, in particular Layers 1 to 3, that drive the conduct, to Layer 6. Skilful improvisation requires drawing on deep, internal personal resources that this type of development endeavours to develop.

The knowledge organisations produce in our leadership growth and development programmes must be in the service of enabling leadership action with regard to Layer 6. Two expressions of such learning are (i) *double-loop learning*, aimed at getting to the mental models comprising underlying beliefs, values and attitudes (Layers 1 to 4) that perpetuate ineffective leadership action, in conjunction with (ii) *action learning*, focusing on conduct change through reflection on real stakeholder and organisational challenges (in other words, Layers 5 and 6) (see Figure 21.3). In the words of Argyris, Putnam, and McLain Smith,[4] methods will have to be employed "to make known what is known so well that we no longer know it, ... so that it might be critiqued, ... and to make known what is unknown, ... the discovery of alternatives so that they too might be critiqued". Skilful improvisation contains such reflexive qualities.

Bridging the science-practice gap

Such leadership growth and development, based on sound scientific principles, will have the potential to respond adequately to bridging the perennial, ongoing science–practice gap. *Leadership Excellence* abounds with many such exemplars. In practice, this growth and development in organisations can be self-driven, technology-enabled, classroom- based, experiential and/or coaching, provided it conforms to its purposes: deep, inside-out growth and development from Layer 1 "upwards" towards Layer 6. Then and only then will organisations be preparing and delivering the right leadership in the right numbers at the right time and place, able, willing and empowered to perform effectively within the VICCAS Context.

Fundamental to this leadership growth and learning will be the need for academics and development practitioners to do less "esoteric", practice-estranged work that results in the growing gap between theory – the proverbial ivory tower – and practice. Within the VICCAS Context, real action research partnerships between academic institutions and business/non-governmental institutions/public sector are essential, focusing on leadership growth and development that is useful to leadership in the moment of action where it matters and will make a real difference. In other words, leadership growth and development that is characteristic of reflective practice, reflecting-in- and -on-action. Given financial pressures, organisations need to place a much greater emphasis on evidence-based, actionable knowledge to drive their change efforts. The speed of practice-referenced and -informed research delivery by academics will have to match the speed of change in the practical world. Otherwise, academics and academic institutions will rapidly become irrelevant to a VICCAS Context "running away" from them. They will become the extinct dinosaurs going into the future.

Conclusion

Having explored tomorrow's VICCAS Leadership Context with its features resulting in "wicked" leadership challenges, issues and problem, answering the remaining ultimate question posed in the Introduction is: "Is there a future for leadership?" Yes, there is a future for leadership, but it is conditional on:

- A *deep understanding of the unfolding VICCAS Context* going into the future in terms of leadership's fourfold relationships with the World, Organisation, Others and Self;
- *Adoption of a complexity vantage point* to leadership;
- From this complexity perspective, *re-imagine at a deep level leaders in a holistic, organic, integrated and dynamic way as a whole person,* in terms of their ability, intelligence, maturity, ethics and authenticity, as embedded in their fourfold relationships, all of which have to be dynamically aligned simultaneously in real time;
- Enabling and empowering leaders to engage with the Context through *Skilful Improvisation*;
- *Growing and developing leadership from the inside-out*, commencing with the deeper layers of leadership's lived world: Layer 1: Worldview through double-loop learning, progressing through action learning towards Layer 6: Everyday Lived Experiences and Actions; and
- *Forming vibrant two-way interactions between the academic and practice worlds,* producing just-in-time, evidence-based, actionable knowledge to drive change efforts to make leaders future-fit.

What a challenge lies ahead of all of us to make it happen in a world that is in desperate need of leadership excellence in order to ensure a sustainable, flourishing future for all.

Endnotes

1 "The situation talks back, the [leader] listens, and as he appreciates what he hears, he reframes the situation once again": *cf.* Schön, DA. 1983. *The reflective practitioner.* New York, NY: Basic Books.
2 *cf.* Also (a) Warren Bennis on jazz and leadership: "I used to think that running an organization was equivalent to conducting a symphony orchestra. But I don't think that's quite it; it's more like jazz. There is more improvisation"; (b) the leadership development training, styled on UK Channel 4s "Whose line is it anyway?", *Workplace IMPROV*, designed by stand-up comedian, Nadiem Solomon. The fundamental rule in this training is "pay attention".
3 Harris, S. 2011. *There are no mistakes on the bandstand.* TEDSalon NY2011.
4 Argyris, C, Putnam, R & McLain Smith, D. 1985. *Action science: concepts, methods, and skills for research and intervention.* San Francisco, CA: Jossey-Bass Inc. 237.

INDEX

A

accountability, 23, 60, 64–65, 68, 131, 157, 160, 184, 235, 237, 242, 246, 249, 265
action lenses, 4
action tools, 4
affirmative action, 41
African humanity, 148, 150, 152
African leadership, 8, 35, 39, 146–153, 155, 157–158, 160
African leadership wisdom, 147, 150, 153
agile flexibility, 15, 21–22, 24, 27
ambiguity and uncertainty, 101
approach to ethics, 130, 138
assertiveness, 35, 171
assessment, 2, 10, 19, 25, 53, 57, 108, 136, 140–141, 195, 200, 227, 243–244, 246–247, 257–263
attitudinal change, 200
attribute/credit ideas, 200
authentic, 21, 60–66, 68–72, 92, 113, 122–123, 147–148, 150, 210–212, 273, 275, 283, 285–286, 294, 296
authentic and confident leader, 273, 285–286
authenticity, 14–15, 20–23, 27, 29, 55, 57, 62–63, 65–68, 70–72, 87–88, 114–115, 122, 211, 294–295, 297
authentic leadership, 8, 60–63, 66, 68–72, 113, 122–123, 294
authentic leadership defined, 62

B

baby boomers, 178–179, 181, 185
black swans, 240
board attributes, 247–248
board coaching, 244, 246
Board Evaluation Assessment Model, 243
board leadership, 8, 235, 244, 246–247, 249
board profile, 247
boundary spanning, 32, 43, 50
brand promise, 53–54
brand promise and leadership, 53–54
bridging the gap, 79

bridging the science-practice gap, 297
business case, 135, 144, 192, 194, 196, 201
business unusual, 235
business value add, 258, 260–261, 264

C

capability and intervention, 2–4, 9
change leadership, 8, 203–209, 211–213
change processes, 206, 209–210
change the rules, 104, 170
charismatic leadership, 39
clash of generations, 178
cognitive and affective, 154
cognitive biases, 77–78
cognitive complexity, 14–15, 17–18, 22–23, 27–28, 44–46, 101–102
Cognitive Intelligence (IQ), 45–46
collaboration, 37–39, 45, 54, 99, 104, 106–107, 174, 202, 206, 246, 254, 294
competencies and knowledge, 100
competencies for leading inclusively, 196, 199, 201
competencies required by change leaders, 209–210
competitive landscape, 10, 13, 268
complexity, 14–15, 17–18, 22–24, 27–29, 31–32, 43–48, 73–74, 100–103, 154–155, 203–206, 210, 236–237, 239–240, 290–291, 297
component frameworks, 217
components of emotional intelligence, 19
concept of African leadership, 146–147
conceptual leadership, 257–258
conceptual lens, 3–4, 6
confidence, 19, 37, 44, 61–62, 85–86, 116, 135, 140, 155, 171–173, 180, 224, 254, 285, 293
confronting our baggage, 197
connect on a personal level, 200
Contextual Intelligence (CQ2), 46
continuous multiplicity, 43
contribution of directors, 244, 246
contribution of women leaders, 164

control and power, 208
core positive values, 115–117, 120
core values for a spiritual leader, 116–117
corporate entrepreneurship, 231–232, 234
corporate governance, 112, 120, 131, 160, 235, 237–239, 241–242, 246, 249–250, 288
corporate governance codes, 235, 237
courage, 20, 61–62, 69–71, 83, 85, 87–89, 91, 93, 105, 137, 139–140, 155, 281–283, 285, 292–293
creating movement as a leader, 273
critical paradigm shifts, 207
cross-cultural influences, 32, 42
cross-cultural leadership, 7, 10, 31–33, 35, 40, 43, 50
cultivating a global mindset, 42
cultural influences, 31–32, 34–35, 40, 42
cultural influences on leadership, 32, 35, 42
Cultural Intelligence (CQ1), 46
cultural renaissance, 148–150
cultural values on leadership, 35
culture, 31–37, 39–40, 42–43, 50, 75–76, 119–120, 131–134, 149–150, 155–158, 161–163, 168–170, 191–200, 212, 232, 257–261
culture building, 212
customer satisfaction, 106, 267–268

D

deep learning, 296
defining "change leadership", 205
defining diversity, 192–194
defining leadership, 3, 5
degrees of complexity, 210
destroying talent, 192, 197
destructive behaviours, 23
developing authentic leadership, 66
developing the 'being' of leadership, 12, 24
developing wise leaders, 106–107
development frameworks, 150, 216
diagnostic-driven, 207
dialogic organisational change, 207–208
dimensions of a global mindset, 31, 44
director attributes, 247–248
diversity leadership, 8, 191–192, 194–195, 197–201

E

ecological context, 218
economic and structural reform, 148
emergent states, 223–224
emerging leadership theories, 111, 113
emerging risks, 240
emerging world, 235
emotional exchange, 192, 198
Emotional Intelligence (EI), 45
emotional response, 21
emotional wisdom, 14–15, 18, 22–24, 27, 56
employee engagement, 10, 13, 26, 65, 76, 192, 206, 210, 259, 266–268, 270
employment equity, 41, 50
empowerment, 93, 137, 163, 165–166, 168, 175, 207, 232
energy2economics, 25
engaging, 2–3, 16, 18, 20, 107, 117, 184, 191–192, 198, 208, 242–243, 246, 276, 285, 293
engaging and communicating, 192, 198
entrepreneurial economy, 229–230, 234
entrepreneurial leadership, 8, 229–233
entrepreneurship and leadership, 229, 231
equity, 40–41, 50, 57–58, 194, 237, 242
ethical, 15, 44, 48–49, 60–62, 70–71, 83–85, 91, 94–95, 97, 111–113, 120, 122, 125–144, 238–239, 292–294
ethical behaviour, 15, 60, 91, 95, 125–126, 131–134, 136–139
ethical challenge, 130, 139
ethical decision-making, 126, 131, 137–139, 142–143
ethical leadership, 8, 83, 97, 112–113, 122, 125, 131, 136, 138–139, 292
ethics, 71, 83–86, 96–97, 100, 113, 122, 125–126, 130–144, 147, 157, 160–162, 242, 292, 294–295, 297
ethics awareness, 126, 131–132, 136, 138–141, 144
ethics competence deficiency, 136
ethics in organisations, 132
ethics management, 126, 134, 138, 140–144
ethics risk assessment, 140–141
ethics strategy, 140–142
excellence measurement model, 258
executive leadership effectiveness, 35, 39, 63

executive resilience, 25
expectations, 12–13, 31–33, 39–42, 47, 54–55, 139, 168–170, 177–178, 180–181, 189, 225–226, 256–257, 259–260, 262, 288

F

financial capitalism, 238
flexibility, 15, 21–22, 24, 27, 45, 179, 181–185, 248
follower expectations, 31–33, 41–42
foreign nationals, 41
Fourth Industrial Revolution, 235, 247–249, 290–291
future-fit leadership, 4, 8, 10, 288, 293–296
future of leadership, 8, 287–288
future orientation, 35
future world of work, 58, 177, 185, 187

G

generational differences, 33, 41
generational theory, 177–178, 184, 189
Generations@Work, 181
generation Xers, 179, 182–183
generation Y, 105, 178, 180–182, 185, 190
generation Z, 178, 180
global arena, 44
global ethical relational practice, 44
global intellectual capital, 44
global psychological capital, 44
global social capital, 44
global systems competencies, 44
GLOBE universal culture dimensions, 35
growing and developing future-fit leadership, 288, 295
growing and developing talent, 192, 197
growing leadership crisis, 288–289

H

hierarchy to heterarchy, 187
higher purpose, 84, 90, 113–117, 120
high-performing boards, 235, 239, 246
HIV/Aids epidemic, 41
holacracy, 188, 190
homophobic sentiments, 41

humane orientation, 35–36, 39
humanity, 83, 86, 88, 91, 93–94, 101, 105, 147–150, 152–153, 155, 158, 164, 167, 169, 274–275
human nature and national culture, 34

I

ignorance, 131, 135–136
impact of authentic leadership, 63
importance of inner work, 197
inclusion, 3, 152, 169, 192–197, 199–202, 254
inclusive capitalism, 238
individual context, 134, 218
individual leader maturity, 24
individual leadership effectiveness, 63
individual virtue competencies, 90, 92
innovation, 35, 105–106, 146–148, 153, 155, 158, 199, 204, 207, 212, 229–234, 239, 241, 243, 289–291
institutionalisation, 140–141
integrated reporting, 238–239
integrated spiritual leadership, 111, 114–115
inter-generational leadership competencies, 186
international initiatives, 165
interpretative lens, 4
inter-relational trust, 63–68
investing emotionally, 192, 197
involve and mobilise people, 209
iQ Business Value Model, 253, 265, 267–268

J

justice, 48, 83–85, 87–88, 91, 93, 129, 146, 157, 161, 194, 290

K

key departure points, 85
King III Report, 238
King IV Report, 238
Kirkpatrick 4 level model, 254

L

leader of the future, 154

leadership assessment and development, 258–261, 263
leadership attributes, 6–8, 10, 32, 35, 37, 39, 42, 59
leadership brand, 4–9, 13, 24, 26–27, 53–58, 255–262, 264
leadership brand behaviours, 55–56, 260, 262
leadership brand modelling, 8, 27, 53
leadership capability, 14, 16, 24, 27, 205, 213, 252, 261–265, 269
leadership capability maturity, 252, 261–265, 269
leadership capacity, 94, 157, 258, 260–261, 263–264, 266, 269
leadership characteristics, 36, 51
leadership contextual challenges, 289
leadership dashboard framework, 260
leadership dimensions, 14, 37–38
leadership engagement, 288, 294
leadership ethics inadequacy, 130, 135
leadership excellence, 2, 4–13, 24, 26–27, 31–32, 44–46, 57, 252–254, 257–260, 262, 264–266, 268, 270, 274, 297
leadership excellence across cultural settings, 8, 31–32
leadership excellence and branding, 8, 11
leadership excellence dimensions, 6, 8, 10, 12–13, 57, 253
leadership excellence measurement, 8, 27, 57, 252, 258, 265
leadership for the future, 293
leadership mindset, 15
leadership model, 111, 114–115
leadership outcomes and impact, 5–10, 251
leadership philosophy, 152, 162, 258, 260–261, 263–264
leadership questionnaire, 90–91
leadership reflective practice, 93
leadership settings, 8, 150, 215
leadership stories, 5–6, 8, 271–273
leadership strategy, 146, 256–258, 260–263, 265–268
leadership strategy model, 256
leadership style, 4, 28, 75, 177, 211–212, 252, 283
leadership types, 7–8, 145
learning the r.e.a.l. dialogue, 25
levels of leading, 31–32

leveraging cultural difference, 44
limitation, 77, 79, 92, 296
long-term sustainability, 102, 238
looking ahead, 103, 161, 236, 252, 288
loyalty, 36, 38, 63, 134, 181–182, 232, 254, 277

M

male champion, 173
management of social institutions, 102
measures and outcomes, 231
measuring individual virtue competencies, 90
mega trends, 236
mentor, 173, 186, 211
midpoint transition, 225–226
millennials, 178, 180, 183–185, 188, 190
mindful board, 244–246, 250
mindful leadership, 8, 73–74, 81–82
mindset of entrepreneurial leadership, 230
mission-driven leadership, 42
model for diversity leadership, 192
modesty and unobtrusiveness, 101
more women into government, 165
multicultural organisations, 42
multi-generational implications, 177, 180
multi-generational leadership, 8, 177, 189

N

narratives, 4, 192, 194–195, 208
national culture, 32–35, 40, 42, 162
need for change leadership, 206, 212
negative leadership impact, 268
new business responses, 235–236
next generation, 177, 184, 276

O

openness and reflectiveness, 101
optimal performance, 226
organisational action processes, 4
organisational context, 40, 112, 131–132, 153, 218, 222
organisational contingency factors, 40
organisational level, 115, 119–120, 252
organisational outcomes, 65, 115, 120
organisational strategy, 120, 195, 218

oversight and supervision, 183

P

pace of change, 175, 203–206, 210–211
Panama Papers, 237
performance orientation, 35, 39
personal intelligences, 114–115, 117, 120
personal lives, 134, 183, 204
perspective of risk, 240
PESTLE systems, 44
political legacy, 148
positioning for success, 171
predictive abilities, 210
proactivity, 182
problem-solving, 104, 117, 155, 207, 221, 226
psychological frameworks, 217
punishment, 133–135
pyramid of positive leadership, 66–67

R

reconfiguring leadership, 206
refocusing the future, 147, 153
regulatory compliance, 239, 241
relevance of spiritual leadership, 111–112
reliable, 20, 199
respond constructively, 201
responsible global leadership, 31, 48
revisiting business and leadership goals, 157
rewards and incentives, 133
rewards and recognition, 183
rise of African woman, 166
risk oversight, 239
root of positive leadership, 62

S

safe space for dialogue, 192, 198
seize the opportunity, 169
self-awareness, 16, 19, 45, 47,
　　61–63, 66–67, 154
self-evaluations, 244, 246–247
self-motivation, 16
self-regulation, 16, 19, 62, 66, 68, 87, 89, 154
service-profit model chain, 13
shareholder activism, 239, 241
silent generation, 179

silo reporting, 238
skilful improvisation, 288, 294–297
skills wastage, 41
social elements, 229, 233–234
social identities, 32, 34, 42
Social Intelligence (SQ1), 45–46
social skills, 101, 106–107
societal fault-lines, 41, 43
solicit opinions, 200
sound diagnostic, 210
spiritual authenticity, 14–15, 20–23, 27
Spiritual Intelligence (SQ2), 46–47
spirituality and religion, 112
spiritual leadership, 8, 29, 62,
　　111–116, 119–123
spiritual leadership model, 111, 114–115
status quo bias, 78
strategic board, 244–246
strategic intent, 22, 40, 55, 102, 252, 290
strategic leadership framework, 4–5, 262–264
strategic leadership value chain, 2–6, 9, 272
sub-cultures, 32–34, 44
sub-cultures/social categories, 34
superficial notions, 208
sustainability, 48, 55, 86, 93, 99, 102, 138, 146,
　　157, 160, 202, 209, 233, 238–239, 242
sustainable entrepreneurial leadership, 232
systemic change, 200–201, 208
systems framework, 217

T

take risks, 155, 169
task-work and teamwork, 220, 222, 227
team context, 218, 227
team effectiveness, 64–65, 123
team ineffectiveness, 64
team leadership, 8, 63–65, 67, 147, 152, 163,
　　216, 218, 220, 222, 224, 226–227
team leadership effectiveness, 63–64, 67
team level, 80, 115, 119
team-orientated leadership, 37, 39
technological innovation, 148,
　　239, 241, 289–290
technology and social networks, 184
temperance, 83, 85, 87, 89, 91, 93
thinking framework, 3–4, 265
traditionalist, 178

traditional organisations, 188, 233
transcendence, 83, 87, 89, 94,
    113–115, 120–121, 123
transformation, 2, 85, 112, 114–115,
    120, 122, 137, 146, 153–154,
    195–196, 203, 205, 238, 240, 245
transparency, 62–63, 65–66, 79,
    111, 121, 123, 130, 144, 181,
    186, 235, 237, 242, 246
trusting, 44, 65, 198–199, 285

U

uncomfortable settings, 44
unconscious bias, 197, 201
understanding teams, 216
unethically, 126, 130, 134–135

V

values-driven, 121, 198
virtue and virtuous leadership, 83
virtue of humility, 79
virtue strengths and competency, 86–90
virtue themes and competencies, 86
virtuous leadership, 8, 83–86, 90–97

W

wisdom and knowledge, 83, 86–87
wise leadership, 8, 99, 101–102
women in leadership, 163–164,
    166–168, 170, 174, 176
women's power, 172
working board, 244–246

www.ingramcontent.com/pod-product-compliance
Lightning Source LLC
Chambersburg PA
CBHW071315150426
43191CB00007B/634